Buying Happiness

BUYING HAPPINESS

The Emergence of Consumer Consciousness in English Canada

Bettina Liverant

UBCPress · Vancouver · Toronto

27 26 25 24 23 22 21 20 19 18   5 4 3 2 1

Printed in Canada on FSC-certified ancient-forest-free paper
(100% post-consumer recycled) that is processed chlorine- and acid-free.

Library and Archives Canada Cataloguing in Publication

Liverant, Bettina, author
Buying happiness: the emergence of consumer consciousness in English Canada /
Bettina Liverant.

Includes bibliographical references and index.
Issued in print and electronic formats.
ISBN 978-0-7748-3513-8 (cloth). – ISBN 978-0-7748-3515-2 (PDF).
ISBN 978-0-7748-3516-9 (EPUB). – ISBN 978-0-7748-3517-6 (Kindle).

1. Consumption (Economics) – Canada – History – 20th century. 2. Consumers –
Canada – History – 20th century. I. Title.

HC79.C6L58 2018   339.4'709710904   C2018-900855-5
C2018-900856-3

Canadä

UBC Press gratefully acknowledges the financial support for our publishing program
of the Government of Canada (through the Canada Book Fund),
the Canada Council for the Arts, and the British Columbia Arts Council.

This book has been published with the help of a grant from the Canadian Federation for the
Humanities and Social Sciences, through the Awards to Scholarly Publications Program, using
funds provided by the Social Sciences and Humanities Research Council of Canada.

Printed and bound in Canada by Friesens
Set in Caslon and Fournier by Artegraphica Design Co. Ltd.
Copy editor: Barbara Tessman
Proofreader: Judith Earnshaw
Indexer: Cheryl Lemmens

UBC Press
The University of British Columbia
2029 West Mall
Vancouver, BC V6T 1Z2
www.ubcpress.ca

FOR LEIB

... because he is always changing the story.

CONTENTS

ACKNOWLEDGMENTS

This book began with a visit to Cody's Books in Berkeley, California, and a chance encounter with Warren Susman's *Culture as History*. I was unfamiliar with his work but, like so many, I was immediately captivated by Susman's understanding that things we buy are part of a larger cultural pattern and a way of life that is about so much more than just shopping. I started thinking about what "culture with us in it" meant, and what a study of this sort might look like for Canada.

And so, what began as a visit to a bookstore became this book. I am indebted, first and foremost, to Doug Owram at the University of Alberta, who provided an ideal mix of challenge and academic freedom; and to Beverly Lemire, who willingly reviewed the manuscript when Doug left Edmonton for new challenges and a warmer climate. Beverly shared generously of her time and her expertise in material culture, with extensive comments and encouragement. I would also like to thank Joy Parr, who brought genuine enthusiasm, a keen eye, and new insights to bear on both the work and the writer. All three provided questions and suggestions that were invaluable in extending my thinking; of equal importance, they are models of academic commitment, intellectual rigour, and outstanding scholarship who continue to inspire.

Over the years, discussions, both formal and informal, with colleagues in the Department of History and Classics at the University of Alberta and, afterwards, in the Department of History at the University of Calgary, provided many opportunities to test and develop ideas. I am deeply appreciative of the generous funding and resources provided by both universities.

The process of peer review went beyond improving the manuscript, helping me grow as a scholar and a writer. I benefited from opportunities to present research at several meetings of the Canadian Historical Association and at the symposium "Consumerism on the Home Front during the Second World War," organized by the German Historical Institute in London, England. Readers who commented on various aspects of this research along the way, and most especially those arranged by UBC Press for the final manuscript, were tremendously helpful, providing detailed, astute, and very generous readings.

Publication would not have been possible without the support of UBC Press, including the guidance provided by the ever-energetic Darcy Cullen and copy editor Barbara Tessman, who fine-tuned the manuscript with keen intellect and great care.

A community of friends also sustained me over the years, first as the manuscript was written, and then when it was transformed into a book. Thank you to Ruth, Bev, Sandy, and Ena – they never wavered in their belief that I was doing something of value. Thanks are also due to the numerous barristas and servers in coffee shops at home and abroad who allowed me to huddle in corners for hours on end, writing and rewriting chapter drafts.

And thank you to my children – Forrest, Royce, and Alyssa – who were my very best study buddies as we worked together on our respective academic and life challenges. My husband Leib knows how difficult it is for me to express in words all that his support has meant to me. The solution is simply to dedicate this book to him.

An earlier version of Chapter 2 appeared as "The Promise of a More Abundant Life: Canadian Consumer Society and the Rise of the Managerial State," *Journal of the Canadian Historical Association* 19, 1 (2008): 229–51. Parts of Chapter 3 appeared previously in "1935: The Forgotten Consumer Election," in *Consuming Modernity, Changing Gendered Behaviours and Consumerism, 1919–1940*, ed. Cheryl Warsh and Dan Malleck (Vancouver: UBC Press, 2013), 11–33. Part of Chapter 6 appeared previously in "Strategic Austerity: The Canadian Middle Path," in *Consumption on the Home Front*

during the Second World War: A Transnational Perspective, ed. Hartmut Berghoff, Jan Logemann, and Felix Roemer (London: Oxford University Press, 2016) and is reproduced by permission of Oxford University Press and The German Historical Institute, London. Part of Chapter 7 appeared many years ago as my first scholarly publication: "From Budgeting to Buying: Post War Canadian Consumerism," *Past Imperfect* 8 (1999–2000): 62–92. Thank you to the Canadian Historical Association, Oxford University Press, and UBC Press for the opportunity to publish these works initially and for granting permission for their reuse.

Buying Happiness

INTRODUCTION

When people think about consumer society, they usually think about buying things or throwing them away. I believe that living in a consumer society involves a particular way of thinking about ourselves, our relationships with others, and our relationships with things. This book is about the history of Canadian consumer society as an idea. When did we begin thinking about ourselves in this way? How did the idea spread? Why does it matter?

The idea of Canada as a consumer society was largely absent before 1890 when changes in spending and a rising surplus of goods began to put the "consumer" on the public agenda. By the early 1960s, the idea that Canada was becoming a "consumer society" had gained widespread acceptance.[1] *Buying Happiness* examines the emergence and development of consumer society as a way of thinking about Canadian society during this period, utilizing a series of case studies. Each chapter examines how different influential Canadians engaged with the pressing social questions of their day in ways that brought consumer society into focus and into being. The emphasis is on concepts and categories rather than on the buying and selling of goods – an approach that is still relatively unusual in histories of consumption. As this book shows, the rise of consumer society was not simply the result of economic changes in productivity and affluence; it involved and required changes in the way people think.

In the last decades of the nineteenth century, social commentators became concerned about the dissolution of social bonds. Society was changing and fragmenting: traditional moral standards of hard work, self-reliance, and deference were being challenged or abandoned as young people moved from the country to the city, as immigrants speaking new languages arrived with new values and religions, as industrialization increased and urban slums appeared. Overall standards of living were rising, new patterns of success were developing, and older social hierarchies were losing their force. For the next seven decades, social critics, statisticians, politicians, policy-makers, academics, writers, and artists responded to the dramatic changes under way in Canadian society by doing what intellectuals do: they moralized, analyzed, told stories, made public policies, and theorized about changing patterns of consumption. As they thought about and developed new ways of representing Canadians during a time when more of everyday life was being reorganized around commercially sold, mass-distributed goods, they generated new concepts that in turn helped to shape social life. Changes within religious, cultural, civic, governmental, economic, and academic thought and practice reinforced each other. New understandings of Canadian society emerged. The cumulative result of these and other factors was that Canadian society came to be described as a "consumer society."

The public thinkers whose writings are at the core of this study are historically situated amid different social, political, and economic conditions that present different challenges and possibilities.[2] The sequence of chapters moves forward in time, sometimes more slowly, sometimes more rapidly, drawing on different sources because different kinds of intellectual work matter more at different times. As society changes so too do the roles and occupations filled by intellectuals and their social and cultural influence. For example, religious authorities became less important while government policy-makers became more so; the authority of sociologists as scholar-experts rose as the discipline developed into a science within Canada's expanding university system; and the influence of the mass media grew progressively stronger.

Consumption was variously a topic for consideration and opinion making by social commentators, a frame of reference for government policies, a fact to be studied by social scientists, and a virtue to be attached to "universal" ideals such as citizenship. Governmental and academic inquiries reinforced new ways of understanding society and legitimized changes in behaviour that traditionalists considered controversial. Episodes of crisis provided occasions to extend the reach of the state. New knowledge and understandings were produced, including by governments generating cost of living indexes and sociologists examining the role of consumer goods in suburban life. Persuading Canadians of the benefits of change, experts in modern living prescribed appropriate ways to participate in consumer culture, teaching families how to balance debt loads and desires through carefully planned spending. By the 1960s, mass media, academics, cultural elites, and policymakers commonly addressed Canadians as consumers. Consumer society had emerged as an accepted frame of reference. What had once been described as novel came to be seen as normative and then as ordinary and pervasive. Regardless of whether the intention was to restrict, redirect, or encourage changes in spending, intellectual practices put the consumer on the public agenda. Seeing Canadians as consumers was – and is – an evolving process.

There was no pattern of coercion, but over time people were increasingly encouraged to think of themselves as consumers making choices within the framework of a consumption-oriented society. The understanding of what was good for society, what was good for individuals and their moral development, and what was good for the economy became aligned with the increased consumption of goods and services. For most people, the vision of the good life came to involve the acquisition of a continuing stream of goods and services. Certainly there was ongoing debate, including outright dissent, about what the right kind of consumption should be; nonetheless, the terms of reference became those of consumer society.

Collectively, the chapters of this book suggest the possibility of an "intellectual gaze." Intellectuals, as they look at society, are not simply observing but are also imposing order on new phenomena, converting data into knowledge and organizing concepts in ways that encourage certain ways of being and impede the path to alternatives. Intellectual practice, *Buying Happiness* contends, must be understood as an active as well as a contemplative exercise. By engaging with society – that is, by describing and debating, by measuring and categorizing, and by making new social models and new public policies – the intellectual and cultural communities came to represent Canadians as consumers and gave specific form to Canadian consumer society.

This study builds on other consumer histories as well as recent studies in cultural theory.[3] Although consumer history is a relatively new field, decades of scholarship, initially in pursuit of the "birth" of consumer society, have addressed more time periods, more national stories, and more and different consumers.[4] Much has been discovered about *who* consumed *what, when,* and *where.*[5] However, the figure of the consumer as an active historical agent was slower to appear. In the 1960s and 1970s, theorists of modern society associated advances in consumption with industrial progress, in some cases painting an optimistic vision of the future with rising standards of living and increasing freedom, in others associating changes in consumption with the rise of mass society, political apathy, and psychological manipulation. Historians similarly tended to regard consumers as the largely passive creations of corporate capitalism, necessary to ensure the profitability of mass production, and most often portrayed them as the victims, rather than the agents, of change.[6] In the 1980s and 1990s, a new generation of scholars more comfortable with mass culture challenged this emphasis on the oppressive nature of capitalism, acknowledging that consumption and abundant goods were at least potentially liberating. They wrote new histories showing that consumers did not simply internalize the values promulgated by advertising but used goods in creative ways, only some of which were intended and anticipated by producers. Celebrating acts of creativity and resistance in everyday life, some scholars shifted scale, exploring more intimate settings and smaller communities. A decade later, other scholars began to connect private consumption more directly with civil society, politics, and the economy.[7] New scholarship raised new questions. British historian John Brewer raised one that intrigued me: How do we get from acts of consumption to consumer society?[8] In the context of Canadian consumer history, this question became specific: How is it that the concept of "consumer" and the idea that Canada is a "consumer society" – notions that were barely visible on the margins of public discussion prior to the 1890s – came to be widely recognized as accurate representations of modern Canada by the early 1960s? I hoped that an answer (or at least insight) could be found by studying the making of these new understandings rather than the mechanisms of advertising and retail exchange.[9]

Approaches from other fields pointed the way: concepts such as *mentalité*, *habitus* (developed by Pierre Bourdieu), *governmentality* (Michel Foucault), and *social imaginary* (Charles Taylor) provided different but compatible approaches to exploring frameworks of social meaning. Although they focused on mechanisms of social cohesion and social stability, these theorists offered practical methodologies that could be used to investigate "consumer society" as a conceptual framework that developed over time.[10]

New representations of modern Canada emerged and were entrenched with new ways of thinking about society and new public policies. The choices available to people change – due in part to real material changes (for example, changes in technology) and in part to changes in their sense of themselves and in what philosophers call "a vision of the good life." Material changes and new ideas are mutually influential: changes in the material world initiate new patterns of thought, and new ways of thinking influence behaviour. In Canada, as this period progressed, the new vision of the good life came to involve the ability to buy things. By the mid-1960s, such consumerism became taken for granted. This study looks at some of the processes through which it was built up and diffused.

There was no single factor or turning point in the emergence of consumer society as a dominant category of social analysis. Observing the development and diffusion of consumer society as a set of values and understandings, we can observe gradual changes in people's awareness of themselves and others as consumers. Rather than having a single moment of birth, consumer society emerges as a dynamic category that is not "once and for all," but cumulative and shifting. Theorists of intellectual history discuss the role of intellectuals as agents of change, often distinguishing between conservative intellectuals serving the interests of the established order and radical intellectuals promoting the transformation of society.[11] Canada's intellectual community, at least during the period of this study, is less easily categorized. In many different roles, with varied vocations and responsibilities, intellectuals helped shape consumer society. Even those thinkers who fundamentally and loudly opposed mass consumerism played a part in making the consumer a common point of reference.

Studying a topic framed as the development of consumer consciousness implies the existence of a prior pre-consumer world. However, as many historians have observed, images of rural self-sufficiency with consumption dependent on the production of one's own family were always more myth than reality.[12] Douglas McCalla debunks accounts of Canadian settlers living Robinson Crusoe–like lives of self-sufficiency at near subsistence levels.[13] His study of the account books of general stores located in Upper Canada during the period of colonial settlement shows that settlers shopped, that goods had set prices, that cash was involved in store transactions, and that women were visible in the account books. Luxury goods did not abound, but there were small luxuries, such as ribbons and trim, as well as room for the exercise of preference and choice among multiple flavours of tea, sizes and colours of buttons, and the like. Over the course of his study, from 1808 to 1861, he documents a gradual evolution and expansion in the number and sorts of goods settlers bought but sees no dramatic revolution. When department stores arrived in the 1890s, he suggests, there was a gain in scale, but the combination of homemade and store-bought goods began well before and lasted long after this arrival. Upper Canada may have been on the edge of an expanding world economy, but its inhabitants were still a part of it. Colonial Canada should not be regarded as a "before" to a modern later. Canadians – regardless of whether they dwelt in rural, village, or urban settings – had long been participants in extended marketplaces linked to regional and global economies.

There was no consumer revolution, but, in the years close to turn of the century, increases in the availability of consumer goods and visible changes in purchasing practices did begin to come to the attention of essayists and moralists. Canada's conservative intellectuals, progressive religious leaders, and economic theorists are usually studied separately as having unique responses to the challenges of modernity. Chapter 1 pursues a more complex vision, showing how each group engaged with the implications of new spending practices: Who was doing the buying, where did they shop, what did they buy? How much was enough? How much was too much? In a world where more goods were being produced, what (or who) determined who got what? While social conservatives regarded rising affluence and the easy availability of goods as a social problem, leaders in the social gospel movement called on Canadians to seize opportunities created by increasing productivity to build the Kingdom of God on Earth, insisting that adequate consumption was the foundation of a full spiritual life. The small community of political economists acknowledged the power of changing consumption patterns but did not believe that increases in domestic consumption could act as a significant vehicle for economic growth in Canada. Yet, in their writings, the consumer is slowly coming into focus, both as individuals and in aggregate. While the notion of consumer society had not yet been formulated, the practices of consumers were moving from the margins to the centre of concerns about modernity.

In the decade after the turn of the century, the economy boomed and rising prices became a subject of controversy in Canada and, indeed, throughout much of the industrialized world. Rising prices exacerbated wage disputes and intensified the tension between traditional producer values of hard work, self-restraint, and thrift and the acceptance of new comforts and patterns of purchasing. Although not all Canadians agreed on the definition of basic necessities, cost of living concerns put household provisioning, rather than luxury consumption, at the centre of national discussion. The federal government responded to social unrest with two inquiries into the cost of living, the first in 1909–10 and a second in 1913–14. These studies are the subject of the second chapter. Establishing a Canadian standard of living that was independent of the purchasing decisions of any one family built awareness of a common consumer interest. Presenting the purchase of domestic goods as normal, ordinary, and widely shared undercut reactionary interpretations of consumption as the product of self-indulgent or irrational behaviour. By measuring and categorizing the changing purchasing practices of Canadians, the state expanded its mandate and helped to shape the way Canadians came to see themselves as consumers.

During the interwar period, producers of high culture saw their work as nation-making and disparaged popular commercially driven, mass-reproduced culture as standardized, feminized, and Americanized. Chapter 3 proposes that elite culture was also commoditized at this time, produced, marketed, and sold by a new generation of cultural entrepreneurs to select audiences. The aesthetics of authenticity, purity, and wilderness gained meaning and value in distinction to the mass produced and the commercially sold.

In the late 1920s, economic expansion came to an abrupt halt. The depression that followed was widely perceived as a crisis not of scarcity but of surplus. Production seemingly had begun, at least in the short term, to outstrip consumption. What was not clear was why. Had production accelerated beyond the world's capacity to absorb goods and services, or were gluts due to temporary imbalances in supply and demand that would, over time, correct themselves? Were the causes largely monetary – involving problems of money supply, credit, and foreign exchange – rather than fundamental limits in demand? There was ample discussion but no consensus. However, as politicians, economists, and self-proclaimed experts turned their attention to the consumption problems of ordinary Canadians, it was evident that poverty was no longer associated with the scarcity of goods but rather with the scarcity of sufficient means to buy goods.

Canadians were still struggling to escape the grip of the Depression in 1934, when the federal minister of trade and commerce launched an aggressive and widely publicized attack on big business, charging that the struggles of ordinary hard-working Canadians were the result of unfair business practices. As public interest swelled, the government quickly established a commission of inquiry, which subsequently became the Royal Commission on Price Spreads and Mass Buying. This drawn-out period of investigation, which included the initial inquiry, the subsequent Royal Commission, the commission's official report in April 1935, and the responses that followed publication, is the subject of Chapter 4.

For over a year, Canadians were scandalized and captivated by revelations of corporate practices that kept profits high and wages low. The public ritual of calling the economically powerful to account was an important factor in the 1935 federal election campaign. Traditionally, historians have associated the expansion of consumerism with times of prosperity and the period of the Great Depression with the expansion of government. However, it was the crisis of the Depression that forged a connection between consumers and politicians, accelerating the incorporation of mass consumption into the mainstream of political and economic policy.[14] The right to a minimum standard of living was central to the rhetoric of the election campaign, with all parties pledging action on behalf of the Canadian consumer.

For the intellectual community, the late 1930s was a time of introspection and reappraisal. Although the worst of the Depression had passed, the spectre of war was rising. Chapter 5 examines the work of social scientists and literary writers who surveyed Canadian society and documented a new social structure oriented towards consumption, with anxious families and budgets stretched between limited resources and increasing choices. They located themselves within this framework, discussing the pressures to commodify intellectual work and their own struggles to resist the allures of the marketplace. Was commitment to high ideals compatible with commerce? Was the disinterested pursuit of knowledge only an artefact of an earlier time? These doubts particularly troubled the nation's economists. The severity of the Depression had called the value of economics as a discipline into question. In the post-Depression period, economists struggled to define their professional worth: were they social scientists focused on the pursuit of truth or experts available for hire, equally able, as one put it, to support "the Stalin model," "the Hitler model," "the Mussolini model," or "the Aberhart model?"[15] There was a common thread in these narratives: regardless of whether the concern was the family budget or government spending, there were too many wants and not enough dollars.

The Great Depression had forged a connection between politicians and consumers as voters; however, it was only during the Second World War that the Canadian state fully acknowledged the economic power of consumers. Chapter 6 examines how the state reached out to Canadians as citizen-consumers during the war and immediate postwar period, seeking in some cases to restrict and in other cases to mobilize their purchasing power. Canada's universal price freeze, implemented in August 1941, was the most severe program to be implemented by any of the allied nations during the war. The system was simultaneously technocratic and participatory. Experts regarded a universal freeze as simple, fair, speedy, and administratively effective; however, they also understood that extensive controls would require a huge bureaucracy and dictatorial tactics unless significant efforts were made to moderate demand and encourage voluntary compliance. The state used tools of market research, including surveys and polling, to gauge public support. A steady stream of propaganda promoted restraint and appealed for compliance on the home front. Hailing housewives as the nation's "House Soldiers," government advertisements, signs, and pamphlets encouraged shoppers to track spending, eliminate impulse buying, monitor prices, and report infractions. Canadian families, particularly Canadian housewives, were enlisted as active partners by the government, called on to exercise their power as consumers to help win the war.

After six years of conflict, the tension between the ideal citizen-consumer, whose constrained patterns of consumption reflected the obligations of patriotic duty, and the private consumer, with pent-up demands and desires cultivated by business, was considerable. Shortages of goods, dating back well before the Depression, had created a backlog in consumer demand. Meanwhile, gains in incomes and the nation's impressive commitment to war savings had built up a significant reservoir of purchasing power. In 1945, the consequences for the postwar period were unknown: Would deferred spending provide a positive stimulus to the economy, creating a temporary boom to be followed by economic collapse, or spur dangerous levels of inflation? Determined to avoid economic stagnation and convinced that sustainable economic growth depended primarily on capital investment and exports, postwar planners recommended policies that would continue to constrain consumers and limit demands for wage increases. Rejecting an expansive, American-style vision of a consumer-oriented society as unsuited to the Canadian economy, the federal government adopted moderate goals, promising adequate access to basic goods with living standards supported by secure jobs and modest social welfare programs. Going forward, growth would depend on the return of international trade.

By the late 1940s, fears of a postwar recession had begun to dissipate. Domestic spending was increasing amid uneven but rising affluence. Chapter 7 explores changing representations of Canadian families in the period following the war, focusing on the new norms of responsible spending promulgated by daily papers and mass-market magazines. The transition from a regime of austerity to cautious consumerism is encapsulated in a series of articles that appeared in the women's magazine *Chatelaine,* each of which focused on the spending practices of a family identified as typically Canadian, beginning with the Menzies in 1949 (self-reliant, self-disciplined, thrifty, and creative), continuing to the Woodses in 1954 (bewildered consumers, in debt and in need of advice, eventually empowered by the professional expertise provided by the magazine), and concluding with the Roses in 1962 (subjects of "101 Ways to Save Money and Look Better, Dress Better, Eat Better and Live Better"). Canadians did not stop valuing hard work, thrift, and self-discipline, but they did begin to place new importance on personal comfort and convenience. In the mass media, experts gave Canadians permission to spend responsibly, within the limits of the family budget, after carefully researching their choices.

Even though family-centred consumer spending began to be met with cautious approval, increases in spending on movies, mass magazines, comic books, pulp novels, and professional sports continued to trouble the nation's intellectual and cultural elites. In 1949, the Royal Commission on National Development in the Arts, Letters and Sciences was empowered to investigate Canadian cultural affairs and institutions of education. The commission acknowledged that the economics of mass production operated to the disadvantage of higher forms of culture: the standards that gave high culture its social significance inherently limited its appeal. Because the commissioners believed that consumption choices were shaped as much by the supply of goods as by demand, they called on the state to intervene in cultural production and distribution, supporting the production of Canadian high culture primarily through investments in the non-profit sector and at the same time imposing a variety of restrictions on commercial mass culture, particularly on American imports.

The final chapter of *Buying Happiness* picks up a different stream of postwar thought, examining the ways in which a rising generation of academics helped to construct and popularize the image of Canada as an affluent consumer society. While hardly supportive of mass consumption, social scientists claimed a role in helping Canadians negotiate the pressures and tensions of mass commercial society. The emphasis was often on the way Canadians made choices – and therefore on questions of education and taste – rather than on questions of access. Consumer behaviour and consumer society became a legitimate topic of academic study. Narratives in the mass media and in academic studies represented the Canadian household as an economic unit dedicated to increasing consumption. The division of labour into gender-specific roles, with a specialized wage-earner and a specialized wage-spender, was understood as fundamentally supportive of increased productivity and increased expertise in spending.

The coming into being of consumer society required more than simply creating impulses to buy; it also involved Canadians' new ways of thinking about themselves and their social relationships. Concepts of identity, citizenship, class, gender, sociability, aesthetics, well-being, and morality were reworked within a changing and expanding economy. New frameworks of understanding were developed and shared. Certain experiences were encouraged or discouraged and given institutional support or marginalized. Through discussion, measurement, policymaking, storytelling, and academic study, consumer identities became central to social life, and consumer values were woven deeply into the Canadian social imagination.

Chapter One

THE MEANING IS IN THE SPENDING

At the end of the nineteenth century, although Canada was not a wealthy country, there were more people, more buildings, and more things to be had than there had been in earlier generations. Some people had experienced impressive gains in living standards: millionaires were constructing mansions along tree-lined boulevards in rapidly growing cities; the middle-class families of white-collar workers were moving into modest homes in newly subdivided suburban neighbourhoods. At the same time, the distributive logic of large-scale capitalism meant that the costs and benefits of growth were allocated unevenly. Real weekly income for skilled labourers remained stable, even as hours of work began to slowly decline.[1] At the poorest levels of society, burgeoning urban slums and industrial labour camps offered shelter of a sort for unskilled labourers and their families, but low wages and job insecurity meant that acquisition of even basic necessities was often a challenge.

Beginning in 1896, economic expansion accelerated dramatically. Annual per capita real GDP growth in the 1896–1913 period averaged 4.7 percent. The population increased from just over 5 million in 1896 to over 7.6 million in 1913. Of the more than 2.5 million people who immigrated to Canada during this period, nearly 50 percent settled in the cities and worked in industrial employment. There was also a marked drift of population from rural to urban areas. The percentage of Canadians living in towns and cities grew from roughly 23 percent in 1881, to 35 percent in 1901, and to 41.8 percent by 1911.[2]

The supply of manufactured goods increased as industrialists modernized systems of production and distribution in the face of growing competition and rising costs. Canada was not at the forefront of change, but businesses began to seek new ways to reach customers. Many became involved in the direct selling of their products: meat packers and boot- and shoemakers, for example, established their own chains of retail stores.[3] Autumn fairs and industrial exhibitions expanded in scale, adding popular entertainments and increasingly elaborate displays of mass-produced, branded consumer goods.[4] In small towns and villages, general stores found themselves in competition with mail-order catalogues, circulars, and travelling sales agents. The use of brands and trademarks increased.[5] In urban centres, elaborate window displays featuring pyramids of products and presenting new brands and packages tempted pedestrians.[6] After the 1870s, department stores began to place full-page advertisements in daily newspapers, often several times a week. From the 1890s, brand-name advertising became common. Estimates suggest that, by 1900, two-thirds of the typical daily newspaper consisted of advertisements.[7] Advertising practices were also becoming more sophisticated, exploiting (and perhaps creating) modern anxieties over hygiene, digestion, and complexion to sell branded goods.

Retail merchandising became increasingly complex. Department stores expanded in number and in size and adopted more sophisticated marketing techniques.[8] Eaton's, for example, began to target different groups of consumers, offering comfortable tea rooms in relatively lavish settings for urban middle-class women, moving "Bargain Day" sales to the Friday following the Thursday evening pay schedule common to many waged workers, and distributing mail order catalogues to rural dwellers.[9] Ready-to-wear garments had long been available, but the number of garments an individual was likely to possess had been steadily increasing. An Eaton's advertisement suggests changing values: "At our prices you are able to have two hats otherwise you could only buy one."[10] As Canadians discussed these changes, they differed in their assessment of what had been lost and what might be possible. Changes in spending patterns were not the foremost concern of those who regularly commented on public affairs, but they were a topic of rising interest.

By convention, Canada's intellectual community in the decades framing the turn of the century has been studied as three distinct groups, with the histories of social conservatives, progressive social gospellers, and political economists (considered as agents of the emergent state and expanding universities as well as practitioners of the developing science of economics) each treated as separate fields. However, if their responses to the challenges of modernity are considered collectively and comparatively, we can make several useful observations. First, we see considerable similarity and overlap in the characteristics of individuals in all three groups. They were almost all of Anglo-Saxon origin, born and raised in production-oriented rural households before relocating to rapidly growing cities, first in pursuit of higher education and then for career opportunities. They were observers of and participants in a rapidly changing world, not simply as consumers of new goods but also as producers and distributers of commodities gaining in market value. Although they had been born in one era, they made their livings in another. Regardless of whether they were social conservatives who idealized rural life or progressives who emphasized the benefits of modernity, they found new opportunities for influence and income as writers, clergymen, authorities on social reform, academics in growing universities, senior civil servants, and consultants to expanding governments and industry. They were well respected, with personal as well as professional ties to the governing classes. Second, they were influential because they had audiences. Increasing literacy and leisure, rising levels of wealth, and an impressive range of technological developments opened the way to growing audiences being reached through the secular daily press, church publications, journals of public opinion (published both in and outside Canada), and fiction and non-fiction books.[11]

There was no consensus about the value of the transformations underway, but there were common concerns. Elite observers were preoccupied with some of the same questions that would interest later historians, particularly with "*who* consumed *what* and *when*."[12] Other concerns were more specific to their time: In a world where more goods were being produced, what should determine access to goods? Should the allocation of goods be left to the market, or should some goods and services be provided as a matter of social justice, citizenship, or Christian fellowship? What was the moral impact of an increasing surplus of goods? How much is enough? How much is too much? Listening to these men and women as they describe, complain about, speculate on, and sometimes celebrate their times – all the while seeking to persuade others of the rightness of their particular interpretation of the transformations under way – we hear the vocabulary of consumer society taking shape.

Voices of Resistance

Canada's loudest critics of new consumer behaviours were conservative, not necessarily in their political affiliations – they supported various political parties – but in their defence of ideals threatened by modernity. As the self-appointed guardians of the nation, Canada's conservative moralists passed judgment on a wide range of topics, writing in support of tradition, patriotism, the British Empire, and the benefits of hard work in general and farm work in particular; objecting to the growth of cities, the rise of department stores, and the spread of business values; and, opposing non-Anglo-Saxon immigration and changes to the roles of women. Industrialization and rapidly rising wealth, they agreed, had brought disorder as well as affluence.

Objections to new consumer practices were a widening strand in the conservative critique of modernity. Such commentators saw growing numbers of middle-class and working-class consumers less as evidence of rising prosperity than as a challenge to the security of the nation, unmaking the social order that underpinned the accomplishments of Western civilization. Business leaders celebrated the growth of industry and trade, but Canada's most committed conservatives saw increasing material abundance as a threat to the ethic of hard work and self-discipline that had made the nation strong. They feared that prosperity would subvert principles of thrift, savings, and self-restraint; that the private pursuit of commercialized novelty distracted from public duty; that abundance encouraged wasteful and dissolute behaviours; and that access to luxuries undermined self-control. Conservative critics most often associated increased leisure time not with opportunities for self-improvement, but with idleness and a lack of labour discipline. Ease of consumption, they warned, comes before the fall.

Against the threats of modernity, conservative thinkers invoked the merits of an idealized past. In agrarian settlements, needs were simple, identities stable, and the bonds of family and community strong. This celebration of rural virtue was as much strategic as it was nostalgic. It was a way of thinking about modernity that turned on the contrast between two ways of life.[13] Hard work was more than a way to acquire money, goods, or social position: it was a virtue in itself. Moneymaking was not the goal but the by-product of sound character, self-discipline, and hard work. The economic and social development of Canada as a nation was intertwined with the moral and intellectual development of individuals. Materialism and the quest for affluence pulled people away from essential values that needed to be maintained.[14]

The values and practices that social conservatives celebrated and promoted were a reflection of their concerns. They valorized hard work at a time when developments in technology and industrial organization (including electricity and running water in the home) were making life more comfortable and increasing leisure time. They insisted on the need for thrift when mass production and modest gains in wages were increasing opportunities to spend. They emphasized inner character at a time when external appearances were gaining more attention. The keywords associated with the development of "character" were both implicitly and explicitly juxtaposed against the perceived vices of a nascent consumer society. Conservative moralists argued in favour of self-discipline, self-sufficiency, industry, prudence, and restraint, calling upon Canadians to reject impulsiveness, self-indulgence, wasteful expenditure, and the pursuit of novelty. A life of ease was synonymous with degeneration, while, over time, struggle led to gradual, cumulative gains.[15]

For conservatives, hard work, thrift, and self-reliance were not simply tools of household management but were critical to the survival of civilization. Malthusian fears that growing populations would outrun agricultural production lingered for social conservatives. The threat of scarcity overshadowed increasing prosperity, which they regarded as temporary and, indeed, as the harbinger of eventual economic and social collapse. Gains in private consumption were not just evidence of growing hedonism: the increasingly easy availability of goods undermined self-discipline and undercut the responsibilities citizens had to society as owners and producers. Personal thrift, both in the expenditure of income and in the management of time, was a necessary aspect of self-improvement and financial independence critical to the security of one's family in an uncertain world. The implications of more relaxed behaviours, if adopted on a broad scale, were ominous. Pointing to the examples of Greece and Rome, well-known Liberal Arnold Haultain linked the decline of ancient civilizations with material excess, warning that, "It is when the mob get their *panis* free that nothing will satisfy them but *circenses*."[16] The "healthiest bodies and the happiest minds are those working hardest," he insisted.

In the late nineteenth and early twentieth centuries, during a period when women's role in society was a subject of intense debate, manufacturers, retailers, and advertisers increasingly portrayed shopping as a primarily female activity, often as a form of leisure rather than work. The discourse surrounding acts of purchasing became explicitly sexualized: merchants "wooed" and "courted" female shoppers, appealing to sentiment and passion to sell goods.[17] Conservative moralists identified and denounced three different types of problem consumers: the "New Woman," the single "working girl," and the bargain-seeking housewife. Their criticism frequently associated challenges to social boundaries with changes in consumption practices.[18]

Andrew Macphail, foremost among Canada's conservative critics, targeted the New Woman in a series of essays, the most notorious of which was "American Woman," printed in the British journal the *Spectator* in 1908.[19] The term "American woman," Macphail explained, referred not to citizenship but rather to a social type defined by a life of independent "luxurious idleness." Performing no "useful function," the American or New Woman was a "restless" campaigner for social reforms of questionable value (including suffrage); alternatively, overwhelmed by her feminine weakness for trivial accessories, she embraced shopping as a leisure-time pursuit.[20] Some argued that the New Woman had been displaced from her role in the family unit by modern conveniences and rising incomes; others charged that she had abandoned the family, seeking out manly jobs in the professions. Either way, critics such as Macphail argued that the New Woman was the "unnatural" antithesis of traditional values, a non-producer responsible for declining birth rates and the erosion of the family unit.[21] "The country has grown rich," Macphail wrote, "but the family is destroyed," undone by industrial progress and commercial development.[22]

The wage-earning working girl represented a different moral danger. Changes in the job market related to industrialization and urbanization opened new opportunities for young women to leave domestic service (including unpaid work in the family home and paid work in the homes of others) for better-paying jobs and greater freedom in Canada's growing urban centres. In the minds of concerned moralists, young single working women were adrift, living without the benefit of close supervision.[23] All but ignoring the problem of low wages and the health and safety risks associated with industrial work, conservative critics tended to focus on the moral threat of leisure time. It "was in leisure pursuits" – not in the workplace, but in non-work hours – "that moral choices were made."[24] Tempted by small vanities and inexpensive commercial amusements, young working girls might be easily lured into committing immoral acts.[25] Department store employees were particularly at risk, as they worked in regular contact with questionable men in an environment that stimulated the desire for fancy goods – a combination seen as fatal to virtue.[26]

Criticism of the New Woman and the single wage-earning girl connected changes in production and consumption with the changing role of women, including greater sexual freedom and the commercialization of leisure. Criticism directed at women in their role as housewives was more specifically connected with changes in retailing and household provisioning. In her pursuit of the lowest price, critics charged that the bargain-hunting housewife put pressure on wages and profits, threatening the independent merchants long regarded as the backbone of the local community.[27]

In 1897, Joseph Clark, editor of *Saturday Night* magazine, launched an attack on department stores, detailing their destructive impact on long-standing patterns of community life. Clark's wide-ranging critique was well received, and a number of his columns were collected and reprinted in pamphlet form as *The Barnums of Business*. Clark identified a number of villains, including beneficial postal rates and the general susceptibility of consumers – men as well as women – to advertised bargains. Purchasers, he objected, were being "lured beyond 'their natural markets'" by false promises. "People no longer shop for necessaries ... but for the things that happen to be offered at apparent or pretended reductions in price."[28] As the series gained momentum, Clark's tone became increasingly strident, and he began to focus on housewives whose purchasing preferences, he argued, were destroying the independent shopkeepers critical to the well-being of the local community and exerting downward pressure on the wages of breadwinners. Women who patronized department stores, Clark charged, were irresponsible and shortsighted. They placed their neighbours, their communities, and their husbands' jobs at risk. Clark attributed this in part to feminine nature: women, he proposed, were especially susceptible to the lure of loss leaders, the false promises of advertising, and the pleasant surroundings offered by department stores.

Clark's attack was articulate and extended but not uncommon. Certainly, as historian Donica Belisle suggests, criticism of women shoppers can be understood as a specific expression of generalized anxieties about modernization. Responding to changes in long-standing relationships between buyers and sellers by stigmatizing women shoppers was one way to reaffirm traditional male authority.[29] But these critiques were also reactions to changing practices in household provisioning. According to historian David Monod, retailers at this time were becoming increasingly aware of a new class of customer: married women who did not work outside the home. Monod points to several reasons for this development: improved access to downtown streets and the increasing number of stores in urban centres meant that more women were travelling downtown to shop; increases in leisure time alternatives may have reduced the time allocated to Saturday as a family shopping day; and, more intriguingly, the "anonymity of cash payments" was altering the shopping experience. In the past, even women who shopped alone tended to be known and identified as the wives of familiar husbands; now shopkeepers were selling goods to women whose families, homes, and character were unknown.[30]

Once regarded as pillars of their community, local retailers increasingly found themselves competing against national chains in a struggle for survival, abandoned by women customers searching for low prices, seemingly unaware of the larger consequences of their choices. Department stores – the arch-enemy of the independent retailer – were especially associated with women shoppers. Social critics continued to see local retailers as good neighbours, men of integrity, and contributing members of the community. Shopping at the store in one's neighbourhood, Clark explained, "You work each other mutual good."[31] Small business was not simply a commercial enterprise, it was a moral enterprise and one primarily coded as male. Abandoning the local retailer for the department store to save a few cents destroyed the vitality of neighbourhoods and violated the moral codes that kept communities strong. As the housewife's responsibilities expanded, taking her out of the home and into the commercial marketplace, she was exposed to accusations of extravagance, vanity, and promiscuity in a way that husbands were not.[32] As turn-of-the-century studies of the New Woman, the wage-earning working girl, and bargain-hunting housewife show, moral critics were prone to seeing women consumers across a broad range of classes as a social problem.

For Canada's most conservative commentators, opposition to changing consumption practices was rooted in personal taste as well as moral conviction. Daily life brought constant affronts to sensibilities nurtured in an earlier age. "In the country," one observer explained,

> everybody knew everybody else. Everyone had a recognized place in the community. In the town no one knew or cared to know his next door neighbour. In the country there was little ostentatious display of wealth ... [and] definite obligations attached to its possession ... In the town the vulgar display abounds; there is much wealth and poverty ... [and] commercial keenness is looked upon with approval.[33]

Another recalled that, "in most places the old pier or hotel you loved in the nineties disappeared by the end of the century ... The shop in which you used to linger, perhaps unconsciously, over old prints or buy the rarer sorts of books in is gone ... and the spacious emporium with many departments that occupies its place hardly keeps anything that does not sell at the rate of a hundred in the season."[34] An idealized version of life on the family farms and in the small towns of mid-century Ontario and the Maritimes provided the yardstick to determine appropriate consumption. Expenditures beyond replacement (whether by the rich or the poor) were regarded as unnecessarily extravagant. Andrew Macphail presented an extreme example of resistance, upholding the virtues of small-town life not only in his essays but also in his personal appearance, by pointedly wearing suits that had been cut from cloth woven by his mother in Orwell, Prince Edward Island.[35] His example was not typical, but his tenacious commitment to past ideals was a physical manifestation of the values other conservatives shared, even as they found their habits and preferences increasingly out of step with the rhythms of the times.

Canadian conservatives took surprisingly little pleasure in rising rates of literacy, because they associated the proliferation of daily papers and mass-market magazines with declining civility and morals. Sir John George Bourinot, a noted constitutional expert and the first secretary of Canada's Royal Society, observed in his study of Canadian culture that, "These are days of many cyclopaedias, historical summaries, scientific digests, reviews of reviews, French in a few lessons, and interest tables. All is digested and made easy."[36] Writers, he objected, responded to "the demands of the publishers to meet the requirements of a public which must have its new novel as regularly as the Scotchman must have his porridge, the English-man his egg and toast, and the American his ice-water." The result was a "veneer of knowledge, which easily wears off in the activities of life."[37] Several of Canada's foremost poets used their newspaper columns to protest the influence of magazines published for readers "who demanded little" and therefore received only brief efforts with "polish but no feeling."[38] Macphail went even further: the misery of the poor, he suggested, was merely a literary creation designed by the daily press to increase sales. Middle-class busybodies, he argued, "driven by satiety in search of new emotions," gorged on the spectacle of urban suffering.[39] The true explanation for modern discontent was not poverty but plenty: "Sorrow begins when the possession of bread is sure, and leisure remains for the magnification of common ills," he maintained.[40]

Regarding themselves the custodians of civilization's highest values, Canada's literary elite insisted they had a duty to safeguard the moral virtues threatened by commercial distractions. Commemorating the achievements of people and important occasions would keep alive the essential values that lay beneath passing events, encouraging humankind to emulate the best of what had gone before.[41] As well-known moral reformer Agnes Maule Machar insisted, "Above all, Canada wants writers with noble ideals. The tendency of too many writers, now-a-days, is to lose these under the undermining influence of debasing materialism, but without the noblest ideals, the noblest work can never be done!"[42]

In spite of their commitment to an idealized past, Canada's conservative moralists did not deny the possibility of positive change. The honour accorded to an agrarian social order should be understood not simply as resistance but as a call to future greatness rooted in the ongoing development of the highest standards of Western tradition.[43] Objecting to the pace, rather than the principle, of change, Canada's conservative moralists minimized the extreme hardships of the settlement period, highlighting the merits of the past to illuminate the flaws of the present.[44] They preferred to characterize hard work as uplifting, seldom as back breaking. The burdens of mortgages and debts to storekeepers were ignored by those (like Andrew Macphail) who preferred to see farmers as the model of the self-sufficient individual, "who lives on his own land and owes no man anything."[45] At issue was not change as such, but the nation's commitment to maintaining the traditional regulatory virtues.[46] If the imperatives of self-discipline, freedom from debt, the dignity of work, abstinence, and the delay of personal gratification became optional rather than mandatory, conservatives believed that social disintegration was sure to follow.

Heading into the Great War, social conservatives perceived an opportunity for redemption and regeneration.[47] The cataclysm of war, they hoped, would break through the superficial trappings of modern life and return Canadians to more fundamental values. The sacrifices needed for victory represented opportunities for purification, offering the possibility of self-correction and the rediscovery of purpose. As the poet Wilfred Campbell explained to members of Toronto's elite Canadian Club, the recent era had been "given over to the pursuit of wealth and pleasure, stock, mine and land gambling of the wildest nature and a craze for motor cars ... but now the tents of gain and mirth are furled." In the postwar period, he predicted, "a new era would dawn."[48] Self-denial, forethought, and thrift would replace the hunger for material gain and vulgar pleasures. Home, family, parenthood, country life, and simple dignity would be revered once more. Although the people of Canada had lost touch with their inner essence, the radical rupture of war might restore society to its true path.[49]

In the early years of the war, as Canadians united in the face of crisis, new attention was indeed paid to moral issues: programs of temperance and electoral and political reform were widely embraced. The rhetoric of sacrifice and restraint rang loud. Political parties were dismissed as frivolous by new voices calling for service, efficiency, and sound management.[50] But at the same time, the practical necessities of waging war hastened the pace of change, increasing mechanization on the farm and in the factory, speeding urbanization, and raising wages. The dynamics of the war effort transformed the economy and society in ways incompatible with a return to prewar ideals.

After a sharp and relatively brief postwar recession, the pattern of rising wages and declining hours of work resumed.[51] In this context of growing prosperity and changing norms, excessive thrift and reliance on homemade goods came to be seen as evidence of insufficient income rather than strength of character, particularly in urban centres, where over 47 percent of Canadians now lived. Preaching simplicity and thrift, and wearing homespun and Victorian black, Canada's most conservative intellectuals represented a shrinking minority, out of step and often vaguely ridiculous in appearance, rigid, uncompromising, and idiosyncratic, rather than models of ideal behaviour.[52] Dismissing change as extravagance, the nation's most conservative critics refused to acknowledge either the pervasiveness or the legitimacy of changes in household spending. Refusing to acknowledge abundance, they also refused to see consumption as the possible basis for social life. The vehemence of their denunciations of material progress as decadence, and rapid change as decline, marginalized their position as leading thinkers in the community. They continued to call for a return to past ideals, advocating increasingly impractical approaches to social reform while their constituency drifted away. Ultimately, they cast themselves in the role of Jeremiah (the broken-hearted prophet), predicting doom would follow from the worship of false idols.

Prophets of Possibility

While social conservatives prophesized civilization's imminent decline, the progressive activists and theologians associated with the social gospel movement had a strongly positive vision, seeing the decades framing the turn of the century as a time of great opportunity. The movement was a collective effort of religious and social reform that swept through North America beginning in the later decades of the nineteenth century. Awakened to the possibilities of social salvation, men and women committed their lives to reconstructing society according to the teachings of Jesus. Social gospellers did not endorse unlimited consumption or encourage Canadians to find happiness through buying things, but they did acknowledge the importance of access to material necessities as the foundation of a moral life.

The rise of the social gospel movement has most often been studied as a reaction to the problems, rather than the possibilities, of modernity. Profound theological doubts coupled with a heartfelt response to the poverty and distress that accompanied rapid industrialization led a diverse group of Canadians to embrace secular objectives.[53] Although the focus of their religiosity shifted from the afterworld to the present, secularization should not be understood solely as a process of disenchantment – that is, of falling away from the spiritual and miraculous. It was equally one of falling towards a greater interest in the world. Reformers were energized by the possibilities of modernity and the perceived opportunity to create the Kingdom of God "within time." Canadians were, as one minister explained, "living in the midst of a great progressive revolution and the inescapable consequence must be the reconstruction of society on a better basis."[54]

Material things had no importance in themselves, but they did have value insofar as poverty was seen as a threat to spirituality. After observing slum conditions first hand as a mission worker and minister to impoverished immigrant communities, the progressive clergyman J.S. Woodsworth became convinced that, "in this world, souls are always incorporated in bodies and to save a man you must save him body, soul and spirit."[55] Other ministers shared Woodsworth's conviction that a full spiritual life required access to resources that had previously been regarded as comforts and luxuries, including sufficient leisure time, education, and, for some commentators, a garden. The Reverend Murdoch Mackinnon of Regina explained in an address delivered to the 1913 Pre-Assembly Congress of the Presbyterian Church that provision for the soul necessarily included provision for "the temple in which the soul is enshrined; if it be worthwhile preparing man for the hereafter, it should be worthwhile making a beginning here. If the 'here' has no value, neither has the 'hereafter.'"[56] In a talk entitled "The Family at Home" delivered to the same congress, Reverend A.G. Sinclair noted that, although "bricks and mortar do not make a home," the soul cannot "reach its highest development unless this base be adequate."[57] "The condition of home-life," he continued, "is the test of all civilization and all progress."[58] Because they saw material and spiritual well-being as closely related, reform-minded ministers insisted that it was not enough to merely sustain life with the bare minimum of food, shelter, and clothing. The opportunity to develop one's God-given gifts required a degree of material security. With consumption recast as the basis for spiritual growth and respectable lives, discussion of the pathologies associated with consumption (hedonism, selfishness, and status-driven buying) received less attention.

Social gospel leaders urged Canadians to regard the material relations of society as the visible manifestation of their spiritual commitments. While economists saw self-interest and competition as vital to progress, social gospellers regarded cooperation, selflessness, and promotion of the common good as the fundamental principals of a Christian economy. Because economic abundance was possible, poverty was no longer acceptable.[59] Ensuring decent living standards for the poorest members of society was the ethical responsibility of a Christian community and not merely the function of personal production. Progressive ministers shared conservative concerns about the growing ethos of materialism and increasing extremes of wealth, but they identified different solutions. Conservative moralists called for a return to past standards of thrift and industriousness; ministers of the social gospel movement denounced the exploitation of labour, insisting that the spiritual interests of the community were best served when workers were paid a fair, living wage. Certainly ministers and social reformers continued to emphasize the importance of work, thrift, and sobriety; however, they also insisted that wages and prices should be determined by the needs of working-class families rather than by the labour markets.[60]

Calls for greater equality accompanied demands for a larger material base. An influential sermon by a leading Methodist churchman, Reverend Dr. Albert Carman, was severe in its condemnation of wealth but confident about prospects for change. In "The Gospel of Justice," Carman urged his prosperous Toronto congregation to look closely at the "hideous wrongs, mighty injustice and cruel dishonesty" in society.[61] He condemned the excesses of wealth but did not specifically call for increases in charity or the return to a more modest way of life. Rather, he challenged listeners to engage in social change. It was, Carman insisted, inappropriate to counsel the poor to wait for "a fairer distribution" in the afterlife when their condition could be improved in the present. As Carman's address suggests, determinations of injustice followed from the belief that abundance was available. Asserting that every individual belonged to a common Christian fellowship and was equal in God's sight helped to detach the right to consume from wages and work. Other moderate leaders were similarly direct when discussing the role of money in social reform. In an exhortation delivered to the Pre-Assembly Congress of the Presbyterian Church, the Reverend Charles Gordon (well known to many as Ralph Connor, the author of best-selling novels) admonished listeners that you can "tell a Christian, not by the way he uses the Bible, but by the way he uses his bankbook; not by the way he spends his Sabbaths, but by the way he spends his money."[62] The great moral problem, another minister explained, "was not poverty but prosperity."[63]

Material and spiritual concerns were often conflated in practical missionary work. The Fred Victor Mission in Toronto, the most prominent of the Methodist settlement houses, offered lessons in elocution, manual training (for boys), and household management (for girls). Facilities included an employment agency, a penny savings bank, a drug dispensary, an inexpensive restaurant, and a boardinghouse.[64] Picnics, special suppers, and a gymnasium encouraged the appropriate use of leisure time. The All People's Mission in Winnipeg offered a popular Sunday afternoon lecture series that included musical concerts and "conversational talks on helpful subjects" such as architecture, the single tax, the nervous system, and contagious diseases, held in surroundings hung with beautiful pictures. The expressed goal of domestic missions was to alleviate poverty by creating moral, upright, and progressive Canadian citizens. Their supporters regarded the standard of living as a tool of integration, serving equally to Christianize and Canadianize immigrants. Respectability had a strong material component, including cleanliness, adequate privacy, and appropriate clothing. Habits of temperance, savings, self-restraint, and personal time management led to economic and spiritual advancement. Inculcating appropriate behaviours, including the proper use of money and suitable consumption choices, was central to the religious project.[65]

Abject poverty was not the only consumption-related concern. Commercialized entertainments – including magazines, popular novels, dance halls, radio programs, and, increasingly, films – were regarded as "rivals" competing for the time, attention, and loyalties of congregants and potential congregants, particularly in larger urban centres.[66] Ministers responded by modernizing their methods and updating their sermon topics to attract and keep the attention of congregants. Many forms of commercial entertainment – including lantern shows, body building, novels, and the sale of religiously themed souvenirs – were recognized as potential evangelical tools that could bring the message of the gospel to new audiences and Canadians closer to God. Other outreach strategies inspired by secular developments included the formation of literary and debate clubs, enlisting endorsements from famous people, and paying greater attention to potential newspaper coverage.[67] Ministers, particularly within the Methodist Church, loosened restrictions on leisure pursuits such as dancing, card playing, and attending theatre performances.[68] Church bureaucracies grew and adopted more systematic approaches to fundraising in order to support programs that placed new demands on their financial and human resources. Increasingly sophisticated campaigns were organized around specific themes, supported by advertising materials, bulletins, pledge cards, and denominational literature distributed through centralized communications departments.[69]

In *Secularizing the Faith*, historian David Marshall argues that, by adopting the methods of commercial culture to advance Christian causes, churches turned their message into a commodity. Other historians have offered more sympathetic interpretations, proposing that progressive ministers embraced the tools of mass culture as opportunities to extend the influence of the church and ensure that Christianity remained within the mainstream of Canadian culture.[70] Whether these efforts were ultimately self-defeating, easing the acceptance of values and lifestyles fundamentally incompatible with Christian objectives, remains moot: in either case, it is not clear what alternative measures were possible.[71] What is clear is that progressive ministers recognized and embraced the socializing potential of consumer experiences and welcomed tools of mass communication as a means to extend their reach. Creating the Kingdom of God in the present required activating and sustaining a broadly based body of public opinion in support of demands for legislative change. The ability to reach mass audiences and to attract a broader range of congregants was critical to the mission of social reform.

The place of consumption in the message of the social gospel movement should not be overstated. Few ministers or lay leaders questioned the importance of behavioural restraints such as sobriety, self-discipline, and thrift. Consumerist themes were an extension of, but certainly not a replacement for, older themes. Anticipating the dawning of a new age, social gospellers imbued material relations with moral significance. As Nellie McClung (prairie Methodist, activist, and feminist) explained, men and women should "live their lives here in such a way that other men and women will find life sweeter for their having lived. Incidentally, we will win heaven, but it must be a result, not an objective."[72] Attention to improving the lives of others in the present moved consumer concerns towards the foreground of progressive religious reform. Some of the negative connotations surrounding consumption were neutralized and replaced with more positive understandings. By insisting that all people had a natural right to material well-being, regardless of their role in production, ministers advanced consumerist values into the mainstream of public discussion.

As long as consumption was considered immoral, it would be impossible to champion an economic order dedicated to increasing consumption. American historian Kathleen Donohue argues that it was necessary to distinguish between legitimate and illegitimate forms of consumption if consumerist perspectives were to become widely accepted.[73] The social gospel movement was a critical force in making and publicizing this difference. Social gospellers, whether radical or conservative, did not seek to justify consumption as such.[74] However, they did play an important role in shifting the focus of discussion from the consumption of luxury goods to "ordinary" consumption. Promoting fuller lives supported by spending beyond the minimum level required for basic sustenance aligned the message of the gospel with capitalism's need for growing markets. Supporting aspirations for material well-being helped to diffuse the image of a society bound together not by common faith but by common consumption practices. By identifying consumption as a field where social relations play out and where reform was possible, the social gospel movement contributed to the creation of a climate of opinion favourable to new practices and new values, helping to create the conditions that would allow for the gradual rise to dominance of a consumer orientation.

The Meaning Is in the Spending

Economic thinking about consumption evolved through the later nineteenth and early twentieth century as increasing productivity in industry and manufacturing called into question theories that had been developed in conditions of scarcity. Focused on capital, labour, markets, and trade, classical economists understood the value of a commodity as primarily a function of the resources and labour necessary to produce it. Increases in consumption were regarded as something that occurred naturally ("supply creates its own demand"), or as the consequence of succumbing to what the influential British economist Alfred Marshall referred to as "unwholesome desire for wealth as a means of display."[75] Classical economists regarded economies as self-regulating: the free operation of the market would ensure a balance between supply and demand. According to traditional economic theory, then, policies to stimulate consumption were unnecessary.[76]

In the last quarter of the nineteenth century, however, investment in capital goods stalled, commodity prices fell, and the global economy entered a prolonged recession. Industrialists, mass retailers, and some economists began to see increasing consumer demand as the key to restoring growth. Professional economists, led by Marshall in England and John Bates Clark in the United States, began to shift their emphasis from the study of production and profit to the study of spending and the conditions of consumption. Output was recognized as the outcome of demand and supply operating in tandem. Demand, along with capital investment, for goods and the satisfaction of the habits, appetites, and desires of consumers could play an important role in driving economic activity.[77]

The economic potential of domestic consumption was less apparent in Canada than in the United States, Britain, or Europe. Seeing a domestic market of limited size, political economists regarded Canada as a country with more resources than population and therefore ample, but constrained, opportunities. Although they were aware of new theories, Canadian economists tended to regard these developments as "valid but remote" for a country "on the fringes" of the industrial giants, dependent on foreign capital, and with a comparatively small industrial base and a limited supply of skilled labour.[78] Instead, mainstream Canadian economists continued to associate economic growth with capital investment and external trade. They identified the consumption of basic necessities as a social good that would benefit individuals and reduce labour unrest; however, they did not regard either the principles of a demand-driven economy or the economic value of ever-increasing rates of consumption as relevant to the Canadian context.

The dominant figures in what was effectively the first generation of professional economists in Canada were Adam Shortt at Queen's, James Mavor at the University of Toronto, Stephen Leacock at McGill, and O.D. Skelton, who succeeded Shortt at Queen's in 1908.[79] Each had begun his studies in the era when the broad discipline of political economy was dividing into the more specialized fields of economics and political science. Their interests and aptitudes, however, lay less in the realm of theory than in policy solutions to practical problems in government, business, and society.[80] Although their ages, training, and education varied somewhat, they were uniformly committed to capitalism and strongly opposed to socialism, believing that competition led to improvements in communication, mechanization, and productivity. They recognized the pursuit of material betterment as a necessary spur to individual incentive but criticized extravagance as both socially disruptive and economically inefficient. They accepted inequality as the natural reward for hard work and good management, but they also believed that greater production and greater consumption could co-exist, and they called for the benefits of increasing productivity to be more broadly distributed throughout society. Because Canada's total wealth was visibly increasing, they regarded imbalances in distribution, rather than a fundamental scarcity of goods, as the principal cause of social unrest. Addressing these imbalances and raising standards of consumption (rather than simply increasing the quantity of goods consumed) would improve individuals and elevate society, solving many of the social problems created by industrial capitalism. They were, for the most part, optimists, believing in the advance of civilization and the promise of Canada. Mavor was something of an outlier among his peers (although not among business leaders) in disparaging the potential role of government. In contrast, Shortt, Leacock, and Skelton believed that legislation could be used to ameliorate problems created during the production process and to improve social well-being.

Adam Shortt was Canada's first native-born economist and the first academic economist to make Canada's domestic economy his primary field of study. Born and educated in the villages of Ontario, he began his studies in religion and philosophy, intending a career in the ministry. Like many who approached political economy from this background, Shortt deplored the separation of economic theory from ethics and politics. The subject of wealth, he objected, should not be "in itself a kind of final object." The sciences of wealth and government were not independent; consideration of the development of civilization required attention to the desired ends as well as to the available means.[81]

Despite his concerns about labour unrest, Shortt credited millionaires and captains of industry with the advance of civilization, believing they were best able to organize and use capital effectively. He wrote approvingly of those who spent their private wealth on museums, art galleries, and gracious surroundings for civic benefit. In an early essay, he expressed the hope that increasing productivity might allow every Canadian sufficient leisure time for self-development and a higher quality of life. Shortt did not doubt the fundamental importance of production, capital investment, and exports to economic growth in Canada, but he also believed that consumption could be an agent of social progress. Insofar as the goods desired by the ordinary men and women of Canada influenced the conditions of production, consumer preferences had the power to change society:

> The kinds of work which the labour classes must do are fixed by the kinds of wares, and the quantities of them, which people will buy. If they buy an unnecessary amount of food, clothing and other mere bodily gratification, if they build unneeded railroads, factories and similar works, but want little good literature, art, entertainment and instruction, then great numbers of men must live by the lower forms of labour and few by the higher.[82]

Like many of his peers, Shortt regarded profit sharing between capital and labour as a means to increase productivity; however, he argued that improved working conditions, even more than wage increases, were the key to reducing labour unrest. Gains in productivity that increased profits would make it possible to redirect a share of capital investment from machinery to the moral and aesthetic advancement of individuals and of society as a whole. The nation, Shortt insisted, should concentrate on increasing those occupations that were the least degrading and on developing machinery and mechanical appliances to relieve people of the worst sorts of toil.[83] Familiar with the small towns of mid-nineteenth-century Ontario, he saw little to celebrate in pioneer life and its regime of mind-deadening labour.[84] When Canadians accumulated "means beyond the needs of the day," he believed that they would turn from the cultivation of the land to the cultivation of the self. As he observed in 1898, "We have spent no end of time and talent in learning, better perhaps than in any other part of the world, how most effectively to acquire wealth, but we have not considered it worth our while to make any serious study as to how most perfectly to spend it. Yet after all its only meaning is in its spending."[85] Insofar as gains in improving forms of consumption would provide access to a more spiritual life for more Canadians, increases in consumption were to be welcomed as possible agents of moral advance.

Shortt recognized that consumer demands, when considered in aggregate, had the economic power to influence the sorts of goods that would be produced, the demand for labour, and the nature of working conditions, yet at the same time he strongly opposed innovations in economic theory that linked the value of goods to demand rather than to production costs. Shortt's early career at Queen's coincided with the rise and gradual acceptance of new economic theories, which held that large-scale industrial capitalism fundamentally altered the dynamics of the economy in developed nations, reducing and stabilizing the costs of manufacturing and vastly increasing the quantities of goods being produced. When economies were organized around mass production, demand was more easily satisfied; as a consequence, prices dropped, reducing the profit per unit sold. As the capacity of production increased, it was the abundance of commodities – rather than their scarcity – that posed the greatest challenge to economic stability. Trying to maintain revenues, manufacturers competed to expand market share, either by taking over competitors or by dropping prices even further. Another solution lay in cultivating mass markets. In a highly competitive mass market, the utility of a good to the manufacturer reflected its ability to satisfy the tastes of consumers in preference to other available goods. The utility of any single item diminished as more and more items were produced: the cost of manufacturing (wages, raw materials, machinery, etc.) became less important than demand in establishing price and profit. While the problem of scarcity had been solved, the problem of profit had increased.[86]

Shortt, however, rejected this notion of "diminishing utility" as a general economic principle, arguing that it held true "for only the barest necessaries of life." In particular, he rejected the market as a mechanism for measuring the value of those wants that society regarded as "distinctively human." Prices might in a general way reflect desire, but they could never measure the true value of "the higher satisfactions." The "pleasure which one derives from a fine picture or a well written book ... may largely determine the price which one will pay for such things"; however, that price gave "no ground for determining with any accuracy worth mentioning, the amount of pleasure or satisfaction one gets for a given amount of money, or how much money one will spend to get a certain kind of pleasure."[87] The products of high culture, he insisted, were not open to commodification. The things most worth having – the things most distinctively human – occupied a realm apart from the market economy and the laws of supply and demand.

As he took up a post in political economy at the University of Toronto in 1893, James Mavor stood similarly poised between old and new economic theories. In the United Kingdom, Mavor was known for his interest in social reform movements, primarily those led by prominent left-leaning thinkers rather than those led by labour unionists.[88] His published articles sounded a modern note, insisting that morals should be removed from the science of economics. The allocation of profits, he asserted, should be determined by return on investment and not the struggle for power between capital and labour. Higher wages should be recognized as an investment in worker productivity. Calling for the collection of data on wage rates and living costs, Mavor focused attention on the ordinary, rather than improving or exceptional, forms of consumption. Economists, he argued, should deal not with what ought to be, but with reality as it actually existed.[89]

As incoming professor of political economy and constitutional history, Mavor was expected to give an inaugural address. His chosen topic was consistent with his reputation as a pragmatist interested in social issues. In a speech entitled "The Relation of Economic Study to Public and Private Charity," Mavor asserted that poverty was not a reflection of moral weakness but simply a matter of "unsatisfied need." Poverty was the "condition of those who live at a low level, whose food, clothing and shelter are relatively inadequate ... [compared] to the resources and consumption of those who are living at a higher level." The solution to poverty was a practical matter of attaining the requisite resources, and thus poverty should be studied as a part "of the economic life of the people as a whole." The study of wealth, he explained, lay in the departments of production and distribution; the study of poverty belonged "in the department of consumption."[90]

Mavor accepted that a national system of government aid might be needed to support the elderly and the ill at respectable levels, but he believed that the solution to urban poverty lay primarily in the laws of supply and demand. He called for a business-like approach to charity. Putting people to work artificially, he objected, distorted the economy. Instead he favoured organizing farm colonies in "neglected" locations, where the able bodied could be self-supporting, producing goods for one another. Establishing new colonies would restore economic equilibrium and rescue the urban poor from the degradations of poverty and dependency.[91]

Although Mavor considered poverty to be a relative social and economic condition rather than a moral weakness, he had little sympathy for Canadians challenged by rising costs. Writing decades later, in the midst of Canada's boom during the First World War, he objected that all classes in the community were "infected by the desire to raise their standard of comfort." Increasing wages encouraged the relaxation of moral codes; ethics turned "from fixed facts to shifting standards that change from age to age like the fashion of our clothes" in an "orgy of extravagance." The pendulum, he warned, would swing the other way when the war ended.[92] If production and consumption were held in balance, a community might effect slow gains over time; Mavor rejected the possibility of an upward spiral of economic growth, with gains in production fuelled by increasing consumer demand.

In marginalist economic theory, the moral significance of a particular good was irrelevant – it was the economic significance of goods as generators of demand that mattered. Adam Shortt and James Mavor welcomed advances in technology and increases in productivity but held misgivings about unfettered demand. It is not clear if they failed to grasp or simply disagreed with the underlying economic assumptions of an economy driven by mass production and mass consumption. They certainly disagreed with the ethical implications.

On the other hand, Stephen Leacock and O.D. Skelton, almost a generation younger, were enthusiastic about the capacity of the industrial economy to provide material abundance for all. As graduates of the nascent University of Chicago School of Economics, they took a complicated view of modern society, seeing interest groups struggling for power in an economy constrained by its prevailing social institutions amid oscillating business cycles. Both advocated strong but very different roles for government in the improvement of society. Leacock associated social mobility with adequate access to education, food, shelter, and opportunities for work. He urged government to provide these basic necessities as a matter of right to its citizens. Skelton emphasized the role of government in the industrial economy, calling on the state to mediate conflicts between vested interest groups and regulate monopolies to prevent the undue exploitation of labour. Both Leacock and Skelton recognized the democratic implications of an economy producing more goods and championed the policies they believed would improve the material welfare of ordinary Canadians.

Best known today as a humorist, Stephen Leacock was a well-regarded economist in the early decades of the twentieth century. He joined the Department of Political Economy at McGill University in Montreal in 1903 and rose quickly to become department head. He was a prolific essayist and a popular speaker, particularly for conservative and imperialist causes. His 1906 textbook, *Elements of Political Science*, became a standard in universities throughout North America and, as Leacock himself often liked to point out, was his most profitable book.[93] Leacock was less positive about the role of concentrated capital than either Adam Shortt or James Mavor, but he was considerably more optimistic about the power of the industrial economy to effect substantial and permanent social change.

Leacock's antipathy to the materialism of his day was well known. In critical essays and fictional stories, he condemned the spread of commercial values and pilloried the consumption habits of wealthy plutocrats who, he alleged, controlled the nation's economy. "We have gone astray," he wrote. "Our whole conception of individual merit and of national progress has been expressed in dollars and cents."[94] What separated Leacock from the purely conservative critics of his day was his acknowledgment that significant gains had been achieved and his insistence that even more were possible.[95]

Although Leacock condemned the erosion of traditional values under the onslaught of industrial capitalism, he championed what was essentially a consumption-centred model of social justice. His strongest critiques were aimed at the morals of the wealthy and those who wanted to be wealthy.

Ordinary Canadians, he insisted, were victims, denied basic necessities of life by an economic system that misdirected the machinery of industry to produce profits rather than plenty.[96] Unlike many social conservatives, Leacock did not call for a return to rural life. In any case, his fiction portrayed the residents of Canada's villages and towns as no strangers to materialism: his stories lambasted status-driven consumption and skewered the pretensions of the wealthy in both town and city. Leacock accepted self-interest as the motive force necessary for economic progress, but he did not share Shortt's and Mavor's faith in elites. Insofar as the moneyed classes had abandoned the ideals of hard work, self-discipline, and creative investment, further increases in wealth were unlikely to foster a spirit of generosity. Leacock believed that the true measure of national progress was not the attainment of fine things by the wealthy but improvements in the living conditions of the masses of working people. The destructive power of modern industry could not be ameliorated, but it could at least be used for the benefit of the ordinary men and women of Canada. Leacock condemned materialism but accepted that Canada had moved beyond scarcity, and he called for the benefits of industrial and technological progress to be spread more evenly. Adequate consumption was identified with citizenship.

O.D. Skelton was the youngest, most optimistic, and most politically progressive member of this founding group. Whereas Leacock regarded ordinary Canadians as victims of capital, impoverished by the rapacity of profiteers, Skelton identified a pattern of gradually rising wages, increasing material well-being, and expanding opportunity.[97] In a critique of socialism based on his prize-winning dissertation, Skelton asserted that the stimulus of private enterprise had "so perfected production as to lower prices of goods and services in nearly every line, and to bring within the reach of the many of to-day what were the luxuries of the few of yesterday."[98] Conservative social critics viewed the market as a moral instrument that held people responsible for their own lives and choices: success or failure was a reflection of character. In contrast, Skelton wrote about the market as a highly efficient mechanism, able to maximize the social utility of productive power and, therefore, of economic and social well-being. The market system, he asserted, was unique in its ability to match production with consumption, avoiding the dangers of excess planning on the one hand and coercion on the other. It was capitalism that "best meets the needs of the millions who every day grow more ambitious in their standards and more insistent in their demands."[99]

As productivity rose, Skelton recognized that competition for market share
was becoming increasingly cut-throat. Bankruptcies, mergers, and monopolies were common in the struggle for profit. Yet he considered a generalized
crisis of overproduction to be impossible. Rejecting socialist theories that
connected economic crises to inadequate consuming power, he proposed
that, "so long as the wants of men are capable of infinite expansion, there
can be no question of the ability of society as a whole to increase its desires
to equal whatever tremendous increase of products and services may be ef-
fected; in the quantitative as aside from the value aspect, over-production is
clearly impossible."[100] Skelton further suggested that rising social unrest was
the outcome not of problems inherent to capitalism, but of its success. It was

> beyond question that wages were higher, hours were shorter, housing
> is better, the death-rate lower ... Yet all these betterments have merely
> served to whet the appetite for more ... The higher pedestal has opened
> new horizons ... Standards have advanced faster than incomes. The
> luxuries of yesterday become to-day's necessities ... Speed and up-to-
> datedness must be had at any cost.[101]

Although his own assessment of the Canadian economy was positive,
Skelton noticed a growing sense of "public uneasiness as to the genuineness
of the seemingly abounding prosperity." The question of the distribution of
wealth was becoming acute. Some groups, including manufacturers, farmers, and those in financial services had flourished, giving "the tone and
colour of prosperity to the period." Other classes gained by an increase in
steady employment but lost purchasing power due to rising costs. Although
Canada was a prosperous nation, discontent and inequality were growing.
Democracy had "levelled tastes and heightened ambitions. Growing leisure
meant, for the poor of soul, need for more expenditure on outward things."
Although he condemned speculation and excess spending as destabilizing,
Skelton insisted that broadly increasing wealth was benefiting the whole of
society, with "at least a proportionate share falling to the working classes."
Private motivations, whether for pre-eminence, fireside comforts, or basic
survival, supplied the "needful stimulus" for economic development. Moreover, under conditions of modern industry, society would be able to meet
basic needs with a smaller and smaller proportion of labour. The rest of
the productive system would be free to meet demands for new services
and commodities.[102] Unlike Canada's conservative critics, Skelton expressed

few reservations about seeking personal gratification, holding that individual choice was paramount.

A decade of economic expansion in much of the industrialized world ended abruptly in 1913 with a sharp recession, followed soon after by the declaration of war in 1914. From the perspective of Canada's economic community, most urgent challenges of the war effort were financial. Prior to the war, the government of Canada had raised revenues from tariffs and capital borrowed almost entirely from British investors. When war broke out, capital inflows fell and imports plummeted. The government turned to Canadians for new sources of revenue, introducing personal income and corporate profit taxes and selling war bonds to domestic investors. Victory Loan campaigns raised tremendous, and completely unanticipated, amounts of revenue. The first domestic savings campaign in 1915 set a target of $50 million and raised $100 million, primarily from wealthier Canadians and corporate investors. Beginning in 1917, the government reached out to ordinary citizens. As casualties mounted on the front, distinctions between needs and luxuries (which were seldom precisely defined but generally referenced things that, a decade earlier, did not exist or that ordinary people did not typically own) took on heightened moral significance. Thrift became a civic obligation rather than simply an economic virtue. The war enlarged the power and the presence of the state in the lives of Canadians. At the same time, massive increases in exports, not only of industrial goods and munitions but also of wheat and timber, reinforced the understanding of Canada as having an export-driven economy.

Professional economists filled a variety of roles during the war. Shortt, Skelton, and Leacock were especially prominent as writers and speakers, encouraging the purchase of Victory Bonds and explaining the need for new taxes. Wartime addresses provided an opportunity to set out postwar visions. Adam Shortt was particularly impressed by the amount of capital raised in domestic markets to support the war effort. Haunted by the image of an army of soldiers "turned loose with nothing to do and no means," he called upon Canadians to further develop their capital reserves. Addressing the influential Canadian Club in April 1915, Shortt warned that foreign investment would remain limited and urged his audience to adopt a regime of plain living and high thinking, promising that, if

a spiritual and educational wave were to pass over this country, we should save immense amounts, and be able to finance ourselves ... We have had

immense attention paid in our educational institutions to training people
for the production of life, but very little attention paid to the training of
people for the consumption of life ... It takes a great deal of training and
a great deal of reflection and a great deal of self-educating and culture in
order to lead the complex, the high life, to get ... up into the loftier regions
[where] the demand is for goods which are not consumed in the enjoyment of life.[103]

Even though Shortt predicted declines in international investment and
trade, he did not suggest that domestic consumption could become a vehicle of economic growth. Instead, he championed reduced consumption
and increased investment as the keys to financial stability and economic
independence.

Stephen Leacock shared Shortt's concerns about wasteful spending but
took a different lesson from Canada's wartime experiences. In a series of
widely publicized essays prepared for the War Department, Leacock drew
a rigid line between necessity and excess. "Tens of thousands, millions of
our men, women and children," he noted disapprovingly, continued to be
engaged in

making pianos, gramophones, motor cars, jewellery, books, pictures,
clothes in millions of yards and millions of dollars, that are mere needless luxuries, furniture that could be waited for, new houses where our
old ones would still do, new railroads that lead nowhere ... Such people,
though they work fourteen hours a day, are mere drones in the hive as
far as the war is concerned ... The farmer who raises food and exchanges
it for pianos, pianolas, victrolas, trotting buggies, books, moving pictures,
pleasure cars, and so on, is just as much a war-drone as the man who
made them.[104]

Equally condemning consumers and the workers who made consumer
goods, Leacock called for the nation-wide reorganization of the economy
and a campaign of thrift: "Save every cent. Live plainly. Do without everything. Rise early, work hard, and content yourself with a bare living."[105]
New clothes, he contended, should be regarded as a badge of shame.

Looking ahead to the postwar period, Leacock proposed that the state's
role in the economy be carried forward to achieve social justice in Canada.[106] He did not propose altering the fundamental structures of capitalism;

self-interest would continue to drive economic progress. However, the state could use its power to ensure a livelihood for every Canadian: employment for the able-bodied, maintenance for the elderly and the infirm, and adequate education for every child. It was equality of opportunity, rather than material equality, that Leacock held up as the measure of social justice. The state's ability to marshal the nation's resources for the war effort had shown that this ideal was attainable. Leacock did not promote consumption as a driver of economic growth; however, he insisted that the modern economy had the capacity to provide for all, and he called on the state to ensure that all citizens had access to basic necessities.

While Shortt and Leacock discussed the economic challenges of war in terms of consumption, Skelton wrote about the war as a crisis of production: "It is goods and services, not money, that are the prime requisite in waging a great war. It is not a question of how to get a billion dollars in money, but how to get a billion dollars' worth of goods and services where they will be most effective in winning the war."[107] The financial task, although immense, was secondary to the task of organizing the nation's resources: "Every bit of human effort, every yard of khaki, every pound of steel that is to count must come out of current production."[108] The problem was how to effect this change in a free society. Opposed in principle to compulsion, Skelton favoured a pragmatic combination of inducements to thrift, savings bond campaigns, and tax reform. The war, he suggested, provided an opportunity to address long-standing inequalities and inefficiencies in the tax system that disproportionately burdened large families and working-class Canadians.[109] New taxes on income, excess corporate profits, and inheritance would be more efficient in directing purchasing power towards the state, effectively transferring labour from non-essential to essential occupations without the need for coercive measures. In the postwar period, higher levels of taxation should be continued in order to support the expanding responsibilities of government and growing expectations for pensions and other socially progressive measures. If the postwar economy were managed with "foresight," Skelton was certain that Canada would become "a land where every man and woman among us will have a fair chance to share in the decencies and comforts and the possibilities of development that have hitherto been restricted to the few."[110]

Amid the crisis of war, a number of the nation's most prominent economists clarified their thinking about the implications of changing patterns of consumption. There was no consensus; however, there was a growing awareness of the power of consumer spending. Canadian economists did not discuss the mass market as such. Although they saw the choices consumers made as heavily influenced by advertising and social considerations, they regarded consumers as independent economic actors. They described the impact of consumer spending as a function of the aggregated power of many individual decisions rather than the workings of a homogeneous mass mind. While they did not hold spending itself to be a virtue, most believed that increased spending could open the way to moral, educational, and social improvements. Canada's leading economic thinkers had begun to modify the producerist paradigm, looking beyond the interests of capitalists and manufacturers, but they had not yet embraced a consumerist one.

Conclusion

At the beginning of the twentieth century, Canada's leading thinkers certainly did not celebrate the pleasures of spending, nor did they support seeking personal gratification through material goods. The growing capacity of the industrial economy, together with innovations in agriculture and resource extraction, promised increasing prosperity, challenging traditional assumptions about the relationship of frugality and success, restraint and indulgence. The consumption preferences of the masses of ordinary people were recognized as a growing force, and anxieties about changes in spending patterns were widely apparent. While some saw growing material abundance as the precursor to a more harmonious social order, others predicted moral decline and increasing class tensions. Observers acknowledged that consumption patterns influenced the structure of the economy, but they did not yet discuss increased spending as a vehicle of economic growth for Canada. Many acknowledged, albeit often with disapproval, that consumption standards were socially determined. The recalibration of need versus want was another related theme. While many observers were concerned about rising inequality, they also commonly noted that the luxuries of yesterday had become the necessities of today – although whether this was to the benefit or detriment of society certainly remained contested.

Conservative moralists advocated resistance to changing consumption practices. Concerned about the corrosive effects of abundance on character, they insisted that the progress of civilization depended on a regime of self-denial, thrift, and hard work. Industrial capitalism was treated with suspicion, blamed for the rise of urban slums and the decline of moral fibre. However, conservative concerns were being marginalized by the economic realities of urbanization and industrialization.

Ministers in the social gospel movement and many of the nation's leading economic thinkers believed that gains in productivity were permanent, leading them to champion a more participatory vision of material abundance. Social gospellers insisted that increases in leisure time and improved access to basic goods and services held the potential for material, moral, and spiritual advancement. Although thrift remained the prescribed route to respectability – especially for the poor – the more progressive commentators proposed that thriving required a bit more spending.[111] The focus of moral concerns gradually shifted: while social conservatives continued to emphasize the need for work, thrift, and self-control among the working classes, social reformers were more likely to criticize the lifestyles of the wealthy and the injustices of the economic system.[112] They associated increasing prosperity with new virtues, including cleanliness, privacy, literacy, household management, and time for study. Commitments to a vision of Christianized capitalism did not displace beliefs in the traditional virtues of temperance, industriousness, thrift, and savings; however, poverty was no longer seen as good for the soul. Progressive thinkers saw material abundance as the precursor to a more harmonious social order. Economists wrote in secular terms but similarly associated growing consumption opportunities with possibilities for self-development and social harmony. Increased personal spending, most accepted, could coexist with economic growth.[113]

These positive views of consumers and consumption were an important step towards creating a frame of reference that would authorize new behaviours, values, and policies. The meaning, as Shortt had already expressed it in 1898, was no longer in the accumulation of wealth, but in the spending.[114]

Chapter Two

THE PROMISE
OF A MORE ABUNDANT LIFE

As the nation's conservative moralists, religious leaders, and economists debated the merits and potential dangers of increased access to consumer goods, prices were rising. Inflation, particularly in the cost of foodstuffs, became a source of concern for many Canadians and, indeed, for working-class families throughout the developed world in the years immediately prior to the First World War. Rioters took to the streets in Europe and the United States to protest rising prices.[1] In Canada, rising prices exacerbated wage disputes and intensified the struggle between traditional producer values of hard work, self-restraint, and thrift and the acceptance of new comforts, conveniences, and novelties. No other topic, observers often noted, commanded more attention. With so many affected and no clear under-standing of causes or solutions, appeals for government intervention mounted. Those purporting to speak on behalf of the consumer – the press, social reform and labour leaders, women's groups – called for investigation and regulation. In response to public outcry, the federal government con-ducted two inquiries into the cost of living, the first in 1909–10 and a second in 1913–14. These investigations helped legitimize new practices of household provisioning dependent on store-bought goods. The nation-wide effort to measure living costs was, in effect, an acknowledgment that the well-being of Canadians was now connected to their ability to buy every-day goods. Once collected, official statistics were available to be used not only by the state but also by consumers seeking government intervention, politicians appealing for votes, and unions bargaining for wages. Politicizing the domestic domain of household provisioning opened the door to political power for consumers and, perhaps more significantly, to the possibility of mobilizing consumers for political purposes.

The processes of investigation and the application of administrative techniques to consumer practices created a new relationship between Canadian consumers and the emergent managerial state. In order to measure changes in the costs of goods and services, it was necessary to measure the consumption habits of Canadians. Collecting and collating these data helped to normalize new consumer behaviours and to embed the category of the Canadian citizen as a wage spender, as well as a wage earner, in the workings of government. By engaging with consumption – that is, by representing, measuring, and categorizing the changing purchasing practices of Canadians – the state expanded its mandate and helped shape the ways Canadians came to see themselves as consumers.[2]

As industrial productivity increased in the decades around the turn of the century, the struggle over the distribution of rising profits and surplus goods intensified. Many accounts of working-class conditions, including contemporary and subsequent historical studies, reveal lives of ongoing struggle but others suggest rising consumption patterns and changes in preference indicative of an economy moving beyond scarcity. Modest gains in hourly earnings and more regular employment enabled skilled wage-labourers to gradually increase their purchasing power.[3] Other Canadians, particularly unskilled workers and those on fixed incomes, were less fortunate. In general, shifts in the economy benefited financiers, manufacturers, and farmers; meanwhile salaried middle-class professionals struggled to keep up with inflationary increases.

Increasing urbanization meant that Canadians were becoming more dependent on store-bought purchases and less able to offset rising prices with home-made clothes and backyard gardens. Changing retail practices, notably the copious use of advertised prices in the daily press by department and chain stores, also encouraged price awareness.[4] Overall, between 1896 and 1915, inflation in store-bought goods averaged 6 percent annually. The Department of Labour estimated that, between 1900 and 1910, the cost of food rose by one-third. Rents increased even more dramatically. Wage-earning families spent substantial portions of their income on food and rent. In 1910, a workingman's family spent 46.8 percent of their total income on food and 22.4 percent on rent, according to Department of Labour estimates. By 1913, these percentages had increased to 47.2 and 24.7, respectively. Because household budgets had little room to absorb price increases, the department believed that poorer families were compelled to lower their standard of housing and expenditure to make ends meet.[5]

American historians have suggested that public outrage directed at escalating living costs marked a turning point in that nation's social and political history, adding to the strength of movements for political reform. High prices created a focus of common concern among interest groups "who had little else to unite them." Once mobilized, consumer consciousness "cut across occupational and class lines, and did a great deal to dissolve the old nineteenth-century American habit of viewing political issues solely from the standpoint of the producer."[6] In newspapers from the early twentieth century, historian Richard Hofstadter observes, one began to read considerably less about the "effects on the working class, the middle class, and the farmer, and a great deal more about 'the plain people,' 'the common man,' 'the taxpayer,' 'the ultimate consumer,' and 'the man on the street.'"[7]

In Canada, by comparison, the controversy over rising prices and the search for an explanation or, failing that, a suitable scapegoat, served less to unify public opinion than to highlight the ways in which the new industrial order advantaged or disadvantaged different groups. Industrialists blamed rising prices on unions and increasing wages. Workers blamed the rise of monopolies. Economists suggested that increases in the world's supply of gold accounted for most of the change. Middle-class moralists pointed to the extravagant expenditures of the wealthy and rising expectations among the working classes. Everyone blamed the proliferation of middlemen involved in expanded networks of distribution and retail sales that characterized modern commerce. The *Canadian Annual Review* devoted six pages of its 1910 edition to a survey of the increasingly intense and wide-ranging discussions, citing numerous experts and opinion leaders, as well as the results of inquiries conducted by the press and various levels of government across the nation.[8] Mackenzie King, newly appointed as minister of labour, noted six possible factors related to rising prices, including increases in the population through immigration, an increase in the supply of gold, large expenditures in public works, and rising wages.[9]

Certainly rapid price increases were fundamentally disorienting, calling into question the value of goods and the meaning of money. But the breadth and vehemence of these responses suggest that rising prices and changing consumption practices provided a focus for social and economic anxieties related to many broader changes in Canadian life. Changes in standards and styles of living, rapid urbanization occurring in tandem with rural depopulation, the commodification of goods and services that families used to provide on their own, modernization of social relationships, and a host of other concerns – in some cases only loosely related to rising prices – were yoked to the visible, everyday problem of rising costs. Different responses to the rising cost of living provide a useful prism through which to view ideological differences among reactionary, populist, and progressive constituencies as they debated the morality of material progress in the emerging political economy of industrial Canada.

For many social critics, particularly the most conservative, concerns about social change began to coalesce around the rising cost of living and the figure of the Canadian consumer. Insofar as these thinkers regarded inflation as a problem driven by unrestricted desire, the solution was to be found in the realm of morality rather than economics. If people regulated their personal desires, there would be enough for all; if they failed to regulate desire, there would never be enough. In any case, more did not bring greater happiness.

Andrew Macphail, physician, author, and one of the nation's pre-eminent champions of conservative values, wrote a passionate critique for *University Magazine*, suggesting that rising costs were symptomatic of an epochal struggle for survival. The cost of living, he contended, was "a reflex, or reflection, of civilization." It invariably rose with the rise of luxury and "rises fastest where luxury is most widespread." For Macphail, luxury was not solely a question of material comfort; it also involved the non-productive use of time and resources. "It does not matter whether that waste is perpetrated by the housemaid in the pantry, by her mistress at the milliner's, or by her employer at the club," he wrote. "The farmer who indulges himself with an unnecessary 'buggy' pays for his indulgence with his hard won labour. The rich man who amuses himself with a motor car distributes the cost of his amusement over the whole country." Macphail set out an apocalyptic vision of a society divided into producers and consumers. "There is, in reality, only one serious question which confronts all created beings," he insisted: "What shall we eat, What shall we drink, Where withal shall we be clothed? ... To-day the war is between those, on the one hand, who consume more than they produce, and those who produce more than they consume. Rising prices are a sign of the rising conflict."[10]

Occupying different points along the political spectrum, consumer activists organized to increase household purchasing power and minimize potential tensions between higher wages and lower prices. Associations of housewives, farmers, and workers – each group self-consciously identifying as consumers – took up a variety of projects designed to counter the perceived inefficiencies of the marketplace. Although working conditions remained a significant concern, unions, particularly those representing skilled labour in Canada's largest cities, began to emphasize wage demands rather than working conditions.[11] In Toronto, the Railway Brotherhood opened a butcher shop and a small grocery store open to members of all railway brotherhoods and other unionists.[12] In Calgary, middle-class women organized the first branch of the Consumers' League in Canada. They breathed new life into a moribund public market, where their ability to offer fresh produce at lower than existing retail costs attracted widespread interest.[13] On the Prairies, a wave of consumer cooperatives sprang up to fight high prices.[14] Outraged over rising costs, women and men mobilized around common interests and took practical action in their local communities. These various acts of protest did not coalesce into nation-wide political action; however, the publicity that attended each effort raised awareness of common consumer interests that spanned boundaries of class, gender, and region.

Ensuring the ability of working-class Canadians to acquire the necessaries of a respectable life, as well as enthusiasm for statistical inquiry, were fundamental themes in Canadian progressivism. Between 1910 and 1915, social surveyors compiled data on the ethnic origin, material circumstances, and moral state of the poor in many of Canada's major urban centres, primarily under the auspices of the Methodist and Presbyterian churches. Statistics on abysmal housing conditions, overcrowding, poor sanitation, and a host of social evils (including improper sleeping arrangements, the number of pool rooms, and prostitution) were carefully documented as threats to spiritual and moral well-being. By amalgamating statistics and moral judgments, sociologist Mariana Valverde argues, social surveys advanced a new way of conceptualizing the problems of the collective. Areas of life once regarded as matters of private responsibility became the subjects of investigation and, potentially, of regulation. Linking social reform to measurable indicators helped progressives identify common goals and define a broad national interest associated with living conditions.[15]

The Managerial State

Studies of consumption practices were only one of many new areas of government intervention in a period characterized by the growth of the state.[16] The expansion of government services since the turn of the century had been rapid but uncoordinated. Evidence of government waste and poor planning had been the subject of probes by the press, the opposition, and the government itself in 1906, 1908, and 1912.[17] The example, and even more importantly, the ideals of industrial management fuelled demands for civil service reform.[18] In short order, bureaucratic values such as economy, efficiency, organization, and effectiveness were imported from business directly into government.[19]

In both the corporate and the civic realms, developments in administration had the effect of opening a middle ground, which, like the growing interest in consumption, shifted attention and power away from conflicts between labour and capital.[20] In the realm of industry, the emergence of the corporate form and innovations in business administration were fundamentally linked with increases in productivity and expanded possibilities of consumption. In the realm of public administration, measurement and analysis became integrated into the working of the managerial state. As Robert H. Coats, Canada's first dominion statistician observed, "The Government is more than a congeries of departments: it is a single agency having as a paramount duty the guiding of economic policy ... The economic body is one, not several; and its observations must be on that basis."[21]

Inquiries into the cost of living were part of a larger initiative to create a centralized national bureau of statistics. Such an institution, Coats explained, would constitute a "central thinking office" with the necessary "inquisitorial powers," machinery, and expertise to act as a "national laboratory" for the observation and interpretation of economic trends.[22] The development of national statistics and the appointment of boards of inquiry should be situated within Canadian progressivism; they were responses to the demand for politically neutral information that would transcend class and ethnic divisions by providing the basis for objective answers to divisive questions.[23] In this sense, collecting data was fundamentally democratic in orientation, undertaken to furnish information for public discussion.[24] Insofar as the high cost of living was fundamentally a political issue involving the relative rates of change in prices and wages, statistics would provide a seemingly objective alternative to the wide-ranging opinions and inquiries undertaken by the daily press, private organizations, and numerous concerned individuals.[25] Seeking a position between the critics and the activists, the Liberal government turned to the civil service. The tools that would be used to measure the cost of living, and the category of consumer that would be constructed through the process of statistical inquiry, contained the possibility of transcending social divisions. Political interest connected rising cost consciousness with state building.

Calculating the Cost of Living

When Canada's Department of Labour was established in 1900, its mandate was to "collect, digest, and publish" information that would be useful in the negotiation and settlement of trade disputes.[26] A monthly journal, the *Labour Gazette,* was created for this purpose, as a "medium for ... the registration of facts."[27] Initially articles in the *Labour Gazette* focused on general industrial conditions, including employment opportunities, wage rates, union activities, the outcome of strikes, and the passage of labour legislation. A young social reformer with an interest in politics, W.L. Mackenzie King, was hired to edit the new journal. When King's interests turned to conciliation and special investigations, the day-to-day work involved in the preparation of the *Gazette* fell to his close friend Henry ("Bert") Harper and, after Harper's untimely death in 1902, to Robert Hamilton Coats, a young journalist.[28]

In these early years, work in the Department of Labour unfolded along two distinct, but still parallel, paths. Both King and Coats were interested in the science of management and the possibilities of increasing consumption. King's interest in labour relations led him to develop new practices of arbitration that directly involved the state in labour disputes. Coats campaigned for new statistical efforts to measure purchasing power, wages, and working conditions. Both the system of industrial relations devised by King and the statistical work carried out by Coats were part of the same effort to manage escalating conflicts between labour and capital. Committed to the management ideal, both men advocated processes of neutral investigation as a strategy to depoliticize inequality.[29] The vision of Canada as a nation of consumers, whether conceived of collectively as the beneficiaries of industrial production (as King saw it) or statistically as the aggregate of individual acts of buying (as Coats did), emerged in conjunction with initiatives that aimed to reduce social unrest to manageable problems in human relations and technical measurement. Conflicts in the realm of production would be de-emphasized by focusing on the common interests Canadians shared as consumers.

The Special Report on Wholesale Prices

Shortly after his appointment, Coats began to campaign for the production and presentation of statistics related to wages and the cost of living. Although wage data had been tracked by the department and made available in the pages of the *Labour Gazette* since 1900, Coats argued that more effort was needed to produce statistics directly related to the cost of living and to record the variations that existed from region to region.[30] He insisted that labour unrest, wages, and the cost of living were interrelated issues. While industry considered wages in relation to profits, workers were interested in what wages bought. "To a labouring man," he wrote, "the first question is the obtaining of employment, the second is the amount of remuneration he is to receive, and its relation to what he has to spend for subsistence."[31] For this reason, Coats believed that attention to purchasing power was the key to minimizing social and political instability. However, due to a lack of resources (and possibly insufficient interest from King at this time), little action was taken until 1909.[32]

At that time, the government responded to public outcry over rising prices with two initiatives. Acknowledging that "no public question at the present moment equals in general interest the abnormal cost of living," the *Labour Gazette* announced that a "more comprehensive and systematic" method of analysis would be introduced to determine the degree of change Canadians were actually experiencing. Henceforth, the monthly review of wholesale prices already published in the *Labour Gazette* as a general indicator of economic strength would be supplemented with price summaries of 230 wholesale and 34 retail commodities selected to reveal trends in living costs.[33] The second initiative was to prepare a special report measuring "as accurately as possible" changes in prices over the past two decades.[34] The investigation would create a benchmark for future comparisons. Despite the desire for precision, it would be necessary for Coats to rely on wholesale prices "to construct a sample of adequate breadth and depth."[35] Data on retail prices, when they existed at all, were not readily available. While the inquiry was, for practical reasons, confined to fluctuations in wholesale prices, it would, Coats promised readers, still serve to "indicate general tendencies" in the cost of living in Canada.

When the *Report on Wholesale Prices* was released in 1910, it established a point of reference for measuring changes in the cost of daily life "of the community as a whole."[36] The methods used in constructing the index, the selection of goods, and the merits of weighted versus unweighted indices, were discussed in detail in both the report and the press.[37] Although consumption choices were the outcome of personal decision-making, the aggregation of individual acts of spending into collective patterns of expenditure was instrumental in producing a collective consumer interest. Consumer protests leveraged the affordability of basic foods, especially those with strong cultural associations such as milk, eggs, and meat, to make rising living costs a political issue. The government, in turn, sought to diffuse public anger by the application of statistical techniques.[38] The individual, Coats observed, was a "law unto himself and ... no pronouncement based on averages can apply individually except by accident."[39] Yet, the process of representing the purchasing choices of individual Canadians statistically normalized new patterns of expenditure, transmuting spending decisions that were unpredictable when considered on an individual basis into a coherent picture of collective practice.[40] By integrating consumption into the workings of the state, the inquiry began to forge a link between citizenship and new consumer practices.

The construction of the general index revealed that wholesale prices had risen 35 percent from the baseline decade of 1890–99. This number was widely cited as a benchmark. The new index positioned the Department of Labour as an authority on the cost of living and brought the problem of living costs into formal government reports.[41] The government had hoped the study would calm discussion; however, by confirming what was widely suspected, the publication of *Wholesale Prices in Canada* had the effect of fuelling debate. Over the next two years, the issue simmered in the press.[42] Some commentators identified the source of the problem as reductions in the supply of foodstuffs (arguing, for example, that rising beef prices were caused by the end of open-range cattle ranching) and in the shift in population from rural to urban settings, with the consequent shift in labour from agricultural production to new service industries. Others focused on the increasing production of extravagances, which, they insisted, occurred at the expense of necessities. Still others emphasized increases in demand as a result of immigration, wage gains, and rising standards of living. There was no consensus. The return of strong economic growth diffused the debate, although the high cost of manufactured goods, particularly when compared with the wholesale prices obtained by farmers for agricultural products, was a significant factor in the 1911 federal election. In 1913, an economic recession caused a sharp decrease in employment, which, in conjunction with continuing high prices, brought the cost of living to the forefront of public discussion once again.[43] The volume of these discussions inflated along with the cost of living. Coats dryly noted that one writer had recently enumerated over eighty possible causes for the increase.[44]

The Report of the Board of Inquiry into the Cost of Living

In 1913, protests in Canada and earlier well-publicized food riots in northern France (1911), Lisbon (1911), Vienna (1911), and Berlin (1912) motivated the government to appoint a board of inquiry to investigate "the causes which have occasioned or contributed to" rising prices.[45] The board was composed of four permanent officials of the government: John McDougald, commissioner of customs (appointed as chair), C.C. James, agricultural commissioner, J.U. Vincent, deputy minister of inland revenue, and R.H. Coats, chief statistician of the Department of Labour. After the board finished collecting evidence in June 1914, Coats proposed that the Department of Labour prepare a memorandum discussing the general economic tendencies behind the rise in prices; however, with the declaration of war in August 1914, board members seemed to believe that the need for a final report had been indefinitely postponed. When Prime Minister Borden requested a submission in late December, the committee seemed to have been caught by surprise. McDougald prepared a summary of the findings and requested that Coats submit his material for inclusion. Coats, objecting both to the narrative style of McDougald's draft and the haste with which the chair sought to push the report through, called for the inclusion of a lengthy exhibit of facts and analysis. McDougald added some of Coats' data, but not his analysis, to the existing summary. Coats, dissatisfied with the absence of analysis, refused to sign the report. After a protracted discussion, a compromise was reached and two volumes were published.[46]

This final report, when tabled on 16 February 1916, was over two thousand pages long and contained considerable duplication, reflecting the tension between McDougald and Coats. The divide between the two was marked not by political affiliation but rather by methodology, age, and orientation.[47] McDougald, in his late sixties, represented the moral framework of late-Victorian Canada. A local merchant and a former Liberal-Conservative member of Parliament for Pictou County, Nova Scotia (a renowned stronghold of Scotch Presbyterianism dedicated to higher education and national service), John McDougald had held the post of commissioner of customs since 1896. As the voice of tradition and experience, he emphasized the costs of progress.[48] Coats, committed to the principles of scientific management and a professionalized civil service, expressed concern about the ad hoc nature of the board's approach and the absence of "any framework" within which to assess the evidence the committee had gathered.[49]

The final report clearly reflected two different responses to changing patterns of consumption, represented by the views of McDougald and Coats. McDougald focused on the rising cost of foodstuffs, changes in methods of distribution, and changes in the standard of living that affected demand. His tone was frequently disapproving, suggesting that if Canadians were in stringent circumstances, they had only themselves to blame. Prosperity, he complained, had been accompanied by increasing waste and excessive advertising.[50] Buying foods out of season added to costs. Cold storage opened the way to hoarding and price manipulation. The shift from bulk purchasing to wrapped packages increased opportunities to mislead consumers. Such innovations added convenience and cleanliness (which were in themselves relatively recent values) but also raised prices.

Canada, McDougald observed, had become a country where people could afford to buy "for flavour or tenderness instead of nutrition." "Thrift is no longer inculcated," he protested. "It is easier and quicker to buy a new article than to repair the old." At the dinner table, abundance was praised more than wholesomeness. The "wants of the people" he observed, "have been multiplied and diversified on every side. They demand more and better things. Their requirements are larger, more varied and more exacting."[51]

The changes McDougald objected to were not solely in the realm of consumption. Canadians, he observed, were working fewer hours. Children rejected manual labour, seemingly ashamed of the honest occupations of their fathers.[52] New services, including ready-made foods, laundry services, and the use of the telephone "to demand frequent deliveries of parcels of small value at irregular times," transformed labour once provided free of charge by the housewife into commodities to be purchased. Both producers

Your "General Manager"

The wise man leaves the management of his home to his real General Manager—the wife who buys the food and who makes a study of its nutritive value. The housewife who knows

SHREDDED WHEAT

has already solved the servant problem and the problem of the high cost of living. Its daily use means health and strength and decreased household expense. Combined with sliced bananas, stewed prunes or other fruits it furnishes the highest food value at the lowest cost. Make it your "meat" for a few days and see how much better you feel.

Always heat the Biscuit in oven to restore crispness. Two Shredded Wheat Biscuits with hot milk or cream will supply all the energy needed for a half day's work. Deliciously nourishing when eaten in combination with baked apples, stewed prunes, sliced bananas, canned or preserved fruits. Try toasted Triscuit, the Shredded Wheat wafer, for luncheon with butter, cheese or marmalade.

The Canadian Shredded Wheat Company, Limited

Niagara Falls, Ontario

Toronto Office: 49 Wellington St. East

70A

FIGURE 1   Changing household shopping practices were a source of contention at a time of rising prices. While traditionalists argued that new ways were expensive luxuries, companies such as Canadian Shredded Wheat insisted they were selling solutions to the problems of modern life: convenience, cost effectiveness, and nutrition. | *Toronto Globe,* 11 June 1914, 4. Courtesy of Post Consumer Brands LLC.

and consumers were exploited by middlemen. New technologies, like the combustion engine, which should have been dedicated to commercial purposes, were used instead in the production of luxuries and for recreation.[53] Inflation provided traditionalists like McDougald an opportunity to reassert the value of conservative principles, including the centrality of work, the dangers of desire, and the need for personal prudence, thrift, and self-restraint. McDougald did not ignore evidence that standards of living were rising and that the country was gaining in wealth. However, he insisted that the "spirit that has won success is the spirit of duty and work. The lessons of history teach ... that a life of ease is not conducive to individual or national well-being."[54] Rising costs were primarily an individual responsibility, requiring self-control and tight management of the household budget.

While McDougald emphasized social and cultural explanations for rising prices, Coats stressed the larger economic transformations underway. Applying the systematic practices of modern government and the tools of statistical analysis, Coats set out to measure and give form to new norms of consumption.[55] Rises in the cost of living were examined sector by sector. Numerous tables and charts were prepared, showing that per capita consumption had increased in every category since 1900. The consumption of luxury goods, from liquor to ribbons and billiard tables, had risen. The value of imported books, magazines, and newspapers had increased by almost 300 percent in the past fifteen years, supported, no doubt, by an increase in literacy rates. Charitable contributions had risen, and the purchase of life insurance policies (regarded as a barometer of savings and thrift) was up by over 75 percent. Housing conditions had deteriorated for unskilled labourers and most immigrants, but had improved for other classes.[56]

Because increases in expenditure were not confined to luxuries and extravagances, Coats argued that shifts in the Canadian way of life were in "their origin ... not psychological alone, but economic ... rendered possible in the first instance by increased incomes."[57] Social phenomena were "in the main incidental," he insisted: "They are not the tide, they are rather waves upon the tide."[58] Coats sought to remove morality from the discussion of the cost of living by employing statistical methods to document behaviours and measure trends. Because standards of consumption varied throughout the nation and, indeed, from family to family, the process of measuring changes in the cost of living, he argued, would require a standardized basket of goods and a baseline concept of "enough." Coats' goal, however, was not so much to defend as to normalize new consumption patterns. The process of collecting, tabulating, and charting data on spending practices, and the development of new abstractions such as the standard basket of goods, helped to create the illusion of value-free purchasing.

Coats resisted suggesting remedies for inflation. He acknowledged that efforts to encourage food production and reduce waste would diminish the impact of high prices, but he believed that such efforts did not address the true causes of inflation, which were not moral but structural. Shifts in the labour force away from food production and towards construction, manufacturing, and mining exacerbated distribution problems. Rises in wages and prices in advance of profits skewed the balance between supply and demand. One solution, Coats proposed, would be to shift the economy away from growth driven by capital investment towards a more balanced economy involved in the making and selling of things. Orienting the economy towards domestic consumption would help reduce prices.

Building up an independent national bureau of statistics was critical.[59] Without a system of comprehensive and up-to-date measurements, Coats argued, it was "impossible to grasp the significance of current phenomenon" or to coordinate economic decision-making.

While McDougald situated his investigation in the context of pre-existing moral standards, Coats deployed the rational methods and vocabulary of management and economics. Coats' report privileged systematically gathered information analysed by professionals, in marked contrast to the personal interviews, first-hand observations, and anecdotal information presented as evidence by McDougald. As bureaucratic modes of thinking "invaded the realm of ethics," the sorts of overtly moral interpretations offered by McDougald were gradually being displaced.[60] Objectifying consumer behaviours as a series of spending practices, rather than moral choices, made new sorts of data available for management by government – and, in time, for management by industry.[61]

The Managerial State and the Community of Canadian Consumers

It is useful at this point to return to Coats' early associate at the Department of Labour, Mackenzie King. While McDougald and Coats were preparing their contributions to the *Report of the Board of Inquiry*, King had begun work on a manuscript, soon to be titled *Industry and Humanity*. This book, which King regarded as his magnum opus, offers another avenue for examining the parallel development of the managerial state and consumer society. If Coats can be said to represent the practices of bureaucratic rationality, King can be seen as an advocate of the managerial function. King argued that the organization of industry on a large scale under scientific management had fundamentally altered relations of production, vastly increasing the material wealth of society with a gradual lessening of human effort.[62] Goods were cheaper and more plentiful than ever before. Standards of living were rising. For these reasons, King explained, industry was not merely a revenue-producing process but also a social service.[63] In King's view, it was the manager, both in business and in government, who was most aligned with the social good. Order and stability benefited all classes of society: assuring jobs, increasing profits, and creating a steady and abundant supply of goods and services for the benefit of the community.

Like most Canadian intellectuals before the First World War, King did
not envision a consumer-driven economy, with growth and high profits
fuelled by abundant consumer purchasing. He thought continually increasing rates of consumption were not the basis of a strong economy, but the
reward for cooperation and sound management. Increased productivity,
falling costs, and rising standards of living were the benefits of scientific
management and industrial peace, made possible by techniques of impartial
investigation. "Investigation," King explained, "is a letting in of light ...
for it assumes that collective opinion will approve the right, and condemn
the wrong. It does not attempt to award punishments or to affix blame; it
aims simply at disclosing facts."[64] Once the facts were revealed, the parties
could negotiate their differences. Conciliation would address "the human
element," resolving personal antipathies that kept disputants apart.[65]

King's enthusiasm for impartial investigation bore a close affinity to
Coats' emphasis on the collection of statistics. Both men believed that the
facts, if objectively gathered and clearly presented, would reveal the
common economic interests underlying the industrial order. King insisted
that all the parties to industry were fundamentally aligned in their obligation to maintain production for the benefit of the whole of society. It was
consumption, he wrote, that formed "the arena within which a people share
a common interest." The rights of capital and labour were secondary to
the rights of the community, "which creates the demand for commodities
and services, through which Labour is provided with remunerative employment, and Capital with a return on its investment."[66] The consumer interest,
as King conceived it, was a comprehensive social category that included
all Canadians. King asserted that the right of the community to consumption served as the point of entry for expanded government responsibilities
and the justification for government intervention in the economy. The
legitimacy of government was linked to the provision of essential goods
and services as a matter of social good.[67]

In the concluding passages of *Industry and Humanity*, King developed
these ideas further, explaining that the ultimate goal of industry was not
profit but "the well-being of mankind." Industry did not affect wage earners "merely as persons possessing labour which they dispose of." Instead,
"the conditions which surround Industry, and the output of Industry,
represent all that is possible for them [most men and women] in the way
of health, happiness, and life itself."[68] Management was the key; the state,
as the guardian and guarantor of social progress, had the responsibility

to manage the economy for the benefit of the community as a whole. Concluding the writing of *Industry and Humanity* during the horrors of world war, King predicted that labour and capital, united by management and inspired by high purpose, would "bring to a disconsolate and broken hearted world the one hope that is theirs alone to bring ... the promise of ... resurrection to a more abundant life." Resolving conflicts between capital and labour would mark "the dawn of a new era in ... which material production would be vastly increased and life and happiness abound."[69]

While McDougald emphasized the problems and negative consequences of modern consumption practices, King and Coats proposed that the consumer interest had the potential to align the interests of workers and capitalists with the whole of society. A national system of statistics, like the consumer interest, would transcend divisions of wealth and region. Thus, the rise of the managerial state was linked to the study of prices and the possibility that social harmony might be obtained through rising standards of living.

Conclusion

"The fundamental tendency of all bureaucratic thought," Karl Mannheim observed in developing a sociology of knowledge, is "to turn all problems of politics into problems of administration."[70] Reports prepared by the Department of Labour and the Board of Inquiry were part of an extended effort to identify, and in this way to categorize and stabilize, new patterns of living and to bring them under government control. As data were collected, tabulated, and charted, individual purchases were aggregated into collective practices. The statistical process itself offered a sense of stability, revealing order amid the disorder of daily life and directing attention away from polarizing debates. The distinction between needs and wants, luxuries and necessities, extravagances and thrift were irrelevant to the statistician seeking to determine common practices. The regular use of normative terms such as "the consumer," "the cost of living," and "a basket of goods" by government and in the daily press began to free consumption of its pejorative connotations. The development of a nation-wide index revealed common consumer experiences. The notion of a widely shared standard of living, with an emphasis on the consumption of bought goods, was incorporated into the workings of the state and publicized in the media.

Before the right to a particular standard of living came the calculation of living standards. Only after general tendencies were turned into objective realities could it become possible for government to manage them.

The state assumed an expanded role, but it was also true that Canadians called for their government to become involved, in effect empowering the bureaucracy to investigate and regulate at least some aspects of daily consumption. While concerns about rising costs directed attention to changes in the social order, the manner in which government responded to the challenges of inflation reinforced the transition to a consumption-oriented society. McDougald, Coats, and King were among those who called for more government, be it in the form of an enlarged bureau of statistics, the systematic management of human relations, or the improved regulation of consumer goods, labelling, and packaging. They also called for government to become involved in the education of consumers, emphasizing the need for individuals to take on a measure of responsibility for their purchasing habits.

Political acknowledgment of the consumer was an important part of the process by which Canada evolved from a late-Victorian, producerist society emphasizing self-sufficiency to a consumer society anchored by the managerial state. Yet, the role of the consumer in the larger economy remained in dispute. Access to bought goods was recognized as an interest that transcended social boundaries; at the same time, attention to a normalized standard of living rather than property ownership was compatible with persistent inequalities in power. Few were willing, as yet, to consider consumers as a significant force capable of driving economic growth, and fewer still considered increased consumption, rather than increased production, as the appropriate ends of industry. Democratic rights remained distinct from consumer rights, but the trajectory that would lead to the blurring of citizen and consumer had begun. Ultimately, the Department of Labour inquiries from this period demonstrate the power of knowing as a form of intervention. Identifying the welfare of Canadian families with their ability to consume goods and services opened the way to increased management of the economy and laid the groundwork for modes of measurement that have become integral to Canada's political and economic system. In the long run, regular reporting of the cost of living by government would increase the political power of consumers.

One of the ways a state maintains its legitimacy is by establishing definitions of equity and community that are able to capture widespread allegiance.[71] During this period, when citizenship became linked with consumption and Canadians came increasingly to be seen as consumers of goods, the role of government expanded to include measuring and monitoring domestic spending. Its task was not yet to ensure consumption – that awaited the arrival of the welfare state after the Second World War – but clearly a new pattern of emphasis had emerged that had the potential to capture wider loyalties. The state had begun to identify its citizens as consumers.

Chapter Three

CULTURING CANADIAN
PATRIOTISM

Historians often explain the development of culture in interwar Canada by way of two distinct class narratives.[1] The first involves the increasing participation of "ordinary" Canadians in commercialized amusements and leisure experiences as they tuned in to radio broadcasts, followed professional sports, bought inexpensive magazines and pulp novels, and gathered to watch made-in-Hollywood motion pictures. The second recounts the rise of a heroic, modern, and, above all, national culture. Feeling that Canada "was as yet unwritten, unpainted, unsung," an aspiring cultural elite set out to make the nation through culture.[2] Between these two discourses lay a great divide: the producers of mass culture ignored highbrow culture; elites denounced the popular entertainments produced by the cultural industries.

More recently, scholars have begun to challenge this division, revealing practices of high culture to be considerably less than "pure." Elites did not, in fact, transcend the commercial concerns they denounced. Canadians of all classes were becoming less involved in the making and exchange of cultural experiences and instead were beginning to buy cultural goods in forms that were produced and distributed in accordance with distinctive economic logics. Although popular mass culture is more commonly associated with the emergence of consumer society, high culture was no less affected by the economic imperatives, practices, and values of consumer capitalism. To borrow cultural theorist Andreas Huyssen's phrasing, developments in both elite and mass culture should be understood as "different impulses within the same cultural moment," both shaped by the structures of capitalism.[3]

Culture wars of this sort are not specific to interwar Canada; however, battles are fought in particular times and places. As provisioning through shopping became recognized as a normal, if not fully accepted practice, attention shifted to the use of what can be broadly defined as discretionary wage-earnings and leisure time. Trade in cultural goods was not a new phenomenon, but it was increasing in scale and specialization. The conditions necessary for mass culture were slowly emerging in Canada.[4] There were more consumers: Canada's population grew from 5.4 million in 1901 to 8.8 million in 1921 and almost 10.4 million by 1931. Although the 1920s were, to use labour historian Bryan Palmer's phrasing, "hardly a decade of unambiguous advance" for Canadian families, a host of economic and social changes were disrupting the markers that had previously denoted class affiliation. These included high rates of literacy, new opportunities for employment in white-collar clerical and professional-managerial roles, shifts in population from the countryside to the city, and the arrival of new immigrants at the bottom of the social hierarchy. Gains in real wages, leisure time, and employment stability, and innovations in technology, management, and distribution, were making commercialized leisure more affordable, particularly for English-speaking, central Canadian city-dwellers.[5]

Seeking to maximize their profits, producers of commercial entertainment reached across barriers of language, ethnicity, geography, and income to build mass audiences. Canadians responded with enthusiasm, watching motion pictures and professional spectator sports (from baseball to boxing), buying best-selling novels and mass-circulation magazines, and listening to radio broadcasts. By 1929, almost 300,000 Canadians had purchased licences to own radio sets, and the 1,100 movie theatres in the country were selling two million tickets a week. By 1936, the average Canadian attended twelve movies every year.[6]

Specialization and professionalization in elite culture were different aspects of the same economic transformation. Entertainments once privately exchanged by friends were being professionalized and made available in newly built concert halls and museums, in newly founded national associations and clubs, in aspiring intellectual journals, and in English departments in growing postsecondary institutions.[7] Subscriptions, memberships, donations, and collecting (rather than "buying" art or artefacts) camouflaged the exchange of money. The status-signifying potential of cultural goods was inherent in these different production and distribution processes.[8] The higher dollar value placed on goods and experiences associated with elite culture was in part a function of their perceived distance from mass commercial markets. Profits made in cultural industries aimed at mass audiences increased with the numbers sold. Profits in elite cultural production depended on judgments of value by recognized experts. Affordability was seen as a threat to high standards.[9] Works produced in limited quantities were deemed rare and valuable – in contrast to mass-produced items, which were considered vulgar and common – and could command higher prices. And yet, the growth in audiences and patrons for elite cultural goods was also an aspect of corporate capitalism. New audiences came from the expanding ranks of higher-level managers and administrators in industry and government, a growing professoriate, and rising numbers of medical and other professionals, including high-culture professionals. Patrons included newly wealthy plutocrats, growing national corporations (especially banks and railroad companies), and, increasingly, new and enlarging state institutions.

Rather than distinguishing between two distinct fields of cultural practice, it is useful to see a broad spectrum of different strategies and responses. At one end of the spectrum, commercially driven cultural industries produced large-scale cultural experiences, characterized by mass distribution and a short production cycle, geared to earning immediate returns through rapid circulation and obsolescence. At the other end, were producers of "pure" art, increasingly professionalized and specialized but claiming autonomy from market forces. Denigrating commerce and refusing short-term immediate economic gains, producers of elite culture and their supporters emphasized the charisma of original creation. Selectivity, rather than accessibility, determined the relationship between a work of art and its audience. Acquiring high culture was (and is) a long-term investment in symbolic capital, position, and power. Of course, neither mode of practice existed in absolute form: the anti-economy of "pure" art was achieved through the exaggerated denial of economic self-interest rather than absolute independence from the market, and the successful production of popular culture required more than cynical calculation of the lowest common denominator.[10] Cultural entrepreneurs, much like entrepreneurs in other fields of enterprise, are successful economic innovators. Both mass and elite culture flourished by cultivating new consumers.[11]

At the time when Canada was moving towards greater political, constitutional, and economic independence from Britain, a loose network of aspiring intellectual and cultural authorities asserted that experts, rather than the market and the mass of ordinary Canadians, should determine which cultural forms would represent "Canada." Cultural disputes of this sort, American sociologist Herbert Gans speculates, are an expression of class conflict: arguing which culture and whose culture should dominate society is a debate about whether the cultural life of the country should be run by a cultured elite or determined by the market.[12] By disparaging popular preferences for commercially driven, mass-reproduced culture, Canada's aspiring intellectual, cultural, and academic elites, and the affiliated rising class of professionals-managers and bureaucrats, reinforced their collective claims to higher social status. Affirming their appreciation for forms of high culture sanctioned by cultural commentators, curators, and gallery owners was also a mechanism by which individual members of the rising class could establish distance from personal origins, often as the sons and daughters of small businessmen, independent professionals, prosperous farmers, and skilled labour.[13] Gender was another tool in the tactical arsenal of elite cultural authorities, who tended to describe their preferences in masculinist terms associated with conquering wilderness and building the nation while simultaneously devaluing mass culture as sensational, emotional, sentimental, and romantic in sensibility.[14]

Citizen and consumer are often understood as opposites; however, in interwar Canada, the consumption of the right sort of cultural goods and experiences became associated with patriotism and good citizenship. A new generation of aspiring cultural providers (including artists, authors, critics, gallery owners, and publishers) formulated and diffused their vision of a new national culture. Among the primary virtues of this culture was its rejection of commercial values and mass-produced culture associated with Americanization. Cultural elites disparaged poor cultural choices, such as attending movies or professional sporting events and reading commercially successful novels, as evidence of aesthetic impoverishment. The stigma associated with participation in mass culture reinforced its critics' claims to superior social and intellectual status. The new generation of cultural and intellectual elites was preoccupied with making national culture. Many of the cultural forms they innovated or identified as appropriately Canadian also suited the political agendas and budgets of the rising class of professionals-managers, bureaucrats, and academics. Claims of cultural authority reinforced claims to social power at a time when traditional cultural and social hierarchies were losing influence. And yet, the objects and images that would become the touchstones of national culture were also created as consumer goods. The emerging distinction between popular/mass culture and elite culture was constructed within the consumer economy.[15]

Print Culture

The formalization and institutionalization of relationships among members of Canada's intellectual and cultural elite during the interwar years has been well studied. The organizations they established served to bolster feelings of community and common purpose, in addition to promoting the nationalist goals of their founders.[16] One of the most visible aspects of these organizing efforts was the creation of serious journals devoted to culture and public affairs. The *Canadian Forum,* the *Dalhousie Review,* the *Canadian Bookman,* the *McGill Fortnightly,* and the *Canadian Mercury* — names that came to be associated with the birth of modern Canadian culture — were launched between 1919 and 1930.

Acutely aware that they were operating within new economic realities, the editors of these periodicals complained that it was an age of too many publications and too little time. Sir John George Bourinot, one of the nation's earliest and foremost promoters of intellectual endeavour, had mocked the idea of a "review" in the early 1890s as offering only "predigested" thoughts. The new generation of intellectual leaders was more likely to describe it as a useful tool. The *Dalhousie Review,* for example, assured readers that the "ever increasing mass of books issuing from the press" would be "sifted by critics for those who have little leisure to sift for themselves." A contributor to the *Canadian Bookman* similarly noted the need for a journal that would "guide the Canadian mind to a wise selection from among the myriad publications which invite attention."[17] At a time when the expansion of publishing was making it more difficult to "discern the best," the editors offered their expertise to readers bewildered by an abundance of choice.[18]

It has been estimated that, by the mid-1920s, over three hundred American publications (excluding newspapers) were circulating in Canada. For every Canadian magazine printed, eight were imported from the United States. The bestsellers were the *Ladies' Home Journal,* the *Saturday Evening*

Post, the *Pictorial Review,* and *McCall's Maga{ine,* with a combined circulation more than double that of the four leading Canadian counterparts. Although Canadian periodicals lagged, the 1920s saw a number of new entries. Notably, *Chatelaine, Canadian Homes and Gardens,* and *Mayfair* appeared, offering smaller made-in-Canada versions of familiar American women's magazines. Mass-circulation periodicals addressed the hobbies, interests, and domestic concerns of the expanding middle class. Technological advances underwritten by expanding advertising revenue reduced costs and made for colourful, attractive visual experiences promoting an "aesthetic of upward mobility."[19] The consumer culture that these magazines embodied and promoted suggested new ways for readers, particularly women, to spend leisure time and money.[20] It was no coincidence that the first editors of *Chatelaine* and *Homes and Gardens* had backgrounds in department store advertising.[21]

Against this background, the editors and backers of Canada's intellectual journals envisioned a growing, but still select, community of high-minded writers and readers. The *Dalhousie Review,* for example, promised to open "a channel of expression" for "anyone who has an opportune comment to make upon the affairs of the day," specifically inviting contributions from scholars, teachers, and men of affairs desirous of speaking "to a wide audience upon the things of supreme consequence." The *Canadian Historical Review* explained that its object was "to provide a forum for the discussion of questions relating to Canadian history" and that it hoped to present a wide expression of opinion in both contributions and correspondence. In the inaugural issue of the *Canadian Forum,* the editors explained that their journal had its origins in the "desire to secure a freer and more informal discussion of public questions." Situating the *Forum* as part of the made-in-Canada movement, the editors deployed the rhetoric of production to distinguish their journal from the easily consumed mass media. Describing the *Forum* as a "monthly journal of opinion," they proclaimed, "No country has reached its full stature, which makes its goods at home, but not its faith and its philosophy." Readers were assured that at least one page would be set aside in each issue for their contributions. The *Canadian Bookman* similarly promised to provide a "forum for the discussion of all bookish matters," pledging to bring "the producers and consumers of the Book into a more sympathetic and understanding relation," that would go beyond the promotion of literature and make and strengthen the Canadian nation. In ancient

Rome, the forum included market stalls as well as opportunities for political discussion; in interwar Canada, the term evoked high-minded discussion of important topics and the exchange of ideas, rather than goods, in a cultural space set apart from the pressures and diversions of the mass market.[22]

Claims to national importance went hand in hand with strident denunciations of mass-oriented culture. Editors and contributors commonly referred to mass-market magazines as an addiction rather than a choice, identifying them as both a symptom and the cause of society's disintegration. "The great bulk of the 'literature' which comes into this country in periodical form," the *Canadian Bookman* told readers, "is not only useless, it is destructive – as a narcotic is destructive to the mental energies of the taker."[23] Indeed the *Bookman*'s inaugural issue contained multiple attacks on the mass media. Contributors uniformly condemned the sentimental, idealess books that "formed the literary food" of too many Canadians.[24] In that issue, Thomas McGarry, the provincial treasurer of Ontario, dramatically linked "the increase of crime and insanity in our midst" to the effects of "cheap magazines that blunt our finer feelings and thus cause vulgarity and coarseness." Canadians "who in their idle and receptive hours consume ... emotional and lurid stuff as the majority of magazines contain" were morally at risk.[25]

Those involved in publishing, writing for, and reading serious journals conceived of their efforts as markedly different from the processes required to produce, circulate, and consume mass-market magazines and the advertisement-filled daily press. Mass-market publications required little attention from readers, dated quickly, and were meant to be replaced rather than cherished. By comparison, reading journals of quality was understood to require a commitment of time because the subjects under discussion were matters of significance. Quarterly and monthly journals circulated in limited numbers.[26] Subscribing to and reading (that is, paying attention to) these periodicals denoted membership in a relatively small community with shared values. Editors and contributors addressed the readers of intellectual and culturally oriented periodicals as engaged, alert, articulate, and participatory readers. The publishers of serious journals strove to create a distinctive social space for intellectual and cultural encounters, one they perceived as very different from the exchanges of the market that aimed only to entertain. Success in popular journalism, intellectual commentators insisted, required the dumbing down of content and the ramping up of sensationalism and novelty to encourage sales. Attacks on mass-market periodicals were not necessarily explicitly gendered; however, popular magazines were often disparaged as sentimental and sensational, and as providing temporary distractions by appealing to the emotions. Serious journals, by comparison, were masculinist locations, associated with reason and nation building, home to discussions of serious themes: politics, commerce, current affairs, history, and literature.

Trading in Books

Historian Clarence Karr describes the period 1890–1920 as the "golden age" of the mass market for authors of popular fiction. The notion of the "best-seller" was rapidly entrenched in the consciousness of publishers, booksellers, and readers, as gains in literacy and leisure time, falling production costs, and new channels of distribution opened the door to commercial success.[27] Popular novels could be bought in department stores, bookstores, drugstores, and railway bookstalls, ordered from catalogues, and borrowed from an increasing number of public libraries. As expanding markets and new outlets created opportunities for financially astute publishers and commercially aware authors, the tension between economic success and literary prestige mounted.[28]

The market for popular fiction continued to expand after the war, lifted by postwar prosperity, the achievement of almost full literacy, the expansion of secondary and postsecondary education, and the spread of electricity, all of which helped to further the practice of reading as a leisure activity.[29] Responses to this trend from the nation's cultural community diverged: one group sought a degree of accommodation with the business of professional authorship and the cultivation of a broad reading public; the other claimed a "gatekeeper" role. In a relevant analysis of literary taste in England, Mary Hammond observes that the ideological values attributed to sales figures, advertising, and financial success, rather than the formal properties of writing, led to harsh evaluations of popular authors: commercial success called the literary merits of popular works into question.[30]

The tension between the book as culture and the book as commodity was acutely felt. B.K. Sandwell, editor of the *Canadian Bookman,* insisted that books were more than "masses of paper and binding" and "so many square inches of type." Books, he protested, were not "speculative" ventures seeking to become best-sellers, but "vessels for the containing of and imparting of ideas."[31] And yet the *Bookman* did not shun commerce. Rather, it addressed itself to the educated book-buying public, offering reviews, trade advertisements, and lists of new books (with books by Canadian authors starred), alongside serious articles on related cultural themes. In the pages of the *Canadian Bookman*, Sandwell explained, books would have the opportunity to battle their rivals – "the player-piano, the phonograph, and the moving picture," and the publicity experts who aggressively promote them with high-pressure sales campaigns costing millions of dollars – for readers' time and attention.[32] Publishers believed that readers and buyers would emerge if audiences were made aware of works by Canadian authors.[33]

The creation of the Canadian Authors' Association (CAA) in 1921 by a group of Canada's most commercially successful writers was motivated in equal parts by the profits generated by the sale of books in expanding Canadian markets and by the spirit of postwar patriotism sweeping the nation. Caught between British and American publishing interests, Canadian authors organized to lobby government for stronger copyright laws to ensure that they received a share of the income generated by the sale of their work.[34] The founders of the CAA pledged that the organization would "act for the mutual benefit and protection of the interests of Canadian Authors and for the maintenance of high ideals and practice in the literary profession." Although they did not see any inconsistency in these goals, the *Canadian Forum* argued otherwise, noting that one of the objectives called for "vigorous self-protection and the other for vigorous self-criticism."[35]

The CAA's launch of "Book Week" later that year provided the occasion for an extended debate on the culture-or-commerce question. Writing for the *Canadian Forum*, literary editor Barker Fairley issued a forceful condemnation of Book Week, even before it occurred:

> When violent methods of publicity are employed in almost every other sphere of life it is difficult to object to them in a really worthy cause ... But there remains a word to be said. Shock tactics do not in the long run serve the best interests of literature ... The fact is that sales of books, whatever temporary satisfaction they bring, are ultimately fruitless unless enlightened interest is behind them, and enlightened interest cannot be created in a week. It must have time.[36]

Sandwell defended the CAA vigorously in both the *Canadian Forum* letters page and in the *Canadian Bookman,* arguing that "enlightened interest must be preceded by attention, and ... attention is a thing for which there is more competition, in this age, than for anything else."[37] Buying a book, Sandwell proposed, was an "act of judgment expressed in the only way in which most Canadians can express their judgment of books, namely by acts of purchase." Transactions that resulted in the purchase of books involved more than "mere dollars and cents." Canadian literature, Sandwell declared, "is made when a Canadian with two dollars goes into a bookstore and buys a book of poems or a novel or a biography or an essay collection because it gives the picture or the attitude or the view which he as a Canadian thinks needs to be given. Without that act by the Canadian reader, Canadian literature will never be made at all ... The Canadian authors cannot do it alone."[38] Barker Fairley remained unconvinced. Canadians desired literature, but too often they were willing to accept "reading matter at any cost, cheap novels rather than no novels, anything to kill time in a streetcar." Cheap literature, he declared, was "the most ineradicable narcotic of our modern life." The CAA should not pander to the weakness of "spiritual 'dope-fiends'" or indulge in "an orgy of mutual congratulation," but provide a "means of distinguishing the chaff from the grain."[39]

Basil King, a former clergyman, popular author of spiritual novels, and one of the founding members of the CAA, came forward to defend Book Week. The Canadian market for books, he observed, was so small that the monetary benefits of even doubling sales was negligible. Book Week was not about generating sales but about calling attention to "the cultural side of our life." King concluded by describing Canada as an infant country with an infant culture that needed time to grow.[40]

The discussion unleashed by Book Week and by King's summary judgment of Canadian culture raged on for the remainder of the decade. Against the background of rising competition from American publishing giants producing affordable magazines and fiction, Canadian authors, critics, and readers debated the nature of national literature. Was it a matter of explicit Canadian content, such as the setting, subject matter, or birthplace of the author? Were the interests of Canadian literature aligned with the sale of books? And, of equal importance, would the quality of Canadian writing be improved by better writers or by better, more critically aware, readers?

Six years later, the debate was still underway. Poets A.J.M. Smith and F.R. Scott joined in common cause, attacking the CAA while offering different solutions to the perceived problem of quality. Noting that tradition guided the development of literature in older countries, Smith called for principles of critical inquiry to direct writers in younger countries. He dismissed the literary boosterism of the CAA as a mercantile approach, akin to the Canadian Manufacturers' Association slogan calling on shoppers to "Buy Made in Canada Goods." Such an approach, Smith objected, was unsuited to things of mind and spirit. "Whatever sympathy one may feel for the aims of the Canadian Authors' Association and however eagerly one may hope for the creation of a worthy national literature," he argued, "it is impossible to view the excesses of 'Canadian Book Week' in a favourable light. Publicity, advertising and the methods of big business are not what is required to foster the art and literature of a young country such as Canada, while the commercial boosting of mediocre Canadian books not only reduces the Authors' Association to the level of an advertising agency but does considerable harm to good literature." Smith objected that the search for audiences turned artists into merchants, and he mocked bourgeois audiences who bought Canadian authors "from the same patriotic motive that prompts the purchaser of Eddy's matches or a Massey-Harris farm implement."[41] Canadian literature, he asserted, could be freed from market pressures by the development of a critical system and the application of intelligence. F.R. Scott supported Smith's attack on the CAA but argued against the call to formulate a critical system. Even the effort to establish principles of poetic production, Scott protested, was an attribute of commerce rather than culture. A nation, he maintained, "cannot be deliberate about its art."[42] Claiming to represent the cause of literature in a battle against the pressures of the marketplace, both men argued that the significance of a book should be determined by cultural authorities rather than by sales.

Smith and Scott were not alone in associating the CAA with uncritical, "noisy boosterism."[43] Other young poets and authors situated, like Scott and Smith, in Canadian universities agreed that the greater threat to literature was not the popularity of mass culture but the distorting influence of commerce on writers and the "nagging problem" of critical standards.[44] Faced with dramatic increases in book publishing, book selling, and book buying, both the CAA and the aspiring literary elite represented by Scott and Smith recognized that the stakes were rising. The problem of copyright, which had motivated more established authors to organize the CAA, and the efforts of a younger generation of academic writers to establish a Canadian canon were both responses to the growing market for books. While one group organized to protect the economic rights of authors in the commercial marketplace, the other strove to assert authority over the field they designated as "important Canadian literature." The *Bookman* and the CAA aligned themselves, and the interests of Canadian literature as a whole, with the sale of books. Academic critics, modernist poets, and avant-garde writers argued that the merits of Canadian literature needed to be considered apart from the market. Interestingly, both groups were explicitly concerned with the problem of national sovereignty: it was the question of Canadian copyright that had spurred the formation of the CAA; it was the search for distinctively Canadian qualities that drove discussion in literary circles.

Sociologist Pierre Bourdieu proposes that disagreements about aesthetic judgement are grounded in social class. The boundary between commercial and non-commercial practice – that is, the distinction between what is art and what is not – comes down to how readers are recruited. This distinction is not simply a matter of positioning one's efforts for a particular audience; it also involves determining which audience is important. At stake is the nature of literary legitimacy.[45] At one end of the literary spectrum, the CAA identified itself with professional authorship, which was seen as primarily commercially driven – that is, aiming to sell books to as wide an audience as possible, with success measured by the number of readers and the financial viability of production. At the other end, recognition as a writer or critic of consequence depended on judgments made by a small, almost exclusively male, circle of academics, editors, and publishers. Privileging the judgments of cultural authorities went hand in hand with devaluing the general reader. This disagreement was not an abstract war of words: the growing gulf between professional writers of best-selling fiction and the literary elite associated with academia was embodied in interwar anthologies that promoted preferred authors, themes, and values. Leaving both the mass and middle-brow markets to large-scale publishers and book-sellers, a rising generation of writers and critics associated with academia cultivated their authority as the gatekeepers of important Canadian literature.

The boundary between "culture" and mass commercial reading was constructed with a distinct gender as well as class bias. Critics persistently and systematically devalued women authors and readers. They privileged works with masculine overtones and national themes: virile men, physical feats, triumph over nature – the literary equivalent of landscape paintings by the Group of Seven. Works by popular authors were dismissed as sentimental, romantic, and emotional. Feminine literary themes were dismissed as domestic or personal and of little interest aesthetically.[46] F.R. Scott's 1927 satirical poem "The Canadian Authors Meet," often celebrated by later generations as the "birth announcement" of Canadian literary modernism, is a particularly mean-spirited example, with Scott using the image of middle-class, middle-aged women devoid of creative passion, clinging to tradition, to trivialize both the literary establishment and female poets and their poetry.[47]

The young poets and authors who attacked commerce did not, for the most part, join forces with those who advocated for political change. They mocked amateur writers as unprofessional even as they criticized commercial culture. The drive for recognition by the academy, rather than success in the marketplace, meant that future success would be a function of postsecondary and particularly university expansion. Insofar as salaries earned as academics and editors, rather than sales, supported their literary work, authors were freed from the constraints of the popular market. Recognition brought financial security in the form of tenure, further negating the need for income from sales. Personal connections with key players in the literary "power structure" helped fortify the literary value of preferred authors.[48] Going forward, judgments of literary value, particularly of nationally important work, would be made by members of the professoriate and a small circle of influential friends and colleagues and not the book-buying public. Over time, rising levels of education and changes in the book trade would occasionally allow authors to cross over and attain commercial as well as symbolic success, at least as intellectual celebrities if not as widely read authors.

Aesthetics: Artists and Audiences, Collectors and Artefacts

When aspiring intellectual and cultural leaders self-consciously took up the project of culturing Canada, they found the essence of the nation in the wilderness landscape and in the experiences of those they perceived as living closest to nature. Their preferred descriptive categories included terms such as "authentic," "primitive," "genuine," and "elementary." These terms took on meaning, not from any properties inherent in the land (or in the lives of Indigenous peoples, the Maritime folk, or the Québécois peasant), but in relation to rapid transformations taking place in the present.[49]

The separation of the sacred from the profane is fundamental to culture; it is also historically specific. As consumer capitalism expanded, this distinction was represented as the difference between high culture and mere "merchandise." Regardless of whether they painted, sculpted, or assembled collections, much of the work of cultural production lay in the creation of a new schema of values that distinguished preferred goods as "culture" rather than as simple objects or commercial merchandise. Adopting the trope of the "romantic quest," painters, collectors, and curators camouflaged their commercial interests by presenting themselves as gatekeepers, saviours, prospectors, and treasure hunters. And yet, as German cultural theorist Theodor Adorno observed at that time, producers in both mass culture and elite culture treated culture as a resource, drawing it into the economic system of market relations.[50]

In spite of their disdain for commodified goods and entertainments and for those who enjoyed them, Canada's aspiring cultural elite did not advocate a return to the wilderness or to primitive ways of life, except for occasional weekend excursions and summer holidays. Instead, artists and rare goods collectors began to build their practices around themes and values understood as the opposite of mass-produced, mass-distributed entertainments and modern technologies. This stance of "anti-modernity" offered multiple strategic advantages. First, the promotion of an aesthetic that valued the primitive and the genuine helped professionals working in the field of high culture remain free from the taint of commerce, even as they engaged in the promotion and marketing of fine art and artefacts. Second, by claiming the high social purpose of nation making, a younger generation of artists, writers, and critics were able to position themselves favourably in relation to the producers and sellers of traditional European culture then admired and collected by Canada's older elites.

Travelling from Canada's major cities to locations perceived as remote, interwar cultural entrepreneurs (including artists, collectors, and their intermediaries) found images, artefacts, songs, and stories to bring back for eventual sale to urban audiences. Re-presenting the landscape, Indigenous peoples, rural residents, and indeed themselves according to the tropes of anti-modernism required acts of imagination, selection, and silencing.

Artists and collectors displayed a "wilful blindness" to their own commercial involvements and the structure of commodity relations that underlay elite as well as mass culture. The desire for unique first-hand experiences meant overlooking the presence of others and the mass availability of tourist experiences.[51] The critique of modernity was linked with the creation of alternative consumer choices rather than a retreat from the market. As Sharon Wall has pointedly observed in her recent study of Indigenous-themed summer camps, "authentic" experiences were being made available "for a price."[52]

Anti-modernist aesthetics were not unique to interwar Canada. Similar reactions occurred in the United States and in Europe in the late nineteenth and early twentieth centuries. Anti-modern impulses accompany modernization as reactions to the losses and dislocations created by rapid change. As they sought to undo the "disenchantments" of science, reason, and technological advance, intellectuals and artists pursued intense experiences and turned their attention to the primitive, the genuine, and the authentic.[53] In Canada (and also in interwar Britain and Germany), experiences of the Great War generated intense reactionary and patriotic impulses, directing cultural preferences towards similar outcomes. The search for the "genuine" coincided with and was reinforced by an upsurge in patriotism in many nations.[54]

Commenting on anti-modernism in general, and on the works of Canada's Group of Seven landscape artists in particular, political theorist Benedict Anderson explains that patriotism favours idioms that "denote something to which one is naturally tied." Symbols such as the wilderness and "the Folk" have the appearance of timelessness: they seem "un-chosen."[55] Searching for symbols of a still-missing nationhood, Canadian painters, critics, collectors, and curators favoured narratives that supported the idea of Canada as an autonomous nation. The grandeur of the untouched wilderness was dramatically different from the overcivilized, wartorn landscapes of Europe. Artefacts and accounts of Indigenous peoples represented as leading premodern lives, as well as references to the hardships of colonial settlement, provided backstories for an aspiring nation-state separate from Britain. Ways of life that an earlier generation had scorned as primitive, deprived, and impoverished were re-described as genuine, authentic, fundamental, and real.[56] A 1924 address to the Empire Club of Canada by the Reverend R.P. Bowles, chancellor of Toronto's Victoria College, makes the shift explicit:

Those early pioneering days of our fathers ought to be an inspiration to us. They lived very close to Nature, and were hard-working, God-fearing men and women. They were happy, too, in their little log shanties. Of amusements, as we know them today, there were practically none ... I hope that no great building up of the cities, no in rush of immigration, will tear the roots of this country from the things that are real, primitive and elementary ... Our fathers did not write their history. They were too busy bringing vast tracts of country under civilization's sway. I hope to see it written some day ... [with] all the finer meanings brought out for the culturing of today's patriotism.[57]

As Bowles' address suggests, nationalist goals and anti-modern aesthetics were mutually reinforcing. In this period, transformations in capitalism and society, the perceived need for a national cultural project, new audiences and opportunities, and inter-personal ties fostered similar values and approaches in many different fields of cultural practice.

The pre-eminent makers of elite visual culture in Canada at this time (both as a material good and as an aesthetic) were the artists affiliated with the Group of Seven and their promoters and institutional supporters. The Group's favourite subjects were "untouched," "virgin" landscapes, solitary pine trees in primordial settings, rocky shorelines, all rendered in vigorous, virile brush strokes. The stories they told of themselves involved strenuous efforts to paint the land and the triumph over hazardous conditions. They represented their success as earned by honest labour rather than expert marketing or skill in meeting audience expectations.[58] The qualities of the Canadian landscape, and equally of those who painted it, were described by Group members and supportive critics in explicitly masculine terms: rugged, vigorous, and bold. Art historian Anne Whitelaw observes that the basis of the Group's claim to artistic distinctiveness lay not in their stylistic achievements but in their treatment of the Canadian landscape and their belief that their aesthetic captured the essence of the Canadian spirit.[59] They claimed that their paintings presented a "transparent record" of their direct encounters with nature, unmediated by the infrastructure of commerce. Engagement with these works promised to re-enact the original authentic experience.[60] As an account in the *Canadian Forum* explained, "Our health and worth as a nation depends ultimately on the self-knowledge that comes from ... recognition." Seeing the paintings of the Group of Seven, made one "feel Canadian."[61] Through art, the Canadian people would find themselves.[62] They would become "Home-conscious."[63]

The tendency to offset the perceived enervating and feminizing effects of urbanization and mass culture with hyper-masculinity is evident in Tom Thomson's posthumous transformation from a commercial artist to an icon of "backwoods masculinity."[64] Although Thomson lived in Toronto, worked in the graphic arts industry, and only travelled to the woodlands, members of the Group of Seven and prominent Toronto- and Ottawa-based writers and critics who supported the group consistently described him as a "natural artist," "childlike" in his emotional responses, practically self-taught, ignorant of any formal style or school, uncontaminated by professionalism or European training, and lacking in acquisitive instincts. They reframed potential character deficits as strengths: Thomson was not anti-social, but stoic and silent, living "truly with Nature." His champions celebrated his apparent indifference to money and honour as confirmation of authenticity, and they minimized Thomson's links with commercial art. His seeming self-isolation in the wilderness became the embodiment of masculine prowess. His experiences in the bush were seen to give an additional level of legitimacy to his paintings. Thomson's character, the Group's foremost promoter enthused, was "the antithesis of commercialism."[65]

As individuals, most members of the Group earned income as professional artists and educators. Yet, they cultivated a stance of rebels and outsiders, motivated by love of nature and love of country, driven by force of instinct rather than the search for profit. Identifying the nation with a wild and savage northern landscape, they celebrated the physical effort needed to capture its images, portraying themselves as the modern embodiment of a "*coureur de bois*," describing their art making as an energetic, manly activity that involved "love of adventure" and exploring.[66] Describing the relationship of artist and audience, the group's unofficial leader, Lawren Harris insisted that the true artist was not interested merely in "what the public wants," which he dismissed as "superficial, external, sensual, the concern of the appetites, the job of the panderer, the shrewd seeker after money or fame."[67] From such a perspective, gains in cultural status were directly associated with the refusal – or at least the apparent refusal – of economic rewards. Despite their success, many Group members continued to insist in public that they were uninterested in financial rewards. Their lives, like the unpeopled landscapes they painted, were to be seen as untainted by association with commercial interests.

The Group's insistence on their integrity as disinterested painters of pure subjects was also a challenge aimed at already established competitors in the cultural field. As Toronto journalist and Group of Seven supporter F.B. Housser explained in his account of the Group's rise, expressing the essence of Canada required "a new type of artist; one who divests himself of the velvet coat and flowing tie of his caste, puts on the outfit of the bush-whacker and prospector; closes with his environment, paddles, portages and makes camp, sleeps in the out-of-doors under the sky, climbs mountains with his sketch box on his back."[68] Distancing themselves from already established competitors, the Group insisted that "art is not a professional practice but a way of life," not "a form of technique" but "a form of intui-tion."[69] As Arthur Lismer recounted to members of the prestigious Canadian Club, the Canadian artist was one who "loved to stick his tongue out at tradition and go gaily on his own livelier road through his own native bush instead of following the shady, flower-strewn ways of older countries." Encouraging his audience to reject the "pseudo art news" of the sale room and discard the commonplace conventions of familiar art, Lismer recom-mended painting in nature as an "anodyne for mental sickness and distaste of our modern man-made efficiency."[70] Defining themselves as authentically uncommercial artists and investing their art with the authority of the "real" Canada, the Group and its supporters claimed a role as nation makers. As Harris explained, one of the distinguishing strengths of the great artist lay in his ability to perceive the finer impulses of his audience, "its aspirations, half formed visions and high dreams." In this way, wrote Harris, the experi-ence of collective purpose was expressed in the creation of works of art.[71]

Denouncing both traditional European-oriented high culture and mass culture, the Group cultivated the middle-brow middle ground, producing representations of the Canadian landscape as wilderness that resonated with expanding audiences and the interests of those building national corporations and institutions.[72] They situated their work within the bound-aries of respectable good taste, aiming to express "the sane and healthy outlook of Canada, neither academic nor super-refined and erotic."[73] Their aesthetic was compatible with an emerging consumer sensibility on a number of levels, not the least of which was affordability.[74] The Group's style was well received by metropolitan audiences who shared their anti-modern anxieties and associated wilderness landscapes with recreation and rejuvenation. Indeed, the Group prospered on the commercial appeal of anti-commercialism.

Historians Mary Vipond and Maria Tippett have shown that rising attention to culture in the interwar period was intertwined with nationalist
cultural aspirations.[75] The goal of producing a distinct national aesthetic
was shared by Canada's political and cultural elites, and the Group of Seven
successfully built strong relationships with museums, art schools, and
corporations.[76] Their specifically Canadian art-making provided cultural
validation to a rising generation of civil servants and industrialists. A nation-state, after all, requires national art.

The dynamic guiding other areas of collecting was also structured around
the polarities of commercial and non-commercial production. Collectors
were not the makers of rare goods, but they did make the context in which
certain objects were seen as especially valuable while others were dismissed
as "strictly commercial merchandise." The most important criteria sought
by those building collections were rarity, genuineness, and authenticity –
qualities that were not inherent in goods but that were defined in contrast
to their industrially made "baser counterparts."[77] As art historian Ruth
Phillips explains, authenticity was equated with the handmade and the
singular; inauthenticity was linked to the industrial production of goods
for profit in external markets. As the category of authenticity became
dominant in the discourse of collecting, it created a double bind for Indigenous craftspeople: when they resisted commodification of their culture,
they retained the respect of ethnologists and collectors but doomed themselves to perpetuating the forms of a static past. When they successfully
analysed the demands of urban audiences for Native goods – producing,
for example, a steady supply of beaded pincushions and moccasins to generate the cash needed to purchase the necessities of modern life – they were
characterized as a degraded people and a doomed race.

Studying the correspondence of the young anthropologist Edward Sapir,
head of the newly established Division of Anthropology within the Geological Survey of Canada, Phillips found details of negotiations over price,
competition among buyers, the role of agents in the acquisition of goods,
and the commissioning of replicas by museums in order to complete collections with items that were no longer commonly made.[78] Collectors made
distinctions between true artefacts, acceptable replicas, and false souvenirs
without regard to the role they personally played in selecting and acquiring
artefacts. The value of producing souvenir art for the Indigenous creator
lay in its potential use as an exchange commodity. For professional ethnologists building collections for museums, evidence that goods were made to

be sold, or that designs had been influenced by contact with Western civilization, was problematic. Rarity and commodity were mutually exclusive categories. The absence of trade goods in museum collections of the period illuminates the same commitments in reverse: there was an ample supply of souvenir goods and tourist art, but no place for these goods within the strict taxonomy of the museum collection, even if they were made by the same people using the same techniques as "authentic" artefacts. The exclusion of objects that showed evidence of contact (including, for example, goods that were stylistically hybrid or produced in multiples) led to the exclusion of contemporary artists and devalued creativity.[79] The commitment to presentation of a static rather than a living people, represented solely by goods from the pre-contact period, conveniently reinforced the "myth of imminent demise" and the availability of tribal lands for others.

In *Quest of the Folk*, Canadian historian Ian McKay identifies the same pattern of opposition between culture and commerce in the work of journalists, collectors, and handicraft revivalists travelling to remote Maritime fishing villages in the interwar period. By re-imagining those they encountered as "Folk," these cultural entrepreneurs found marketable images for urban audiences. McKay proposes that the ability of these entrepreneurs to see the inhabitants of fishing villages as pre-modern depended not on empirical observation, but on the exclusion of evidence of modernity (including coal mines, lumber camps, a large-scale fishing industry, banks, department stores, newspapers, radios, books, and even their own presence), and a willingness to reframe poverty and deprivation as simplicity. The value placed on the culture of "the Folk," like that placed on Indigenous crafts, reflected urban anxieties and the longing for idealized communities, presumed to be free from class tensions and immune to the pressures of industrial capitalism.[80]

The same values are evident in descriptions of the Québécois, portrayed as an organic traditional community, suspended in time and distanced from modern life. Group of Seven painter and art educator Arthur Lismer was one of those who praised the simplicity and integrity of the Québécois. "There are still places in Canada," he wrote, "where simple people live natural, hardworking lives without the grayness and futility that so often accompanies life in newer settlements ... Life in a community where ... art is exercised as a common every day task, is infinitely brighter than in those communities where the machine-made products of factories abound. It is not much to the credit of Canada that the department store with its multitudinous variety of unnecessary things has invaded and swamped the simpler, home-made products of the people." Peasant peoples, he continued, respond to the necessity of nature rather than the demands of the market. "Primitive, or let us say, simple people feel beauty naturally. Children are like this. It is not acquired. It is not merely taste. It is intuitive." Lismer recommended that the government should bring more peasants to Canada to teach others the "desire for expression which all real peasant people have."[81] Others shared Lismer's vision of the Québécois as peasant-spiritual people, including the historian Arthur Lower and the folk-culture enthusiast and Canadian Pacific Railway (CPR) publicity agent John Murray Gibbon, who organized folk-song and handicraft festivals at various hotels across Canada under the sponsorship of the CPR. The Québécois peasant, like the Maritime folk, the Indigenous artisan, and the wilderness landscape, were approached as cultural resources: sources of material and inspiration for the development of cultural goods and the tourism industry.

Amateur Practice and Anti-Modernism: Developing a New Market Niche

The same pattern of opposition between culture and commerce structures the writings of two key interwar social scientists.[82] Anthropologist and linguist Edward Sapir and sociologist Robert MacIver were long-time sojourners in Canada, who went on to play important roles in building up the institutional and theoretical underpinnings of their respective fields, first in Canada and later in the United States.[83] Working independently, Sapir and MacIver developed theories of Indigenous North American societies of the past, societies they imagined as more authentic and fulfilling than the present, and used their theories of these past societies to critique and potentially heal the malaise they identified in modern society. Each postulated that, in the cultured societies of the past, workplace and home, communal and private life, productive effort and personal recreation had been integrated in a totally harmonious way of life. Such integration was impossible in advanced capitalist societies, where increased productivity grew from task specialization. Because industrial society reduced individuals to mindless workers and passive consumers, the technological benefits of modernity were inherently incompatible with a cultured life. The antidote to machine-shaped urban life, they each concluded, could be found in the past, particularly in the example of Indigenous North American society.

Coming to Canada as a young and ambitious anthropologist, Edward Sapir was an active member of Ottawa's cultural community, a well-regarded poet, and a frequent contributor to the *Canadian Forum, Queen's Quarterly,* the *Canadian Magazine,* and the *Dalhousie Review.* He was one of a handful of writers singled out by the critic A.J.M. Smith for significant contributions to modern Canadian poetry.[84] Sapir arrived in Ottawa in 1910 to establish and direct the Anthropology Division of the Geological Survey of Canada. The culmination of his professional experiences in Canada (he left in 1925 for a position at the University of Chicago) appeared in a seminal article entitled "Culture, Genuine and Spurious," published in the *Dalhousie Review* two years prior to its better-known appearance in the *American Journal of Sociology.*[85] It was Sapir's contention that "Every profound change in the flow of civilization, particularly every change in its economic bases, tends to bring about an unsettling and readjustment of culture values."[86] Modern society, where rapid material progress had been won through processes of specialization and fragmentation, defeated individual efforts to lead a fully integrated life. The apparent accomplishments of machine civilization offered only a "spurious" sense of progress when measured against criteria of a "harmonious, balanced, self-satisfactory culture ... Part of the time we are dray horses," Sapir despaired, "the rest of the time we are listless consumers of goods which have received no ... impress of our personality."[87]

Robert MacIver came from Scotland in 1915 to fill the position of associate professor in the Department of Political Economy at the University of Toronto. He headed the department from 1922 until he left Canada in 1927 to take up a position at Columbia University, where he gained a reputation as one of the world's leading sociologists, later becoming president and then chancellor of the New School of Social Research in New York. MacIver was a progressive in his politics, and he and his family were close friends with several members of the Group of Seven, taking painting lessons and sharing summers in neighbouring cottages on Georgian Bay. Much like Sapir, MacIver questioned the value of specialization, quantification, and positivism. Instead, he argued that community was the fundamental law of social life.[88] In the essay "Civilization versus Culture," one of his best-known works, he insisted that the individual and the social organization must be compatible for life to be satisfying. In primitive society, whatever its disadvantages, "men have the sense of being at home ... their mental world is secure." In such a world, "the arts and crafts, the rules and techniques," were embedded in the social system. Every object had social as well as technical significance and belonged to the total culture of the community. In primitive life, culture and civilization were harmonized. In modern society, culture and civilization were unreconciled and antithetical; the apparatus of means had become separated from the system of ends they serve. "Culture is what we are, civilization is what we use," he explained.[89] Utility demanded standardization, mass production, ugliness, and haste, and therefore could not provide spiritual satisfaction. The absence of larger goals left individuals in an alienated state of being. "The maladjustment of culture and civilization is the outstanding characteristic of our age. We do not feel at home." Cultural significance infused the whole apparatus of primitive peoples but was absent in large portions of modern civilization, where objects and activities were devoid of any significance beyond their direct instrumental function. "Civilization is too much with us," he concluded, paraphrasing the English poet William Wordsworth. "Getting and spending we lay waste to culture."[90]

Both Sapir and MacIver drew on similar romanticized notions of primitive culture to provide models for resistance and renewal, proposing that amateur practices could provide the solution to modern urban ills. Sapir suggested that the "spiritual heightening" gained through acts of creativity could compensate for the losses of modernity.[91] Technological mastery was associated with cultural impoverishment, but self-mastery in the "non-economic, the non-utilitarian" spheres of existence could act as an antidote to the "remorseless leveling force of average mind on average mind."[92] MacIver similarly identified the separation of the technical from the spiritual as the source of modern alienation. And, much like Sapir, he recommended the pursuit of culture during leisure time as the vehicle to restore spiritual wholeness. Somewhat paradoxically, MacIver argued that the separation of culture from civilization offered the solution to modern alienation by allowing the spiritual to be preserved in a distinctive sphere of life rather than fully eliminated. Spiritual unity could then be re-created on an individual basis, in "the will of each to be himself and achieve the objects that are dear to him."[93]

The emphasis both men placed on the liberatory and transformative potential of "making" rather than "buying" echoed the critiques of earlier generations who warned against taking pleasure in material things. For Sapir and MacIver, however, the purpose of "making" was to restore well-being. Becoming cultured was not the end goal but the means to regenerate the "self" and reconnect the physical and spiritual aspects of life. Self-improvement was no longer a matter of learning the "best that had been thought and said," but instead was associated with acts of personal creativity carried out in the present. The spiritual wholeness that had been lost in daily work-life could be recaptured in leisure time. Although a spender of dollars, the true amateur did not produce for profit. As was the case with other discussions of elite culture, financial disinterest was the test of authentic creativity. Amateur acts of culture making were recommended as the antidote to economism. The lessons Sapir and MacIver took from their study of primitive society were therapeutic: the objective was not to overturn modern society but to help individuals accommodate themselves to the challenges of modernity. Although modern society as a whole was no longer "cultured," individuals could approach wholeness by pursuing culture as a means to an end. The balance and harmony lost in society could be restored, to some degree, at the personal level in private life.

A pair of essays appearing in the *Canadian Forum* at this time, written by social critic and musician-composer Marcus Adeney, offer additional insights. Asking readers to join him in a thought experiment, Adeney described a small town cut off from the modern world and meditated on the virtues of the amateur spirit and communal life. "Who derives the most satisfaction," he asked, "the man who creates or the man who buys the use of a man-created thing?" Adeney marvelled at "the utopian possibilities of the small town" and celebrated the spirit of the amateur as "essential to man's ultimate victory over expediency." Today's culture, he complained, was standardized, commercialized, and "devitalized." The true amateur was bound neither by tradition nor by "the imposition of worthless machine-made literature and films." He or she was "a spiritually articulate human being," unlike those who consumed goods produced mechanically and who, therefore, possessed only mechanical values. It is perhaps a surprise to realize that the inspiration for Adeney's small town was Paris, Ontario, a community very much in the mainstream of industrialization.[94]

As older practices of entertainment, where the roles of producer and consumer were interchangeable, were displaced by professional performances, the value of amateur practice could be, in theory at least, recaptured

as personal re-creation, outside of the market.[95] For the individual, amateurism promised personal and remedial benefits rather than radical change.
Return on investment came in the non-material realms of the psychological
and the spiritual: a skilled amateur might build up a store of symbolic and
cultural capital but must necessarily refuse to convert expertise into economic capital. And yet, even though Adeney, Sapir, MacIver, and others
theorized amateurism as non-commercial practice, the fulfilment of more
complex needs had economic potential. The therapeutic values of self-
development aligned with an emergent consumer culture and an economy
promoting spending on goods and services.[96] Self-fulfilment as an amateur
required expenditures of time and money on travel and hobbies, including
such items as art supplies, musical instruments, lessons, cottages, and summer camps. The commercial potential of middle- and working-class amateur
activities was evident in the increasing number of hobby columns in newspapers; in the rise of manufacturers, magazines, and national and local
organizations devoted to various specialized hobbies, ranging from pho-
tography and stamp collecting to theatrical productions; and in the growing
popularity of recreational hunting, camping, and fishing.[97] The new cultural
intelligentsia imagined the experiences of the amateur, like those of "the
Folk," as authentic, intense, meaningful, and located outside the disciplines
of the modern economy. In lived experience, however, amateur activities,
like those in other fields of interwar culture, were a growing part of that
"commerce in things which are not commercial."[98]

Conclusion

Canadian elites reacted with dismay to the surge in mass-produced, commercially sold forms of popular entertainment. But in spite of, or perhaps
because of, their misgivings, social observers could not simply dismiss the
economic implications of mass culture. As University of Toronto economist
C.R. Fay observed, the problem was fundamental: "mass production without mass consumption is useless. It is mass consumption which makes mass
production both possible and profitable." What concerned Fay was that
the advertisements that made the newspapers profitable threatened to
overwhelm coverage of the political news that he regarded as their true
social function. Similarly, he complained that in sports the virtues of team
effort were being sacrificed to the demands of managers who operated
"with an eye on results." The consumer, Fay objected, was being "drenched

with standardized novelties." At the same, time, although these changes were lamentable, the strength of the modern economy was dependent on modes of consumption that undermined traditional aesthetic and moral values. As Fay begrudgingly acknowledged, volume of sales had replaced standards of judgment as the measure of success. The contrast between past and present, he observed, was clear: "A thing of beauty is a joy for ever, said the poet Keats. That is bad economics. For economic progress prescribes a new model every year as soon as the old one has been paid for, if not before."[99]

Maintaining standards in the face of increasing standardization was also a matter of maintaining and reworking class distinctions. At a time when the American way of life was coming to be associated with mass consumption, Canadian elites rejected such consumption as the basis for national identity. Artists, writers, and intellectuals asserted their autonomy from the market and from commercial influence, claiming indifference to monetary profit. The repositioning of the amateur was another response to the increasing professionalization of culture and the perceived malaise of modern life. Each of the different fields of high culture production was organized around the same fundamental opposition between the commercial and the non-commercial. The discourses that developed around discretionary spending on cultural goods correlated differences in class and gender with different forms of cultural consumption, creating an "approved list" of commodities.

This "commerce in things that are not commercial" offered different opportunities for careers and incomes.[100] There was a correlation between those who produced "culture" and the social group on which they depended for economic support, which included other cultural producers (that is, other artists, writers, critics, intellectuals, and promoters) but also audiences and clientele drawn from the educated higher ranks of the professional-managerial class, the business elite, and the upper echelons of the civil service. Bonds of kinship, friendship, business, and personal history reinforced the schema of values that structured different culture fields.[101]

Ideas about cultural nationalism and the incompatibility of culture and commerce served many purposes. Elite critics associated national culture with the prestige of high culture rather than the widespread appeal of commercial entertainments. They denigrated consumption of mass culture by ordinary Canadians as general commodity consumption. Consumption of the right sorts of cultural goods enhanced class claims as well as assertions of good citizenship. Cultural nationalism contained "a claim of equality" but was erected on a structure of values that challenged the leisure time choices ordinary Canadians were making on a daily basis. Those who consumed mass culture were not disenfranchised, but the sincerity and value of their citizenship was called into question.

Chapter Four

MORALIZING THE ECONOMY

Early in 1934, while the country was still struggling to escape the grip of economic depression, Trade and Commerce Minister H.H. (Harry) Stevens launched an aggressive and widely publicized attack on big business. Present hardships, Stevens charged, were the result of monopolies of distribution. Large organizations used their power to crush small manufacturers and independent workers. Big businesses were "a canker" threatening the economic life of the nation by controlling markets, dictating prices, and forcing down wages.

A story on Stevens' address appeared on the front page of the *Toronto Star* the next morning under the headline "Evils of Big Interests Challenged by Stevens: Trade Minister Deplores Greed and Avarice, Calls for Correction." Noting that the prime minister had asked Stevens to fulfil a speaking engagement at the National Shoe Retailers convention, the reporter emphasized the novelty of a sweeping attack on big business by the cabinet minister in charge of trade and commerce. The story gathered momentum the following day, when both the *Star* and the *Globe* printed front-page rebuttals by prominent business leaders.[1]

Over the next week, both sides used morally charged language to make their cases. Stevens alleged that big businesses were colluding to "dictate," "coerce," "demand," "exploit," and "hold hostage" the independent workers and small businesses that formed the backbone of the nation. Casting current economic turmoil as a war of the large against the small, he declared that the economy had been "demoralized" by the fixing of prices and the restriction of supply and demand. Business spokesmen responded in kind. Responding to Stevens under the headline "Quantity Buying Beneficial Not Unmoral" in the *Toronto Daily Star*, R.Y. Eaton, the president of Eaton's department stores, insisted that lower prices for the consumer were in the interest of the entire community.[2] After five years of depression, Stevens' attacks on big business captured the attention of the press and the public, leading to the immediate appointment of a parliamentary inquiry investigating in detail the structure of the national economy, which subsequently became the Royal Commission on Price Spreads and Mass Buying.[3] For the next fifteen months, Canadians were captivated and scandalized by revelations of corporate practices that kept profits and prices high and wages low. Then, in the spring of 1935, the commission presented its report to Parliament and disbanded. In spite of the prolonged controversy, the federal election held in the fall of 1935 largely renewed the nation's commitment to capitalism – albeit with a new Liberal government replacing Prime Minister Bennett's Conservative one. In the months that followed, the intense emotions associated with the Price Spreads Inquiry evaporated. Much of the legislation increasing government intervention in the economy was disallowed by the courts. The economy limped along, shrugging off the Depression only when wartime spending kicked in.

Although historians commonly note that Canadians were transfixed by the revelations of the Price Spreads Inquiry, they tend to reduce the episode to the story of H.H. Stevens, the Conservative politician who helped the Liberal Party return to power, the unlikely political spoiler of the 1935 federal election. At the time, however, political and social observers were convinced of the importance of the inquiry itself, frequently predicting that its revelations would alter the balance of economic power in Canada. To some extent, the gap between later interpretation and contemporary experience can be attributed to the biases of traditional political historiography, focused on the fates of elites and on election results. However, such interpretations, which reduce widespread public outrage to irrational scapegoating, leave many questions unanswered – in particular, why did the relatively technical question of price spreads emerge as the focus of Depression-era frustrations?

The Depression years were the climax for shifts underway since before the turn of the century. A critical point had been reached in the movement away from an idealized agrarian society, rooted in independent labour, property ownership, and personal relationships, and towards a future of large-scale corporate capitalism. The balance of wealth and power had shifted in favour of large enterprises. The Price Spreads Inquiry gave voice to the disappointments and fears associated with new economic conditions.

The shift in the balance of power between large and small producers was a political and social issue as well as an economic one. The perception that large-scale industrial capitalism destroyed loyalties, eroded the bonds of mutual economic interest, and devalued labour was widely shared. Job losses, bankruptcies, and foreclosures threatened long-standing associations between manliness and independent labour, and between property ownership and citizenship. Jobs that appeared in new sectors of the economy (such as light manufacturing, clerical work, and the service sector) were often perceived as geared towards women, offering lower wages, less stability, and less prestige. It is undoubtedly true that some workers were able to compensate for their loss of autonomy and their value as skilled craftsmen by emphasizing their roles as breadwinners, but losses in control over the value of one's own labour and life were real nonetheless, the result of changes that began long before and continued long after the Depression years.[4]

The primary value of the Price Spreads Inquiry and the subsequent report was not in specific recommendations but in changing the significance attached to acts of consumption in Canadian political discourse. By confirming the political legitimacy and economic significance of consumers and their interests, the inquiry helped shape the themes of the next federal election. In the wake of the inquiry, politicians addressed voters as consumers, promising to protect consumer interests and to ensure a minimum (albeit vaguely defined) standard of living. Highlighting the connection between earnings and spending power validated a new role for ordinary Canadians in a corporate industrial economy geared towards higher productivity. Managing the economy to ensure adequate private consumption, politicians promised, would minimize future conflicts among social groups and secure social stability. Identifying a consumer interest avoided a direct assault on corporate power.

In thinking about the outburst of public anger that accompanied the Stevens Commission, it is useful to consider how scholars have conceptualized similar episodes of populist protest. According to historian Adam

Ashforth, commissions of inquiry should be regarded as special investigative techniques created by governments to solve particular problems.[5] Government inquiries, he proposes, promise to pursue truth in situations where citizens do not see truth to be forthcoming. Matters under dispute are investigated, testimony is compelled, findings are publicized, issues are held up for public scrutiny and debate, interests are discussed, and possible solutions are considered. While in existence, the inquiry removes the problem from the arena of daily politics; however, commissions of inquiry are also a form of political theatre, offering evidence of the state's interest in the concerns of the people. Although they end in formal reports and recommendations, they perform the ritual of calling the powerful to account.

Considering the Price Spreads Inquiry, from its beginning in 1934 to its end in 1935, through the prism of the moral economy locates these events in the tradition of populist protest linked to changes in economic regimes. Within this tradition, discussions of resistance to economic transformation most frequently involve the transition from pre-market to market society. The extension of the market threatens the material well-being of ordinary people, as well as their shared values and traditions. Tensions mount along with uncertainty. Hunger, whether due to inequality in distribution or shortages in supply, is often a factor. The state is finally called upon to intervene, mediating between interest groups, protecting citizens from the most disruptive impacts of monopoly capital and the commodification of labour. The depth of popular concerns must be recognized and accommodated, hegemony must be re-negotiated and defended, and consent must be obtained in order for government to function.[6]

Popular protest takes historically specific forms. In a liberal democracy in the 1930s, the process of government inquiry offered a ritual link between the state and the public, providing a vehicle of legitimization by which the state – and the elected political leadership – could demonstrate that it was listening to the concerns of its citizens. The dynamic of the 1930s was not the transition into capitalism, but rather a transition *within* capitalism, with conglomerates and monopolies displacing proprietary capitalism, small businesses, and independent workers. The economies of scale introduced by mass production and the collapse of commodity prices meant that distribution and commercial costs made up a larger percentage of the total cost of goods. While increased competition, shrinking markets, and falling prices squeezed all retailers, these conditions tended to favour mass producers and mass merchandisers over the small independents. Social bonds were eroded by increases in scale and competition, which the Depression exacerbated. The profit-maximizing behaviour of larger corporations was at odds with historic commitments to property and self-sufficiency.

The problem, as Stevens represented it, was not one of structural change but of greed and avarice. He declared that the ordinary men and women of Canada – industrial workers, farmers, and fishermen – were being exploited by corporations, both in their roles as producers and consumers. They were confronted, on the one hand, by fiercely competitive practices that erased profit margins and drove down wages and, on the other, by misleading commercial practices that eroded real purchasing power. Canada Packers, Stevens charged, exploited farmers by driving down the price of beef, while chains such as Tamblyns drugstores used loss leaders to drive neighbourhood stores out of business. He claimed that Eaton's exploited its dressmakers to keep prices low and that the owners of Simpson's department stores sold shares that yielded no return to unsuspecting investors but created high profits for owners and stockbrokers. Oppressed by combinations and big business, small businessmen and independent workers could not sell their products or their labour at prices that enabled them to afford a decent standard of living. For the many Canadians who agreed with Stevens, these changes came to symbolize the dislocations of modernity.

The commission of inquiry and the subsequent Royal Commission were ideal vehicles through which to examine in detail the vast changes underway in the Canadian economy since before the war and to reconsider notions of fairness. A large public audience of voters and potential voters was mobilized and kept engaged for over a year, as much by the moral tone of the proceedings as by the factual findings.[7] The visible misery of Canada's working people and the high rate of unemployment challenged conventional claims that government could not, or should not, intervene in the workings of the economy. Seeking to channel public opinion, political leaders pledged to expand the role of the state. These commitments helped maintain the legitimacy of government, but also required politicians to acknowledge new rights and claims on the state. The consumer in the economic realm was identified with the citizen in the political realm.

In the week immediately following Stevens' speech to the delegates at the national convention of the Retail Shoe Merchants and Shoe Manufacturers Association, letters and wires from farmers, retail merchants, bakers, shopgirls, consumers, and manufacturers flooded into his office and that of Prime Minister Bennett. Most were supportive of Stevens' claims.[8] The ceremonial opening of Parliament took place on 25 January 1934. The following week, Bennett added a resolution to the first order paper of the new session, calling for the appointment of a select Committee of the House to investigate the minister's charges. The eleven members of the committee were mandated to "investigate the causes of the large spread between the prices received for commodities by the producer thereof, and the price paid by the consumers therefore." Specific topics for investigation included the effects of mass buying by chain and department stores, the relationship between the flour-milling industry and bakeries, and how the system of marketing animal products "affords or restricts the opportunity for fair return to producers."[9] The committee, with representatives from all political parties, was given the right to summon witnesses, to commission special reports, and to secure evidence as necessary to carry out its task. It was to be the most comprehensive review of Canadian trade and commerce ever conducted. The scope, Bennett explained, was broad and would be dictated by public interest. Stevens would be the chair.

The committee began hearings almost immediately.[10] Members of Parliament, leaders of industry, and the general public attended the proceedings. Details of witness testimony were published regularly in daily and weekly papers nation-wide. The evidence and tone of the investigation were considered closely in lengthy articles in important national journals. The inquiry was by far the most popular initiative undertaken by the Conservative government.[11] When Parliament was prorogued in July, an order in council transformed the committee into a Royal Commission, again to be chaired by Stevens. Political turmoil during the summer months ensured that public interest remained high. Stevens' regular attacks on the practices of big business were creating tensions within the Conservative Party, especially at the cabinet level, where links with Canada's business community were strong. The breaking point came when an address Stevens had delivered to a Conservative study club in June was reprinted in pamphlet form for public distribution. Bennett ordered the pamphlets destroyed, but Stevens' allegations became public knowledge when the contents of the pamphlet were printed in the *Winnipeg Free Press*.[12] Stevens was forced to

Hon. H. H. Stevens Addresses Capacity Audience in Toronto

FIGURE 2 Canadians were captivated by the revelations of the Price Spreads Inquiry, chaired for a time by Conservative Trade and Commerce Minister H.H. Stevens. The investigation exposed the inner workings of modern mass retailing, including abusive business practices that leveraged the advantages of size to squeeze out small independent firms and exploit workers. | *Globe,* 6 November 1934, 1.

resign as chair of the Royal Commission, although he retained his seat in the House and his Conservative Party membership. Many Canadians saw Stevens' resignation as a victory for powerful industrial interests. Not surprisingly, then, he continued to be well received as a public speaker and was greeted with rousing welcomes in a subsequent tour of eastern Canada. His audiences filled large halls, and loud speakers had to be provided for meetings that overflowed into the street.[13]

In October, the commission resumed hearings with a new chair. It would meet sixty-five more times before retiring in January 1935 to prepare a report of its findings and recommendations. The publication of the *Report* in April triggered another round of press coverage, ensuring that the findings of the inquiry would be a prominent issue heading into the summer recess and a fall election.

Several times each week for over a year, stories about the inquiry appeared – often on the front page – of Canada's major papers.[14] Wire services distributed highlights across the nation. Particularly sensational revelations generated additional coverage in the op-ed pages, including editorials and letters to the editor. Journalists described aggressive interrogation of business leaders and managers, and the respectful questioning of oppressed employees and independent workers struggling to earn subsistence wages in miserable conditions. Other testimony was more analytical and involved the detailed questioning of expert witnesses, including academics and accountants commissioned by the inquiry to prepare special reports. Expert reports added a sense of impartiality and authority to the proceedings, lending support to Stevens' accounts of impoverished working people and business wrongdoing.

Media attention extended beyond the testimony presented at the inquiry. The press widely reported opinions delivered by politicians inside and outside the House of Commons. Stevens himself was greatly in demand as a speaker. After resigning as the chair of the commission, he toured eastern Canada, promising "not to white wash" the findings of the inquiry. His addresses were a dependable source of dramatic headlines: "Industrial Chisellers Slammed by Stevens in Sizzling Phrases" and "Stevens Would Padlock 'Shortweight Stores.'"[15] The revelations of the investigation were topics of intense discussion in federal by-elections and provincial election campaigns, providing ample material for speeches by aspiring leaders on both the left and the right of the political spectrum. The press also reported on submissions prepared by special interest groups; these included lengthy formal reports prepared by the Canadian Manufacturers' Association, the Retail Merchants' Association, and the Conference of the United Church of Canada, as well as those submitted by independent business organizations, including associations of hairdressers, of professional photographers, and of furniture makers. The space devoted to reporting such submissions varied, but the attention contributed to the sense that the proceedings held an importance that extended well beyond the industries directly under investigation.[16]

In addition to coverage in the daily press, the inquiry was reviewed in detail in lengthier, more analytical articles in *Saturday Night*, the *Canadian Forum*, *Queen's Quarterly*, and the *Round Table*. The tone of Stevens' interrogations while in his role as chair aroused considerable misgivings in the intellectual community. Many expressed dismay at the spectacle of prominent people being treated aggressively. Journalist and author Wilfrid Eggleston, for example, described "the Stevens episode" as "one of the most baffling chapters of our political and economic history."[17] Others described the inquiry as an "inquisition," a "crusade," and a "witch-hunt."[18] But intellectuals, no less than the popular press, were inclined to find moral lessons in the evidence uncovered by the inquiry. Eggleston directly linked individual accounts of poverty with the unequal distribution of economic power. Because corporations and independent businesses differed in their ability to resist the effects of lost income, Eggleston argued that government should intervene to ensure that the burden of depression was fairly shared. Queen's University professor Duncan McArthur considered the social consequences of the concentration of economic power the inquiry had revealed, and similarly concluded that the antisocial behaviours of industry should be restrained in the interests of the community. Freedom, he argued, was no longer an "issue concerned with the protection of political rights but rather with the right of those engaged in various processes of production and distribution to obtain an adequate return for their efforts."[19] While they disapproved of the emotional tone of popular protest, many economists acknowledged the existence of legitimate economic grievances. Entrenched elites and new-money plutocrats had monopolized the wealth created by technological improvements and the reorganization of industry. Structural changes in the economy had tilted the balance of economic power disproportionately in favour of the wealthy.

Over the course of nine months, the inquiry worked its way through the Canadian economy on an industry-by-industry basis, examining the steps by which primary products and raw materials were transformed into retail goods and sold to Canadian consumers. Key sectors for investigation were the textile, clothing, and needle trades; flour milling and baking; tobacco; car and agricultural-implement manufacturing; fishing; livestock and meat packing; furniture manufacturing; rubber goods; canning; and retail distribution. The investigation of each new sector generated banner headlines and revelations that kept the inquiry on the front pages. Together, these investigations showed the disruptive impact of new technologies and of the reorganization of production and distribution on a mass scale.

A closer look at the investigation of a single sector gives a good sense of the nature and tone of the revelations. In 1934, the commissioners examined milling and bread baking for several weeks, interviewing owners and managers, receiving briefs from different organizations of bakers, reviewing advertisements submitted as evidence of unfair trade practices, analyzing bread samples, circulating questions to Canadian mills, and sending out teams of investigators and auditors. As part of its inquiry, the commission produced seventy-one charts with information on this sector. Modernization and anticipation of profits had created vast overcapacity in the flour-milling industry. For every two barrels of flour produced, Canadian manufacturers had the ability to produce an additional three and a half barrels. Two-thirds of the nations' flour needs were being met by 23 of 1,292 flour mills, and even many of these operated at a loss. In an effort to raise returns, the mills had begun to acquire bakeries. The development of large-scale milling brought about the development of equally large-scale selling organizations. In recent years, several bakers testified, the largest factor in the cost of a loaf of bread was no longer the ingredients but the costs of selling and distribution. The effects of the entry of flour mills into the baking industry was compounded by the arrival of chain stores and the adoption of national advertising programs. The price of a loaf of bread was often set in the Toronto head office, regardless of the cost of wheat and flour in other centres. Toronto baker James Dempster complained that new practices violated long-standing customs that allowed bakers to set and lower prices within each community in unison, a practice that had helped to stabilize the local market and maintain wages and profits. Chains and department stores sold bread at below cost as loss leaders. One chain was reported to have bought a thousand loaves of bread at seven cents a loaf and sold them at five cents each. Examples were given of bakers throughout the nation dropping prices below the costs of production. In some Toronto grocery stores, bread was being given away with the purchase of groceries. The industry was described as "demoralized" and "chaotic." Bakers were pitted against one another; quality was declining. It was reported that, with prices so low, housewives had stopped baking their own bread.[20]

Similar stories were told, with variations, in every sector of the economy: the wages and earnings of independent workers and primary producers were collapsing. The pricing policies of mass merchandisers squeezed suppliers, forcing even well-intentioned businessmen to cut wages and speed up work routines. Witnesses with first-hand experience testified to the ways chains manipulated and cheated "Mr. and Mrs. Consumer."[21] Mass producers and mass retailers had seemingly sustained their profits during the Depression by exploiting ordinary Canadians.

In the flour-milling and baking industries, changes in the price spreads reflected shifts in the economy that were reducing the cost of primary commodities at the same time that consumer goods and services were becoming more important. In 1930, it was calculated that the difference between the price of one pound of wheat and the price of the flour used in one pound of bread was less than one cent, but that the difference between the price of flour used to make the pound of bread and the price of the pound of bread had risen by more than five cents. The spread between flour and bread prices rose from 2.33 cents per pound in 1916 to 5.13 cents per pound in 1930.[22] Changes in scale and innovations in technology, transportation, and business organization increased both the volume of production and productivity, putting downward pressure on the incomes of small producers and wage earners. The price charged for goods became less dependent on the costs of production (including labour), and more dependent on demand. With margins under pressure, the share of the profits was larger at the point of sale than at the point of production. The commission, after meeting in its two different forms for a total of 123 days, generating over seven million words of evidence, and reviewing more than a dozen industries, adjourned to prepare its report.

The Report Arrives

In the spring of 1935, the Price Spreads Commission returned to the front pages of the daily press and the inner pages of academic journals with the presentation of its report to Parliament.[23] While Stevens had been the moving force behind the inquiry, the preparation of the 500-page report consolidating the commission's findings and recommendations was the work of members of the professional federal civil service.[24] Although the tone of the inquiry had often been adversarial, the report's authors insisted that Canada's economic problems were not moral but economic in origin. Modern business methods were rational and efficient, with lower cost structures and improved productivity; however, they also concentrated economic power. The report attributed abuses largely to impersonal mechanisms and the long-term structural changes that had "set the stage" for predatory practices in an economy undergoing transition, an economy "in which simple competition still prevailed in some parts, monopoly had succeeded it in others and monopolistic or imperfect competition characterized the rest."[25] The collapse of income from exports intensified competition, adding pressure to businesses already struggling. The commissioners concluded that these problems would not be corrected over time by "automatic forces," but rather required the creation of a federal trade and industry commission with broad powers to supervise and regulate industrial and commercial activity.

By analysing the issues in this way, the report identified problems to which more government intervention seemed the obvious and necessary solution. Given the impersonal nature of the modern economy and the antisocial nature of the corporate form, the state needed to enter the market to mediate asymmetries of power to restore competition where possible, and regulate monopoly when necessary. Specific recommendations included an extensive regime of commissions, trade boards, and standards to regulate wages, working conditions, products, and selling practices. Waged workers and primary producers would be assured of a larger return for their labour. Consumers and small investors would be protected against profiteering, whether by the sale of inferior goods, the manipulation of markets, or deceptive sales practices.

Chapter 8 of the report made a strong case for the importance of the consumer in the modern economy, observing that it

> is now a commonplace of economic thought that the significance of the wage-earner is not confined to his activities as a producer. Production cannot continue without profitable markets; business activity of every sort ceases without prosperous buyers. Despite the importance of certain export markets, our own workers constitute the biggest market for Canadian products. On the stability of their income and purchasing power depend the profits of business enterprise. On their standards of living rests the possibility of commercial prosperity.[26]

In spite of this strong statement, the report did not call for government to directly fund consumption by creating jobs; rather, it envisioned that consumption would increase if consumers were informed and were protected from fraudulent practices. Modern production, the report explained, helped the consumer by reducing costs and increasing the availability of goods. In the new world of industry and trade, transactions were no longer direct and face to face; consequently, "*caveat emptor*" had taken on "a new and pertinent meaning."[27] Describing consumers as the frequent victims of false advertising, adulterated goods, inferior substitutes, short-weighted scales, and a host of other deceptive practices, the report called on government to standardize, control, and grade the output of industry. The majority of recommendations sought to aid producers by restraining competition and supporting prices. When the authors used the language of consumer rights, they envisioned policies that would encourage economic activity rather than bring about economic equality.

In spite of broad unanimity among the commission members, three Liberal representatives signed the report subject to a memorandum of reservations, and another member, also a Liberal, dissented altogether and submitted a minority report.[28] All four Liberals contended that the report had not sufficiently emphasized the importance of external trade to the Canadian economy. They also insisted that the recommendations failed to adequately consider the interests of the consumer. Noting a tendency "to think of the various subdivisions of society entirely in the capacity of producers," the dissenting Liberals argued that consumers were alike in a way that producers were not. It was, they proposed, the consumer who constituted "the main general interest, as distinguished from particular interests."[29] Deeming increased competition more important than increased regulation, Liberals saw less need for government intervention in the economy.

Manitoba Liberal E.J. Young made an even stronger case for a common consumer interest in his dissenting minority report. Young maintained that the consumer "exercising his right not to buy" had the power to force the readjustment between supply and demand. The test of the efficiency of any merchandising system, Young insisted, must be "'how does it serve the consumer,' and in this test the consumer, himself, will be the judge."[30] Young argued that any form of regulation, whether by government or industry, served only to protect the obsolete. It was up to the people to judge whether they wanted a particular service or not. Efforts to legislate improvements in working conditions and wages on the grounds that "we are all producers" were fundamentally misguided. "The only common ground on which we all stand is as consumers ... The only interest that is not a class interest is the consumer interest. The only legislation that is not class legislation is legislation in the interests of the consumer. In seeking the remedy for our economic ills, we should always keep the consumer's interest uppermost in our minds for 'the consumer's interest is the interest of the human race.'"[31] Despite his pro-consumer rhetoric, Young linked his advocacy of the consumer interest to the elimination of protective tariffs and the restoration of international trade rather than to policies such as higher wages that would directly increase domestic spending. The role of the consumer was to regulate supply and demand, not to stimulate economic growth.

The 1935 Federal Election Campaign

The report of the Price Spreads Commission was presented to Parliament in April 1935. When the House of Commons recessed for the summer, members left knowing that an election would have to be called before the fall. The turmoil of the Depression and the prolonged drama of the Price Spreads Inquiry, concluding with its report, altered the political landscape, generating heroes and villains and new tactical opportunities.[32] Conditions eased somewhat through 1934 and 1935, but employment, income, and gross productivity failed to recover to 1929 levels. When the federal election campaign began in earnest in September 1935, there was broad agreement on the need for government to intervene in the economy in order to secure a minimum standard of living for the people of Canada, with each party drawing on evidence presented in the inquiry to support its particular agenda. Different political parties called for different degrees and areas of regulation, but all agreed that the days of laissez-faire were over.[33] There were other points of consensus: politicians now addressed Canadian voters as consumers as well as workers, integrating consumer concerns into their campaign platforms and pledging to defend consumer interests in the marketplace. The government, all parties agreed, had a responsibility to protect consumers from fraudulent and misleading commercial practices. Growing attention to purchasing power and consumer interests did not replace traditional commitments to production, but it added new themes and inflected ongoing patterns of emphasis. On the campaign trail, politicians might address women as a group with a special interest in consumer concerns, but, more often, speakers ignored differences of income, gender, class, and region, and addressed their remarks to a homogenized "Canadian consumer." Used in this way, the term "consumer" emerged as a general category, less politically charged than "labour," with the potential to reach across party loyalties already shaken by the economic crisis.

THE CONSERVATIVE CAMPAIGN

Prime Minister Bennett sought to re-energize the Conservative Party's election prospects in a series of five radio speeches to the nation in January 1935. "The old order is gone," he announced dramatically. "It will not return. We are living amidst conditions which are new and strange to us." Proclaiming that free competition and the open marketplace had vanished, he insisted that the only option was increased government regulation and control. The influence of the Price Spreads Inquiry was evident in his declaration of war on "avaricious industrialists, unscrupulous big business wizards and financial promoters." Selfish men and corporations without souls "will whisper against us ... We fear them not. The lives and the happiness of too many people depend upon our success to allow the selfishness of a few individuals to endanger it."[34] Bennett acknowledged that every Canadian had the right to a decent standard of living; however, he never wavered in his belief that increases in consumption had to arise from increases in profits and commodity prices. Making industry profitable, Bennett insisted, would increase employment. When jobs appeared, workers would be able to buy what they needed. Many listeners doubted Bennett's sincerity, and key members of the Conservative establishment opposed his proposed program of regulation and reform, but reaction was, on the whole, favourable. The government introduced legislation to support this program but, in most cases, failed to provide the staffing and funding that would ensure effectiveness. It was not clear whether the lack of support was temporary and the legislation regarded as interim, pending the determination of constitutionality by the Supreme Court and the Privy Council, or rather was a deliberate effort to sabotage reform.[35] In any case, the question was rendered moot by the upcoming election.

Bennett campaigned strenuously through the summer months, emphasizing the government's record and its commitment to maintain living standards by supporting price levels and restoring trade. "I did my best for the producers and exporters in this country," he often declared.[36] During the campaign, the prime minister made little mention of social reform, calling instead for rigid economy, a balanced budget, hard work, and patriotism (which included the vigorous prosecution of communist agitators).[37] While pledging to introduce the protective legislation recommended by the Royal Commission, Bennett largely ignored consumption as a significant force in the economy. Declaring that "the basis of all our civilization must be the maintenance of what we have come to consider law and order," Bennett insisted that property was the only source of real wealth. Committed to maintaining the financial integrity of the country and "the good name of Canada before the world," Bennett promised that economic equality, "in the reasonable meaning of the word," would be spread by conservative policies of "saneness and fair play." "We will get nowhere by recklessly and stupidly clouting capitalism into a paralysis of ineffectiveness," he cautioned Canadians. "Treat capitalism decently, not for its own sake but for your own sake. For it can serve you well." Increasing consumption was not an end in itself but would follow from increases in the well-being of producers.[38]

THE LIBERAL PARTY

Of all the parties competing in the election, the Liberals were the least concerned with the fate of capitalism as an economic system. Party leader Mackenzie King consistently argued that mismanagement, rather than fundamental flaws, was responsible for the ongoing economic crisis. Campaign literature drew from an address King had made to the House in February 1933, often highlighting the non-specific but vaguely consumerist pledge King had made at that time:

> The Liberal party recognizes that the problem of distribution has become more important than that of production, and believes that personality is more sacred than property. It will devote itself to find ways and means of effecting a fair and just distribution of wealth with increasing regard to *human needs*, to the furtherance of *social justice*, and to the promotion of the *common good*.[39]

Recognizing the trend away from laissez-faire liberalism and towards intervention, but seeing only limited consensus between young and old Liberals, King steered the party cautiously. In spite of the desire for reform, he was reluctant to open discussions that might lead to dissension within the party. Instead, the campaign publicized King's record as a reformer and the party's historical commitment to progressive social action.[40] The Liberals pledged to eliminate economic insecurity and fear of poverty by offering Canadians a middle course, one that would balance "the pull of tradition and the urge of innovation ... so to organize our social and economic life as to make possible a more abundant life for all members of the community."[41] Both the Liberal and Conservative parties maintained that material security depended primarily on employment; only in the absence of jobs were government measures needed. The fundamental difference between the two campaign platforms lay in King's highly positive vision of the productive capacity of capitalism. He insisted that industrialists and consumers shared a common interest in abundant consumption. A strong economy, he argued, offered the greatest possibility for individual improvement: what was good for business was also good for the consumer. The reason, King explained, could be found in the pages of *Industry and Humanity*, reissued for the election in an abridged version:

> Whatever increases production tends to enhance purchasing power, and so to benefit the parties to Industry. Whatever enhances purchasing power tends, in turn, to increase production. Instead, therefore, of a vicious circle, bred of fears and narrowing continually towards destruction and extermination, the substitution of Faith for Fear provides an enchanted circle widening ever towards increase of effort and increase of enjoyment as well.[42]

The presence of Liberal members on the Price Spreads Commission created challenges as well as opportunities for the party. In the face of tremendous public interest, it was imperative that Liberals be seen to support the process but also to develop an independent position. After the report was issued, the Liberal memorandum of reservations became the basis of the campaign strategy.[43] While always careful not to exacerbate divisions within the Liberal Party, King was eager to wreak havoc among the Conservatives by casting doubt on Stevens' sincerity as a crusader for social justice. Party strategists sought to position the Liberals as the preferred choice by aggressively questioning the constitutionality of the government's legislative program, even as they insisted that Conservative efforts did not go far enough to help ordinary Canadians. At the same time, the Liberals condemned each of the new parties for proposing excessive regulations, which, King insisted, would move the country along the path to dictatorship.

Consumer issues took on heightened visibility in the final weeks leading up to election day, when Liberal activists seized on the consumer concerns raised by their party's members on the Price Spreads Commission to launch a "Forgotten Consumer Crusade." The slogan referenced the term the "Forgotten Man," a well-known theme in popular culture and American politics, used by Franklin Roosevelt in the 1932 presidential election. Although often associated with the unemployed, the Forgotten Man was the average citizen at the bottom of the economic pyramid: "the forgotten, the unorganized but indispensible unit of economic power," who formed "the infantry of our economic army."[44] In the American context, the Forgotten Man was the industrious, self-supporting worker. Amended and redeployed in Canadian politics as the Forgotten Consumer, the term was applied to the shopper, most often the housewife, caught up in a daily struggle to stretch the household budget.

In the lead-up to election day, radio addresses, newspaper advertisements, and prominent speakers (including the Liberal members of the Price Spreads Commission) urged Canadians to "Vote Liberal and lower the cost of living." A circular, beginning with a phrase popularized in E.J. Young's dissenting report ("the consumers' interest is the interest of the human race"), was distributed at rallies and reprinted in the *Toronto Daily Star*.[45] One of the most visible speakers on the subject was Mrs. Thorburn, a prominent Ottawa Liberal and officer of the National Council of Women. Her message was crafted to appeal to women in their role as household managers. As the centrepiece of her address, Thorburn compared American and Canadian prices on many common household items, blaming the difference on Tory tariffs (see Figure 3). Pointing out that, for the same price, American wives could give their husbands two cups of coffee while Canadian women could serve only one, she added, "We can't compete with that handicap." Thorburn encouraged Canadian women to consider questions of politics and economics from the standpoint of the pantry shelf when marking their ballots. Through the requirements of the home, women could gain insight into the economic needs of the country as a whole. "Let us acquire the habit of regarding ourselves as consumers, a wider term than housewives," she urged.[46]

In appealing to women as voters and to voters as consumers, the Liberal campaign sought to bridge traditional producer ethics (thrift, hard work, discipline) and modern spending practices.[47] Although consumption was an issue of concern to all voters, leading Liberals believed that it could be an especially motivating consideration for women, with the potential to recruit voters – particularly newer female voters whose party loyalties might not yet be firmly established – to the Liberal cause. The party characterized shopping, like voting, as an informed practice of skilful decision making. Indeed, shoppers and citizens were seen as sharing similar rights, including the right to freedom of choice, the protection of the state, and formal equality in the marketplace and the voting booth.

FIGURE 3   Politicians across the political spectrum addressed Canadian voters as consumers in the 1935 election cycle. Competing for the votes of women, the Liberal Party promoted itself as a champion of consumer rights in the closing weeks of the campaign. | "The Forgotten Consumer," *Globe*, 9 October 1935, 9.

OTHER PARTIES

Three new parties emerged out of the turmoil of the Depression. In the summer of 1935, Harry Stevens made a final break with the Tories and announced the formation of the Reconstruction Party. Presenting Reconstruction policies to *Maclean's Magazine*, Stevens described Canada as "a country of homes" and the family as "the unit and basis of society."[48] The party pledged to open up "avenues of opportunity for all who are willing to work ... to enable them to retain their self-respect and earn a moderate living." Recognizing that "the responsibility of making the consumer's dollar go as far as possible rests largely with the women," the party promised to ensure "that in every way possible exploitation of the public through unwarranted profits shall be vigorously restricted."[49] Restraining cut-throat competition would allow wages to rise. Eliminating fraud would assure consumers value for their money.

The Co-operative Commonwealth Federation (CCF), a coalition of left-leaning farm and labour interests, welcomed the high productivity achieved by advances in mechanization and expert management but deplored the chronic tendency towards overproduction. The price spreads investigation was a frequent point of reference, drawn on for examples of wrongdoing and to demonstrate the need for vastly increased federal regulation.[50] The party proposed to manage the Canadian economy as a self-contained unit, with a sustainable balance in producing and consumer power. By favouring production geared to the needs of the community rather than private profits, the CCF platform implied that ordinary Canadians could expect to see modest increases in the availability of some goods and services.

The campaign platform of the new Social Credit party also hinged on the promise of government intervention, but it offered a dramatically different vision of the role aggregate consumption should play in the economy. Under a Social Credit government, Canada would be a nation of citizen-consumers in which everyone was entitled – and, indeed, had a responsibility – to consume the products of industry and agriculture. The most sensational aspect of the party's platform was the promise of a "social credit" or dividend to be paid to every man, woman, and child, regardless of their personal wealth and whether or not they were employed. As described by party leader William Aberhart, the dividend was both a social program designed to ameliorate poverty and an economic measure intended to stimulate job creation. Dividends would never have to be paid back, but they would have to be spent. Indeed, as credits expired at the end of the year in which they were paid, they existed only to be spent. The credits would work in conjunction with a fixed "Just Price" and increased government spending to ensure that the productive capacity of the industrial system would be used and developed to the fullest. The greatest feature of the whole remedy, Aberhart asserted, was that men, women, and children would be given sufficient purchasing power to guarantee adequate food, clothing, and shelter. Public welfare would be measured in the consumption of goods rather than in business profits. Every individual, the party insisted, had the right to economic security and a share in the common cultural heritage and resource wealth of the nation.[51]

THE ELECTION RESULTS

Interest in the election was high; record crowds had turned out to hear the leaders, and 75 percent of eligible voters went to the polls. The frustrations of the Depression and the distinctive positions advanced by new parties suggested that change was at hand, but the results – the Liberals were elected with an overwhelming majority – largely reaffirmed Canada's commitment to minimally regulated capitalism. Parties on both the left and the right that had advocated highly amplified roles for the state received limited support at the polls.[52] Considered solely from the standpoint of competing efforts to win power, the election changed little. It is possible, however, to evaluate the election campaign differently – not as a race between winners and losers, but as part of an extended discussion in which politicians advanced and debated ideas, attempting to persuade voters of the value of different solutions to the challenges raised by the modern economy.

During the campaign, all parties identified consumers as a legitimate political constituency. Candidates discussed material security rather than property ownership as the basis of an orderly society. At a time when few Canadian economists endorsed the power of mass consumption to revitalize the economy, politicians recognized the power of the consumer as voter.[53] Measures to protect consumers from exploitation due to fraud were endorsed by every leader and were identified with the promotion of the public good. Similarly, every party committed itself to ensuring the economic security of individual Canadians and a decent standard of living. The details of what this standard would be were scanty, but assurances that every Canadian would have the basic necessities of food, clothing, and shelter were now obligatory. As they sought to mobilize consumers in order to win votes, politicians made consumption a legitimate public concern and a political rather than a personal, private matter.

Chapter Five

CHARTING THE CONTOURS
OF MODERN SOCIETY

Throughout the 1930s, particularly in the waning shadow of the Depression in the latter part of the decade, sociologists, social workers, economists, and literary writers set out to document Canadian society, describing value conflicts between classes, genders, and generations. Working as professional observers of society, they took upon themselves the task of charting the contours of society, while also struggling to determine their own place in it.[1] The expenditure patterns of ordinary families were the subject of statistical studies, surveys, and fictional narratives. The ability to consume goods and services was described as a fundamental marker of class.

The Depression had exacerbated tensions that many observers now regarded as fundamental to modern society. Fictional narratives in particular revealed a society struggling to recover from economic crisis, defined more by its tensions than by consensus.[2] The strain between limited financial resources and potentially unlimited consumer needs, the role of goods as indicators of social status, and the fundamental instability of both wages and wants were key themes in new models of the social order, which were central to fictional stories of domestic life and to economic theory. Indeed, many sociological studies and fictional stories told essentially the same narrative, albeit in different ways, reinforcing the growing sense of Canada as a consumption-oriented society. Consumer society was emerging as an idea, a way of thinking about relations between people and between people and things.

The Structure of Consumer Society

"Paramount among the results of industrialization," one of Canada's pre-eminent social scientists noted in a study of the late 1930s, was "that it creates wage-earners."[3] Although the persistence of agriculturalists and farm labourers slowed the emergence of new middle-class and working-class patterns of consumption, Canada was inexorably changing from a nation of family farms and small businesses to one of wage earners dwelling in urban settings. During the 1920s, the number of wage earners increased twice as rapidly as the general population.[4] By the late 1920s, over half the population lived in areas that the government considered to be urban. The experiences of the Depression revealed the degree to which daily life in Canada was now shaped less by *how* than by *how much* income was obtained.

New questions asked in the 1931 census made it possible to compare the earnings of occupations previously seen as belonging to different social strata.[5] The decision to analyze census data by grouping categories of earnings reveals new assumptions about social relationships that emphasized purchasing power. Data for the mid-range stratum with average earnings of between $20 and $25 per week included the incomes of bakers, butchers, and furniture makers, as well as longshoremen, stevedores, coal miners, painters, decorators, tailors, tinsmiths, clergymen, and priests. At the lower end of the scale were males between the ages of twenty and forty-four who were earning between $15 and $20 per week as unskilled workers, labourers, seamen, sailors and deckhands, waiters, weavers, messengers, cooks, teamsters, carriage drivers, janitors, sextons, boot and shoe opera-tives, barbers and hairdressers, chauffeurs, and bus and truck drivers. At the higher end were policemen, detectives, brakemen, foremen, and a variety of sales agents reporting average earnings of between $30 and $35. Grouping occupations according to earnings highlighted the erosion of traditional distinctions between education, ownership, and physical labour. As Canadian society became consumption-oriented, the quantity and sta-bility of income, as well as borrowing ability, were becoming critical factors in the establishment of social status. As traditional class distinctions lost significance, relative earning power became more important.

If they looked back in time from the perspective of the late 1930s, working-class families fortunate enough to have steady employment would see that their hours of labour had decreased and that their purchasing power had increased modestly.[6] However, Canadian statisticians and economists believed that comparisons with the past held little interest for wage-earning families. As J.C. Cameron, the head of the new Industrial Relations Section at Queen's University, explained, "In the last analysis ... from the point of view of employees, their present economic position depends not only on its relation to that of the past, but also upon its relation to that of other groups in the community ... The question of 'status' is one of satisfactions, and satisfactions are relative."[7] As a study conducted by the Dominion Bureau of Statistics at the start of the 1930s explained, even concepts of luxury had become relative and were continually undergoing change. "Silk stockings, for example, which formerly were considered a luxury, are today considered a necessity even by girls who are getting as low a wage as possible. The same is true of many other articles of food, clothing and furniture ... The conception of luxuries also differ[s] from place to place. Higher priced clothes, for example, which to an office employee in the city are a necessity become a luxury to a person similarly employed in a rural district."[8] Those compiling Canada's social statistics were coming to regard income and the goods that income could buy as a key determinant of social position. Consumer behaviors were in transition and purchasing decisions took on importance relative to the purchasing decisions of others.

The relationship between earning power and status lay at the centre of the first comprehensive study of Canada's class structure, conducted by Leonard Marsh, director of social research at McGill University. After engaging in what he described as a lengthy process of "social arithmetic," Marsh's correlations revealed a structure of eleven occupational status divisions grouped into four social classes.[9] Canada's class structure, he proposed, was unlike that in the Old World, in which rank reflected one's position at birth in an established social hierarchy. It was also unlike that in Marxist theory, which divided society into owners (whether of property or the means of production) and the proletariat. Instead, Canadian social classes reflected occupational incomes and the patterns of consumption that these incomes allowed. Because the amount of money an individual had to spend "directly determined his command over the actual symbols of status," social ranking proceeded "outwards from occupation" to include standards of living, levels of education, and differences of attitude and opinion. Money, Marsh asserted, "not only measures status but helps to buy it."[10]

Marsh's portrayal of Canadian society as "a pyramid with a ladder running through it" was not simply a new metaphor for pre-existing conditions but a description of an entirely new structure of social connections.[11] The "social aura" of individuals or families, Marsh asserted, was directly related to the economic facts of their life.[12] Status was not an abstract concept but was embodied in markers of class difference, including possessions, reactions to social situations, and in the scope of opportunity and experiences an individual might encounter in life. The socially important aspect of occupation, Marsh explained, was the level of consumption it allowed and the "differences in freedom" the person experienced. Members of a class shared "the same kind of reaction" in social situations because they "live similar kinds of lives."[13] Social position was the sum of experiences that money could buy.

Marsh's analysis was echoed in other studies. R.H. Coats, still Canada's chief statistician and the current president of the American Statistical Association, observed that skill and occupation, and the income these factors generated, had become the greatest considerations in determining class differences. They were, he claimed, more important than race or gender in explaining the growing gap between the wage-earning abilities of the least skilled employees in the lowest wage classes and those of better-trained, higher-waged Canadians.[14] The effect, Coats noted, was the "crystallization" or "hardening" of lines between two classes of workers: "the one seldom employed, the other seldom unemployed."[15] Marsh observed similar gaps within the salaried classes. Those able to reach positions in the middle ranks of modern business and administrative organizations found that the "educational ladder" that had allowed them entry did not lead to further advancement. The chance to move upward "came early on and then closed," limiting access to the higher professions.[16] Insofar as the occupations associated with higher levels of social status required training, experience, and connections, living standards were increasingly passed from parent to child. As Marsh explained, "habits of behaviour" reinforced and reproduced each family's place within the existing class structure.[17] Although older class distinctions had eroded, upward mobility was limited.

Professionals earning good incomes confronted somewhat different, but related, status challenges. British sociologist T.H. Marshall, addressing the annual meeting of the Canadian Association of Political Scientists, observed that modern conditions had undermined the relevance of traditional markers of achievement and success. Once conceived of as a member of a select body, the professional has been distinguished by pecuniary indifference, the availability of leisure time, and the freedom to work according to his own sense of what was right rather than what might be profitable. But in the late 1930s, Marshall explained, leisure was no longer a spiritual quality denoting a higher calling, but "merely the way one spends one's money when the day's work is done ... The business man's leisure is as good as anyone else's because leisure is simply the antithesis to work."[18] Professionals were no longer able to ignore their wage-earning aspect; in response, they sought to redefine their task as one of service, involving labour of a special and superior kind that involved demonstrations of judgment rather than the sale of commodities. Professional services were those that could not be mass-produced or offered in cheaper lines to broader markets; therefore, they should be accorded extra social value.

The form of the social structure Marsh described – with sloping sides rather than steps – seemed to have softened class boundaries. Divisions were "shaded rather than abrupt," with extended margins that were not absolutely set.[19] Although Marsh characterized status as a function of income rather than ownership or birth, class tension had not disappeared. Instead, the former security of knowing one's place had been replaced by an illusion of social mobility and increased fear of falling status, particularly for those who entered the middle class by way of new occupations in administrative roles. Tensions within the family unit rose as those families positioned on the margins of each class discovered that their spending abilities failed to coincide with their aspirations. Marsh concluded that each "class" was defined by reference to two social areas: the "area" or members of society subject to a certain set of economic conditions and that "area" or part of the community that accepted a particular set of conventions and valuations as its own. He described the gap between these two criteria (the one based on economic limits and the other on cultural aspirations) as "the discrepancy between fact and belief."[20] Marsh identified the psychological tensions generated by this discrepancy as one of the most important phenomenon of modern society.

During the 1930s the concepts of "an American way of life" and an "American standard of living" emerged and became familiar within and well beyond the borders of the United States. Marsh argued that there was, however, no corresponding widely shared middle-class standard of living in Canada. Although there was a common vision of a Canadian standard, the wages needed to support it were not the wages of the majority.[21] A middle-class standard of living, with access to the "amenities of modern civilized life" (which Marsh described as a liberal and varied diet, ownership of a few domestic labour-saving devices, and reasonable provision for health and recreation) required, "at the most frugal," $2,000 annually.[22] This level of income was enjoyed only by managers, professionals, and the uppermost levels of wage earners, who collectively constituted not more than a quarter of all Canadian families.[23] Marsh also observed that wages paid for similar occupations were generally lower in Canada than in the United States, increasing the gap between income and images of middle-class life made familiar in magazines and movies that were made in the United States and circulated in Canada. In view of the statistical evidence, Marsh proposed that the pervasiveness of the middle-class image was the result of increased visibility rather than numerical strength. Middle-class families in Canada were concentrated in urban centres, tended to dominate the new trades and services, and, because they travelled frequently, spread their example throughout the country and abroad. Industrial wage-earners were the largest class numerically, but were immobilized by the absence of leisure time and by limited financial resources. Advertisers adopted the image of the middle-class family for sales campaigns, but Marsh emphasized that this was not representative of life as led by the majority of Canadians.

Marsh explored connections between between spending patterns and social status but seldom addressed in detail the ways families managed their budgets. A number of statisticians and social workers, however, were examining patterns of family expenditure, studying farm families, salaried workers, and wage earners as distinct spending categories. These studies of living expenses had a number of different uses, providing information for the construction of family budgets by welfare agencies and home economists, for analyses of nutrition by public health authorities, for use in the calculation of cost-of-living bonuses, for government agencies making international comparisons, and by businesses for marketing and advertising.

In the largest of these surveys, the Dominion Bureau of Statistics sampled 6,252 households in twelve cities across Canada, chosen through census data and random selection.[24] The study – the first family-expenditure survey carried out by the bureau – focused on households of urban wage-earners, each with a husband and a wife living together as joint heads in a self-contained dwelling unit, with one to five children, and no more than one lodger or domestic living in the home.[25] Family earnings ranged from $450 to $2,500 for the survey year.[26] A subset of 1,439 households was enlisted to track their living costs in detail on a ten-page schedule.[27] The bureau supervised the entire project, sending out specially trained field workers to work with the families.

In this survey, the government was, for the first time, studying Canada as a nation of consumer families with different spending abilities and propensities. The most striking findings, from the point of view of those undertaking the study, lay in the data about family finances. Living standards were not solely the result of income but, increasingly, also involved the use of credit, and that use varied considerably, even among families within the same narrow income range. Introducing their findings, the authors observed that a "statement of goods and services purchased in any given period does not provide an accurate gauge of a family's level of living. Some families habitually strain credit resources to the limit, while others adjust their levels of living to make provision for the future and may continue to do so in the face of repeated reductions in income."[28] One in three families recorded debits in excess of savings during the survey year. However, results were not consistent across the country: in some cities, families with high earnings levels had debit increases; in other cities, even where earnings were comparatively low, fewer families reported debit excesses.[29] Contrary to expectations, as income per person increased, so did the family's total debt load. However, families earning greater income incurred debits for different purposes. Poorer families incurred debits for groceries and medical care; better-off families used credit to buy motor cars and household furniture and equipment. In fact, cars accounted for 33 percent of new debits for families with incomes greater than $600 per person, while medical care accounted for close to 33 percent of new debits for those with incomes of $100 to $199 per person.[30] Meanwhile, there was a "surprisingly" low correlation between gross savings and family income.[31] The authors believed that wide differences in net savings and debits within narrow income ranges pointed to differences in thrift that revealed "more strikingly than living expenditure patterns the importance of personal preferences in determining family living expenditures" among Canada's wage-earning families.[32]

Other commentators also remarked on the change in attitudes towards spending and thrift. University of Toronto economist D.C. MacGregor had been impressed by the technical advancements in the work carried out by the Dominion Bureau of Statistics, but strongly objected to the methodology and conclusions reached in a similar study produced by the Toronto Welfare Council, titled "The Cost of Living: A Study of the Cost of a Standard of Living in Toronto Which Should Maintain Health and Self-Respect." MacGregor argued that the standard of "self-respect" used by these agencies was arbitrary, with no basis in reality.[33] Making ends meet was a concern for most Canadians, he insisted, who sought out "bargain sales, 'seconds,' second-hand shops" and studied the "articles for sale" column in the evening papers. "Is the standard of self-respect endangered ... by trying to make a dollar go as far as possible? ... A world in which everyone could ... buy only new, branded articles at standard prices, in which no one patronized second-hand shops and in which no one need rely on free clinics or other government assistance would be one kind of Utopia." This utopia, he noted, was well beyond the reach of a male adult earning minimum wage.

Other observers shared MacGregor's concerns about rising expectations and the declining practice of thrift. In a brief prepared for the Royal Commission on Dominion-Provincial Relations, J.A. Corry, a professor of economics and political science at Queen's University, linked the decline of thrift to the shift towards salaries and waged income and the collapse of many farms and small businesses during the Depression.[34] In a wage-earning economy, without the incentive of ownership, Corry believed, the propensity to save was diminished.[35] An "increasing proportion of our population live in urban centers, where all sorts of attractive gadgets and diversions are always on display. The daily contact with these things multiplies wants and, combined with the blandishments of modern advertising, it breaks down sales resistance. People become so much less able to sacrifice the enjoyment of today for the security of tomorrow." The greater thriftiness of rural and village folk, he claimed, was not the result of moral rectitude but "lack of temptations."[36]

These observers concurred that the imperatives of thrift, savings, and living within one's means — traditionally seen as the essential traits of middle-class respectability — were being challenged by a new emphasis on an achieved standard of living. Class differences — for Canada's social scientists and seemingly for the households they studied — were determined more by patterns of expenditure and the consumption of goods and services than by property ownership or savings in the bank.

Consuming Families

While social scientists documented the social structure, literary writers were interested in answering the question "How does this economy feel?" For most Canadians, hard work and thrift were not merely institutionalized values but daily practices driven by necessity. The limits of family incomes continued to require prudent choices. While meagre funds encouraged thrift, intensive advertising and images in movies, magazines, and store windows stimulated desire. Increasing consumption opportunities pitted wage spenders against wage earners, threatening the peaceful cohesion of the family unit, particularly during the hard years of the Depression.

From 1930 to 1933, the unemployment rate rose from 12 percent to close to 30 percent. No family was untouched. And yet there was what American scholar Rita Barnard has aptly called a "doubleness" to the lived experience of the Depression.[37] The abundance made possible by large-scale production may have been unaffordable for many Canadians, but it remained visible. The paradox of poverty in the midst of plenty was not an abstract metaphor but a characterization of daily experience. Motion pictures, magazines, and department stores continued to promote visions of consumer abundance. Indeed, many businesses responded to depressed profits with cost-cutting measures and more intensive advertising.[38] Fascination with consumer goods did not decline during the Depression, and financial hardships did not halt the advance of consumer culture.[39] Indeed, the coexistence of plenty and scarcity frequently animated fiction of the period.[40] The cultural counterpart of the social scientific and statistical surveys that flourished during the 1930s was a new aesthetic of documentary-style realism.[41] This "documentary impulse" motivated non-fiction and fiction writers, photographers, playwrights, and film makers, directing their attention to the realities of everyday life and towards the average or common person.[42] John Grierson, the future head of Canada's National Film Board, described the documentary form as the "creative treatment of actuality."[43]

Canadian literary scholar Evelyn MacLure has described the years 1935–40 as a transitional period "when tradition was strong, but the story shift[ed] its concerns to man in society."[44] Commercial fiction at this time was formulaic, committed to idyllic happy-ending stories of romantic adventure. The authors writing for Canada's literary, academic, and political journals, however, favoured a tone of direct reportage, seeking to present the everyday lives of working- and middle-class families simply and directly.[45] Writing in a straightforward style, authors aimed to strip away the illusions of capitalism. Concerns related to consumption were often central to character and plot. Such stories do not focus on household provisioning per se; rather, authors were interested in bought goods as a means to express identity, relationships, hopes, and dreams. Regardless of whether or not the objects of desire could be acquired, thinking about consumer goods could free the imagination from the constraints of poverty, the drudgery of housework, or the limits of rural life on failing farms. Character is often revealed by the ways in which people related to material goods. New tensions developed between generations and genders divided by new spending practices. Lack of money led to problems in communication that drove husbands and wives apart. Short stories and novels featured conflicts involving the purchase of, or yearning for, objects of consumer culture, particularly new mass-produced goods. While these tensions are accentuated by the lingering poverty of the Depression, the primary focus is on the emotional impact of "the budgetary poverty of ordinary families."[46]

In the genre of realistic fiction, consumer goods are frequently objects of desire that symbolize a more romantic and exciting world of colour, glamour, and gaiety beyond the drab confines of working-class and farm life. Yet, those who reach for these goods seldom find contentment. In one story, a blue kimono that once symbolized "bright dreams and aspirations" becomes ragged. In another, a woman purchases the red shoes she has been admiring in a shop window but must dye them black to attend a funeral. In a third, a wife succumbs to the temptation of a stylish hat but is berated by her husband for her foolish purchase.[47]

Insofar as new purchases and acquisitions link each subject, however briefly, with a larger world of romance and imagination, writers seemed to sympathize with those who yearned for more. Store-bought goods transfix those who desired them, offering the illusion of escape, but the consequences of giving into temptation are never beneficial. These authors were not especially interested in shopping as part of the daily routine; instead, characters' consumer desires reach to items that, however modestly priced, lie beyond the realm of basic necessity. Often, objects of desire pit selfish yearnings against the traditional order of the family. Women, children, and young lovers return again and again to gaze through shop windows at the goods they desire but that prudence and lack of income prevent them from acquiring. Insofar as the value of these goods comes not from their potential utility but from their symbolic power, yearning for goods underscores the shift from a production-oriented to a consumer culture.

The grittiness of social realism is often associated with urban settings, but portraits of rural life were equally grim, showing beleaguered farmers unable to compete against mechanization and overproduction. Those trapped in drab rural settings also yearn for the colour and glamour of city life, isolated by the lack of money even more than by distance. In "The Wind Our Enemy," a poem by Anne Marriott, a wife gazing out of her kitchen window transforms the fields of grain into store-bought goods –

> A woman's eyes could kiss the soil
> From her kitchen window,
> Turning its black depths to unchipped cups – a silk crepe dress –
> (Two-ninety-eight, Sale Catalogue)

– until the wind and sun dry up the land and the possibilities of new things.[48]

Cultural theorists argue that consumption can be a means to agency and an opportunity for self-determination that is eroded or contested in other areas.[49] Writing during the Depression and immediate post-Depression era, Canada's documentary novelists did not present consumption as an act of liberation, but rather as an act fraught with confusion and multiple meanings. In these stories, husbands and fathers are reluctant to give up their work identities and their authority as breadwinners. Decisions to spend money generate tensions and are often the cause of family conflicts. The transition from window shopping to buying and owning is empowering, but often only temporarily so: baseball caps are stolen, red shoes dyed black, and stylish hats brutally destroyed. In Morley Callaghan's stories, the desired items are almost always personal clothing, suggesting that identity rather than agency is involved; however, the distinction is not entirely clear. Generally, those who dream more widely, about circuses and trips to Paris, have the least ability to make actual purchases. In stories by Mary Quayle Innis, imaginative consumption provides an opportunity to escape the drudgery of housework: an impoverished mother imagines her children in pretty clothes, and a weary housewife dreams of wearing pretty dresses that will win the attention of her family.[50] Goods help people imagine lives beyond the limits of their daily routines, and the denial of gratification intensifies the "imaginative passion" for consumer goods.[51]

The symbolic economy of class difference is manifest in descriptions of store windows and displays that allowed people to see the goods they desire but cannot afford. The tired mother in a short story by Mary Quayle Innis is typical. Wandering the aisles of the home furnishings section in a large department store, she dreams of what might have been and what will never be. Forced by the store clerks to keep moving, she leaves the displays and returns to her own life.[52] The story highlights the powerlessness of poverty and the tensions that come from living in a world with an abundance of goods and an unequal distribution of spending power.

Consumption in Canadian fiction was generally not represented as the dreams of wage earners seeking compensation for the monotony of routine labour (except the unpaid labour of household drudgery). Most often, the yearnings for new experiences in the form of goods were the dreams of those who earned no wages, regardless of whether they were in positions of dependency as wives and children or were unemployed. Resistance to the temptations of commodity consumption came not from self-aware individuals rejecting pressures to buy, but from those whose authority and stature in the family were threatened by economic change. The dreamers (most often, but not always, women and children) are pitted against the wage earners (most often, but not always, men). While consumption is gendered in these works, neither gender is particularly empowered or fulfilled by the dynamic of working and buying. Producers and consumers were both, in different ways, written as victims of economic and social processes.

In these narratives, the satisfactions attained by consumption are fleeting, and the larger moral lessons of consumption experiences remain ambiguous. Did these writers regard the possibilities of consumption, the transformations of identity, and the gratification of desire as opportunities or traps? Did they believe that romantic consumption offered meaningful resistance or only the illusion of escape? Were characters who dreamt of goods selfish, or were they able to dream because they had thus far escaped the soul-destroying rhythms of the assembly line or the disheartening struggle with the land? Writers of fictional realism did not focus explicitly or exclusively on "consumer culture": their concerns remained those of family identity and relationships: husbands and wives argue, lovers quarrel and make up, sons disappoint their mothers, and daughters resent their fathers. However, the problem of identity and relationships in a world with an abundance of goods and a shortage of purchasing power was a new and increasingly frequent theme. Traditional family identities are destabilized by unemployment and by the increasing importance of bought goods. The yearnings of working-class children and women for goods and experiences threaten the stability of the family unit, forcing husbands and fathers to acknowledge their own weakness. Desire is often represented as a threat to the moral and social order of the traditional family, yet efforts to contain desire and repress dreams are often quite brutal – denying the values of consumption brought no honour. Authors were ambiguous in their message: they sympathized with the yearning for more but continued to present desire for store-bought things as destabilizing and not entirely legitimate. It is unclear if empowerment came with the earning or the spending of money, or to what degree these processes could be separated. What is evident is that themes of consumption and the tensions created between wage earner and wage spender were now capturing the imaginations of Canadian authors.

In these fictional representations of the Canadian family, parents – especially fathers – tended to represent thrift, savings, self-restraint, and other traditional values associated with a restricted economy where resources are scarce, while children pushed for spending, novelty, and expanded participation in the new economy of consumer experiences. Wives and mothers found themselves in an ambiguous position. The spending decisions they made on behalf of the household were dutiful, but personal spending continued to be regarded as self-indulgent. And, in advertisements touting the value of new labour-saving devices, packaged foods, and store-bought clothing – in both fictional and real marketplaces – it was not always clear which purchases belonged in which category. Insofar as society and authors identified women with spending, their choices became the locus of doubts about consumption. Their choices were psychologically understandable but often frivolous in the context of the family budget.

Studies of leftist fiction written during the Depression and the immediate post-Depression years show that the working man was often presented as a victim of capitalism, trapped in hopeless situations that end in the urge towards either self-annihilation or illusory escape.[53] In such fiction, manual labour was physically and psychologically degrading – working on an assembly line reduced men to unthinking cogs in industrial machines.

The family farm, meanwhile, was an economic impossibility in a world dominated by large-scale producers and processors. In the economy of industrial capitalism, as portrayed by authors of leftist fiction, hard work was no longer a source of status or meaningful identity. Moreover, the spectre of unemployment loomed large. Whether employed or unemployed, fictional workers were frustrated by mechanized society and unable to adapt. It was no longer "true that a man is *worth* what he gets and gets what he's *worth*."[54] The fictional unemployed did not form a militant class but seemed frustrated by free time without money.[55] In Frederick Philip Grove's *The Master of the Mill*, the decision to suspend collection of rents and give the workers displaced by machines free access to the company store precipitated armed revolt. The men wanted meaningful work – jobs, not charity.[56]

Middle-class jobs in support of the capitalist economy were no better. Andrew Aikenhead, one of the central characters in Morley Callaghan's *They Shall Inherit the Earth*, came to doubt the value of his work as an advertising executive: "It was a terrible thing for a man to feel suddenly that he had devoted his life to convincing people they wanted things they really did not want, that he had created imaginary passions and lusts in the breasts of millions just to provide them with imaginary satisfaction."[57] Aikenhead's son is an engineer hired by the city's electric company to devise plans that will encourage homeowners to install electric heaters, in order to stimulate the economy.[58] It is his paycheque, rather than the work itself, that offers some fulfilment, enabling him to purchase a new dress for his lover.

Although they most often depicted women and children yearning for consumer goods, other authors also showed the effect of consumer desire on men. The plot of Irene Baird's novel *Waste Heritage* turns on one man's desperation to own a decent pair of shoes. The failures of industrial capitalism and the promise of liberation associated with consumer goods converge as the story unfolds. Misunderstanding an advertisement for a "one cent sale," the character Eddy does not realize that customers first have to buy a pair of shoes at full price. As Eddy argues that he is being cheated out of a one-cent pair of shoes, a crowd gathers. Confused and scared, Eddy flees and deliberately stands in the path of an oncoming locomotive.[59] Baird recognized that, in the shift to a consumer oriented culture, the unemployed were doubly disadvantaged: to the extent that the work ethic still ran deep, the loss of one's job also meant the loss of identity, authority, and meaningful work; to the extent that identity had come to involve consumer goods, and that consumer goods had taken on social values well beyond their basic materiality, loss of income led to a loss of status and identity.

While statisticians measured the actual expenditures being made by Canadian families, literary authors, through their characters, examined the significance of acquisition, whether through purchases deferred, or not made at all, or those that required trade-offs in tight family budgets. In these stories, the yearning for consumer goods is connected with the yearning for experiences and opportunities beyond the menialities of daily life. Desires may have been stimulated by the presence of goods in Hollywood movies, department store windows, shop displays, and glossy magazine advertisements, but they are still deeply felt. Consumer goods at the centre of these novels were not just things – rather, they held psychological importance, representing the possibility of escape, even if the opportunity was only momentary or imaginary. An impoverished life was not only a matter of falling short of nutritional standards but also of lacking red shoes and new hats. Fantasies of more were made especially poignant by their economic impossibility.

The Commodification of Intellectual Work

Growing markets for works of fiction and for social science reports by governments and industry challenged successful authors and academics to think about their relationship to money and markets. There was a "new self-consciousness" about the assumptions and purposes of intellectual inquiry and growing awareness of the "new social roles and agendas" made possible by opportunities not only in the commercial mass media, but in writing for political journals, professional organizations, university departments, and government commissions and agencies.[60] Writers, artists, experts, and academics articulately discussed an apparently keenly felt conflict between their integrity as intellectuals and new opportunities to earn money. In a 1938 essay entitled "The Plight of Canadian Fiction," Morley Callaghan contrasted a hypothetical young writer who could choose to "sit down and study the fiction market offered by the big magazines ... If he is intelligent and not impatient and has the gift at all, he may succeed in giving the editors the thing they want. He meets the market ... In no time at all he may have an enormous income, because there are vast profits to be made from writing for the big slick magazines." The enterprising young author would have to purge his stories of personal qualities that might separate him "from the masses." He would have to make no demands on his readers and avoid making them feel uncomfortable or unhappy. The reader should never be deeply moved, as "he might start brooding. And no magazine ever had a big circulation of brooders." Callaghan described this sort of writing as "a field of entertainment like vaudeville." The other kind of writer was one "who wanted to have his own growth and look at reality with his own eyes." This writer might, over time, win an audience, but not within Canada. The market was too small – indeed, Callaghan claimed there was no demand in Canada for thoughtful works. Canadians bought books much as they bought any other commodity – tea bags was the example Callaghan used to make his point – and not for spiritual gratification. In such an environment, he asked, "If there was no demand, was Canadian literature really necessary?"[61]

Leading economists wrote of similar challenges. As their salaries and social status gradually eroded after the Great War, new opportunities in contract work offered influence and income beyond academia.[62] Some, like University of Toronto economist Gilbert Jackson, consulted directly for industry.[63] Others prepared reports and studies for churches, foundations, business associations, and governments, often for presentation to the many special inquiries and Royal Commissions created in response to the economic crisis of the Depression.[64] As University of Toronto economist Harold Innis caustically observed, social scientists were "in great demand at the prevailing rate among business firms, including publishers, governments, and political parties."[65] The "call to management" was transforming universities into reserve pools of labour. As they moved beyond theorizing to consulting, academic economists wondered if they were becoming wage earners rather than members of the intellectual elite. What were the goals of intellectual work: scientific truth or technical solutions? Was pecuniary indifference a viable stance in a society where consumer goods were of increasing social importance? Was success the result of publicity and promotion or merit?

The relationship between the social sciences and society was the central theme in a series of influential articles published in 1934 and 1935. In an essay contributed to the *University of Toronto Quarterly*, senior American economist Frank Knight complained that trained economists were being put, and were putting themselves, in the position of appealing to the crowd, "competing to sell to the public ideas and doctrines which they could not sell to each other."[66] Truth seeking was displaced by public debate, and intellectual discourse was geared towards the identification of "marketable products."[67] The appeal of charismatic leaders and the movement for planning and control, Knight argued, were both symptoms of the loss of faith in intelligence as an agency for social problem-solving.[68] The challenge was not to fight for truth (because to resort to techniques of persuasion was to join the enemy) but to stand against the trend. Knight called on his colleagues to preserve in their small area an atmosphere where reasonable people could engage in the process of cooperative discussion.

E.J. Urwick, head of the Department of Political Economy at the University of Toronto, similarly deplored the "disastrous results" of what he termed "the Age of Reason." Social science, Urwick objected, was a contradiction in terms, as the so-called scientists were necessarily caught up in the processes they were trying to examine. While Knight called on economists to preserve objectivity and continue to search for fundamental truths, Urwick argued that objectivity in the social sciences was impossible and, in any case, increasingly irrelevant. In the face of public pressure for more (*more* protection, *more* supervision, and especially *more* utilities and services), government was becoming a "Universal Service Organization." "WANTING things," he objected, had replaced thinking about things.[69] With support for radical parties on both the left and right of the political spectrum gaining strength, Urwick was concerned that the public's "unlimited and illimitable" demand for more was leading inexorably to increases in bureaucratic management and control. Excessive bureaucracy, he warned, was fundamentally incompatible with thoughtful democracy.

In the same twelve-month period, Stephen Leacock, then chair of the Economics Department at McGill University, addressed the members of the Canadian Political Science Association, asking "What Is Left of Adam Smith?" The first question of political economy, Leacock asserted, was "How does mankind produce enough goods for the wants of mankind?" This question, he insisted, had been answered long ago. Meanwhile, a second question – "How can mankind adjust its production so as not to over satisfy some, under satisfy others and break down in the process?" – remained unanswered. Adam Smith's economics of scarcity had been exchanged for a new "economics of abundance," but these developments in economic theory had not improved social welfare.[70]

Leacock urged economists to move beyond laissez-faire and to "faire-faire," not to "let things happen but 'make things happen.'"[71] Knight called for dedication to truth seeking apart from the realm of politics. Urwick denounced the drift to planning and the reduction of economics to an exercise in problem solving, urging greater attention to feelings informed by intelligent discussion. Each of these responses – the call for action, the call for seclusion, and the call for informed intuition – was positioned against prevailing trends towards measurement, prediction, and regulation. Leacock, Knight, and Urwick rejected managerial, statistical, and quantitative approaches as vehicles for social progress. Technocratic tendencies and paid expert advisers were inimical to the philosophical and ethical concerns they believed lay at the heart of the social sciences.[72]

The economist and cultural theorist Harold Innis, a generation younger, grouped these three thinkers together to create a counterpoint for his own analysis of the profession in an article for the *Canadian Journal of Economics and Political Science*.[73] In that essay and another published the following year in the *Dalhousie Review*, Innis wrote that the intellectual had indeed become a "tragi-comic figure," the "vestige" of a passed era, and a symbol of commitments to freedoms no longer supported in fact.[74] Consulting for political parties, government, church groups, and charitable foundations biased thinking, leading to recommendations for controls and to plans that favoured the goals desired by the particular institution. Belief in progress reinforced the importance of change and intensified pressures to innovate. Focus on the present diminished attention to long-term consequences. The situation in the universities, he claimed, was little better: departmental routines interfered with the search for truth, and the university itself encouraged professors to be visible.

Although Innis suggested that the pervasive tone of pessimism common to Knight, Urwick, and Leacock was the result of psychological disillusionment rooted in the anxieties of war and depression, his vision of the future was similarly grim. The dynamic of industrial capitalism, he argued, undermined informed public discussion. Phenomenal increases in goods required more efficient methods of distribution, pushing manufacturers and retailers to advertise, which in turn stimulated the expansion of newspaper production. In order to meet the high overhead costs associated with the modern printing presses, newspapers needed to expand advertising revenue and, for this reason, were pressured to reach the widest possible audiences. The quality of informed discussion, Innis asserted, weakened in proportion to the expansion of efforts to stimulate mass consumption.[75] At the same time, Innis rejected what he saw as a false distinction between the possibilities of objectivity and subjectivity that had troubled Knight and Urwick. Social scientists, Innis believed, could not be "scientific" or "objective" in the conventional sense.[76] But they could struggle against becoming mere producers of commodities, preoccupied with the problems of social adjustment and technical management and smoothing the way for governments and business profits.

Frank Underhill, a well-known political journalist and historian, wrote a rejoinder to Innis, denouncing his position as "retirement to the ivory tower."[77] "The picture of the disinterested scientist," Underhill argued, was "only possible in an era of complacent stability ... when all the ultimate values and objectives of society were taken for granted ... To-day in an era when values and ends are again in question the social scientist, however he may pose, cannot disassociate himself from considering them." The ideal of the detached scientist was, according to Underhill, "the opiate of our academic intellectuals."[78] The times required that intellectuals step forward and having identified the ends and objectives most consistent with the progressive and democratic thrust of Canadian history, devise the means to reach them.

This discussion, circling around the proper role of the economist in society, continued to preoccupy both economists and political scientists.[79] In influential essays, D.A. MacGibbon and W.A. Mackintosh, both trained economists working as civil servants for the federal government, sought to move beyond the limited choices of ivory tower idealism, commoditization, and social planning. Rejecting Underhill's call-to-arms, both men defended the scientific basis of economics and insisted that a morally neutral, instrumental practice was possible. Offered a choice between resistance and collaboration, they proposed a path of technocratic accommodation.

MacGibbon argued that the problem of objectivity was not a problem of the science of economics but a failure of the ideal of progress.[80] The experiences of war and depression had called the quality of modern civilization and the nature of its economic arrangements into doubt. Different social groups held different values, often antipathetic to each other. As there appeared to be no criteria for determining which set of values was superior to another, MacGibbon argued that economics must either forgo judgments on social progress or forgo its claims to science. It was not the task of the economist to choose between "the Stalin model," "the Hitler model," "the Mussolini model," or "the Aberhart model." The responsibility of the economist, according to MacGibbon, was "to observe, to collect data, to verify hypotheses, and to analyze these phenomena."

While always ready to render assistance when asked, economists worked within the framework of "an organized community which has determined its own ends." Insofar as values were relative and specific to each society, MacGibbon argued, ends and objectives were a matter of social choice. Economists could offer technical support by making careful studies of the "new social models now on the market." But economists offered no truths independent of society's goals. Indeed, MacGibbon argued that it was "arrogance" to believe that economists should determine and dictate society's ends.[81]

The following year, when Queen's economist W.A. Mackintosh addressed a joint meeting of the Canadian Political Science Association (CPSA) and the Canadian Historical Association as the president of the CPSA, he similarly spoke of the promise of an economic practice that was morally neutral and limited in scope.[82] "Economics is not the science of welfare," Mackintosh insisted, but rather "an application of reason and systematic thought to a limited field of human relations. Apart from the facts with which it deals, it leads to no definite program." Economists should be neither the "protagonists nor antagonists" in political debates; they must reject the temptations and rewards of public life. Economic theory, he asserted, prescribed no policy and enunciated no doctrine apart from the analysis of the particular facts of a problem. Insofar as an economist "responds to a political party, to a social movement, or to a class interest, he does it as an individual citizen and not as an economist."[83] In an age threatened by overproduction, with an abundance of goods, a lack of jobs, and limited purchasing power, the economist was no longer a truth seeker but an expert offering practical solutions to pressing problems.

Conclusion

In their articles, both MacGibbon and Mackintosh referred to a definition of economics that had recently been proposed by British economist Lionel Robbins. Economics, Robbins wrote, was "a science which studies human behaviour as a relationship between ends and scarce means which have alternative uses."[84] MacGibbon connected Robbins' definition to the study of economic life under different types of social organization, and thus to the alternative uses. Mackintosh suggested that the ends should be determined by society through its political leadership and not by economists. Robbins' definition is also relevant to the dilemmas confronting the fictional families depicted by Canadian authors. There was real scarcity, but feelings of scarcity were also the result of having so many new choices. The tensions between wage earning and wage spending that Canadian novelists explored were the same as the problems of limited resources and unlimited wants identified by economists. Decisions about the allocation of resources that society once regarded as holding moral significance were being reframed as matters of choice by a wide range of intellectual and cultural commentators. In the wake of the Depression, leading professional economists embraced the principle of detachment, proposing to abdicate their role as moral authorities as they considered that commitment inconsistent with scientific objectivity.[85]

Both social scientists and literary writers identified and explored the gap between limited means and expanding, indeterminate ends in the social, emotional, and economic structures of the emerging consumer society. In a class structure characterized by sloping sides, there was an absence of firm footing and the ever-present danger of sliding. Earnings were limited while spending opportunities were increasing, and the emotionally compelling qualities of consumer goods complicated decision-making. After decades of material change, and even after the Great Depression, the line between necessity and want continued to blur.

Chapter Six

REGULATING THE CONSUMER

The relationship between the state and the Canadian consumer changed dramatically during the Second World War. The crisis of the Depression had elevated consumer concerns; however, the mainstream parties had addressed consumers as a voting interest with political rather than economic clout. In the worst years of the economic crisis, an estimated 30 percent of the labour force was unemployed and as much as one-fifth of the population dependent on some form of government assistance, but the level of aid was minimal, designed to prevent starvation and discourage dependency rather than to stimulate the economy. During the war, policymakers accepted that consumer spending was a significant component of the Canadian economy. However, they engaged with purchasing power as a matter of economic management rather than growth – that is, as something to be controlled and directed rather than encouraged.

Awareness of consumer spending played a critical role in policies of wartime finance, which sought in some situations to restrict and in others to mobilize the buying power of Canadians for specific purposes. During wartime, the government's policy objectives were straightforward: suppress the price mechanism and minimize inflation, leaving the government as the dominant force in the economy. The key was a universal freeze on prices and wages that would work hand in hand with new high levels of taxation and aggressive savings campaigns. The government commissioned extensive market research to guide the development of propaganda promoting restraint and encouraging voluntary compliance. There was a strong gender component to these policies: as the nation's principal consumers, Canadian housewives were recruited as partners in the war effort, exhorted to demonstrate their patriotism by monitoring prices, limiting spending, shopping wisely, and directing every extra dollar towards Victory Bonds and war stamps.

Postwar planning, which was part of wartime policymaking virtually from the outset, displayed the same commitment to economic management. In the early years of the war, government leaders (many of whom were veterans of the Great War) were concerned about avoiding a repetition of the pattern of high unemployment, inflation, and demoralization that had followed the end of hostilities in 1918. As the wartime economy boomed, new concerns arose: Would Canada fall back into a depression when over a million veterans (10 percent of the population) were demobilized, wartime spending ended, and exports to allied nations ground to a halt? Over the course of the war, Canada became a more prosperous nation, with full employment, an enlarged and modernized industrial infrastructure, and considerable personal savings. As they began to address the challenges of reconversion, policymakers continued to regard consumers as a useful tool: their spending could be constrained to prevent inflation or encouraged modestly to support the economy as wartime spending wound down. As the war ended, the state moved to supplement incomes at modest levels, hoping to keep wage demands moderate and exports competitive. Management of the economy during the war and the transition to peace was widely considered a policy success: inflation was held in check, and the nation navigated through the potential dangers of the conversion period to a postwar boom. Through it all, the government addressed Canadians on the home front as consumers, encouraging housewives to monitor their shopping practices carefully. The government message equated good citizenship with responsible consumption. In the uncertain times of the immediate postwar period, the state emphasized the importance of income security rather than higher wages, abundant choices, or increased spending. The lessons and policies of wartime carried forward to set the stage for a postwar era of cautious consumerism. At a time when American policymakers embraced mass consumption as the key to prosperity, their Canadian counterparts continued to see exports and capital investments, rather than domestic spending, as the key to economic growth and job creation.

The Home Front during Wartime

Canada entered the war in September 1939 with minimal preparedness and a high proportion of idle resources. Levels of personal income and gross national production still measured 7–8 percent lower in 1939 than in 1929. Surplus capacity on farms and in factories meant that both consumer and wartime needs could be met with little difficulty.[1] Opportunities for employment in wartime industries and enlistment in the armed forces were expected to increase purchasing power, stimulating the production of consumer goods as well as equipment for war. In the early months of war, it seemed, as Canadian economist A.F.W. Plumptre explained, "There may be more guns, more butter and more churns all at once."[2]

With the fall of France in the summer of 1940, demands on the Canadian economy increased rapidly. As existing factories expanded and new ones were rushed to completion, the economy reached the "zone of full employment." Concerns mounted that higher wages and expanding civilian demand would act to misdirect the nation's productive capacity and drive up the costs of waging war. The challenge was not simply to finance the war through taxes, savings, and printing money but to mould the entire economic system in accordance with the needs of war. These policies embodied new understandings of the economy, ones in which consumer spending played a critical role. As the minister of finance, James Lorimer Ilsley, explained in an address to the House of Commons, in a "deeper sense the task of finance is, by taxation and borrowing, to restrict the civilian demand for economic resources in order that they will be free when the defense or supply departments need them." Increased taxation and new programs of savings would "siphon off" increases of purchasing power from rising wages and steady employment and "immobilize money." R.B. Bryce, one of the government's specialists in wartime finance, later explained that the objective was not simply to borrow idle funds but to borrow "in such a way as will most effectively reduce private consumption." By preventing income from reaching consumers, the government believed that they would be "thus entirely delivered from the temptation of spending."[3] In October 1941, Prime Minister Mackenzie King announced in a dramatic Saturday evening radio broadcast that the time to choose between guns and butter had arrived: "We must face the fact that there are not enough men; there are not enough machines; there are not enough materials to meet the demands of consumers and the needs of war. Since the government, with the full support of the Canadian people, is determined to maintain and to intensify the war effort, we have no choice but to reduce our consumption of goods."[4] Strict price controls, high tax rates, and limits on wage and salary gains would allow for vast increases in output without increasing profits or creating inflationary pressures that would drive up the costs of making war. Domestic consumption would be controlled in order that the needs of war could be fully met.

Policymakers intended price and wage controls and rationing to work hand in hand with savings and tax programs. Sales of Victory Bonds (initially targeted to larger investors and businesses) and war savings certificates (always aimed at small savers) were reorganized in 1941 under the purview of the newly created National War Finance Committee (NWFC). The NWFC was extremely successful in converting support for the war effort into sales, devising new strategies in response to polling results, organizing volunteer and professional commissioned agents, staging high-profile campaign events, and saturating the mass media with publicity and propaganda.

In the early years of conflict, the government promoted war savings bonds and certificates as products that would help end the war. Publicity for these programs initially emphasized patriotism and sacrifice. Public opinion polls conducted by the NWFC, however, suggested that appeals to rational self-interest might be more effective. While the approaches were always many and varied, campaigns began to emphasize bonds as a sound tax-free investment and a source of security and deferred spending that could be directed at the purchase of household goods or even a home when the war ended. Over the course of the war, the NWFC spent $30 million on posters, direct mailings (a letter from the finance minister was sent to every household at the beginning of the 1943 Victory Loan campaign), movie trailers and short films (including films commissioned from the Disney studio), radio spots, campaign kick-off parades and ceremonies (Shirley Temple joined Prime Minister Mackenzie King for one such ceremony on Parliament Hill in 1944), and numerous staged events (including dramatically staged invasions).[5]

By the end of the war, virtually every Canadian who could afford to had bought a bond. One in four Canadians, for example, subscribed to the November 1943 issue of war bonds. By 1945, 97 percent of Canada's industrial workforce subscribed through payroll-deduction programs.

Comparisons with American bond drives give a sense of the success of the NWFC marketing strategy. While individual Canadians purchased half of Canada's Victory Bonds, individual Americans held only 27 percent of US bonds. Similarly, American workers directed less than 5 percent of their total payroll to bond purchases, compared to the average of 16 percent by Canadian workers, who were at the same time paying higher wartime taxes on comparatively lower wages.[6]

Local committees and personal persuasion were essential to success, but just as important was extensive advertising in the major daily, weekly, business, labour, and ethnic newspapers and magazines. An advertising blitz was launched two weeks before each bond drive and continued through the initial three weeks of each campaign, one every spring and fall. Government promotion was supplemented by tax-deductible advertising sponsored by private businesses. The slogan "Buy Victory Bonds" was ever present, featured in full- and quarter-page advertisements, inserted as a tag line in movie listings, and attached to ads for grocery stores, furniture, and fashions as well as to wartime recipes recommended by the nation's food producers (see Figure 4).

Distribution networks were inescapable. During ten wartime and one postwar campaign, bonds were sold at bank branches, in the workplace, and door-to-door, targeting both urban and rural households. The number of Victory Bond buyers rose steadily, from 986,259 in the first Victory Loan drive of 1941, conducted before the creation of the NWFC, to more than three million by the fifth, in 1943.[7] Many Canadians, especially those working in large companies or for the government, bought bonds through payroll deductions. By the autumn of 1941, some 10,000 firms had payroll-deduction schemes. The pressure of workplace solicitation, often carried out by supervisors and managers, could be "intense."[8] Payroll deductions were frequently scheduled to enable the purchase of one $50 bond (the minimum amount) every six months in conjunction with each bond campaign – this at a time when half of Canada's industrial workers earned less than $1,600 annually. The government targeted smaller amounts of disposable income through war savings certificate and war stamp campaigns, raising an additional $318 million for the war effort and involving millions of ordinary Canadians, including school children, in systematic savings.[9]

With high employment and fewer available goods in the war years, ordinary Canadians saved more than ever before. Over the course of the war, per capita personal savings multiplied by a factor of five, rising from

FIGURE 4   Window display at Jenkins' Groceteria, Calgary, Alberta, ca. 1941–45. |
Glenbow Archives, PA-2453-229.

$17.93 in 1939 to $95.05 in 1945 (calculated in constant 1939 dollars).[10] While
the number of large bank accounts, particularly those between $1,000
and $5,000, were reduced as owners shifted their savings into Victory
Bonds, the number of personal savings accounts with modest deposits had
increased by 246,000 since before the war.[11] Collectively, Canadians saved
25 percent of their disposable, after-tax income, during a period of high
taxation.[12]

Bond and certificate campaigns encouraged ordinary Canadians to become systematic savers. In order to urge Canadians, particularly women
and children, to practise restraint, war stamp campaigns, for example, used
dramatic slogans designed to discourage consumer purchasing. One advertisement depicted Hitler reaching into a woman's handbag to pull out
a five dollar bill while whispering into her ear, "GO ON SPEND IT ...
What's the Difference?"[13] But savings campaigns also marketed these investment products in the same manner as commercial goods, often addressing buyers as prospective consumers rather than as savers, with rhetoric
and imagery that urged Canadians to think of their contributions as re-

directed spending rather than savings. One campaign equated the purchase of war stamps with the purchase of armaments: every quarter bought a magazine of bullets for an army rifle; sixteen stamps bought a war savings certificate, and a few certificates would buy the rifle itself; a few more certificates would help buy a machine gun, a gun carrier, or a field gun.[14] By weighing every potential purchase and buying war stamps instead of personal goods, those at home were able to participate in the war effort, in effect "loading a rifle by licking a stamp."[15]

Certain themes, such as patriotism, duty, family, and the enemy threat, were consistently used in advertising and publicity efforts to sell war bonds; other themes evolved over time in response to changing circumstances.[16] In the later years of the war, sales campaigns created by government and by industry increasingly linked the purchase of bonds with deferred personal spending. In one advertisement, a soldier explained to readers that he bought bonds because it would help "to smash the Jerries" and because "I figure on buying a house when I come home, and the wife and boy will need lots of things that they have been going without since I've been away."[17] Victory Bonds provided "a nest egg for your future," another slogan promised.[18] Almost 80 percent of salespeople polled in connection with the eighth Victory Loan campaign in the spring of 1945 reported that people were buying bonds as a good investment rather than to help win the war.[19] Distinctions between thrift, spending, and savings were eroded in the effort to redirect consumer dollars towards the war effort.

Like the savings campaigns, dramatic increases in taxes were intended to raise revenue, discourage spending, contain inflation, and conserve resources.[20] In 1940, Ottawa levied a National Defence Tax, which was deducted by employers at source, before wages could reach consumers. Over time, new sales taxes were added, personal tax rates were raised, and exemptions levels were reduced. The proportion of Canadians paying income tax rose from 2.3 percent in 1939 to 18.7 percent by 1945.[21] Personal income tax totals increased sharply, from $45.8 million in 1939 to $683 million in 1945. The line between savings and taxation was further blurred by the introduction in the 1942 budget of "compulsory savings" of 8 and 10 percent of income, to be paid back by the government, with 2 percent interest, within three fiscal years after the war ended.[22] The refundable compulsory tax provided new revenues during the war and was expected to provide a postwar countercyclical stimulus.

In September 1939, the government established the Wartime Prices and Trade Board (WPTB) under the Department of Labour, with the intention of forestalling inflation and reassuring the public that hoarding (described as "speculative purchasing") was unnecessary. The board initially exercised limited jurisdiction, controlling rents and the prices of a limited number of staple goods regarded as "the necessaries of life."[23] Early measures had limited success: inflation rose rapidly, increasing almost 18 percent over the first two years of the war. In August 1941, responsibility for price controls was transferred to the Department of Finance and extended to include all goods and services. After considering various systems, the government adopted a universal price and wage freeze. Wages and salaries were frozen in place. The price of each good and designated service was fixed at the highest level at which that good or service had been sold in the four-week "basic period" of 15 September to 11 October 1941. Employers would be required to pay their workers a cost-of-living bonus for every 1 percent rise in the cost of living.

Canada's universal price freeze was the most severe program to be implemented by any of the allied nations during the war. Kenneth Taylor, the secretary of the WPTB and formerly a professor of political economy at McMaster University, described Canadian wartime price controls as "a novel experiment" and "a pioneering venture that received considerable interest at home and abroad."[24] Experts regarded a universal freeze as simple, fair, speedy, and administratively effective. Taylor explained that the intent behind the program was twofold: to control inflation but also to deprive the economy of changes in prices that would otherwise trigger shifts in the allocation of resources. He stressed that manipulation of the price system was not a tool to achieve social justice. "The primary function of the price system was to allocate resources and to guide production. If you mix up price control with social justice you are apt to get neither."[25] The price ceiling, together with wage and salary controls, would not reflect improvements in productivity or changes in demand, but rather was intended to preserve the status quo. Cost increases were to be absorbed in the production and distribution chain before reaching the consumer.[26] Without price changes to "signal and induce" increases in supply, production changes would occur primarily at the behest of the government. Policymakers understood that, given the size and complexity of the Canadian economy and the democratic nature of Canadian society, extensive controls would require a huge bureaucracy and dictatorial tactics unless significant efforts were also made to moderate consumer demand and encourage voluntary compliance. Taylor later described the system of price controls as an "illusion" whose

> success depended overwhelmingly on voluntary compliance ... A sort of mass enthusiasm had to be built up. There was a good deal of extravagance and not infrequently a conspicuous lack of qualifying phrases in the argument. But it was a pardonable almost a necessary aspect of speedy mass education, that the price ceiling should be "sold" to the Canadian public as an end in itself.[27]

Voluntarism was Ottawa's preferred approach to all aspects of the war effort, from enlistment to price controls. Indeed, the government considered the patriotic emphasis on voluntary rather than dictatorial methods to be one of the characteristics that distinguished the allies from the enemy. At the WPTB, practical considerations were also a factor: with limited staff for enforcement and considerable potential for backlash, the willingness of Canadians to limit their spending was vital to success. If Canadians believed that price controls worked, enforcement efforts would become unnecessary.

Women were at the core of the WPTB's efforts to manage the domestic economy, mobilized both as shoppers and as adjuncts of government helping to administer wartime regulations by reporting changes in price or quality. The WPTB announced price-checking programs in full-page newspaper ads. Maintaining the ceiling, headlines shouted, was "One Big War Job Which You Alone Can Do." The board distributed blue booklets to help shoppers track prices (see Figure 5). Notices encouraged the women of Canada, described as the "buyers of four out of every five dollars worth of all the goods sold in this country," to plan their purchases before starting out and to review their spending upon returning home. Announcements in the daily press provided guidelines and a sample form to be clipped out and consulted. "We want you to sit down today and make a list of the things you buy from week to week and from month to month," the government instructed. "Make notes about quality ...Write down prices ... Keep this list – use it when you buy."[28] A monthly publication, *Consumers' News,* was widely circulated in both French and English, keeping the public abreast of changing regulations.[29] At the end of 1941, the WPTB organized a Consumer Branch to coordinate the efforts of volunteers. Although

Canadian consumers had organized before the war, action had tended to be local and episodic, associated with protesting or advocating for particular causes and then dwindling.[30] The Consumer Branch brought the leaders of existing women's groups together under the directorship of Byrne Hope Sanders, the dynamic editor of *Chatelaine,* Canada's principal women's magazine, within the wartime government.[31] The branch represented consumers at the policymaking level (for example, advising the WPTB on the timing and scope of food controls), but its involvement in price watching was of primary importance in the war effort. Price-watching programs rallied Canadian women and provided the organizational base for the branch's other efforts, including the distribution of rationing cards.[32] In monitoring the price ceiling, the Consumer Branch encouraged shoppers to record prices and report stores charging above the price ceiling to one of the branch's thirteen Women's Regional Advisory Committees (WRACs) for investigation.

By the end of 1943, the branch had organized almost fourteen thousand women into a network of more than four hundred subcommittees, reaching nationwide into urban and rural Canada. Membership in the branch reached over sixteen thousand by the end of 1944 and peaked at nearly seventeen thousand, with representation from a wide range of groups, including labour union auxiliaries and middle-class women's clubs, and from both anglophone and francophone communities. Because the vast majority of Consumer Branch members were liaison officers affiliated with locally based women's clubs and organizations, the branch's reach was enormous. Liaison officers spoke at meetings in their local communities, distributed educational materials, and channelled grassroots concerns back to the branch. The branch gave Canadian women a direct role in monitoring prices and in the logistics of rationing, and provided feedback to the WPTB on a range of policies that affected domestic spending. In its approach to these responsibilities, the branch promoted a gendered notion of the consumer as an efficient household manager. Indeed, several historians have suggested that this image of price watching as a natural extension of women's household duties helped mute potential opposition from retail merchants to the work of the branch. Of course, this approach also reinforced the notion that consumer concerns were primarily women's issues.[33]

For the most part, government publications represented the household as a centre of consumption and the consumer as female, middle class,

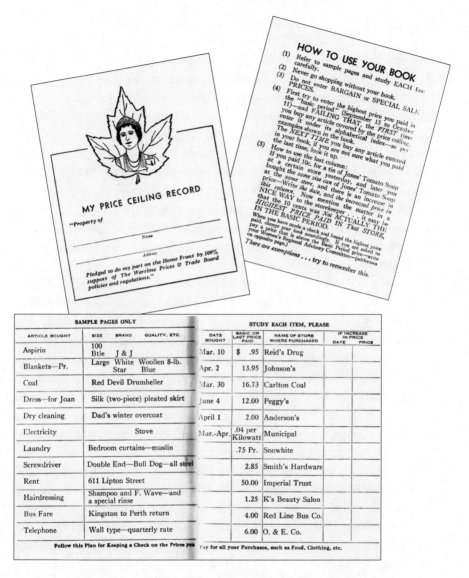

FIGURE 5 *My Price Ceiling Record.* The government called on the women of Canada to serve as the guardians of price controls. Nearly half a million copies of this "Little Blue Book" (so-called because of its blue cover) were distributed by the Consumer Branch of the WPTB in 1942 alone. The inside cover admonished, "Never go shopping without your book." Women were encouraged to record the details of every purchase and report price violations. Home front propaganda encouraged hyperawareness of purchasing habits. Canada Wartime Prices and Trade Board, Ottawa, 1942. | Courtesy of Wartime Canada (wartimecanada.ca).

and married.[34] Variously described as "Canada's Housesoldiers" and the women's "Home Guard,"[35] homemakers were seen as allies in the war effort, practising patriotic consumption through careful household management, including price checking, conserving scarce resources, cooking nutritious meals, raising money for soldier's parcels, recycling scrap, making clothing for the Red Cross, directing savings towards the purchase of war stamps and certificates, and, when the time came, complying with rationing. While government campaigns, as well as the rhetoric favoured by commercial advertising, reinforced gender stereotypes, they also imbued mundane acts of shopping with a new political significance: thoughtful shopping was a way of exercising social responsibility. Ottawa hailed the women of Canada as shoppers, but as shoppers with particular characteristics: they were alert, conscientious, and willing to sacrifice personal pleasure for the greater good. In Canada, as in so many other countries, good citizenship and good consumership came to be seen as inseparable, and, alongside Rosie the Riveter, Mrs. Consumer became one of the iconic images of the Canadian home front.[36]

Both government and the media framed home economics as a process involving rational decision-making that had ethical and political, rather than hedonistic, implications. They acknowledged that the everyday labour women performed as housewives and mothers was critical to the war effort. The women's pages of daily newspapers, women's magazines, and radio programs championed "practical patriotism," engaging women with slogans such as "Eat it up, Wear it out, Make it do" and recipes to stretch rations. Educational pamphlets with titles such as "The Miracle of Making Old Things New" suggested ways in which women could contribute to the war effort at home.[37]

The WPTB, the Consumer Branch, the Wartime Information Board, and the mainstream media produced a steady stream of propaganda promoting policies of restraint and appealing for understanding and compliance. At first these materials, much like bond campaigns, made generic appeals to patriotism. Increasingly, though, the creators of propaganda used the responses to public opinion surveys to help them capture the minds of their audiences.[38] During the war, for the first time, Canadian governments used market research to gauge support for current and prospective measures. Early on, Ottawa drew on surveys conducted by a division of Gallup. Later in the war, the Statistics Branch of the WPTB organized its own surveys in conjunction with the Consumer Branch. Polls that revealed a lack of support for particular programs led, not to changes in policy, but to education and publicity campaigns. Polling, in other words, was not a tool of direct democracy but rather one of governance, deployed to help the state market controls more effectively to the Canadian public.[39] Insofar as public opinion polls indicated solid support for the price freeze through most of the war, "the education of Mr. John Public," as the head of WPTB, Donald Gordon, put it, was successful.[40]

The government used the same combination of polling, education, and publicity to build public support for rationing. Although the Canadian food supply was never substantially threatened, several commodities became scarce. Anti-hoarding regulations had been passed by the government in 1939 as part of the legislation creating the WPTB, but they had no enforcement mechanism. In the spring of 1942, Ottawa enacted voluntary or "honour" rationing on sugar, tea, and coffee, announcing quotas but again without any enforcement mechanisms. Although the government hoped that moral suasion would be enough to curb consumption, the public actually expected some form of rationing. A Gallup poll conducted in January 1942 – before any official statements about rationing had been made – found that 58 percent of respondents believed that rationing would be needed at some point. Yet the government resisted, convinced that a coupon or ration card system would be prohibitively expensive and difficult to carry out effectively in a country whose population was spread across so vast a geographical area. Ultimately, increasing shortages forced the government's hand, and coupon rationing was introduced in the summer of 1942. While the ration amounts were broadly consistent with those set in the United States and the United Kingdom, the number of commodities rationed was, by comparison with other nations, quite limited: rubber, sugar, gasoline, butter, tea, coffee, sweeteners, and beef. Preparations for rationing went beyond organizing logistical and administrative support, and involved a systemic program of publicity that included the use of news reels, magazines, newspapers, radio, and store displays. Popular cooking school hosts on the radio provided advice on food substitutes and conservation. Educational materials such as meat-coupon value charts for consumers and manuals for dealers were printed and distributed by the government. The Consumer Branch played a central role in distributing ration cards and, of course, in promoting compliance.[41]

Shortages created by extensive government intervention on the production side of the consumer goods equation supported policies of price

controls. Regulations prohibited factories from producing new lines of
household equipment after November 1940. Canada's entire food and clothing trade – including manufacturers, processors, and wholesale and retail
distributors – operated under licence after 1941. By the fall of 1942, Ottawa
had suspended the production of refrigerators, stoves, electric washing
machines, and cars for civilian use. Other directives mandated simplifica-
tion and standardization, including the elimination of handles on teacups,
buttons on jacket sleeves, flaps on pockets, and restrictions on the sizes of
tin cans and the colours of thread.

Compliance with all the new wartime regulations and policies was far
from universal.[42] The prospect of restrictions often promoted hoarding, not
only of staples such as butter and sugar, but also of potentially discretionary
goods, including girdles.[43] Announcements emphasizing that hoarding was
a criminal offence began appearing in local papers in 1941, suggesting that
stockpiling of goods by consumers was becoming a concern.[44] Indeed, a
national poll conducted in November 1941 revealed that 18 percent of Canadians admitted they had stockpiled goods they feared would soon be in
short supply, and that 56.5 percent said they knew of others who had done
the same.[45] Alternative markets in rationed goods emerged, including a
flourishing trade in second-hand goods and an illegal black market, most
notably in gasoline coupons and sugar. Swapping of ration coupons was
endemic, and upcharges in the price of cars and rents common. Some retailers inveighed against price checkers as "snoopers."[46] Bond sales in the
workplace could be highly coercive.[47] As income taxes were broadened to
include lower-income workers in 1942, tax avoidance increased, as did the
efforts of the Department of Finance and National Revenue to identify tax
dodges.[48] Nor was resistance solely covert. Workers in heavy industries,
particularly mining and lumber, used their position as essential war workers
to bargain for additional rations of meat, tea, and butter, challenging equal-
share rationing as fundamentally unfair (see Figure 6).[49]

Prosecution for violations of the WPTB rules did occur, but were, on
the whole, limited. The WPTB offices received approximately 35,000 complaints per month. Yet, between 1 September 1939 and 28 February 1946,
a total of 23,416 people were convicted of wrongdoing. Most received fines
of $25 or less, although 253 were given jail terms.[50] Lacking a large staff and
concerned about triggering a backlash, the board was reluctant to prosecute
minor infractions. By 1943, the public's awareness of leniency and its general

Don't be a
CUPBOARD
QUISLING!

"Cupboard Quislings"! Is that too hard a name for people who selfishly lay in unnecessary stocks of clothes or food, or other goods for fear of shortages?

No! The name is not too hard, even though it may be earned through thoughtlessness. For in reality they are doing, in a petty, mean way, what the Quisling does in the open.

Anyone who buys more than is necessary for current needs—

    Is breaking his country's law for personal advantage.
    Is betraying his loyal neighbours and those who are not so well off as he.
    Is, in effect, depriving our fighting men of the munitions and supplies they must have to defend us.
    Is hindering our war effort and helping our enemies.

Loyal citizens avoid putting unnecessary and abnormal strains on our factories. In time of war, loyal citizens do not spend one dollar more on civilian goods than is absolutely necessary for current needs.

The law provides for fines up to $5,000 and imprisonment up to two years for hoarding; and hoarding is just another word for unnecessary selfish buying.

    In cases where it is advisable for you to buy in advance of your immediate requirements — such as your next season's coal supply — you will be encouraged to do so by direct statement from responsible officials.

▶ THE WARTIME PRICES AND TRADE BOARD ◀
OTTAWA, CANADA

FIGURE 6   Canada's Wartime Prices and Trade Board discouraged hoarding and encouraged good consumer practices with aggressive propaganda. This example uses the term "Quisling" – derived from the name of Norway's pro-Nazi wartime leader – to describe traitors who collaborate with the enemy, helping them to become an occupying force. | Wartime Prices and Trade Board, *Globe and Mail*, 12 May 1942, 9.

war-weariness, combined with the growing number of restrictions, led to an increase in violations and conviction rates.[51]

Although the government urged Canadians to adopt habits of thrift and deferred spending, manufacturers and retailers insisted that consumption could be patriotic. Advertising was not reduced, but it was adapted to wartime concerns. "Who said 'You Can't buy happiness'?" Philco Radio asked Canadians in 1942. "Good health is happiness ... and rules for health in wartime call for relaxation! No service other than radio gives you so satisfying respite from daily care and strain." A new radio, Philco promised, would provide "refreshing comfort for all the family in these strenuous times."[52] Whenever possible, advertisements associated products with patriotism. Car owners, for example, were assured that the purchase of Mobiloil, Champion spark plugs, and Sealed Power piston rings would bring victory closer by extending engine life and saving oil and gasoline.[53] Holt Renfrew, a high-end fashion store, advised that proper storage of fur coats was a "patriotic duty."[54] Companies such as General Motors and

FIGURE 7 As victory became more certain, the benefits of buying government savings bonds were explicitly linked to future consumption. Dreams of a privately owned home, its furnishings, a new car, and the benefits of education were central in visions of postwar prosperity. | "Keep on Saving till the Job Is Done," artist unknown, ca. 1939–45, Library and Archives Canada, no. 1983-30-581.

General Steel Wares, restricted by government in their ability to provide consumers with goods, emphasized their contribution to the war effort. As victory approached, advertising shifted from wartime to postwar thinking. In the early years of the war, for example, the Parker Pen Company had urged Canadians to "take up your pen for victory" and buy bonds. Later in the war, the company's ads associated the Parker pen with "the men who are planning the world of tomorrow." Government and business advertising linked wartime sacrifices to the material promise of the postwar era, encouraging Canadians to dream of a world where "the discoveries of war" – that is, the innovative products and technologies developed by military and industry for war use – would be "devoted to the more pleasant task of making the home more livable and more beautiful."[55]

Although prices and wage rates were frozen, taxes high, and savings aggressively encouraged, the war years were a time of full employment, with extended hours of work and new wage-earners. Total personal disposable income rose from $4.2 billion in 1939 to $8.4 billion in 1945.[56] Shortages of durable goods and housing channelled consumer spending towards the goods and services that were available. During a six-year period in which the cost of living rose 20 percent (18 percent from 1939 to 1941 and 2 percent from 1942 to 1945), grocery sales increased by 48 percent, purchases from retail stores increased by 82 per cent, and restaurant business tripled.[57]

During the war, the government encouraged civilians to think like consumers. Constant monitoring attuned Canadians to fluctuations in the prices of common goods.[58] Wartime experiences with economic controls helped to educate Canadians about the mechanisms of prices, profits, supply, and distribution. Price and wage controls set new precedents for government intervention in the marketplace, establishing a legacy of bureaucratic involvement in private life. Government campaigns broadcast images of thrifty, price-conscious Mrs. Consumer, while at the same time associating military victory with material abundance. Aggressive savings programs, shortages, propaganda, and rationing were effective in constraining consumption during wartime, but the policies that had successfully dampened consumption during the war had the potential to magnify it in the postwar period. Neither ordinary Canadians nor policymakers were certain what lay ahead.

Reconstructing Canada

Planning for postwar Canada began shortly after the declaration of war in 1939 and was very much a part of Canada's home-front experience. Initially, postwar plans focused on the efforts that would be required to ensure the smooth re-establishment of members of the armed forces in civilian life. Politicians and policymakers were anxious to avoid the social and economic disruptions that had followed the end of the First World War. They also regarded planning for postwar prosperity as vital to maintaining morale. As Minister of Pensions and National Health Ian Mackenzie noted, "It is widely believed that our fighting men and workers acquire new vigour by the appeal of future blessings to come."[59]

By 1943, the military situation had improved and planning for peacetime was underway. The theme of reconstruction was widely discussed in the media, at academic conferences, by business people, and by politicians at every level of government.[60] The conversations that swirled around the topic were at once apprehensive and aspirational. Public opinion polls indicated that Canadians were becoming increasingly concerned about the economics of the postwar period.[61] There was considerable uncertainty about the end of the war and fear that the country would see a return to conditions of depression. Every Canadian knew that hundreds of thousands of civilians working in wartime industries would be let go and that over a million soldiers (one-tenth of the Canadian population) would be returning home. Conditions of full employment experienced during the war might be anomalous. Politicians filled the void of uncertainty with promises and proposals. Those on the left called for wartime controls to be carried over into peacetime, as permanent, rather than emergency, measures, to secure "the good life" for Canadians. Others, such as C.D. Howe, the minister heading the Department of War Services and the future minister of reconstruction, observed that the war had produced new economic opportunities, particularly in the areas of electronics, transportation, and communication. The war had already reconstructed Canada's economy, Howe insisted; all that was needed was a rapid reconversion that would make the best use of this new infrastructure.[62]

In 1943, however, Howe's positive views were not widely shared by economists in key positions in the federal planning bureaucracy, who were, as one later recalled, "all geared up for an assault on the problems of the Great Depression."[63] The pessimism expressed by political economist D.C. MacGregor was more common. MacGregor was doubtful that "what we can do in war (i.e. in creating and maintaining a boom) we can do in peace." The wartime economy had been dominated by the demands of a single buyer purchasing enormous amounts of war goods, supplemented by the buying from other governments. Heavy borrowing and high taxes had supported the economy in a manner few Canadians would be willing to acquiesce to indefinitely. Intense levels of demand, the absence of seasonal fluctuations, and high levels of productivity were not sustainable over the long term. The war economy, MacGregor insisted, differed so much from that of peacetime that any effort to perpetuate its merits would be exceedingly difficult. Finally, MacGregor emphasized Canada's dependency on decisions made in the United States and Great Britain. The Canadian economy, dependent on trade for prosperity, remained vulnerable to outside conditions. Its key markets were unreliable and likely to be particularly so in the postwar period.[64] Others shared his views. "The kind of world which will emerge after the war," W.A. Mackintosh explained to a Canadian journalist, "will have more effect on Canada's destiny than any changes that are taking place within Canada during the war."[65]

The problems of transition would also, many economists believed, be magnified by long-term economic and social challenges. The war had intensified industrialization. Many old jobs – in agriculture, for example – no longer existed. It was possible that women could be convinced to return home, the elderly persuaded to retire, and the young to attend school, but the nation would still be left with thousands of returning soldiers, many of whom were wage earners. By law, no one would lose his or her job as a result of having served in the Armed Forces. Many economists regarded the wartime boom not as evidence of the ability of the economy to grow, but of the power of the state to achieve set objectives. John Deutsch, a young economist who joined the Bank of Canada during the war and would later chair the Economic Council of Canada, recalled that, at the time, the industrialized world shared the concern that stagnation "represented ... the 'normal' condition to which an advanced capitalistic economy would tend." Although they recognized the potential of domestic spending to stabilize the economy as the war wound down, economists did not believe that spending by Canadian consumers could sustain the economy in the long run. The domestic market could simply not generate sufficient demand to call forth the capital investments needed to provide jobs, particularly the well-paying jobs that supported high standards of living. Population growth and technological progress would slow over time, consumer spending would decline, and savings would outrun the demand for capital.[66]

Alert to the potential dangers of both inflation and depression, most Canadian economic experts recommended a middle path: if inflation were kept under control, there might be sufficient domestic demand to sustain the economy for one to two years following the conclusion of the war. After that, with savings exhausted and pent-up demand satisfied, Canada's prosperity would depend on the restoration of foreign trade, with growth linked to exports and capital investment. Excessive consumer spending at a time when goods remained in short supply was more likely to destabilize than grow the economy, but it could be managed by prolonging economic controls. International competitiveness dictated low wages, with living standards sustained by job security and government programs of social security. Thus, in Canada, attention to domestic consumption did not imply a commitment to economic growth driven by ever-expanding levels of consumer spending; instead, it meant a commitment to policies that sought primarily to restrain and dampen consumption for the greater good of other sectors. In the short term, stability was regarded as more important than growth. Canadians were consumers, but the policy-makers believed that the national economy benefited most when consumers were restrained and thrifty.[67]

Managing for Stability

In December 1939, only a few months after the war had begun, cabinet appointed a special committee to plan for the demobilization of the armed forces. Recognizing that the problems of demobilization would need to be considered with reference to the total postwar economic situation, the committee began to expand, adding subcommittees and advisory committees with representatives from agriculture, business, labour, and academia. The most prominent of these was the Advisory Committee on Reconstruction, commonly referred to as the James Committee after its chair, Cyril James, McGill University principal and a former professor of finance and economic history. When the James Committee presented its final recommendations after two and a half years of investigation and study, it linked the future growth of the Canadian economy to expanding markets at home and abroad, rejecting the idea that the immediate postwar period was "a time for comprehensive social and political revolution."[68]

The most important of the many investigations conducted by the Advisory Committee on Reconstruction led to the *Report on Social Security for Canada*, prepared by economist Leonard Marsh. Although the Marsh report was never formally adopted, it received considerable attention from both progressive and conservative thinkers arguing about the future of social welfare in a changing society.[69] In his report, Marsh explicitly recommended social welfare payments, not as a matter of social justice but as a strategy to provide "economic stability in the maintenance of the flow of purchasing-power at the time when munitions and other factories are closing down and war activity in many other spheres is being liquidated." For the most part, the report did not concern itself with the provision of specific social facilities and services, although Marsh noted that these were worthwhile. Instead, it focused on the family unit and on wage levels as the "critical determinant of well-being."[70]

The campaign waged by conservative social reformer Charlotte Whitton against the Marsh report was extreme in its vehemence but clear in articulating the conflict between progressive and conservative models of Canadian society. In modern society, Marsh wrote, different standards of living were defined on a "budgetary basis" as a series of purchasing decisions made in the privacy of the family unit. Whitton rejected the exchange of money as a meaningful social bond. Assuring every individual a social minimum, Whitton argued, was not only prohibitively expensive, it was also fundamentally misguided. Quality of life, she insisted, was not determined by "so many dollars and cents" per head, but by "a simple, decent, sound, wholesome family life." The goal of full employment, she further objected, assumed a population of urban wage-earners and disregarded the needs of a third of Canadians who continued to be employed in primary industries and agriculture. Ultimately, she argued, a decent social minimum was "something more far-reaching, vital and complex than the hope of a calculated amount of income in currency terms."[71]

Fundamentally, Whitton and Marsh were championing different models of society. Whitton spoke for Canadians concerned about the moral and cultural consequences of a waged, consumption-oriented society. Marsh emphasized the dangers of economic instability, arguing that employment security was a right of citizenship and that ensuring access to a minimum but measurable quantity of goods was the responsibility of the state. Social progressives such as Marsh connected quality of life to quantity of income and called on the government to provide a baseline of material security as a means to increased freedom and opportunity for self-fulfilment. Social conservatives such as Whitton honoured traditional producer values of individual effort, self-sufficiency, and the reciprocal commitments of community. They associated increases in government with decreases in liberty, diminished personal responsibility, rising apathy, and a careless attitude towards civic life.

The debate between Marsh and Whitton is illustrative of the intense battles that swirled around the topic of reconstruction as different ideological groups competed to ensure that their particular postwar visions would prevail.[72] Some opposed the enlargement of the state, while others advocated for central planning, but there was considerable consensus among intellectual and cultural elites of different political persuasions that democratic ideals were threatened by mass production, mass culture, and the mass media. The wartime economic boom confirmed long-held beliefs that growth in the Canadian economy was dependent on exports. Wartime success in regulating consumer spending was another lesson learned.[73] The biases of a narrowly constituted elite of policymakers and cultural authorities, who often lived in the same neighbourhoods, socialized at the same events, and shared the same ideas, reinforced economic understandings, encouraging a carrying forward of regulations and especially of attitudes that would prolong policies that dampened consumer spending.

In 1943, with the end of the war in sight, the James Committee's increasingly interventionist recommendations, which included the creation of a new ministry of reconstruction, began to generate a reaction within the civil service. The Economic Advisory Committee (EAC), an interdepartmental group that had coordinated Canada's war effort at the highest levels of government, asserted its power as the principal agency responsible for developing plans and programs for the postwar transition. Authority for postwar planning moved to the inner circles of the federal government.[74] Going forward, policies would be devised by the same personnel who had been responsible for wartime planning, applying the same theoretical framework and many of the same assumptions. Canada was committed to a free-enterprise economy. The corporations created by the federal government to expedite the war effort were dismantled or sold off. The rapid conversion of industry from wartime to peacetime production was encouraged with tax incentives. Canada aggressively pursued initiatives to re-establish international trade, playing an important role in the Bretton Woods conferences that set postwar currency-exchange rates and advocating for open markets. Policymakers orchestrated a rapid transition for producers, but believed that consumer spending should continue to be carefully managed. New social programs were introduced to act as a floor that would stabilize the economy as wartime spending wound down, while price ceilings and rationing would be prolonged to forestall inflation.[75] To preserve currency reserves and to support Canadian manufacturing, Ottawa discouraged purchases of mass-produced, imported goods in favour of domestically produced, low-cost items. In the face of ongoing shortages of goods, consumers would carry the burden of maintaining stability. This burden was borne particularly by housewives, who were encouraged to stretch limited wages, to postpone needs, and to put desires on hold a bit longer.

Policymakers favoured programs that addressed multiple concerns, meeting aspirations for a better postwar world in ways that provided both economic and political benefits. Planning for veterans, for example, evolved by 1945 into an expansive set of programs collectively known as the Veterans' Charter. Consumerist assumptions were clear in the centrepiece of the Charter, which provided a tax-exempt discharge gratuity to those who had enlisted in the war effort (linked to the length and arena of service) and a clothing allowance voucher. Cash payments would fulfil the nation's moral obligation to help those who had enlisted in the war re-establish themselves in peacetime. These payments would also help stabilize the economy as government spending was withdrawn and, the government anticipated, would build loyalty to the federal state and particularly to the Liberal Party. Additional re-establishment grants were available for job training and education. Those who chose not to claim these benefits could receive a grant to help purchase, furnish, or equip a home or business. Payments to veterans faced no political opposition, and, from the perspective of the Department of Finance, were predictable, controlled, and clearly defined.

Although a universal family allowance had been only a minor feature of the Marsh report, this program was created in 1944 with payments beginning in 1945. Ottawa regarded family allowance benefits as simultaneously "an installment on promises" made for a better postwar future and a fiscal measure that would, as Minister of Health and Welfare Brooke Claxton put it, "increase the buying power of those groups who not only need the money but who are most certain to use it immediately."[76] Indeed, Claxton was so committed to the family allowance program as a measure of economic stimulus that he objected to advertisements by Eaton's department stores encouraging children and families to deposit the monthly allowance cheques in a savings account.[77] Family allowance payments were limited in cost, minimally invasive, and could be implemented without triggering constitutional conflicts over federal and provincial jurisdiction. By supplementing family incomes, they could help forestall demands for wage increases. To be paid whenever possible to mothers, they were tangible evidence of the postwar paternalistic state, with sufficient power, the ruling Liberal Party hoped, to offset the appeal of parties on the left during the next election, due no later than the spring of 1945 (see Figure 8).

The fate of Wartime Housing Limited shows the same commitment to private spending and self-reliance. When shortages of accommodation for industrial workers threatened to delay the war effort, the federal government intervened directly in the housing market, through WPTB rent controls and the establishment of Wartime Housing Limited. This Crown corporation built almost 45,000 modest homes. Mid-war, a government commission estimated that there would be a shortfall of as many as 500,000 dwelling units in urban Canada at the end of the war, the result of fifteen years of deterioration and deferred construction. Although Wartime

FIGURE 8   The new family allowances program was intended to strengthen the Canadian family, the domestic economy, and voter loyalty to the Liberal Party. Modest enhancements to private spending were intended to sustain the economy as wartime spending wound down without committing the government to expensive programs of social welfare. The family became the principal unit of postwar consumer society. | "Hey Mom! Why Haven't You Sent in That Form?" *Hamilton Spectator*, 28 March 1945, Department of National Health and Welfare, Ottawa. Courtesy of *Hamilton Spectator*.

Housing could have been adapted to fill this need, the corporation was systematically dismantled and housing units sold off. The government regarded the direct provision of housing in peacetime as socialistic and dangerous, and it insisted that, without a wartime emergency, the construction of affordable rental housing for low-income families was a provincial and municipal responsibility. Ottawa's approach was to encourage residential construction and private home ownership by offering mortgage insurance to financial institutions.[78] The federal goal in housing, as in other programs, was to return Canada to a free-market economy with minimal redistribution of wealth, and only as much government intervention as was needed to create jobs and social stability – and to ensure the re-election of the Liberal Party.

Although cultural programs did not figure prominently in the government's plans for the transition period, policies to limit mass consumption resonated with the biases of Canada's cultural elites. Intellectual and cultural leaders on both the right and left of the political spectrum hoped that the end of the war would see an extension of regulation rather than a return to consumer choice. They called on the state to invest in infrastructure and create a national cultural ministry in order to limit the influence of mass commercial culture and strengthen support for physical recreation, amateur performances, and opportunities for exposure to high culture. With appropriate government intervention, opponents of mass culture hoped the average Canadian would devote anticipated increases in leisure time to self-improvement rather than commercial entertainments.[79]

With respect to consumption, then, a consistent set of concerns guided postwar planning, casting increases in consumption as potentially counter to the national interest, to be constrained rather than encouraged. The cumulative effect of these programs was to magnify differences in Canadian society. For example, many veterans' benefits were available to both volunteers and conscripts who served overseas but still overwhelmingly benefitted English-speaking over French-speaking Canadians because, for a variety of historical and social reasons, men from Quebec were only half as likely to serve as men from Ontario or other Canadian provinces. Tuition credits were of more help to middle-class individuals and of limited benefit in expanding opportunities for those men and women whose wages were required to support themselves and their families. Similarly, policies that supported access to mortgages, rather than low-income housing, made homes more easily available to those who were steadily employed and earning good wages. Overall, since men had constituted the vast majority of those who had enlisted, veterans' benefits strengthened the position of men, especially middle-class men, in Canadian society.[80] The combination of family allowance payments, veterans' benefits, and the withdrawal of support for daycare programs encouraged women to leave the paid workforce, marry, and start families.[81] Policies that discouraged wage increases in order to promote exports and capital investment disadvantaged working-class Canadians, especially housewives who had to make do with limited supplies and reduced purchasing power when price controls were gradually removed. The full impact of these decisions would become clear in the cautious consumerism of the immediate postwar decade.[82]

Postwar programs had been introduced on an ad hoc basis, each devised for a particular purpose as needs and opportunities arose. In 1945, the economist W.A. Mackintosh, one of the nation's most important wartime civil servants, prepared a comprehensive policy statement, presented to the public as Canada's first White Paper. Mackintosh described the White Paper as a consolidation of commonly held beliefs that was neither revolutionary nor "even novel" in its approach to postwar policy.[83] The government's common-sense Keynesianism promised "high and stable levels of employment" with internationally competitive wage rates, supplemented by a variety of social security payments. During the war, the economy had been mobilized under stringent price controls, with high tax rates and aggressive savings campaigns, to dramatically raise output while minimizing inflation and private profit. The same commitment to comprehensive economic management that characterized wartime planning carried over into planning for postwar Canada; however, the objectives were orderly deregulation and economic stability, defined primarily in terms of employment. Consumption-oriented economic theory and policy did not require more consumer spending. Indeed, Canadians would be urged to practice restraint, thrift, and patience in the face of ongoing shortages. During the immediate transition from wartime to peacetime, the nation would continue to depend on the self-discipline and restraint of Canadian consumers.

Chapter Seven

BUYING HAPPINESS

Through years of depression and war there was considerable continuity in the lived experiences of Canadians in terms of their relationship to consumer goods: in the early 1930s, as the economy contracted, goods were plentiful but income was not; in the war years, when the economy gained strength, income was available but goods were not. The end result, regardless of changing circumstances, was fifteen years of austerity in the home. Victory did not bring immediate change. In order to smooth the transition to a peacetime economy, the government reduced subsidies and lifted direct controls only gradually, adding social programs that could support the economy as wartime spending wound down. The primary focus of government policy was job creation. Ottawa rapidly lifted restrictions on production and devised tax incentives to speed the shift from wartime to peacetime manufacturing. Canadian policymakers were active participants in conferences to restore international trade. The message to Canadian shoppers, however, was one of ongoing caution. In the immediate postwar years, Canadians were encouraged to moderate their expectations and wage demands in support of the government's vision of export-led development. The danger of inflation, officials warned housewives, was "more real now than at any time since the war commenced."[1] Government policies encouraged Rosie the Riveter to leave the workforce to open high-paying industrial jobs for returning male veterans; meanwhile, Mrs. Consumer – the rational, constrained spender recruited for the war effort – remained relevant and was exhorted to work even harder to win the peace. As the pace of decontrol increased towards the end of the decade, consumer spending was mobilized around the purchasing, finishing, and furnishing of new homes. Over one million new dwelling units were constructed in the decade between the 1951 and 1961 census; 702,886 of these were detached, single-family dwellings. By 1961, 44.2 percent of all occupied dwelling units (both owned and rented) had been built since 1945.[2]

Chatelaine, the nation's pre-eminent women's magazine, regularly featured articles examining the money-management challenges faced by Canadian families after the war. Over a fifteen year period, three features in particular showcased changes in the spending and saving practices of "typical" families. This chapter uses these articles as a lens through which to examine changing attitudes towards the family budget, the responsibilities of the housewife, and household debt. *Chatelaine* held the spending decisions of its selected Canadian families up for examination, in some cases as inspiration and in others as a warning, a lesson to other families. As is evident in these series, traditional gender divisions were maintained and refreshed in the postwar period, with the role and responsibilities of housewives shifting from production to financial management and purchasing decisions. Money management, even more than rising wages, was presented as the key to financial freedom and family well-being. Over time, good spending habits came to be seen less a question of character and more a matter of skill – something that could be learned and strengthened with practice.

The end of hostilities did not mean a return to conditions of the past. Canada's industrial and agricultural infrastructure had undergone significant changes; many traditional export markets had been disrupted. The expectations of ordinary Canadians had been changed by wartime rhetoric and experiences. Each of the allied nations approached decontrol differently. In Canada, it would be a gradual process as policymakers sought to navigate a middle path between the rapid deregulation of the American economy and the prolonged shortages and ongoing regulations experienced in the United Kingdom. Indeed, Canadian policymakers and media commentators often pointed to the American example – where the rapid removal of controls was accompanied by dramatic increases in inflation – as a cautionary tale.[3] In Canada, the shift to decontrol began slowly in September 1944 and gained momentum in mid-1945. Restrictions on supply were lifted in stages. Initially the Wartime Prices and Trade Board (WPTB) issued lists of suspensions; then, as the lists grew longer, the approach changed to listing only those products still under control. The process was designed to reaffirm the strength of the WPTB during the transition, particularly given the rapid disintegration of American controls.[4] Rationing of foodstuffs was especially prolonged, in large part due to humanitarian commitments to send supplies overseas. Meat rationing, for example, initially suspended in March 1944, was reimposed in the fall of 1945 on an even wider range of products. Canadians found themselves limited to smaller rations on a wider range of meats in the immediate postwar years than they had been during the war. Restrictions on meat lasted until the summer of 1947; those on sugar and molasses, the final foodstuffs to be removed from the ration list, continued until November of that year. Durable goods remained in short supply for the remainder of the decade, a residual effect of Canadian wartime policies that restricted both the use of materials and innovation in production, particularly in the production of domestic goods. The Emergency Exchange Conservation Act of 1947, which prevented the importation of equipment, further exacerbated shortages of items deemed non-essential, including most domestic appliances.

Every Canadian looked forward to the end of rationing; however, reactions to the gradual withdrawal of price controls were more divided. Manufacturers, retailers, landlords, farmers, and the Conservative Party (the official opposition) called on the government to end controls rapidly and allow prices and profits to rise. Higher prices, it promised consumers, would end postwar shortages. Yet each round of decontrol was also met with critical letters, petitions, and resolutions from women's organizations, trade unions, and individuals calling for the continuation of remaining price controls and subsidies and appealing for the reinstatement of those that had already been removed.[5] From the government's perspective, the system of price controls and subsidies was a solution to wartime problems; the Liberals assumed that, over time, prices and availability would again be determined by the market.[6] Some citizens agreed, but others regarded the relationship that had been cultivated through extensive economic controls, government propaganda, and direct transfers of money from the state to individuals and families as one that should be ongoing.[7]

Well before the end of the war, leaders in the Consumer Branch had begun to discuss the possibility of forming a peacetime organization that would carry forward its work.[8] Members of the branch had different opinions on the purpose and approach of such an association. The moderate mainstream leadership saw an organization that would build on the branch's wartime work in standards and consumer education with new initiatives in product research and development. The radical leaders who had subsumed their political allegiances to support the Consumer Branch in the war effort insisted that the government should continue its wartime role, particularly in ensuring the distribution of household goods at reasonable prices through the continued imposition of price ceilings. In the months immediately after the war's end, the Consumer Branch and most Canadians remained supportive of the decision to prolong controls. But as controls were removed and prices began to rise, the once-unified consumer interest fractured into competing groups.

The Liberals disbanded the Consumer Branch in May 1947, effectively removing the voice of women from the policymaking level of government. Byrne Hope Sanders, who had headed the branch, returned to her work at *Chatelaine* magazine. Other members of the inner circle of the branch's leadership established the Canadian Association of Consumers (CAC) in 1947. The CAC did not, for the most part, challenge the elimination of price and wage controls; rather, it sought to position itself as a liaison between government and consumers, presenting the concerns and recommendations of homemakers to the appropriate government department or agency, and working as an educational force in the development of enlightened public opinion. By acting as a conduit, the CAC proposed to become "a great stabilizing and constructive influence in the practical workings of democracy."[9] Aligned by political commitments and personal ties to the Liberal government, the CAC generally supported the government's postwar policies that privileged the needs of exports and industry before those of the Canadian household. Like the government, the CAC recommended thrift, patience, and household management as the keys to familial and national happiness during the transition.

The CAC had a rival in the more radical Housewives' Consumers Association (HCA). The HCA was organized by left-wing labour activists in 1937 to demand state intervention in a range of household concerns, beginning with high milk prices. During the war, the HCA had supported the Consumers Branch, but, after 1947 it resumed its role as an advocate for working-class consumers. The HCA objected that the burden of making ends meet was falling on individual families, especially housewives, rather than on government or industry. From the perspective of the HCA, the effectiveness of government wartime controls was proof that the state could intervene successfully in the marketplace. The HCA took an activist approach to advancing a class-based agenda, calling for national boycotts and buyers' strikes, organizing petitions, and sending delegations to Ottawa to demand the reinstitution of price controls and subsidies. These initiatives were front-page news and gained the organization new members.[10]

In January 1948, the government announced that it would accelerate decontrol. As more controls were removed, prices rose, as did public unrest.[11] Seeking to build support for policies of decontrol, the government directed funding towards the moderate CAC, while at the same time using the heightened rhetoric of the Cold War to attack those consumer organizations, particularly the HCA, calling for the re-imposition of price and rent controls. Links between HCA leadership and the Communist Party attracted the surveillance of Canada's security services and led to the group's vilification in the mainstream press. Red baiting, in which the leaders of the CAC also took part, undermined the credibility of the HCA and, over time, tainted the entire consumer advocacy movement. Ultimately no consumer organization was able to build a significant peacetime role.[12]

The official federal response to public alarm over price increases was the appointment of a special committee in February 1948, upgraded to a Royal Commission in July, to investigate the reasons behind rising prices. The commission's report supported the government's decision to discontinue wartime controls, contending that price controls were impractical and inadvisable under peacetime conditions. Reimposing price ceilings after the war, it stated, would involve fixing prices at levels "so unrelated to the realities of the economy" as to be "wholly impracticable and undesirable." Moreover, the report added, in a peacetime economy "there could be no discrimination in price setting between essential goods and luxury goods, or essential services and luxury services," raising the question of which goods should be subject to price control.[13] All but ignoring the concerns of low-income families, the commission emphasized the technical problems that would be involved in administering controls. Among the many reasons it gave to explain why controls would not work in peacetime was the absence of the Consumer Branch and its vast volunteer network. Decontrol proceeded uninterrupted; the WPTB was finally dissolved in 1951 when its final responsibility (for rent controls), was handed over to the provinces.[14]

Despite their differences, Canada's leading postwar consumer-organizing initiatives both discussed consumer interests as specifically female.[15] The mobilization of women as consumers as part of the war effort had forged a connection reaching from government policymakers and administrators through the ranks of elite volunteers and women's committees down to thousands of ordinary shoppers. The Consumer Branch had leveraged the stereotype of women as household managers, but it had also garnered a degree of authority for Canadian women in the community and in government through its influence on price controls, rationing, and regulations. Promoting consumer compliance, monitoring prices, and acting as a conduit between government and the consumer were responsibilities that both the government and print media frequently described as crucial to the war effort.[16] Yet, by the early 1950s, it was evident that the women's voice in economic decision-making at the national level had been a uniquely wartime phenomenon, a response to emergency needs rather than a permanent advance for consumer interests. By 1950, the HCA membership base had all but disappeared.[17] The CAC fared little better. By 1952, only 2,200 Canadian women were dues-paying members.[18]

With the end of the war came the end of the home front. Yet, well into the late 1940s, guidance from the CAC, the government, and prominent columnists emphasized the need to make do, echoing the advice offered to women in the preceding decades of depression and war. Promised postwar opportunity, consumers were nonetheless urged to practise thrift and patience.[19] Canadian prosperity, government spokesmen insisted, depended on high productivity and industrial stability. Graham Towers, the governor of the Bank of Canada, assured the women of Canada that efficient production and competitive pricing were critical in a world where success depended on "being able to offer our customers goods at the going world price."[20] Wage increases would make Canadian products uncompetitive; strikes would disrupt the flow of goods. Business and government promoted job security and regular hours, rather than higher wages, as the key to improved standards of living.[21]

In numerous articles written for *Saturday Night* and *Maclean's*, Lillian Millar, Canada's pre-eminent "women's page" columnist, continued to advise women to do without, to question every expense, and, when they did have to buy, to shop wisely. Insofar as "financial difficulties in the home inevitably bring demands for higher wages which in turn often result in strikes and labour unrest ... the peace and prosperity of the nation" were seen to hinge on "whether or not personal finances could be put on a sound financial basis."[22] Limiting demand would limit inflation; limiting inflation would limit class strife. Typically, women's-page experts like Millar proposed three strategies for dealing with rising prices in the immediate postwar period: thrift, "know-how," and united action. Needless buying was discouraged and prudence emphasized.[23] "With so much at stake, no one can afford to buy carelessly or thoughtlessly," admonished Millar.[24] Even a high income was no guarantee of success, for, no matter how large the income might be, it would not buy everything one might need or desire. Instead, the "housewifely arts," "good buymanship," and successful budgeting would provide "peace of mind ... a sense of security ... [and] the thrill of satisfaction which achievement brings."[25] Millar urged the government to reinstitute wartime programs encouraging conscientious consumption practices to meet the postwar "state of emergency," but her primary focus was on private purchasing practices. Other women's page writers agreed with her that, during this transitional period, when the supply of domestic goods was outweighed by demand and employment remained uncertain, "know-how" and "good buymanship" were the housewife's "best allies" in stretching dollars and preventing inflation. A balanced household budget, wrote Millar, was "the only sound foundation upon which a strong and peaceful nation [could] be built."[26]

Despite the pessimistic predictions of many experts, no significant economic downturn followed the end of war. By 1948, five million Canadians were working, 700,000 more than the number of civilians employed at the peak of the war effort in 1943, and 1.3 million more than in 1939 at the end of the Depression. With secure employment, rising incomes, veterans' benefits, family allowances, government mortgage insurance, and easier access to credit, total consumer expenditures rose from $14.1 billion in 1944 to $17.3 billion in 1946 and to $18.5 billion in 1947.[27] In the decade following the war, Canada's gross national product averaged gains of 5.6 percent per year and unemployment remained below 4 percent. Real wages rose and the average workweek shortened (from 48.2 hours in 1945 to 44.8 hours in 1950).[28] Soon Donald Gordon, the former head of the Wartime Prices and Trade Board and now deputy governor of the Bank of Canada, was able to boast that "[we] drank one third more milk, ate two thirds more pork, rang up two thirds more movie admissions and bought 75 percent more new houses in 1948 than in ... 1938 ... We used twice as much gasoline, chewed twice as much gum, bought twice as many refrigerators and ate three times as much ice cream."[29]

Towards Cautious Consumerism

Home and family were central concerns in postwar Canada. The yearning for stability and the idealization of domestic life were a response to decades of emotional uncertainty and financial strain.[30] The family home, its furnishings, and its infrastructure needs were also becoming increasingly important to the Canadian economy. In the decade after the war, household formation rose dramatically. Spiking marriage rates, the subsequent boom in births, and long-deferred need saw the addition of over a million new dwellings in the decade between the 1951 and 1961 census. The phenomenon of the middle-class suburban family captivated the popular media and was the subject of numerous academic studies, several of which will be discussed in the next chapter.[31] As consumption increased, gender divisions within the family were maintained but gradually recast as ideals of responsible consumerism evolved from thrift to responsible spending.

Canada's leading women's magazine, *Chatelaine*, offered a unique forum for the discussion of modern living, marriage, and motherhood. With a monthly readership of almost two million from all regions of the country, *Chatelaine* was something of a national institution.[32] It was also a mass-produced consumer good. Historian Valerie Korinek proposes that reading *Chatelaine* made one part of a particular community; however, she argues that it was the magazine's editors, writers, and advertisers who set the agenda.[33] The topics they selected for attention established a frame of reference for readers in their thinking about Canadian society. By giving certain lifestyles positive attention and, in effect, tacit approval, and by instructing Canadian families how to achieve similar results, the magazine helped to legitimize new patterns of spending and consumption.[34]

From time to time, feature stories in *Chatelaine* examined the spending patterns and lifestyles of young Canadian families, celebrating lives of modest consumption. These stories offered both normative and prescriptive accounts of the Canadian family, describing these families as in some way typical but, at the same time, using them to demonstrate lessons in living that would help other Canadian families bring their own lives closer to the ideal. Close reading of three of *Chatelaine*'s featured family articles published over the period 1949 to 1962 reveals steady increases in material prosperity, a gradual relaxation of stringent self-disciplines, and an increasing encouragement to experiment, albeit in preapproved ways, in the expanding world of commercial possibilities.

Korinek argues that the commercial imperatives of the publication, particularly the advertisements promoting household perfection through consumer spending, should be read separately from the feature articles, editorials, and letters, which, she contends, subversively complicated any simple recipe for affluent domesticity. However, the boundary between the world of goods and the world of feminist ideals was less firm than Korinek indicates. It is, perhaps, more useful to see two consumer discourses running in parallel, with advertisements that sought to stimulate spending set beside articles that taught homemakers how to achieve good results on small budgets. The magazine presented new opportunities for self-expression through the selection and consumption of goods alongside discussions of birth control, divorce, and racism.

A close examination of three of the magazine's lengthier feature stories – "Rich on $40 a Week" (1949), "We Sent an Expert to Help This Family Make Both Ends Meet" (1954), and "101 Ways to Save Money – and Look Better, Dress Better, Eat Better and Live Better" (1962) – shows how new consumption patterns were simultaneously reflected in and authorized by the magazine. Each article presented a family with young children as typical of the Canadian experience at the time, but also as worthy of emulation in the personal struggle to achieve the Canadian ideal. These articles celebrated increasing prosperity and materialism but also, and more importantly, the ideals of family, home, and financial security. The emphasis on careful spending, thrift, and the wisdom of the family budget is persistent, even as the emphasis shifts from a producer to a consumer orientation over the course of thirteen years.

All three of these articles presented their subjects as Canadian success stories. Each family owned a home (albeit with a mortgage) and was financially secure, if challenged in stretching its income to cover all expenses. In addition, all three conformed to the mid-century gendered ideal: the women remained in the home with the children; the men worked. As Doug Owram observed, "Every magazine, every marriage manual, every advertisement, and the entire cultural milieu – from store hours to the absence of such institutions as day-care facilities – indicated a society that assumed the family was based on the single, male wage-earner and the child-rearing, home-managing wife."[35] In each of these stories, stay-at-home mothers were the primary caregivers of two young children, while breadwinner fathers held secure positions in the upper ranks of skilled labour or the lower ranks of the salaried professions. Although occupations, spending patterns, and relationships between spouses differed in each family, *Chatelaine* was consistently interested in the amount each family earned, how they spent, and how they saved. As the magazine made clear, handling money was part of the work of consumption and central to the narrative of the emerging consumer society.[36]

THE MENZIES

The Menzies, featured in "Rich on $40 a Week" (1949), represented the postwar familial ideal.[37] Bill, a veteran working at Bell Telephone Company, and Marie, who had left the workforce and become a stay-at-home mother of two, demonstrated by the strength of their personal example how to live modestly with grace. *Chatelaine*'s "salute" to this family stressed that, while anyone could economize grimly, there was "something special about young people like veteran Bill Menzie and his wife Marie, of Hamilton, who are buying their house, raising their children well, and doing it all with deep and satisfying happiness." While some readers might doubt that it was possible to run an attractive and charming home on so little, *Chatelaine*'s correspondent insisted that the Menzies proved it could be done and "told us *how* they do it." The vocabulary used to describe Bill and Marie emphasized skill, self-sufficiency, thrift, self-discipline, and strength of character – the traditional attributes of success in a producer economy.[38]

The Menzies' income came from Bill's wages as a Bell Telephone lineman plus a monthly $11 family allowance cheque, minus at source deductions for taxes, insurance, and company bonds. The remaining monthly income of $154 covered mortgage payments on a small house in a veterans' housing development, life insurance, utilities, groceries, a $10 monthly payment on a vacuum cleaner, and a few miscellaneous expenses, including a daily paper, tobacco, streetcar fare, and, most recently, a $3 payment to a pediatrician. There was no provision in the budget for clothing and no mention of a car. Both Bill and Marie practised personal thrift, in part because, as children, they had grown up on the prairies during the Depression, "when mere survival seemed an end in itself." Marie was part of a clothing exchange – whenever she received a garment, she gave another away "so that her closet is not filled with dresses of dubious value that she seldom wears."[39] Their son wore pyjamas that she had made from flour sacking, trimmed with colourful fabric. Father and son had matching sport shirts that she had sewn using government surplus cloth, embroidering their initials on the pockets. To eliminate impulse purchases, grocery shopping was limited to one trip a week. The cost of meat was a concern, but Marie had "clever ways" of stretching out the weekend roast ("but not day after day until the family is tired of it"). Marie's cooking skills were the subject of frequent compliments by the writer, and the article included her personal recipe for refrigerator rolls. Bill was finishing the upstairs of the house himself, and the magazine informed readers that he had proven a very competent carpenter.[40] For pleasure there was gardening, potluck dinners, conversation with friends, and occasional games of bridge. Earlier that year, Marie had rented out a room and provided breakfast to a boarder for two weeks, earning the money needed to join a book club: $15 a year paid "proudly" in advance. In a world that increasingly emphasized novelty, the Menzies slept beneath framed pieces of hand embroidery that read, in part, "Let me grow lovely growing old / So many old things do ... Why not I as well as they grow lovely growing old." *Chatelaine* concluded approvingly that these words were the key to the philosophy the Menzies lived every day, "in which things had been passed up but never sacrificed."[41]

The Menzies represented Canada in the early stages of the postwar transition. Their decisions were shaped by their experiences of depression and war. They exemplified traditional values associated with "a culture of character," exhibiting self-control, mastery, and a willingness to work hard.[42] Their skills and their roles were strictly gendered but extended to both production and consumption: Bill was a wage earner and a skilled craftsman; Marie had a broad range of competencies, with an emphasis on household production, supplemental wage-earning, and thrift. The author of the feature lauded Marie's abilities as an artist, seamstress, and cook, and commended Bill for his carpentry skills as well as his contribution to the war effort and steady job with opportunities for advancement.[43]

The Menzies made their way without complaining and without relying on others, thus embodying the attributes of the producer family unit, modestly amended for a world of waged employment that was moving towards higher levels of consumption and a more rapid turnover of goods. Discipline and self-denial remained key themes in a household that blended home-made and store-bought goods. Marie and Bill managed their purchases carefully, expressing themselves by making and doing rather than by buying.

At the same time, the family's participation in the marketplace was increasing. They purchased durable goods – including a refrigerator, a washing machine, and a vacuum cleaner – one item at a time by opening a charge account with reputable dealers of high standing in the community and carefully budgeting monthly payments. They bought quality goods from known manufacturers. "It must be both good and essential or it has no place in the Menzies' scheme of things," explained the writer. The family budget was limited, but *Chatelaine* assured readers that this was "a story of devotion and integrity; the story of two fine young people who have found real happiness for themselves by putting the welfare of their family ahead of their own pleasures."[44]

The Canadian family, however, was on the threshold of a new age. By 1951, two years after celebrating Marie and Bill's prudence, *Chatelaine* enthusiastically described the family budget as "a marvelous bit of household equipment" that promised to make "wishes come true." Money management had become a "successful formula for better living," and the place to begin budgeting was no longer with income but with "wishes."[45] Regardless of the modest role the government had envisioned for the domestic consumer, spending was on the rise. The family wish list was no longer regarded as frivolous or dangerous; it had become the tool that could provide the incentive to make budgeting work.[46]

THE WOODS FAMILY

With purchasing power on the rise and more goods available, Canadians were becoming increasingly comfortable with their role as consumers. Changing expectations, however, created new challenges. In 1954, the *Chatelaine* spotlight focused on Russell and Josephine (Russ and Joie) Woods, who were "in trouble trying to make $300 a month cover upkeep on two children, a new bungalow, a bigger car than they should have bought and a rash payment on a TV set." The Woods family was the subject of a series of three articles written by an expert budget adviser sent by *Chatelaine* to "help this family make both ends meet."[47] While the Menzies had been described as "special" and "interesting" in their ability to make do with limited means, the Woodses were "a family with a universal problem." Striving "to participate in Canada's climb toward a higher standard of living" while fighting the inroads of rising inflation, they were unable to make their income fit their expenses.[48] Young and inexperienced, overwhelmed by impulsive spending and bad budgeting decisions, the Woodses were having difficulty navigating the new world of consumer goods, instalment buying, and rising incomes. In the course of five years, *Chatelaine*'s "typical" Canadian family had become less, rather than more, competent. The focus of the series, entitled "We Sent an Expert to Help," was a "budget experiment with a real family." By following expert advice, the Woods family and *Chatelaine*'s readers would learn how to budget, research, and plan their purchases to obtain whatever they wanted most.[49]

Russ Woods was a music teacher in the Windsor public system, earning $4,450 annually before deductions for insurance, pension, taxes, and the Patriotic Fund – an income the article described as fairly typical of a white-collar family. Although both the Menzies and the Woodses had mortgages on their homes and had bought appliances on the instalment plan, the magazine had presented the Menzies as practised in self-denial and self-discipline. By comparison, it portrayed the Woodses as adrift in the world of consumer goods and easy credit, irresponsible in their money management and prone to impulsive purchases. When Russ, for example, had gone to test-drive a small $500 car, he returned with a $1,400 Pontiac and a debt to the Teachers' Credit Union at 6 percent interest. A few years earlier, Russ had "television fever" and bought a reconditioned set for $25 down. The family had second thoughts about the purchase but was unable to cancel the contract. The sales manager allowed them to apply the down payment towards a less expensive radio-phonograph, which continued to occupy a corner of the living room although it was already broken. While Russ was something of a hapless consumer, Joie was described as "a brave and expert practitioner of the penny-stretching arts." Her specialty dishes, which she nicknamed "conglomerations," combined ingredients to save on food costs (*Chatelaine* did not publish any of her recipes).[50]

The professional adviser, teaching Canadians to become more effective consumers, is central to the story. The expert brought in to help the Woods family was Sid Margolius, the author of the best-selling *How to Buy More for Your Money*.[51] Margolius insisted that the young family start with accurate record keeping and a long-range plan. The overall goal was to pay down debt and develop a cash reserve for replacements and repairs. Margolius described the budget as a muscle: the more it was used, the more effective it became. The problem the Woods family faced was not insufficient income, but insufficient "muscle," experience, and knowledge.[52] The solution was not to stop spending but to research and plan purchases, taking advantage of sales, buying in bulk, and keeping instalment payments to a minimum. The onus to control spending remained with the family, but they needed to serve a period of apprenticeship in order to learn to manage their spending. The objective was not to increase savings, beyond the creation of an emergency reserve fund, but to facilitate the accumulation of material goods. Budgeting was the means to increased consumption.

Chatelaine described readers as "pulling for" the Woodses, and the magazine returned periodically to see how they were making out.[53] By September, the family was one member larger, after the birth of a third son, and was virtually debt free. The budgeting techniques helped, but the family was also able to significantly increase its income. Russ had gained strength in his breadwinner role. He received a raise, started teaching at night school, tutored students, and found paying passengers to defray the costs of the commute to work.[54] The baby bonus, which provided a buffer, was used to help out with other budget items as needed. The family's rising income facilitated debt reduction and encouraged plans for future purchases.

A final report on the family in December 1954 revealed that Russ and Joie had "found new values, new purpose and a new security" through budgeting. Once "baffled," "frustrated," "impatient," and "unsure of themselves," they now had definite aims. "Before we knew what we wanted to do, now we know how to do it," explained Joie. Just as Russ had become a more competent breadwinner, Joie had become a more competent consumer. As the family's purchasing agent, she was planning, in order of desirability, the following acquisitions: an electric floor polisher, a new rug for the living room, and an electric clothes dryer. After making a thorough study of a particular field of merchandise, Joie would determine what type and model to buy, emphasizing quality rather than cheapness.[55] Margolius characterized Joie as "an unusually expert shopper" who believed "quite rightly ... that home management requires as much skill and thought as business management."[56] Although it was Russ' increased earnings that had turned the family budget from debt to surplus, *Chatelaine* emphasized the proficiency gained through planned spending rather than self-denial or increased income. Implicit in this series was the recognition that Canadian attitudes were changing: pejorative associations between excessive spending and the loss of self-control were softening. Yet, the writer suggests thoughtful planning legitimized increases in spending in a way that simple gains in income failed to do.

The stories of the Menzies and the Woodses offer condensed versions of the challenges many Canadian families were experiencing. While the domestic competencies of family members continued to be strictly gendered, they had shifted from the realm of making and production, exemplified by Bill and Marie Menzies, to the realm of buying and consumption. If the Menzies' lives epitomized the material limitations of the immediate postwar years, the Woods' reflected the opportunities of the economic expansion that followed. *Canadian Business Magazine* reported in October 1954 that the typical family income was $4,520.80 (Russ Woods earned $4,450 that year). Although taxes and some prices had increased, the spread between wages and the cost of basic necessities (shelter, clothing, and food) had improved considerably since the 1930s, leaving families with more income for discretionary spending. Accounting for increases in taxes and inflation, spendable income in 1930 dollars climbed from $420.45 in 1930 to $735.06 in 1954. Indeed, with increases in population and income, total spending on consumer goods and services was 261 percent greater in 1954 than in 1930. Savings had also increased: the average Canadian's savings soared from $8.62 in 1930 to $104.41 in 1953. During the same period, the Consumer Price Index rose by 53.4 percent from 1930 to 1953.[57]

Some purchases involved wartime savings and veterans' grants, but many others, particularly those involving durable goods such as cars, refrigerators, and stoves, relied on various forms of instalment debt. According to a 1948 Dominion Bureau of Statistics survey, the average Canadian family was running an annual deficit of $137. By 1956, the average Canadian family owed over 12 percent of its total income and paid out $135 a year just in interest charges. The average per capita instalment debt had increased threefold since 1942. Over 45 percent of owner-occupied single, detached, non-farm dwellings were mortgaged. The biggest users of credit were young middle-income families like the Woodses, who typically bought far more on instalment than did poor families. It was not unusual for young, middle-income families to have 40 percent of their income tied up in mortgage and instalment payments.[58]

The problem was not so much wages, which had generally kept pace with rising prices, but dramatic increases in new opportunities for consumption. Through the 1950s, spending on durable goods (particularly new automobiles) began to plateau, but spending on non-durable goods and services continued to rise. In 1957, Procter and Gamble reported that more than half of it sales volume came from products that had not existed in 1945. David Sarnoff, chairman of the board of RCA, a producer of radios and televisions, observed that, "80 percent of the products we are now selling did not exist ten years ago." For General Foods, the figure was 36 percent, and for the St. Regis Paper Company, 25 percent. The inventory of an average Dominion store rose from 1,000 items in the 1930s to 5,000 items by 1956, including the addition of many non-food items. Similarly, Loblaw stores stocked 4,000 items in regular inventory in 1952, and 6,000 to 8,000 by 1965. By the early 1960s, a typical North American supermarket was being offered 125 new or improved items weekly or about 6,500 annually. From these offerings, some 800 items might be added to the product mix each year while another 600 would be dropped.[59] The first Canadian shopping centres opened in 1949 and 1950; by 1956, there were sixty-four such centres nation-wide, forty-one of which were in Ontario.[60] Some Canadians, like the Woods family, were able to increase their incomes. Others turned to various forms of credit to access this expanding world of consumer goods. Faced with so many new choices, even a family that had once represented the Canadian ideal (white, educated, married, with a salaried, white-collar job) found itself in need of outside expertise. Of course, in the Woods' case, with professional intervention they were able to regain control, both of their "selves" and of their finances.

Chatelaine articles advising "how to borrow wisely" (1951) gave way to those asking "how much money should your family owe?" (1956).[61] In 1957, *Food for Thought,* Canada's magazine of adult education, explained to its readers that, over the past two decades, there had been tremendous strides in production, particularly of consumer goods, so that the "Canadian economy no longer depends on the export of agricultural products and raw materials, but increasingly on the sale of consumer goods at home." Consumption had become the key to prosperity. "Those of us who are now in our forties are often sharply aware of a great gulf between our thinking and that of young people in their twenties. Older Canadians can remember the standards of their childhood; thrift, hard work, 'pay as you go.'" In wartime, we were "expected to 'do without' as a patriotic duty ... In peace time, it is 'patriotic' to buy as much as possible. The financial structure has changed accordingly to encourage buying on time. 'Enjoy while you pay' is the new slogan."[62] Instalment buying, which had been associated with the improvident lower strata of society, was widely adopted by middle-income

Canadians. Spending patterns that previous generations regarded as self-indulgent and irresponsible were becoming more broadly accepted.

Indeed, the series on the Woods family and the responses to it (the article aroused considerable comment among *Chatelaine* readers, which will be examined in more detail later in the chapter) highlight growing tensions between old and new values: many Canadians still believed that taking on debt was wrong.[63] The solution, as *Chatelaine* implied, was to see the dilemma not as a moral problem but as a management problem. If the Woodses learned how to manage their finances, they could have everything they wanted. Of course, as the series itself showed, increases in income made domestic management quite a lot easier. With a steady white-collar job and opportunities to earn additional income, the Woods family was positioned to take advantage of expanding consumer opportunities. Many Canadian families were not as fortunate.

THE ROSES

In 1962, *Chatelaine* editors again selected an "average" Canadian family living in an "average Canadian suburb" as the subject of a feature story. "101 Ways to Save Money – and Look Better, Dress Better, Eat Better and Live Better" focused on the Rose family.[64] While the Woodses had required only a period of tutelage under a single self-help expert, the Rose family were advised by a small team of consultants and the staff of the Chatelaine Institute. The bulk of the feature (thirteen of sixteen pages) used the Roses to showcase expert advice on how to spend, grouping recommendations under headings such as "How to Eat Better and Save $200," "You Can Be Your Own Best Hairdresser and Save $26," "Have the Furniture You Really Want in 5 Years and Save," and so on. While the earlier articles had spent time introducing the feature family, the Rose family, Rita, Stan and their two children, take a back seat to *Chatelaine*'s detailed recommendations for food, fashion, home decorating, and practical spending advice. Stan Rose's near absence is especially noticeable in comparison with the attention given to his predecessors, Bill Menzie and Russ Woods. Stan's relative invisibility is consistent with historian Cynthia Comacchio's observation that fatherhood in the postwar era was associated almost exclusively with breadwinning. It is also an accurate representation of the growing geographic separation between the suburban home and the workplace.[65] The goal of *Chatelaine*'s intervention was to demonstrate how this conscientious family could improve its overall standard of living by improving its spending practices. The family moved to the background of the story, and the magazine itself became the arbiter of appropriate expenditures.

Rita and Stan already practised certain economies and were proud of their home-management skills. According to *Chatelaine*, Stan's salary of $4,900 was close to the national average for salaried workers.[66] Their three-bedroom bungalow, bought for $16,300, exceeded the bank's mortgage-qualification limit, but the bank relented when it took into account their sound financial status and Stan's steady employment record. They had saved a down payment when Rita was working, before starting a family, and, as a matter of principle, had agreed to postpone future purchases until they could pay cash for the items. The family ate meals in the kitchen while the dining area sat unfurnished, and they listened to "semi-classical" records bought at low cost through a record club and played on a standard portable player. Rita looked forward to owning a high fidelity phonograph "some day." Family allowance cheques were not part of the budget, going directly into a trust savings account paying 4.5 percent interest.

Compared with Marie and Joie, Rita was less of a producer or purchasing agent and more of a passive vehicle through whom *Chatelaine* experts could demonstrate ideas that would help Canadian families lead less expensive but considerably more fashionable lives. Most of their recommendations were far from lavish, many involved a combination of bought and do-it-yourself effort. Rita's beauty make-over, for example, began with six cuts a year at a top salon (because "a good cut is worth every penny") but would be maintained with home permanents and the setting and styling techniques demonstrated by the magazine's beauty editor. Similarly, Rita had come to rely on convenience foods in her earlier days as a working wife; now *Chatelaine* redirected her menus towards more time-intensive but less costly dishes. The recipes in the article were devised by *Chatelaine* and were prepared and professionally photographed in the magazine's test kitchen. In a striking comparison with the stringencies required by Marie Menzie, *Chatelaine* showed Rita how to transform two dresses and a light-weight coat described as "three white elephants," into "three of the smartest and most useful outfits in her wardrobe"[67] (see Figure 9). *Chatelaine's* experts incorporated a new aesthetic dimension into many of their suggestions, for example, encouraging Rita to reinvent herself with a new haircut and wardrobe makeovers. At the same time, they continued to point out opportunities to substitute labour for money and reduce costs, recognizing that

FIGURE 9 Even as incomes rose, Canadians remained cautious consumers, with visions of affluence tempered by limited incomes and a legacy of thrift. In 1963, *Chatelaine* examined the spending patterns of Rita and Stan Rose, described as a "typical" Canadian family. The magazine's experts demonstrated how the Roses – and, by extension, all families – could participate more fully as consumers in modern society. | "101 Ways to Save Money – and Look Better, Dress Better, Eat Better and Live Better," *Chatelaine*, January 1962, 38–39.

How to perform a miracle with a make-over— AND SAVE

Two dresses and a suit for $7.19. The miracle of make-over makes it possible. Read how Rita Rose transformed three white elephants into three of the smartest and most useful outfits in her wardrobe

BY VIVIAN WILCOX *Chatelaine Fashion Editor*

29 cents is all it cost to streamline this dress

$3.87 transforms an old coat into a new party dress

$3.03 makes this transformation

PHOTOGRAPHS BY JOHN HERBERT

Chatelaine · January 1962

38

it was still necessary for many readers to negotiate between store-bought and home-made goods, according to their particular circumstances, abilities, and incomes.

Growing affluence allowed for an extended chain of purchasing, involving more goods, a longer time frame with planned purchases, and an ongoing stream of spending to avert obsolescence. The Roses were able to gear their expenditures towards an ideal furniture plan because they were already setting aside $200 annually for furnishings. Their acquisition list, which began with an extension dining table and two chairs in 1962 and concluded with framed prints, plants, and bunching tables in 1966, indicated a level of detail and long-term commitment to spending significantly beyond that contemplated by the earlier families. In fact, many of *Chatelaine*'s recommended ways to save were really different ways to spend. The magazine addressed its readers as consumers in articles like this feature as well as in the advertisements. For example, readers were instructed to pay bills by cash to avoid cheque charges and were advised to buy season tickets rather than individual tickets if they expected to attend entertainment events regularly. In a significant change in attitude and best budgetary practices, *Chatelaine* urged readers to compare the price of repairing durable goods against the price of replacement, noting that many items had dropped in price while repair charges had increased. As the story title implied, saving was not the opposite of spending but the means to leverage spending and obtain more.

The intensification of consumer capitalism and the consolidation of new practices is evident in the progression of the stories on these three families. The Menzies (1949) bought as little as possible and were presented as largely self-sufficient. The Woodses (1954) tended to buy impulsively, a trait they learned to control by training and self-discipline. Once managed, their purchasing plan could extend in small increments into the future. In the Roses' case (1962), the purchasing impulse was directed towards an extended network of objects, including their five-year plan for home furnishings, comprehensive enough to include artwork and accessories.[68] Similarly, the personal shopping of each woman expanded: Marie had a single new dress (her first in four and a half years), whereas Rita was encouraged to update her wardrobe and personal appearance. While Marie valued continuity and making old things new, Rita was self-consciously modern, if not before, then certainly after *Chatelaine*'s intervention. The systematic expansion of domestic consumption was accompanied by a change in emphasis from reliance on one's self to reliance on experts, and a shift in focus from non-pecuniary values to an emphasis on appearances and lifestyles assembled through the increasing, but always judicious, purchase of goods and services. Even while counseling moderation, *Chatelaine* encouraged spending.[69]

The budgeting adjustments recommended by *Chatelaine* for the second and third of its families promised to help the Woodses and the Roses make better use of the opportunities available to them through the mass market. Although the magazine coaxed the families to spend, it also advised that purchases were to be undertaken with caution and calculation and were to involve comparison shopping, expert guidance, and a long-term budget. All three families noted a preference for cash over credit. "We're happier when we know we don't owe anything" Rita Rose explained, "and we don't mind waiting for the things we'd like to have. We don't want many luxuries."[70] Lip service to traditional values lingered, but all three families used instalment payments to advance their standard of living, and each successive family had more of them.

Thinking of the family unit in terms of its consumption practices gave increasing attention to the role of the purchasing wife over that of the breadwinning husband. The 1949 visit to the Menzies had shown both husband and wife in the roles of producer, consumer, and wage earner. By 1954, Russ Woods was a wage earner rather than a producer, with little competence in the modern marketplace. In the course of the series, the husband-as-consumer was further marginalized and pushed out of the home, working evenings as well as days to finance purchases made by the household's increasingly skilled female "consumption expert." By 1963, the home had become a centre of consumption, and Stan Rose was all but absent from the story.

In 1950, the budgeting expert who would soon be advising the Woods family, had already told *Maclean's* readers that "one of the biggest news stories of the decade and one you won't find on the financial page [is that] ... more women are handling family finances than ever before and experts say they make a better job of it than their husbands."[71] Margolius described women as "less sentimental" about money than men. Pride never got in their way; they dealt with whoever gave them the best rates and were persistent in their pursuit of financial goals. Margolius was careful to reassure readers that women's growing expertise in family finances would not change the fundamental order of things. In his own case, he explained, "rather than resigning any male prerogatives I feel like the chairman of the board. As for womanly extravagances, I find my wife is definitely tighter with cash now that she has charge of it than when I doled it out to her. Then, what I gave her she spent. Now ... I can't get my wife to part with a dollar." Husbands, by comparison, were regarded as unlikely to "feel, pull, rub, squeeze, stretch, press and smell" the merchandise or to comparison shop.[72] The value placed on skilled consumption and increasing feminine independence was potentially challenging to male authority. Margolius restored the breadwinner's authority by reframing his role in the household to that of chairman of the board. Although his wife now controlled the shopping, she still had to report to the highest-ranking officer in the family unit. *Maclean's* made a similar point in its discussion of children's allowances, observing that "nearly all educators stress that, whenever possible, the father should pay the allowance personally instead of handing the job to mother. That way a child begins to understand father's place in the home."[73] The role of the housewife, explained the editor of *Food for Thought*, a publication of the Canadian Association for Adult Education, had shifted. The "former attributes of a competent housewife – the ability to sew, to cook, to knit" – were less relevant. "Today the good housewife is one who can *buy* intelligently," navigating the pressures of advertising and a bewildering quantity of goods.[74]

Awareness of the collective impact of the "housewifely dollar" brought renewed attention to the Canadian Association of Consumers. As *Canadian Business Magazine* explained, in "the early days businessmen regarded CAC as a group of overly enthusiastic women who were out to make life difficult for them. Today ... CAC has been successful in divorcing itself from the 'lunatic fringe' and communist-front troublemakers" and has become "a power not to be dismissed lightly by government or industry."[75] Now perceived as, literally, buying into the system, Canadian women and the CAC were celebrated by business.

The shift from managing scarcity to managing relative abundance, and from budgeting to buying, should not be exaggerated. The emphasis on obtaining consumer goods continued to be balanced by messages to plan spending and keep expectations modest. In the pages of *Chatelaine*, a mortgaged home, a car (possibly second-hand), labour-saving devices bought on the installment plan, book clubs, and record collections were the stuff of

Business and government
listen to this consumer's voice

FIGURE 10 As domestic sales rose, Canadian businesses celebrated the power of
the "housewifely dollar." Grocery chains extolled the abundance of frozen, instant,
and prepared foods, and the modern conveniences of the supermarket available to
"today's busy homemakers." | *Canadian Business Magazine*, February 1956, 72.
Used with permission of Rogers Media Inc. All rights reserved.

dreams. Although wives and mothers did the majority of the shopping,
husbands developed areas of masculine specialization, including the purchase
of major appliances, family vacations, recreational real estate, and expenditures associated with lawn and yard care and maintenance of the exterior of
the house.[76] The families that *Chatelaine* selected for presentation remained
modest rather than gaudy. Their materialism was primarily oriented towards
home and family. However, good money management no longer meant
self-denial; instead, it was discussed in the mass media as a matter of making
choices and ordering priorities to ensure that each family was able to direct
its income towards satisfying its needs and achieving its wants. Instalment
loans, home mortgages, and payroll deduction plans – primarily vehicles
for home mortgages and durable goods – blurred the difference between
savings and spending. Taking on debt by instalment payments or department

store credit served to mobilize the small surpluses of working- and middle-class families, incorporating those who were otherwise "unexploitable" as a force for consumption, but it also imposed practical constraints.[77]

Reading about the experiences of the Menzies, the Woodses, and the Roses gave legitimacy to new attitudes, presenting images of a new way of life and instructions on how to achieve it. The baseline of necessity changed, making ends meet remained a persistent theme.[78] The tension between desire and debt was not hidden; it was addressed directly in stories about trade-offs and planned purchasing in which thrift had become less a matter of not spending than of spending wisely. Consumption was valourized as an orderly and disciplined process. The ideal Canadian consumer was rational, restrained, and responsible, with irrational impulses subdued by self-discipline.

A money-management guide issued in 1962 by Household Finance of Canada captured the limits of postwar consumerism, encouraging house-holders to shop "intelligently" by defining their values and goals and knowing their requirements. The guide advised consumers to create a personal buying guide for future purchases by collecting articles, advertisements, and information from various product-rating services.[79] "Responsible consumership," the company assured its readers, was "a goal that can be reached by every shopper." The publication concluded with a checklist that promised to help shoppers evaluate their shopping skills. Questions focused on consumer practices and motivation: "Is your spending an expression of your individual and family values and goals?" "Are you in the habit of using a well-planned shopping list to be sure you get the things you need and want?" "Do you compare prices and quality of various items before you buy?" "Are you using your consumer power effectively in the part you play in our national economy?" Those who answered "yes" were, in effect, given permission to spend. There was no need to merely make do if one followed the rules and spent wisely. The purchase of new goods, whether from cash savings or through regular installment payments, had become a part of being modern.

Resistance

Although expanding consumption practices were publicized and legitimized by the mass media and corroborated by extended discussions in academic studies, positions of resistance and contestation emerged. Many questioned the growing dominance of consumer values – even those who welcomed increasing choice continued to emphasize the need for thrift, the risks of debt, and the significant gap that remained between expectations and achievements.

Chatelaine regularly turned space in its letters page over to readers who disapproved of new trends. Many of the letter writers seemed to view themselves as lone voices holding fast to traditional values. Several objected that *Chatelaine*'s feature families were atypical in their income and unrealistic in their spending patterns. Readers aired such complaints regardless of whether the feature families had incomes generally in line with Canadian medians (like the Roses) or somewhat above the national average (like the Woodses).[80] Lower-income readers, who were often, though not always, from rural regions, argued that the editors had erred in their selection of representative families.[81]

Criticisms that began with the family budget frequently expanded to condemn lifestyle choices. The series on the Woods family aroused particularly strong responses, highlighting moral concerns surrounding new patterns of domestic spending. The two aspects of the series that generated the most comments were the Woods' level of indebtedness and the absence of church contributions in their budget. Often these themes were linked, as in this response by a reader who expressed outrage at the Woods' lifestyle and budgeting efforts: "Tell them ... to get down on their knees and ask God to take away the foolish pride that makes them want to live beyond their means." "Why should a family earning $300 a month require help to budget their income? I will tell you why – because God has been left out of their scheme of things," wrote another reader. Budgeting experts might describe debt as a "useful tool," but a segment of *Chatelaine*'s readership continued to regard debt as evidence of moral weakness. Readers who regarded thrift as a core value of Protestantism, good citizenship, and the key to personal and national prosperity believed that the availability of consumer credit destabilized society by making it easier for people to live lives devoted to instant gratification and hedonism. As one distressed reader observed, "If other families were selfish like the Woods the world would be more pagan than ever."[82]

Even readers who saw debt primarily as a problem of financial management were "appalled at the thought that there were those who could not raise two children and keep out of debt on nearly $300 a month. I would be in heaven on this income ... Getting into debt is entirely out of the question as we could never get along at all if we did." "We pay as we go or do without" was a maxim that continued to have followers.[83] Reader responses revealed a disjuncture between traditional values of savings and self-denial and the growing material aspirations and opportunities of postwar Canada. Those who had scrimped during the Depression and war could be critical of the shift from a household budget built around hard work and thrift to what they criticized as a modern lifestyle geared to leisure. One letter writer, for example, scrutinized the photos accompanying the article on the Woods family, observing that, "according to their picture they have much waste land that could be producing raspberries, strawberries, currants, boysenberries, tomatoes ... To use more stews, soups, puddings ... Out of each cheque to put some in the bank. On less than half his salary I sent my three children to university."[84]

Chatelaine seemed caught off guard by the vehemence of reader responses and mounted a defence of the Woodses. The magazine contacted clergymen to ascertain typical church contributions. Readers were assured that the Woods family budget was in keeping with current charitable practices. In effect, *Chatelaine* moved to defend the Woods against charges of "what ought to be" with evidence of "what is," juxtaposing new normative standards with the moral objections raised by readers. Such an approach avoided a direct battle with traditional morality while still acknowledging the existence of social constraints. Of course, the very fact that these concerns were published in the magazine suggests the degree to which dissent could be expressed and managed within the expanding framework of consumer society.

Chatelaine and a growing number of Canadians were willing to accept that increasing consumption would not subvert the social order. American historian Gary Cross proposes that postwar consumption succeeded in part because it could overcome contradictions that few wanted to choose between.[85] The presentation of these *Chatelaine* families supports Cross' proposition: family enrichment remained central to virtuous consumerism, but responsible spending could involve taking on debt; mass-produced goods could be used to remake personal identity as well as denote group membership, and research and careful planning could bridge the divide between older values of thrift and new aspirations. These were years of cautious consumerism, with families adjusting their roles, attitudes, and practices to take advantage, as best they could, of unprecedented consumer opportunities. Buying things would help Canadians become modern, provided spending was kept within the limits of the family budget.

Chapter Eight

ACADEMIC ENCOUNTERS

When historians consider how Canada's intellectual and cultural community responded to mass consumption, they consistently identify a pattern of concern, distaste, and disapproval. This approach understates the radical changes underway among younger scholars developing new methodologies of investigation in the decades following the war, and also underestimates the powerful legacy of anti-modernism they worked within.[1] After the war, many academics – much like the writers at *Chatelaine* magazine – became interested in the lives of ordinary Canadians. They recognized that mass-produced goods and entertainments were extremely popular and were not about to disappear. Without advocating materialism, a select group of theorists and cultural commentators acknowledged that new consumption practices were a socially necessary and meaningful aspect of life in an affluent society. They did not celebrate or embrace consumerism, but their work marked a significant break with long-standing patterns of elitism and dismissal of mass culture.

The Canadian commentators and academics examined in this chapter made deliberate efforts to reach beyond the ivory tower. Insofar as they saw themselves developing theories that could lay the basis for practical interventions promising to solve the social problems they diagnosed, they welcomed opportunities to reach wider audiences. Approaching consumer society as scholars and educators, they encouraged Canadians to think about their consumer identities and sought to increase rather than decrease consumer consciousness. Greater awareness, postwar intellectuals believed, opened the way to more informed choices. Concerned and intrigued by changes in the daily lives of ordinary families – such as the Menzies, the Woods, and the Roses – some members of this new generation of scholars began to deliberately connect their academic practices with the advance of consumer capitalism. They identified a role for their work in helping Canadians negotiate the pressures and tensions of mass commercial society, while still insisting – either explicitly or by implication – that affluence should have ideals and aspirations beyond material comfort.[2]

The scholars considered in this chapter were aware of each other's ideas; however, they did not form a coordinated movement. Rather, they worked in relatively close proximity in Canada's larger universities, primarily in Toronto and Ottawa, often referencing each other's work. Generational change and wartime service brought younger scholars with more varied backgrounds into the academy. Middle-class consumers were no longer the anonymous masses, but family and neighbours. Most Canadian scholarly studies were popularized in the same few media outlets, most commonly in *Maclean's Magazine*, on CBC radio, and in Canada's major daily papers, particularly the *Toronto Star*. The majority of these academics were Canadian born – the oldest between 1910 and 1913 and the youngest between 1920 and 1923 – though several were British educated. They lived through the Great Depression and the Second World War and emerged as leading intellectual figures in the 1950s and 1960s. The focus of this chapter is on the early stages of their academic careers, some of which evolved in different directions.

The academics who studied Canadian consumer behaviours in the postwar period were also participants in a larger North American discussion. Best-selling books by American thinkers offered competing narratives, with arguments playing out against the rebuilding of Europe and rising Cold War tensions. Capitalism's intellectual boosters, including political scientist Seymour Martin Lipset and modernization theorist Walter Rostow, asserted that material plenty, education, and the widespread ownership of goods were the prerequisites of a strong democracy. They regarded rising levels of consumption, in which basic needs were satisfied and citizens had disposable income for additional goods, as an attribute of advanced societies and saw the United States as the foremost example of such a society.[3] Capitalism's critics, on the other hand, connected material abundance with political apathy, the manipulative power of advertising, the rapid growth of bureaucratic organization, and rising psychological tensions. Choice was an illusion, they argued, and inequality was on the rise. The creation of artificial needs and pressures for social conformity were addressed in a number of controversial best-selling books and in the newspapers, magazines, and television programs that discussed them. Titles included *The Lonely Crowd* (1950) by David Riesman, *The Organization Man* (1956) by William Whyte, *The Hidden Persuaders* (1957) by Vance Packard, and, probably the most influential critique of consumer society, *The Affluent Society* (1958) by John Kenneth Galbraith.[4] Taught to think as consumers, ordinary people, these authors maintained, strove to increase their spending in a futile search for well-being that served only to guarantee profits to industry. These authors found large audiences in Canada, including within the academic community.

In the decade immediately following the war, some young Canadian scholars began developing innovative approaches towards commercial culture and consumer behaviours. Their interest in consumers stood in marked counterpoint to the long-standing refusal of the Canadian intelligentsia to consider mass consumption seriously. For a new generation popular tastes and mass-made goods were no longer simply the negative other of socially correct values, and poverty was no longer a sufficient explanation for consumer preferences. This is not to suggest that a cohort of academics emerged in the aftermath of the war endorsing mass consumption. They did not. They continued to examine society from positions within the academy, rooted in their commitments to intellectual effort, literary theory, and the social sciences. However, they were determined to analyse new modes of consumption rigorously. They did not reject consumer society out of hand; rather, they gave it legitimacy as an important subject of sustained academic attention. With an influence reaching beyond the ivory tower, their work helped establish the image of Canada as a modern consumption-oriented society.

The Social Sciences

After a few years of uncertainty, Canada's postwar economy gained traction. Statistics documenting the construction of new homes and increasing ownership of durable goods, furniture, radio sets, and, increasingly, televisions showed living standards on the rise. Canada's affluence was consistently more modest than that in the United States, but commercial culture spread rapidly across North America. Sociologists were not so much concerned about rising material abundance in itself; rather, they focused on the changing relationship between commercial goods and social status and on the social dynamics they saw as directing consumers to purchase similar goods. Emphasizing the symbolic and communicative dimensions of consumption, they developed new understandings of society that granted consumers and commercial goods a more central place in the social order. Of course, recognition that consumer spending had a social dimension was not new. In *The Theory of the Leisure Class* (1899), Thorstein Veblen had coined the term "conspicuous consumption" to describe spending by the wealthy to build prestige and establish social dominance. Difficult relationships with material goods were a staple of Depression-era literature. Interest in consumption in the late 1940s and 1950s, however, was different, associated neither with great wealth nor with dire poverty but with the expanding middle class. The strong wartime economy, veterans' benefits, and the postwar boom created a broad middle class that lacked status according to traditional markers of family, education, and occupation but that enjoyed considerable (especially by historical standards) economic and organizational resources. And yet, most sociologists refused to simply associate material abundance with well-being and increased choice. In fact, many argued that affluence and rapid change had eroded traditions and introduced new social pressures, increasing psychological tensions. These concerns were often the starting point of their efforts to explain, classify, and categorize consumers and consumer behaviours. Canadian sociologists John Seeley, Alexander Sim, and Elizabeth Loosley, co-authors of *Crestwood Heights*, an important study of suburban life, spoke for many when they speculated that North America was witnessing, not simply the attrition, but the "pulverization" of tradition.[5] While some social scientists proposed a functional role for consumption as a vehicle for social cohesion and belonging, others saw it as a source of differentiation and status competition. And, while some critics belittled consumers as passive shoppers who followed the dictates of the mass media, others argued that, when closely observed, consumers were not especially homogeneous and certainly were not passive in their choices. These differences in interpretation emerged within a common framework that saw consumer behaviours as socially significant and meaningful.[6]

The first of these projects, and perhaps the best-known at the time, began as a study commissioned by the Canadian Mental Health Association to examine child-rearing practices in a typical Canadian suburb. The project, carried out from 1948 to 1953, placed sociologists in seven community schools in an upper-middle-class suburb of a central Canadian city easily recognized as Toronto but treated as an anonymous prototype. Their mission was to investigate the influence of social and cultural factors on mental health of students and also to evaluate the effectiveness of new strategies related to mental health education. Methodologies of data collection included observation and interviews in the school and in the home, psychological testing, diaries, access to census and school records, and regularly scheduled classroom discussions. The results of this work were presented in a number of scholarly papers and also in a book, *Crestwood Heights: A Study of the Culture of Suburban Life,* that became a best-selling sensation in both Canada and the United States in 1951. Sociologist John Seeley was the director of the project.[7]

The community chosen as the subject of this study and given the pseudonym of Crestwood Heights was actually Forest Hill, a thinly disguised and widely recognized upper-middle-class suburb of Toronto. Although this neighbourhood was more affluent than most, the co-authors claimed that it was representative of "what life is *coming to be* in North America." Crestwood Heights, they explained, "*is* normative or 'typical,' not in the sense of the average of an aggregate of such communities," but as the "norm to which middle-class community life" is moving towards, the "familiar approximation" of the North American dream – a dream of material abundance to be achieved and maintained by struggle and sacrifice. Although Crestwood Heights was not representative of how the majority of people lived, it was representative of how they *wanted* to live. It represented the goal of all those who "struggle to translate the promise of America into a concrete reality for themselves, and, even more important, for their children." It was a "thing of dreams" pinned down in time and space, but it was also part of a tradition of dreaming, "a dream of material heaven in the here and now" that was "perhaps as old as the world itself." In Crestwood Heights the authors believed that this dream took on a "specific content."[8]

In presenting the results of their research, Seeley, Sim, and Loosley adopted the tone and level of scrutiny recently popularized by anthropologists such as Margaret Mead discussing the rites and rituals of "primitive tribes" in faraway places. In *Crestwood Heights,* suburban families were specimens once exotic and familiar. Husbands and wives were described as post-industrial workers, with daily occupations that involved managing information and manipulating symbols. While the husband was at work in the city, the wife was responsible for establishing the family's position in suburban society. Each was an expert in his or her own realm.[9] Roles were gender specific within a household, which operated as an economic unit dedicated to consumption, anchored by a specialized wage-earner and a specialized wage-spender. As an expert in the realm of culture, the home-maker had to be aware of current decorating trends but also had to make strategic decisions about which items would be retained (in order to link the family with important traditions) and which needed to be changed to denote upward mobility. This analysis built on Veblen's notion of status competition insofar as social position was validated by public display. Crestwood Heights families were highly deliberate in their efforts to lever-age symbolic goods to maximum advantage. If the home was to be an effective exhibition of status and an aid to the male career, it needed to be symbolically prepared and continually "defended against attack."[10]

The Crestwood home was not a place of peace or ease for any member of the family. "No citizen of Big City or its hinterland, casting a longing and covetous eye towards Crestwood Heights, could easily envisage a life of leisure there. Should he, by some stroke of fortune or through his own exertions, enter the promised land, he will fully accept continuing work and increasing anxiety as the price he must pay if he does not wish to be cast out of his paradise." The stakes surrounding consumption were high, and decisions about home decorating, holiday celebrations, summer camps, and school clubs often became a source of tension in the family. Indeed, the researchers described the suburban home rather dramatically as "a solution to the problem of survival."[11] The dominant institutional emphasis in the community was child rearing. The residents of Crestwood Heights were almost all new arrivals in the upper middle class. In the pursuit of upward mobility, the measure of ultimate success was the production of children who would perpetuate the values and accomplishments of the parents. Children, especially teenagers, were pressured both to express their individuality and to honour the family's commitment to the pursuit of upward mobility by doing well in school and in extracurricular activities. Happiness and success "are often used as though interchangeable terms."[12]

The Crestwood Heights project was intended to be therapeutic and not merely observational. It was the first full-scale sociological study of a suburban community, unique in its psychological focus and in its ambition to improve the life of the community.[13] In the first part of the study, the

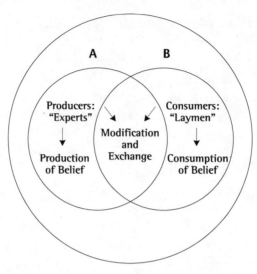

FIGURE 11 Just as the suburban family was a consumption unit for material goods produced elsewhere, it was also a consumption unit for ideas, views, theories, and opinions produced elsewhere by core specialists. Seeley, Sim, and Loosley referred to this as the "Belief Market." As the practices and values of consumer society infiltrated the social sciences, the drive for novelty (on the part of audiences) and recognition (on the part of aspiring experts) led to the abandonment and replacement of one approach after another. Therapy became a consumer commodity. | John R. Seeley, R. Alexander Sim, and Elizabeth W. Loosley, *Crestwood Heights: A Study of the Culture of Suburban Life* (Toronto: University of Toronto Press, 1956), 343. Reprinted with permission of the publisher.

authors described the complex and reciprocal relationship between the residents who stocked their homes with the newest goods and the people who supplied them with these goods. The home had shifted from a production unit to "a consumption unit" relying on "ideas, views, theories, opinions that are produced elsewhere ... by a core of persons specialized for such production." As the study unfolded, the authors found themselves personally being drawn into the socio-economic system of consumerism. Seeley referred to the relationship that evolved between the sociologists and the community as the "transaction system" and the "belief market"[14] (see Figure 11).

The second part of the book took a closer look at this relationship. Seeley observed that, on the supply side of the belief market, the producers of beliefs were the members of the team studying Crestwood Heights. They were specialists in human relations, claiming expertise in the highly competitive and emerging field of childhood mental health. Practitioners in the field of community mental health, which was subject to the vagaries of public funding, tended to be young academics in search of a theory that would establish their reputation. On the demand side of the relationship were well-meaning and caring families who adopted new beliefs in mental health and child rearing with the same speed, enthusiasm, and effort to attain the current best with which they greeted material fads and fashions. The cycle of demand and supply brought a quick succession of experts to the community offering new ideas and solutions that were, Seeley suggested, doomed to failure by high expectations and constant change. Indeed, Seeley concluded that the study had "abundantly made clear" that this community, although "rich in all the means ordinarily thought of as contributory to mental health," showed no improvement, despite five years of effort. "No forcing of the data, no optimism, no sympathy with aims can lead us to suggest that mental health in the community is sensibly better than elsewhere." Methods of child rearing and education were in constant flux in Crestwood Heights and in modern Canadian society. Classroom interventions by the Crestwood Heights team had revealed students struggling with mental tensions but were of no help in resolving them. Seeley concluded that the techniques that had been introduced by the experts were, at best, palliative and, at worst, had exacerbated the situation. More money had not brought more happiness.[15]

Crestwood Heights was widely reviewed in the Canadian mainstream press, the academic press, and in intellectual journals such as the *New York Times Review of Books, Commentary,* and *Public Opinion Quarterly*. It was selected as a choice of the Basic Book Club in the United States.[16] The University of Toronto Press promoted the book before its release with a series of dramatic teaser ads in the *Globe and Mail,* with captions such as "What Counts in Crestwood Heights? What You Are or What You Have?," "Why Do People Want to Move to Crestwood Heights?," and "The School or the Family – Which Counts More in Crestwood Heights?"[17] After the book appeared, controversial headlines in many of the nation's daily papers focused on the mental health issues of suburban residents. The authors' findings were the subject of an extended follow-up series in the *Toronto Star*. For five consecutive months, the book topped the Toronto Public Library's list of books in demand.[18]

The mainstream press tended to focus on Part 1 of the book – that is, on the details of suburban life and the documentation of mental health issues. For the academic community, the key message was different. Seeley's conclusions made it clear that the efforts of social scientists and the ex-tended team of professionals had been overwhelmed by the penetration of marketplace-like mechanisms into the field of raising children. The power of consumer society had transformed sociology into a therapeutic com-modity, circulating like any other consumer good. The cycle of purchase, consumption, and rapid replacement, Seeley found, undermined the sci-entific process. The ideas of experts were tried and abandoned in the drive for novelty by audiences desperate for guidance. In the end, the Crestwood Heights research team came to doubt that their expertise and authority, rooted in academic theory, could be sustained in the setting of consumer society.

The Crestwood authors were not unsympathetic towards their subjects; however, they often interpreted new consumer behaviours as pathological, adopted by Canadian families in response to the erosion of tradition and to the need to establish and defend their status in a highly mobile society, and also as part of the shift to matriarchal dominance in suburban settings. Insofar as the authors approached the community as therapists rather than theorists, a critical bias was embedded in their program of research, intended from the outset to solve social problems.

Other sociologists approached consumer behaviours from a different perspective. In 1955, Howard Roseborough, a Canadian studying at Har-vard, co-authored with David Riesman (author of the surprise 1950 best-seller *The Lonely Crowd*) an influential article that coined the term "standard package."[19] The standard package, as described by Roseborough and Riesman, was less about the possession of material goods than about mem-bership in a particular social group or subgroup. Like the *Crestwood Heights* authors, Riesman and Roseborough believed that contemporary consump-tion choices were socially and culturally driven. However, while Seeley and his co-authors associated postwar consumerism with the fracturing of social bonds, Roseborough and Riesman saw a dynamic evolving society in which individuals used their purchases to create meaning and build social bonds. Consumption choices seemed non-discretionary because many people made similar decisions, but the authors insisted that pursuit of the standard package was an adaptive behaviour and not the result of mass production or advertising. Roseborough and Riesman noted that, while the lowering of social barriers suggested a society moving towards a "fairly uniform middle majority life style," the goods that made up each family's package were assembled over time. Even though the overall structure of choices might suggest social conformity, each purchase was distinct and allowed for variety and self-expression. Indeed, the newest research, they noted, revealed multiple standard packages corresponding to different reference subgroups, localized by region, ethnic group, and occupation. Consumers made selections from a repertoire of available goods. Their selections gained meaning in relationship to other available choices but were also connected to aspects of personal identity, including age, gender, and most especially career. Roseborough and Riesman identified a performative aspect to consumption that foreshadowed later post-modern understandings, as people bought up, down, or in anticipation of their future social standing. The standard package, the authors concluded, was more open ended than its critics claimed. Regardless of "the perception of uniformity, there are real choices to be made." The "specter of uniformity," they insisted, was greatly exaggerated.[20]

Addressing the Canadian Political Science Association in 1960, Roseborough hypothesized that consumer spending was deeply integrated into the functioning of modern society. Purchases of commercial goods and services were instrumental in processes of group integration, motivation, and tension management. Spending was not about status but about belonging. Ownership of the minimum standard package signified to observers that the members of a household were "members in good standing," committed to society's values.[21] Roseborough noted that although the package varied with social status, it was relatively invariant in relation to moderate changes in income. Families tended to level up or level down to different standard packages. Those with incomes below a particular threshold spent somewhat beyond their means; families with incomes above the threshold directed discretionary dollars to prestige goods, impulse purchases, and savings. Propensities to spend (or to save) were structured by social factors rather than by economic needs. People purchased the goods "necessary for cultural, not biological, survival."[22] Far from eroding social solidarities, Roseborough argued, consumer spending played an instrumental role in stabilizing society.

Roseborough and Riesman discussed consumption as a socially necessary and meaningful activity. Identifying functional reasons for consumer behaviours made them more "natural," if not uncontroversial. The authors also asserted that consumers had a high degree of agency. Not every choice was conscious, but, as Roseborough explained, spending decisions took on meaning because they were choices made between alternatives within the scaffolding of the social order.[23] Roseborough especially sought to integrate consumer spending into new analytical models of society, proposing that consumption provided functional solutions to existential social problems, problems that all social systems were required to solve if that society were to survive. The standard package was an effective means of social integration because the goods in the package were simultaneously broadly accessible to the majority of the population and also somewhat flexible, allowing for personal style, regional variation, and leveling "up to" or "down from" according to factors such as age and social position. The ideas developed by Roseborough and Riesman were extremely influential, particularly in advancing academic research into processes of consumer socialization.[24]

Other sociologists, focusing less on the cultural and social frameworks of consumer behaviour, emphasized the economic constraints that restricted spending choices. The notion that suburban residents should be seen as economic pioneers was central to the work of S.D. Clark, a respected mid-career academic working to establish a department of sociology at the University of Toronto. Clark theorized the suburbs as the most recent of a series of economic frontiers. Suburban settlements, he proposed, were the creation of a "great house-hungry population."[25] Young families wanted houses, and they moved to where they were affordable. In the postwar period, this meant the suburbs: suburban housing was produced by large, integrated developers along quasi-industrialized lines on raw land, and new home purchases were eligible for financial assistance as part of the government's support for the postwar economy. The buyers of suburban housing were typically young families, with no substantial savings and modest incomes. The purchase of a new home, Clark observed with some concern, often had the effect of lowering a family's overall standard of living. Taking on the burden of a mortgage committed families to an ongoing stream of expenditures and instalment payments. Suburban migration was creating a debtor society.[26]

And yet Clark insisted that the provision of housing followed the rules of commodity exchange in a free market: consumers made largely rational choices among the goods made available by the market; the market made goods available in response to consumer desires. Families, in other words, were freely exercising their prerogatives. Clark observed, much as Roseborough had, that the majority of families bought up to or slightly beyond what they could afford. Those who could afford more than the down payment required in any particular area tended to look elsewhere. The choice of neighbourhood was determined almost entirely by affordability. Thus, it was the sifting characteristics of housing prices, rather than a suburban mindset, that created relatively homogeneous neighbourhoods. Clark did not deny that suburban society suffered many deprivations, including isolation, financial burdens, and a lack of cultural facilities, but affordability allowed families to own a private home and build a community in a way that was not possible in the city. Suburban stereotypes, Clark maintained, were the creation of "urban loving intellectuals" passing moral judgments that largely ignored the desires of Canadians families. Suburban society was largely a society of choice, and the stream of purchases that a new home implied were also matters of choice.[27]

Other sociologists disagreed, arguing that Clark's free-market interpretation of suburban development minimized the degree to which social background constrained income and life opportunities. Where Clark saw young families pursuing affordable housing, striving to pay for dreams partially attained, his colleague John Porter saw families who would never be able to attain their dreams. Porter, who had begun teaching at Carleton University while conducting research towards his dissertation, began publishing a series of studies on Canadian society in the 1950s.[28] These were ultimately collected in *The Vertical Mosaic* (1965), a landmark study of social and ethnic inequality in Canada.[29] Porter argued that Canada's understanding of itself as a nation of middle-class families was an illusion that ignored both the sacrifices required by low-income earners and the privileges of the wealthy. Porter challenged the perception of Canada as an egalitarian society, arguing that the image of a "middle level of classlessness" with "a general uniformity of possessions" obscured significant structural inequalities in Canadian society. Representations of Canadian families in the mainstream media gave the sense that new consumption practices were widely shared, but Porter insisted this was simply untrue: there was no statistical evidence to support "the validity of the widespread social image of middle classness, or the believed-in high level of affluence."[30]

Porter used class as a descriptive category rooted in measurable inequalities such as education and the value of goods and services that could be purchased with a given income and also as a social category that "becomes real as people experience it."[31] He accepted that industrial capitalism had raised consumption standards for individuals and families, but contended that measuring progress by the ownership of things was problematic and not an accurate measure of the standard of living. The statistical emphasis on increasing per capita consumption, Porter believed, obscured other measures of quality of life. Rising incidences of social and mental disorder, for example, were evidence that "we are not producing human happiness."[32] Society, he argued, had "experienced a great increase in means without a corresponding articulation of ends."[33]

Porter proposed a more nuanced understanding of the relationship between Canadians and their material aspirations. He claimed that preoccupation with the acquisition of durable consumer goods such as cars, refrigerators, and electrical appliances was characteristic only of the lowest levels of the middle class.[34] The higher levels of the middle class, he observed, were less concerned with the "ownership of gadgetry" than with the consumption of services. Access to "the best" obstetricians, pediatricians, and nursery schools, and to ballet and music lessons, ensured the attainment of value-oriented goals such as good health, privacy, security, and a sense of cultural accomplishment. This ability to consume things that could "neither be bought with a small down payment and three years to pay nor be used as security for a chattel mortgage," Porter wrote, identified the "real middle class."[35] Above the middle class were those fortunate enough to rank in the upper levels of Canadian society, who took consumption largely for granted. Porter particularly objected to standardized images of middle-class consumption levels and behaviours constructed by advertisements and articles in popular magazines depicting child rearing, homemaking, sexual behaviour, health, sport, and hobbies. These images were often American in origin, but contributed substantially to Canadian values.[36] Yet, Porter insisted, 54 percent of Canadians had no chance of meeting this made-in-America standard. The disparity between average incomes and media-generated ideals meant that people were trying to define their social identity by a level of consumption they were unlikely to attain in reality.[37]

For Porter, the aspirations of ordinary Canadians for a "standard package" of goods were not a mark of social homogeneity but evidence of social stratification. The image of Canada as a single middle-class social formation, uniform in affluence and desire, was a useful fiction that concealed class differences. The image of a classless society made it possible to treat the poor and the underprivileged as "though they did not exist."[38] Unmasking the illusion of widely shared consumption patterns, Porter believed, would unmask inequalities in class structure, opening the way to a more just society.[39]

Commercial Culture and the Humanities

Canada's cultural elites had muted their criticism of mass commercial culture during the war, when so many other concerns, including the need to keep home-front morale high, took precedence.[40] Yet as Leonard Kuffert's study of visions for postwar reconstruction shows, their concerns were only put on hold. As the war drew to a close, criticism of commercial culture resumed. Framing their opposition as a battle against the dual enemies of totalitarianism and American mass culture, intellectual elites advocated for a broad range of postwar policies that linked active citizenship with the pursuit of worthwhile leisure.[41] Cultural leaders and educational theorists called for ambitious programs of adult education, including government support for public affairs radio forums, community centres, folk culture, amateur arts, and an infrastructure of institutions associated with high culture. Enjoyment of mass culture was denounced as a passive activity, complicit in fostering a homogenized worldview and undermining independent and critical thinking. As educator Hilda Neatby succinctly explained, "If we content ourselves with mere happiness ... we are not bringing up free men and women. We are conditioning units for mass servitude."[42]

With the battle over national culture, Americanization, and public education becoming heated, the government appointed a royal commission in 1949 to investigate the state of the arts, letters, and sciences in Canada and to make recommendations for their protection and development.[43] This authority, known as the Massey Commission after its chair Vincent Massey, received over four hundred briefs from a wide range of interest groups in academia and the arts during hearings held from 1949 to 1951. The commission's final report, and indeed many of the briefs presented to it, showed that the dynamic of cultural production and consumption was now broadly understood as an economic process. Even the traditionalists who associated culture with ennobling experiences accepted that Canadians were consumers. Accepting (however unwillingly) the new context of cultural consumption, the commissioners sought to mount a rear-guard action, borrowing from wartime lessons in economic regulation that restricted some kinds of consumption and encouraged others. Insofar as different forms of culture were in direct competition for the disposable income and leisure time of Canadians, the commissioners called on the state to intervene in the economics of cultural production and consumption by supporting the production of preferred forms of culture and regulating, as much as possible, the importation and distribution of undesirable forms. Going forward, the commissioners explained, Canadian achievement would depend "on the quality of the Canadian mind and spirit. This quality is determined by what Canadians think, and think about; by the books they read, the pictures they see and the programmes they hear ... We believe, however, that the appetite grows by eating. The best must be made available to those who wish it."[44] The result was to institutionalize state support for the antidotes to mass culture and, equally, to institutionalize pejorative associations that linked mass entertainment with passive consumption and Americanization. Substantial investments in education, time, and money would ensure that Canadians had access to a broad range of better cultural opportunities. Popular entertainments, unless they had a regional or folk association, were dismissed as detrimental to good citizenship. Although Canada's cultural elites acknowledged that consumption of high culture could not be forced, they seemingly shared the businessman's understanding that consumption – whether of vacuum cleaners, the latest hairstyles, or classics of literature – could be influenced by persuasion and prices.

The theoretical innovations of Marshall McLuhan and Northrop Frye stand out against this background of conservative resistance. While the Massey commissioners called on the state to use its power to offset commercially driven mass-reproduced culture, McLuhan and Frye, both scholars of English literature at the University of Toronto, focused on improving the skills of individuals. By linking education to the possibilities of resistance, they insisted that reason – in the form of cultural analysis – could restore freedom of choice. Both sought in different ways to transfer techniques of critical interpretation developed in literary theory to the study of mass commercial culture. While neither embraced commercial culture, they acknowledged its power and appeal. To be effective, academics had to be more than gatekeepers: they needed to cross the boundary that separated high culture and daily life in their research and by addressing their work to the educated general public. Canadians need not be passive consumers; they could be armed with the ability to engage with culture systematically. Regarding critical thinking and analysis as forms of political action, McLuhan and Frye both insisted that education had the power to help ordinary Canadians transcend the pressures of commercialized messages.

As a student at Cambridge, McLuhan had gained recognition as a scholar of English Renaissance literature.[45] The defence of high culture against the onslaught of mass civilization was a preoccupation at Cambridge at that time.[46] McLuhan certainly shared these concerns, but he did not agree with the recommended solution, which called for a cadre within the intellectual elite to step forward and preserve the achievements of the past against pressures of the commercial market and the downward pressures of mass civilization. If scholars simply restricted themselves to teaching the past, McLuhan believed that the battle was lost. High culture could not successfully compete with the "unofficial program of education" being carried on by business through the press, radio, and movies. Affluence had a liberating potential: there was a "promise" in new developments "to which moral indignation is a poor guide."[47]

Upon returning to North America and assuming a university post, McLuhan felt an "urgent need to study popular culture in order to meet his students 'on their own ground.'" He developed a new approach to teaching, deploying traditional and modern methods of literary and cultural analysis, and the new techniques of "persuasion" devised by marketing professionals to reveal the distortions of the commercial media. McLuhan worked on this study for several years; gradually *The Mechanical Bride* took shape as a guidebook that would "energize" the mind and train readers to see things as they really are.

The text of *The Mechanical Bride* consisted of fifty-nine short "exhibits" or case studies; each inspected a clipping from a magazine or newspaper, most often an advertisement. The images were accompanied by an ironic running commentary, with McLuhan delivering pointed observations on aesthetics, techniques, and cultural attitudes, sarcastic insights on contemporary social life, and rhetorical questions intended to encourage readers to consider larger issues raised by popular and commercial culture. In his introduction, he explained that the hero of "A Descent into the Maelstrom" by Edgar Allan Poe had inspired his method. Poe's hero, stranded on a ship caught in a whirlpool, saved himself by studying the actions of the water and then cooperating with the currents. The key to his escape was an attitude of detached amusement: responding as a spectator to his situation, rather than with anger or moral indignation, enabled the sailor to extricate himself. McLuhan was convinced that exposing the techniques used by the press, radio, movies, and advertising agencies to manipulate minds and emotions could, in a similar way, break the grip of mass culture and restore freedom of choice.[48]

The Mechanical Bride was innovative in many ways that have since become familiar, including its non-linear structure. But, above all, it was a pioneering academic study of material that had generally been dismissed as ephemera and unworthy of thoughtful consideration. McLuhan gave advertisements, comic strips, and Hollywood movies careful attention, referring to them collectively as the "folklore of industrial man." He appreciated that the techniques being used to sell goods were aesthetically and technologically innovative, but he insisted that more was going on than the simple selling of commodities. Advertisers, he warned, were "getting inside" people's minds, exploiting their insecurities, and manipulating their dreams, desires, and deepest longings – a situation to which he strenuously objected. Their intention was not simply to sell goods but to sell meanings that would legitimize the order of industrialized mass production and consumer capitalism. Although he was aware of recent work in sociology that gave consumer goods a social function, McLuhan saw minimal agency in the spending decisions of Canadians, attributing their choices to psychological manipulation rather than social dynamics.[49]

Gender (particularly weakened males and sexualized women) was one of the organizing categories of McLuhan's analysis, and he was particularly pessimistic about the future of the North American family.[50] In both *The Mechanical Bride*, and in an early essay, "Dagwood in America" (1944), he presented images of husbands reduced from breadwinners to emasculated wage-slaves, seeking the comforting illusion of strength in westerns, war movies, and detective stories. Fathers were absent from the home and, to McLuhan's way of thinking, had been displaced from their proper role as head of the family. Male heroes – strong and silent – were repressed. Women's bodies were commodified, presented in unnatural postures or as objectified parts, sometimes fused with machine images, to sell goods. The exaggerated sexuality of the "love goddess assembly line" had replaced natural physical contact. "Can the feminine body keep pace with the demands of the textile industry?" he queried alongside an advertisement promoting women's undergarments.[51]

McLuhan proposed that the rhetoric of the adman and the Hollywood movie industry influenced behavioural patterns by establishing a common symbolic language that shaped perceptions of reality. Successful advertisements manipulated "sub-rational impulses and appetites" for profit. Under the pressure of these new techniques, society had taken on "the character of the kept women ... Each day brings its addition of silks, trinkets, and shiny gadgets, new pleasure techniques and new pills for pep and pain-lessness." Advertisements linked social status to the consumption of expensive goods rather than to discernment, perception, and judgment. As insidious passivity spread, it required "an exceptional degree of awareness and an especial heroism of effort to be anything but supine consumers of processed goods."[52]

McLuhan argued that the myths of mass consumer society supported the political and economic power structure by discouraging critical thought and directing attention away from social problems.[53] When success was measured by purchasing power, the need for money bound people to jobs and to big cities where most of the jobs were. In this context, educating people to see the techniques used to manipulate their emotions was an act of political as well as cultural resistance. To counteract materialism gone wild, psychological sensationalism, and thrill seeking, McLuhan offered a combination of ironic detachment and critical engagement that reflected his ambivalence towards the dangerous, compelling pleasures of consumer culture.

The Mechanical Bride received generally favourable reviews, dozens of which McLuhan collected and carefully filed.[54] However, critics at the time regarded it as a book that would interest primarily those involved in advertising, rather than cultural or social criticism. After *The Mechanical Bride*, McLuhan shifted his attention from print towards other methods of cultural transmission. In his next works, *The Gutenberg Galaxy* (1961) and *Understanding Media* (1964), he was especially enthusiastic about the potential of electronic mass media to transform human experience.[55] By the mid-1960s, he was an intellectual superstar: the first public intellectual of the electronic age. Yet, by the early 1970s, his fame was in rapid decline; overproduction and overexposure had diluted his value. As Seeley had observed in the context of Crestwood Heights, the market for new ideas turned academic output into a commodity like any other, a trend that was exacerbated in McLuhan's case by his willing participation in the market for cultural commentary.[56]

Northrop Frye developed a very different, but complementary, approach to the challenges of affluence. Acutely aware of each other's writings and ideas, Frye and McLuhan were intellectual competitors rather than friends.[57] Whereas McLuhan brought a range of critical techniques to bear directly on the analysis of commercial messages, Frye theorized an autonomous critical system through which the ideals of literature would be made relevant for the present. Frye did not, for the most part, study commercial media. His goal was to create a systematic unified theory of criticism as a discipline in its own right, independent of any single work of literature. But despite holding fairly elitist attitudes towards popular culture, he insisted that the importance of critical theory lay specifically in its value to consumers.

Frye had gained international attention in 1947 as the author of an innovative commentary on the poet William Blake. The publication of *The Anatomy of Criticism* in 1957 elevated his standing even further.[58] In his introduction to *The Anatomy of Criticism*, Frye dismissed what he described as the popular notion of the critic as a cultural middleman, positioned between the producer and consumer, distributing culture to society for profit. Literary criticism, he insisted, was not an exercise in taste but a scientific practice that revealed values and preserved cultural memory.[59] The value of culture to society, he wrote, emerged through criticism:

> It is the consumer, not the producer, who benefits by culture, the consumer who becomes humanized and liberally educated. There is no reason why a great poet should be a wise and good man, or even a tolerable human being, but there is every reason why his reader should be improved in his humanity as a result of reading him ... What does improve in the arts is the comprehension of them, and the refining of society which results from it.[60]

As an academic project, *The Anatomy of Criticism* sought to establish a classification system for the totality of literary work, identifying a system of modes, symbols, myths, and genres that included folklore and classical antiquity as well as Shakespeare and modern novels. Approached through this structure, literary works stood independent of human history, offering a standpoint from which to appraise the present and a vision of infinite future possibilities that could enable society to rise beyond the compulsion of daily habits and prejudices. Frye accepted the fact of consumer society but positioned literature as the opposite of commodity culture. Indeed, he advocated the thoughtful consumption of literature as an antidote to ordinary lives of passive consumption.

Critical theory, for Frye, was a science of the human imagination and a methodology for improvement.[61] Literature and culture offered the resources and critical tools to sustain, nourish, and perpetuate alternative frames of reference. The tension that emerged between "what is" and "what ought to be" opened a critical path that pointed the way to change.[62] The present value of culture lay in "its interim revolutionary effectiveness" as a vehicle to a better future. The "total experience of criticism" was progressive, leading towards the ideal of "a complete and classless civilization."[63]

By shifting the focus of literary criticism from the author to the reader, Frye proposed to recover a social function for literature in a society of affluence and choice. Considered independently, detached from the particulars of time, place, and authorship, each work of art was transformed from "an object of aesthetic contemplation" into "an ethical instrument." While the success of an individual book might be evaluated as a retail good, the whole of literature provided "an autonomous world that gives us an imaginative perspective on the actual one."[64]

Frye presented a popularized version of *The Anatomy of Criticism* for CBC Radio's Massey Lecture series in 1962, in which he distilled the lessons of systematic critical theory for a broader audience. In the final episode, titled "The Vocation of Eloquence," Frye remarked that "Tonight ... I'm speaking to you as consumers, not producers of literature, as people who read and form the public for literature. It's as consumers that you may want to know more about what literature can do and what its uses are, apart from the pleasure it gives."[65] Approached systematically and scientifically, literature offered a transcendental database of ideals and images that consumers could draw upon but that were never used up. It was through reading, rather than writing, that individuals could transcend the passions of the present and the pressures to conform. It was the appreciative consumer, rather than the romantic poet, who could draw on the imaginative energy of world literature to create a better future.

For this reason, Frye (much like McLuhan) advised his listeners to adopt an ironic approach and "detach" their personal imagination from the illusory grip of "the social imaginary" that was intended "to persuade us to accept our society's standards and values." Irony, Frye explained, helps us to "develop our own vision of society to the point at which we can choose what we want out of what's offered to us and let the rest go."[66] The value of education, for the individual and for society, lay in training the mind to be critical, dispassionate, and tolerant: the "reader as hero" set both the individual and society free.[67] Although people live in both a social and a cultural environment, Frye believed that the ideals provided by the cultural environment enabled individuals to do more than simply adjust to the illusions of middle-class twentieth-century Canadian society.[68] At a time when many were rejecting hierarchies of taste, Frye promised that culture held redemptive value.

Towards an Economics of Consumption

In the late 1940s economists reformulated long-held principles and statistical measures to fit new facts and situations. In a series of articles published between 1949 and 1951, for example, the prominent Canadian economist B.S. Kierstead and the senior American economist C. Reinold Noyes carried on an extended debate on the value of new research in consumer psychology, asking whether consumer decisions were primarily rational or irrational, deliberate or automatic, impulsive or predicable, and what the answers meant for economics as a distinct science.[69] The challenges of measuring disposable income were examined in the *Canadian Journal of Economics and Political Science* in May and November 1949. Did different ways of calculating income alter a consumer's propensity to spend? Other economists grappled with statistical questions, concerned, for example, that data on new house construction were being recorded as business income rather than as consumer spending, while data on durable goods were being recorded as a one-time expenditure rather than as a capital investment that depreciated over time.

The Dominion Bureau of Statistics determined that the entire cost of living index should be reset, beginning a lengthy mathematical exercise that stretched from 1948 until 1952. The previous index, developed in 1938, had been outmoded by developments in sampling techniques and changes in purchasing habits. Moreover, the dramatic rise of that index (which reached a high of 159.6 percent by October 1948) was becoming politically problematic, contributing to public concerns about rising prices. Resetting the index and shifting the nomenclature from a cost of living index to a consumer price index were intended to calm anxieties. The bureau also waged a campaign of public education, explaining how the index worked. The index, Canadians were assured, measured changes in the prices of the goods purchased by representative families and not the overall cost of living in any single location. The sample of representative families that formed the basis of the index was expanded from urban wage-earning families with two to three children to include families ranging in size from two adults with no children to two adults with four children and included more regions of Canada.

The most interesting aspect of the change was the inclusion of forty new items and the elimination of twenty-nine items from the index. The bureau emphasized that the process for inclusion or omission of any particular item in the price index was purely factual. Most of the new items had been added as a result of technological and production changes. Statisticians made "no attempt to distinguish between luxuries and necessities," and had not considered "desirability from a moral or social point of view." The list of omissions and inclusions provides a snapshot of changes in the daily life of ordinary Canadian families: dropped from the list were items such as salt, marmalade, women's woollen hosiery, bedsprings, and frying pans. New additions included margarine, cake mixes, macaroni, peanut butter, bologna, canned pears, chocolate bars, women's fur coats, twelve items of children's wear, vacuum cleaners, lawnmowers, alarm clocks, camera film, phonograph records, and the price of a visit to a women's hairdresser.[70]

The economist David Slater tied together a decade of statistical trends and discussion in a study on consumer expenditure produced for the Royal Commission on Canada's Economic Prospects (1957). Asserting that "in a fundamental sense the consumer is supreme in our society," Slater highlighted the ways in which new information challenged conventional wisdom, driving change in economic theory.[71] Slater observed that, according to traditional economic understandings, if real wages rose and the cost of goods fell, a smaller fraction of income was required to meet the minimal physiological requirements of food, clothing, and shelter. The result should have been more leisure, more savings, or a shift in spending to other goods and services. However, the amounts spent on food, clothing, and shelter took up roughly the same proportion of Canadian budgets in 1955 as they had in 1929. Rather than changing their spending patterns, Canadians had upgraded their choices in the core categories, buying more and better-quality items. Similarly, conventional theory held that consumption varied directly with income. It was evident, Slater concluded, that a much larger range of economic and social forces were involved. Expectations regarding inflation, the availability of credit, and the anticipated availability of new consumer goods also factored into each family's spending decisions. Even more interesting, he added, was new research suggesting "that income may depend on consumption as much as the other way around," with opportunities to buy motivating families to increase their earnings.[72] A decade earlier, Canadian economists planning for postwar reconstruction had been most concerned about stagnation; now, Slater marvelled that Canada had become a nation

of a rich people becoming richer, of households with the time and means
for increased use of sporting and hobby equipment and travel, of a people
with few servants and many items of household equipment, of a nation
with fairly low standards of housing but many automobiles. It is a picture
of an acquisitive society, the members of which are prepared to work for
but expect substantially higher levels of material living.[73]

Slater noted that, although there was insufficient information to determine
whether or not increased consumer spending could replace capital investment as a driver of economic growth, underconsumption was no longer a
concern. There is "little question but that desires for more goods and the
convictions that they are to be had, are part of the Canadian social tastes,"
he concluded. "There is apparently no limit to the desires of our consumers
to spend."[74]

By the mid-1950s, it was common to describe North American society
as "affluent," "opulent," and "advanced." The problem of need, it was often
said, had given way to the problem of want. Some saw this as progress;
others lamented that advertisers deliberately cultivated discontent and
desire, fuelling a spiral of private consumer spending driven by anxiety
and status seeking. Some critics saw the affluence of middle-class sub-
urbanites, rather than the persistence of poverty, as the principal social
challenge. Of the many critiques of economic growth, *The Affluent Society*
(1958), by the Canadian-born economist John Kenneth Galbraith, was
possibly the most influential. After moving to the United States to pursue
graduate studies, Galbraith had come to exercise tremendous power over
the American economy as one of the highest-ranked civilians working
in the US Office of Price Administration during the war. In *The Affluent
Society*, Galbraith, now a well-regarded economist and public figure,
argued that traditional economic theories were obsolete. In the twentieth
century, the ability to produce goods was virtually unlimited; the fundamental economic problem was disposing of these products. Because high
rates of spending were required to keep the machinery of production turning, new wants had to be continually "manufactured" through advertising,
salesmanship, and easy credit. People were working harder to spend more
but never felt satisfied. Conventional economic thinking supported this
imbalance by emphasizing high rates of production as the measure of
prosperity. In *The Affluent Society*, Galbraith specifically connected excessive spending on private consumption with insufficient spending on public

services, and he recommended using government policy to restore the social balance between the public and private realms.[75]

One of the loudest voices raised in opposition to Galbraith was that of Canadian economist Harry G. Johnson. Johnson engaged directly with Galbraith's controversial best-seller, sharing his premises but not his conclusions. Johnson agreed that productivity rather than scarcity had become the driving force in the modern economy, but he rejected Galbraith's moral critique, offering in its place a largely positive narrative. Although he is less well known today, Johnson was one of the most influential economists in the 1960s – a well-regarded and prolific writer and a peripatetic conference-goer with broad interests and a hard-drinking, hard-working lifestyle. Johnson often used Canadian audiences and Canadian occasions to develop his thinking on economic approaches to social questions.[76] He agreed with Galbraith that the theoretical apparatus of classical economics, "formed and shaped by an atmosphere of grinding poverty," was no longer relevant.[77] He disagreed, however, with Galbraith's claims that past conditions of "real scarcity" had been succeeded by present conditions of "contrived scarcity" dependent on the creation of false needs.[78] Galbraith differentiated between a baseline of real needs and the artificial needs stimulated by advertising, but Johnson believed that no such distinction was possible. All needs, Johnson insisted, beyond the most basic requirements for physical survival, were socially determined. All economically relevant wants, he wrote, "are learned." As the wealth of society increases, demand evolves, and the emergence of new, less essential wants was inevitable. As physiological necessities are met, the margin of "want-satisfaction" tended to move to psychological and sociological needs characteristic of a high-consumption economy. In any case, Johnson wrote, "it has yet to be demonstrated that material comfort makes the pursuit of a good life harder instead of easier; the evidence seems to me to suggest, on the contrary, that as the mass of the people become wealthier, society becomes more decent, humane, and civilized, and the average quality of life improves."[79]

Johnson hypothesized that modern North American society was not simply a traditional society with a higher standard of living, but something different. Advanced economies were characterized by rapid innovation, mass scale, and advances in productivity institutionalized in the modern corporation. Consumption no longer involved necessities or even goods that were used up or consumed in the traditional sense: continuing to think about consumption as a flow of goods was an artefact of the economy of scarcity. Modern consumption, Johnson asserted, should be understood as the steady stream of services. "Not tea, but TV," he wrote, should be considered as "the exemplary commodity of the age of opulence."[80] The key to theorizing a new "political economy of opulence" (a term he preferred as more in keeping with the traditions of classical economics) lay in recognizing that economic progress improved both the production function and the consumption function. The economy, he insisted, was a mechanism for the production and distribution of goods and services, not a moral system for the testing and rewarding of desirable character traits. He also asserted, very much against the trend of Galbraith, Vance Packard, and other intellectual critics of the day, that the satisfaction of wants created by advertisers should not be regarded as a social ill. Intensive selling, Johnson noted, was characteristic of advanced societies where wealth was "synonymous with having a wide range of choice," and "choice involves the necessity of decision."[81] Advertising increased as societies became richer and was used not just by commercial enterprises, but also by cultural programs, political parties, charities, churches, and other interest groups to provide information and advice. Johnson did not dispute the need for government controls against fraud, and he agreed that advocacy by organized consumer groups would be beneficial, but he argued against the view that consumers were the brainwashed dupes of ad-men.

At the same time, Johnson believed that changes in wealth creation meant that a purely individualistic conception of consumption decisions was no longer appropriate. Economic risks were built into the structure of opulent society. Factors such as rapid change, innovation, inflation, and specialization also made for greater insecurity of income. The family, rather than the individual, was the basic spending unit, and their decisions would uplift or debase the quality of life for all. The family in its role as a consumer unit faced many challenges. "It is not all that easy to grow rich successfully," Johnson opined. Spending well required a continual process of learning: learning to budget income, to manage one's property and one's self, and to invest in capital goods and the services associated with progressively rising standards of living. Specialization in both the earning and spending functions increased the family's abilities and competencies as a consumer unit, but the possibilities of failure were considerable. Most decisions required knowledge and command of capital beyond the reach of a single family, which was, by its nature, small in economic size and dependent on a specialized wage-earner. In the postwar period, critics of middle-class affluence on both the left and the right of the political spectrum called on the state to restrain excesses of private spending in support of public services. Johnson disagreed. Instead he argued that social policy should be used to help Canadian families manage their risks and maximize their opportunities in a society characterized by rising wealth.[82]

Conclusion

By the early 1960s, academic and other experts had come to see consumers, once marginal to the discussion of society, as central to understanding modern Canada. Such observers understood purchasing decisions – once regarded as private, personal, and constrained by the limits of income – as primarily social experiences. They pointed to social belonging, rather than selfish pleasure seeking, as the principal psychological driver of consumer behaviour. The attention of academic authorities helped to validate the importance of consumers. Sociologists, including Seeley, Clark, and Porter, lifted spending decisions out of the flow of daily life and discussed them scientifically, as facts to be theorized rather than as moral problems. Marshall McLuhan turned advertisements into cultural artefacts. Northrop Frye, already celebrated as one of Canada's great minds, addressed consumers as potential visionaries able to transform society. Economists debated the significance of changing patterns of consumption. Coverage in the national media gave academics a degree of celebrity; at the same time, academic scrutiny imparted a new gravitas to the purchasing decisions being made every day by ordinary Canadian consumers.

In spite of significant differences in political commitments and methodology, the narratives created by this diverse group of scholars are remarkably compatible, validating the role of the consumer by giving consumer behaviours a larger social purpose. And yet, although they acknowledged that Canadians, on average, enjoyed a high standard of living, academic observers – even the most progressive – continued to write about loss: the loss of tradition, of agency, and of social stability. They also expressed concerns about mental health and entrenched inequality. Indeed, these concerns were the basis of their claims to social relevance: their ambivalence towards consumer society allowed them to assert a value for academic work in helping consumers understand their situation and make better choices.

Perhaps, then, it is useful to see their work not simply as descriptions of reality but as narratives of modern Canada that renewed academic purpose within the parameters of a more democratic, more prosperous postwar society.

By the late 1950s and early 1960s, few questioned that (for better or worse) a new stage had been reached in the technological and material progress of humankind. The problem space for thinking about consumer spending had become one of affluence and choice, with the expectations that these changes were – short of nuclear war – irreversible. Within this problem space, academics began to theorize consumer society as a coherent, socially shared set of behaviours and values, and the consumer emerged as an agent of change, making choices among alternatives. Analysts interpreted spending decisions as a social phenomenon, in both socially positive ways (e.g., as purchases that solved social problems) and socially negative ways (e.g., as social images that could misdirect consumer choices). Consumer choices, these academics understood, took on meaning in relationship to the choices made by other consumers within a common matrix. The consumer was both someone who made choices and someone whose ability to choose freely was limited by socially shared images and values. Although their decisions may not have been fully conscious or fully informed – indeed, although were often manipulated and duped – consumers had to have the potential for agency if academic work on the subject was to have significance. For only then could freeing the consumer from the illusions of society become a form of political action.

CONCLUSION

Comparing the start and the end of this study, beginning just before 1900 and reaching to the early 1960s, we see a sequence of changes in perception and thinking, from initial impressions about consumers to sophisticated analyses of consumer society. The consumer is a figure of controversy throughout, seen at the turn of the century by conservative moralists as a harbinger of decline and, at the same time, associated with the promise of the Kingdom of God on Earth by social gospellers. Despite a growing surplus of goods, there was, at that time, no sense of a consumer society as such, although various commentators expressed concern about the impact of the aggregated spending decisions of individual consumers. The interwar period saw national culture emerge as a consumer good, but one explicitly positioned in opposition to mass-produced commercially driven culture. During the Depression and Second World War, the consumer emerged as a recognized political interest. Consumers were voters; they were also citizens with rights, responsibilities, and purchasing behaviours that became the subject of government policy. As a political interest, the consumer was a universal category; however, as a voting interest and a subject of home front economic regulations, the consumer was almost always envisioned and addressed as a middle-class housewife. In the postwar period, observers of consumer society noted that commercial goods had infiltrated social relationships to a degree not thought possible – and certainly not thought desirable – in earlier decades. Consumer behaviours had, by this time, become a topic of fascination and discussion in both the mass media and in academia. In both discourses, the family unit was reframed as a consumer unit with highly specific gender roles. In a high-output economy, new themes, including responsible spending, debt management, and the use of goods to fashion personal identity, displaced older themes of thrift, self-denial, and character. The understanding of need was transformed, so that, by the 1950s, it came to be generally understood as the falling short of social norms rather than the absence of necessities. It became common to characterize Canadians as consumers, but this practice did not usher in a new wave of acceptance or end dissent. Consumer behaviours continued to be a source of concern and resistance, certainly for elites but also, as the letters from *Chatelaine* readers revealed, for ordinary Canadians. Dissent could be easily expressed within consumer societies by writing letters to the editors of mass-market publications, calling in to CBC radio programs, and purchasing best-selling books written by prominent social critics.

In the midst of the heady period of economic expansion that followed the war, there was a tendency to see all of North America as following the same trajectory. Scholarly studies and the mass media both presented Canadians as consumers in an economy marked by relative affluence and choice. In fact, both types of experts – the one claiming practical knowledge in the realm of daily life, the other claiming authority in the realm of science and scholarship – understood their role as one of improving (rather than discouraging) consumption. The overall level of moral censure directed towards individual consumers lessened as the perceived collective significance of consumer behaviours rose.

Visions of abundance tended to be more modest in Canada than in the United States, with goals focusing on security rather than a plentitude of things, given Canadians' experiences in a volatile resource-based economy. Canadian expectations were also shaped by the proximity of the United States and the persistent and significant gap between Canadian purchasing power and made-in-America images of family life. In the postwar period, Canadian per capita incomes were, on average, two-thirds of those of their American neighbours. At the same time, the prices of consumer durable goods in Canada were quite a bit higher, the result of shorter production runs for smaller markets, high transportation costs, and tariffs on imported American parts and products. Canadians were audiences for made-in-America images but had less purchasing power. For this reason,

Joy Parr and Joseph Tohill speak of a Canadian "frugality born of chronic-ally lower disposable incomes" and document the "shrewd economic cal-culus" required to make the most of more limited purchasing power.[1]

Largely accepting the limitations of the family budget, experts in a broad range of fields linked improved consumption to education. While aligning their interests with an expanding consumer society, they positioned their advice in counterpoint to mass consumption. The logic that underpinned this seeming inconsistency was made clear by Elizabeth Loosley, editor of *Food for Thought* and one of the co-authors of the Crestwood Heights study. Loosley observed that the postwar consumer, torn between in-compatible pressures, "tends to lose the sense of 'it is *I* who chooses'."[2] Her solution was broadly echoed by experts ranging from Sid Margolius to Northrup Frye to Harry Johnson. The "I" who chooses, that is, the sub-jectivity of the individual Canadian as a consumer could be fostered and developed by consumer education. Thus, after six decades of discussion, the Canadian discourse surrounding consumerism culminated in support for responsible spending, advice to budget in order to buy, a call for gov-ernment intervention to minimize risk, and scholarly commitments to restore consumer choice. Canada's is a cautious consumerism.

Cultures are defined by their tensions. In discussions of consumption, in Canada and elsewhere, dreams of abundance emerge in counterpoint to warnings of the dangers of over-indulgence and fear of loss of control and loss of self. These discussions are always political and moral (implicitly, if not explicitly), but they are not always the same. At the turn of the century, conservative moralists feared that abundance would erode the character traits and self-discipline necessary for the advance of civilization. By the later 1950s, critics, depending on their perspective, saw mass-produced commercial goods as having the potential either to erode or to stabilize social solidarities. Ambivalence about consumption is part of the dynamic of consumer society.[3] The association of increased consumption with well-being and social status exists alongside the rejection of material things as a path to contentment. We respond to the idea of buying happiness with irony, but also with poignancy.

This project was conceived as an effort to historicize the concept of con-sumer society. Although consumerism is part of the economic system of large-scale industrialization, the representations examined in this study were, for the most part, not generated in order to sell goods. Rather, they emerged as people thought about the impact of new consumer experiences and behaviours on Canadian society. Each generation, in thinking about these issues, was historically situated and preoccupied with different concerns. They, variously, constructed the consumer as an object of moral concern or statistical reckoning; as a subject of public policy, media scrutiny, or academic research: the consumer appeared in essays, indexes, government reports, political party platforms, state policies, novels and short stories, popular magazines, and scholarly research.

As the chapters of this book have shown, different conditions shaped what contemporaries thought were the most consequential and critical problems. In each period, observers asked different questions, perceived different choices as possible, and created new representations. The questions they raised and, even more so, the answers they provided created frameworks for understanding new experiences. Consumer society was embodied in particular narratives, concepts and categories, theories and policies. What was imagined, debated, and reflected on by one generation became an "actually existing" structure of ideas for successor generations.[4] Concepts, as well as goods, advertisements, the constraints of income, and the pressures of everyday life, form the social space in which we live.

In the anthropologist Clifford Geertz's extraordinarily influential formulation of culture, "man" is "suspended in webs of significance he himself has spun."[5] This metaphor can convey an unfortunate sense of determinism – that is, of being stuck in a web. However, I believe that it can be more useful if attention is focused not on the web as a finished thing but on the spinning of the web as a framework of meaning. The framework grows stronger as filaments are added, but it is also transformed as some strands are reinforced and others weaken and fall away. The conceptual framework of consumer society is now deeply embedded in Canadian society, present in our stories, social relationships, state policies, and theories, operating as an almost taken-for-granted set of assumptions. But as this study shows, concepts have a history. And, as such, they also have a future.

NOTES

INTRODUCTION

1 The potential of this line of inquiry was suggested by Frank Trentmann, "Knowing Consumers: Histories, Identities, Practices," in *The Making of the Consumer: Knowledge, Power, and Identity in the Modern World*, ed. Frank Trentmann (Oxford: Berg, 2005), 1–6; and Frank Trentmann, "The Modern Genealogy of the Consumer: Meanings, Identities and Political Synapses," in *Consuming Cultures, Global Perspectives, Historical Trajectories, Transnational Exchanges*, ed. John Brewer and Frank Trentmann (Oxford: Berg, 2006), 19–69.

2 Anthropologist David Scott proposes that intellectual questions and preoccupations and scholarly and political concerns emerge within particular temporal problem-spaces in which there are particular questions that seem worth asking and particular answers that seem worth having. "Problem-spaces alter historically because problems are not timeless"; thus, successive generations have a different relationship to seemingly similar concerns. David Scott, *Conscripts of Modernity: The Tragedy of Colonial Enlightenment* (Durham, NC: Duke University Press, 2004), 4, 43–44; David Scott, "The Temporality of Generations: Dialogue, Tradition, Criticism," *New Literary History* 45, 2 (2014): 157–81.

3 Histories of consumer society by American scholars are particularly relevant to consideration of the Canadian experience, most notably those by Warren Susman (*Culture as History*), Daniel Horowitz (*Morality of Spending; Anxieties of Affluence; Consuming Pleasures*), T. Jackson Lears (*No Place of Grace*), Meg Jacobs (*Pocketbook Politics*), and Liz Cohen (*Consumer Republic*). As is evident throughout this text, I have greatly benefitted by "thinking with and against" them.

4 For an overview of recent historiography, see Frank Trentmann, "Introduction," in *The Oxford Handbook of the History of Consumption,* ed. Frank Trentmann (Oxford: Oxford University Press, 2012), 1–19.

5 This paraphrases an early and often-cited question posed by Carole Shammas – see "Changes in English and Anglo-American Consumption from 1550 to 1800," in *Consumption and the World of Goods,* ed. John Brewer and Roy Porter (London: Routledge, 1993), 177.

6 On the influence of modernization theory on consumer historiography, see John Brewer, "Microhistory and the Histories of Everyday Life," *Cultural and Social History* 7, 1 (2010): 93–95, and Frank Trentmann, "Consumer Society: RIP – A Comment," *Contemporary European History* 20, 1 (2001): 27–31. The debate between agency and conditioning continues to be prominent in American consumer historiography; see David Steigerwald, "All Hail the Republic of Choice: Consumer History as Contemporary Thought," *Journal of American History* 93, 2 (2006): 385–403, and David Blanke, "Consumer Choice, Agency, and New Directions in Rural History," *Agricultural History* 81, 2 (2007): 182–203.

7 On current trends, see Peter Van Dam, "Tales of the Market: New Perspectives on Consumer Society in the 20th Century," in *H-Soz-Kult,* April 12, 2015, http://www.hsozkult.de/literaturereview/id/forschungsberichte-2832.

8 John Brewer, "The Error of Our Ways: Historians and the Birth of Consumer Society," in *Cultures of Consumption,* Working Paper 12 (2004), available at http://www.consume.bbk.ac.uk/working_papers/Brewer%20talk.doc.

9 As Canadian historian Douglas McCalla recently observed, historians are always looking for revolutions, transitions, and transformations, building their narratives around dichotomies that contrast pre-capitalism with market and/or industrial capitalism, needs with luxuries, willing participation with manipulation, and utopian abundance and freedom of choice with profound loss and limited agency. Douglas McCalla, *Consumers in the Bush: Shopping in Rural Upper Canada* (Montreal and Kingston: McGill-Queen's University Press, 2015), 10–15.

10 The concept of cultural and intellectual work as practice builds especially on the observations of Sonya O. Rose, "Cultural Analysis and Moral Discourses: Episodes, Continuities, and Transformations," in *Beyond the Cultural Turn: New Directions in the Study of Society and Culture,* ed. Victoria Bonnell, Lynn Hunt, and Richard Biernacki (Berkeley: University of California Press, 1999), 225–31; William Sewell, "The Concept(s) of Culture," in ibid., 35–61; Michel Foucault, "Politics and the Study of Discourse," in *The Foucault Effect: Studies in Governmentality,* ed. Graham Burchell, Colin Gordon, and Peter Miller (Chicago: University of Chicago Press, 1991), 53–72; and Charles Taylor, *Modern Social Imaginaries* (Durham, NC: Duke University Press, 2004), 31–32.

11 There is an extensive literature discussing the relationship of intellectuals to historical change, beginning with Karl Mannheim, *Ideology and Utopia* (first published in German in 1929). Mannheim argues that intellectuals, unattached to any one class, have "a restricted sort of objectivity" that can be the basis for a sociology of

knowledge and the foundation of ethically responsible political decision-making. Italian Marxist theorist Antonio Gramsci (1891–1937) argued differently, asserting that disinterested inquiry was a pretense that in fact served entrenched interests. Progress required skilled, engaged intellectuals to step forward and lead. While these distinctions remain relevant, it has become less common to dichotomize intellectual efforts intended to sustain and those intended to change society. American historian T. Jackson Lears' study of anti-modernist thought, for example, suggests that the line between protest and accommodation can be ambiguous. Resistance can have unintended consequences that serve to pave the way for the acceptance of new values. British theorist Terry Eagleton, discussing the challenges of colonial intellectuals, similarly proposes that the opposition between traditional intellectuals, who support the status quo, and organic intellectuals, who promote emerging social interests, is highly unstable; roles can shift over time so that the organic revolutionary intellectuals of one era become the traditional stabilizing intellectuals of another, first helping to overturn the existing dominant order and then helping to entrench a new hegemony. Karl Mannheim, *Ideology and Utopia: An Introduction to the Sociology of Knowledge* (New York: Harcourt, 1936), 3, 4, 40; Terry Eagleton, *Ideology: An Introduction* (London: Verso, 1991), 108–10, 112, 119; Raymond Williams, *Problems in Materialism and Culture* (London: Verso, 1980), 37–42; T. Jackson Lears, *No Place of Grace: Antimodernism and the Transformation of American Culture, 1880–1920* (New York: Pantheon, 1981), xiii, xv–xvi, 258; Terry Eagleton, *Scholars and Rebels in Nineteenth Century Ireland* (Oxford: Blackwell, 1999), 2–3, 7, 36–39, 150n7.

12 On the fantasy of "a pre-lapsarian, edenic world," see Brewer, "The Error of Our Ways," 3–8.

13 McCalla, *Consumers in the Bush,* 5–11, 148–53.

14 For a discussion of similar themes in the development of American consumer society, see Lizabeth Cohen, "The New Deal State and the Making of Citizen Consumers," in *Getting and Spending: European and American Consumer Societies in the Twentieth Century,* ed. Susan Strasser, Charles McGovern, and Mattias Judt (Cambridge: Cambridge University Press, 1998), 111; Lizabeth Cohen, *A Consumer's Republic: The Politics of Mass Consumption in Postwar America* (New York: Alfred A. Knopf, 2003), 18; Kathleen G. Donohue, *Freedom from Want: American Liberalism and the Idea of the Consumer* (Baltimore: Johns Hopkins University Press, 2003), 197; and James Livingston, *Pragmatism and the Political Economy of Cultural Revolution, 1850–1940* (Chapel Hill: University of North Carolina Press, 1994), 112, 117.

15 D.A. MacGibbon, "Economics and the Social Order," *Canadian Journal of Economics and Political Science* 2, 1 (1936): 73.

CHAPTER 1: THE MEANING IS IN THE SPENDING

1 Morris Altman, "New Estimates of Hours of Work and Real Income in Canada from the 1880s to 1930: Long-Run Trends and Workers' Preferences," *Review of Income and Wealth* 45, 3 (1999): 353–72.

2 Canada's annual per capita real GDP growth of 4.7 percent for the period 1896–
   1913 should be compared to 1.3 percent for the period 1870 to 1896 and 0.05 percent
   for the period 1913 to 1925. By way of comparison, in the United States, the annual
   per capita GDP growth rate was 2.5 percent for the period 1896–1913; in Germany
   it was 1.6 percent, in France 1.5 percent, in the United Kingdom 1.1 percent, and in
   Australia 2 percent. Morris Altman, "New Estimates of Hours," 355; Ninette Kelley
   and Michael J. Trebilcock, *The Making of the Mosaic: A History of Canadian Immigration Policy*, 2nd ed. (Toronto: University of Toronto Press, 2010), 113–15.

3 Ben Forster, "Finding the Right Size: Markets and Competition in Mid- and Late
   Nineteenth-Century Ontario," in *Patterns of the Past: Interpreting Ontario's History*,
   ed. Roger Hall, William Westfall, and Laurel Sefton MacDowell (Toronto: Dundurn
   Press, 1988), 153.

4 Keith Walden, *Becoming Modern in Toronto: The Industrial Exhibition and the Shaping
   of a Late Victorian Culture* (Toronto: University of Toronto Press, 1997), 120–25;
   E.A. Heaman, *The Inglorious Arts of Peace: Exhibitions in Canadian Society during
   the Nineteenth Century* (Toronto: University of Toronto Press, 1999), 107–11.

5 David Monod, *Store Wars: Shopkeepers and the Culture of Mass Marketing, 1890–1939*
   (Toronto: University of Toronto Press, 1996), 103, 112, 116, 122–23, 140–41; Russell
   Johnston, *Selling Themselves: The Emergence of Canadian Advertising* (Toronto:
   University of Toronto Press, 2001), 183–84.

6 Keith Walden, "Speaking Modern: Language, Culture and Hegemony in Grocery
   Window Displays, 1887–1920," *Canadian Historical Review* 70, 3 (1989): 285–310.

7 In 1872, less than one-half of Canadian families purchased a daily paper; by 1900,
   more papers were sold each day than there were families in the nation. By 1911, in
   some larger cities the average family took two and half papers per day. Behind these
   advances in readership lay fundamental changes in the economics of the newspaper
   business, both in technology and in the role of advertising. Mary Vipond, *The Mass
   Media in Canada*, 4th ed. (Toronto: James Lorimer, 2011), 25–30; Minko Sotiron,
   *From Politics to Profit: The Commercialization of Canadian Daily Newspapers, 1890–
   1920* (Montreal and Kingston: McGill-Queen's University Press, 1997), 52–69.

8 On the rise of department stores and the penetration of mail order, see Donica
   Belisle, *Retail Nation: Department Stores and the Making of Modern Canada* (Vancouver: UBC Press, 2011), 22–35; Monod, *Store Wars*, 122–23.

9 On department stores as women's spaces, see Cynthia Wright, "Feminine Trifles
   of Vast Importance: Writing Gender into the History of Consumption," in *Gender
   Conflicts: New Essays in Women's History*, ed. Franca Iacovetta and Mariana Valverde
   (Toronto: University of Toronto Press, 1992), 245; Belisle, *Retail Nation*, 28; William
   R. Leach, "Transformations in a Culture of Consumption: Women and Depart-
   ment Stores, 1890–1925," *Journal of American History* 71, 2 (1984): 319–42.

10 Joy Santink, *Timothy Eaton and the Rise of His Department Store* (Toronto: University of Toronto Press, 1990), 137.

11 Journals of public opinion published in Canada included the *Canadian Monthly*,
   Queens' Quarterly, and *Saturday Night*; the *Spectator*, originating in Britain, was
   also popular. Technological developments occurred on both the production side

(including changes in print technology) and the consumption side (electrification, for example, increased the time available for reading). On new opportunities for publication, see Janice Fiamengo, *The Woman's Page: Journalism and Rhetoric in Early Canada* (Toronto: University of Toronto Press, 2008), 19; Johnston, *Selling Themselves*, 251–66; Clarence Karr, *Authors and Audiences: Popular Canadian Fiction in the Early Twentieth Century* (Montreal and Kingston: McGill-Queen's University Press, 2000), 26–28.

12 See discussion in McCalla, *Consumers in the Bush,* 5.

13 On the city and country as dialectically related ideals referencing particular relationships of capital, labour, and commodities rather than actual communities, see Raymond Williams, *The Country and the City* (Oxford: Oxford University Press, 1973), 1–12, and Gerald MacLean, Donna Landry, and Joseph P. Ward, eds., *The Country and the City Revisited: England and the Politics of Culture, 1550–1850* (Cambridge: Cambridge University Press, 1999), 1–23. The myth of rural virtue in America is explored in Laurel Thatcher Ulrich, *The Age of Homespun: Objects and Stories in the Creation of an American Myth* (New York: Knopf, 2001). Doug Owram discusses Canadian country and city debates in *The Government Generation: Canadian Intellectuals and the State, 1900–1945* (Toronto: University of Toronto Press, 1986), 20–23.

14 On the views of social conservatives, see Robert Lanning, *National Album: Collective Biography and the Formation of the Canadian Middle Class* (Ottawa: Carleton University Press, 1996), 2, 85, 180–83, 187–88, and Allan Smith, "The Myth of the Self-Made Man in English Canada, 1850–1914," *Canadian Historical Review* 59, 2 (1978): 202–5. On the views of business leaders, see Michael Bliss, *A Living Profit: Studies in the Social History of Canadian Business, 1883–1911* (Toronto: University of Toronto Press, 1974), 16–20, 30, 32. On the social category of the self-made man as a rejection of consumerism, see David Kuchta, "The Making of the Self-Made Man: Class, Clothing and English Masculinity, 1688–1830," in *The Sex of Things: Gender and Consumption in Historical Perspective,* ed. Victoria de Grazia and Ellen Furlough (Berkeley: University of California Press, 1996), 54–78. Robert Lanning's study of several of the "collective biographies" of worthy Canadians that were published in the final decades of the Victorian era argues that these compilations were designed as "tools for socialization." As the Reverend William Cochrane explained, each biography in his series *The Canadian Album* (1891) demonstrated "object lessons for the present generation and examples to posterity." Cited in Lanning, *National Album,* 2.

15 This opposing of traditional producer culture and the culture of abundance by way of key words draws on Warren I. Susman, *Culture as History: The Transformation of American Society in the Twentieth Century* (New York: Pantheon Books, 1984), xx, xxii, xxiv.

16 Arnold Haultain, "Complaining of Our Tools," *Canadian Magazine* (July 1897), 184–85.

17 As women became identified as the principal shopper, the selling of goods became increasingly sexualized: store layouts and displays were gendered, retailers

"courted" customers, advertising was described as seduction, and comparison shopping and trying on goods were characterized as promiscuous behaviours. Monod, *Store Wars*, 89–90, 114–17, 119–20; Kathy L. Peiss, "American Women and the Making of Modern Consumer Culture," *Journal for MultiMedia History* 1, 1 (1998). http://www.albany.edu/jmmh/vol1no1/peiss-text.html.

18 These often vitriolic condemnations of women in new roles can be seen as a form of "moral panic," which is explained by historian Sonya O. Rose as an effort to maintain threatened moral boundaries. Panic occurs when communities face a crisis as boundaries shift and communities become unsure of their identities. Rose, "Cultural Analysis and Moral Discourses: Episodes, Continuities, and Trans-formations," in *Beyond the Cultural Turn: New Directions in the Study of Society and Culture,* ed. Victoria Bonnell, Lynn Hunt, and Richard Biernacki (Berkeley: University of California Press, 1999), 218–19. On the "new woman" and the "work-ing girl" as different categories of concern, see Carolyn Strange, *Toronto's Girl Problem: The Perils and Pleasures of the City, 1880–1930* (Toronto: University of Toronto Press, 1995), 7–10, 212. Also see Donica Belisle, "Crazy for Bargains: Inventing the Irrational Female Shopper in Modernizing English Canada," *Canadian Historical Review* 92, 4 (2011): 581–606.

19 Ian Ross Robertson, *Sir Andrew Macphail: The Life and Legacy of a Canadian Man of Letters* (Montreal and Kingston: McGill-Queen's University Press, 2008), 97–98, 99–102, 119, 133–34. On the essay "American Woman," see 99–102. The editor of the *Spectator* anticipated that "American Woman" would be controversial and later wrote to Macphail that it had provoked "violent letters of protests" from readers.

20 Andrew Macphail, "The Cost of Living," *University Magazine* 11, 4 (1912): 51.

21 See Veronica Strong-Boag, "Independent Women, Problematic Men: First- and Second-Wave Anti-Feminism in Canada from Goldwin Smith to Betty Steele," *Histoire sociale/Social History* 29, 57 (1996): 2–8.

22 Andrew Macphail, "'The Whole Duty of the Canadian Man:' An Address Deliv-ered to the Canadian Club of Saint John, New Brunswick, 26 March 1908," cited in Robertson, *Sir Andrew Macphail,* 97–98.

23 Women, particularly young single women, were the fastest-growing segment of the paid labour force. Monod, *Store Wars,* 113.

24 Carolyn Strange, "From Modern Babylon to a City upon a Hill: The Toronto Social Survey Commission of 1915 and the Search for Sexual Order in the City," in *Patterns of the Past: Interpreting Ontario's History,* ed. Roger Hall, Anthony Westfall, and Laurel Sefton MacDowell (Toronto: Dundurn Press, 1988), 256.

25 Strange, *Toronto's Girl Problem,* 22, 119–20, 136. On the single working girl in American moralism, see Daniel Horowitz, *The Morality of Spending: Attitudes toward the Consumer Society in America, 1875–1940* (Baltimore: Johns Hopkins University Press, 1985), 166.

26 Mariana Valverde, *The Age of Light, Soap and Water: Moral Reform in English Canada, 1885–1925* (Toronto: McClelland and Stewart, 1991), 186n66.

27 On this theme, see Monod, *Store Wars,* 61–67.

28 Mack, *The Barnums of Business: How Departmental Stores Injure Business, Property, and Wages* (Toronto: Sheppard Publishing Company, 1897), 63. The articles originally appeared from 13 February to 24 April 1897. Mack was the pseudonym used by Joseph Clark. Carr situates Clark's articles primarily as a reaction to the impact of department stores on existing merchants; Belisle forefronts his criticisms of women. Angela K. Carr, "New Building Technology in Canada's Late Nineteenth-Century Department Stores: Handmaiden of Monopoly Capitalism," *Journal of the Society for the Study of Architecture in Canada* 23, 4 (1998): 136–38; Belisle, "Crazy for Bargains," 587–88, 593–94, 598–99.

29 Belisle, "Crazy for Bargains," 606; see also Strange, *Toronto's Girl Problem*, 3, 5, 20; and Wright, "Feminine Trifles of Vast Importance," 240–41.

30 Monod, *Store Wars*, 114.

31 Mack, *The Barnums of Business*, 11–12.

32 On this theme, see Amanda Vickery, "His and Hers: Gender, Consumption and Household Accounting in Eighteenth-Century England," *Past and Present* 1 (2006 Supplement): 37.

33 James Mavor, cited in S.E.D. Shortt, *The Search for an Ideal: Six Canadian Intellectuals and Their Convictions in an Age of Transition, 1890–1930* (Toronto: University of Toronto Press, 1976), 120.

34 James Cappon, cited in ibid., 64.

35 Ibid., 32.

36 John George Bourinot, *Our Intellectual Strength and Weakness* (Montreal: Royal Society of Canada, 1893), 1.

37 Ibid., 30, 50.

38 Archibald Lampman, in the *Globe*, 18 June 1892, cited in Barrie Davies, ed., *At the Mermaid Inn: Wilfred Campbell, Archibald Lampman, Duncan Campbell Scott in The Globe, 1892–93* (Toronto: University of Toronto Press, 1979), 96. See also William Wilfred Campbell, cited in Laurel Boone, ed., *William Wilfred Campbell: Selected Poems and Essays* (Waterloo, ON: Wilfrid Laurier University Press, 1987), 169–70.

39 Andrew Macphail, "Unto the Church," *University Magazine* (April 1913): 358.

40 Ibid., 360.

41 Boone, *William Wilfred Campbell*, 1.

42 Fiamengo, *The Woman's Page*, 24. On citing Agnes Machar as a conservative intellectual rather than a social gospeller, see ibid., 34–36. Of course, the process of assigning thinkers to different groups is somewhat artificial. Most individuals can be placed in multiple categories, most movements include a range of opinion, and the commitments of individual thinkers evolve over time.

43 Carl Berger, *The Sense of Power: Studies in the Ideas of Canadian Imperialism, 1867–1914* (Toronto: University of Toronto Press, 1970), 259–60. See Mannheim, *Ideology and Utopia*, 229–33, for a useful discussion of conservative ideology, most often articulated, he proposes, in the face of change. Berger notes that affirmations of the virtues and permanence of agrarianism were being made at the very time when agriculture was in fact losing its primacy in Canada. Berger, *Sense of Power*, 191.

44 See Berger, *The Sense of Power*, 129–33, 177–82.

45 Shortt, *The Search for an Ideal*, 30–32.

46 The concept of "regulatory virtues" draws on Valverde, *The Age of Light, Soap and Water*, 33.

47 The regenerative potential of vigorous military effort as an antidote to the enfeeblements of modern life was a persistent theme in imperialist thought. See Berger, *The Sense of Power*, 251–57, for Canadian imperialists; see Lears, *No Place of Grace*, 114–17, for American imperialists.

48 Campbell, cited in Boone, *William Wilfred Campbell*, 198, 199, 202.

49 On the conservative view of war as offering the possibility of regeneration, see Dominick LaCapra, *Representing the Holocaust: History, Theory, Trauma* (Ithaca, NY: Cornell University Press, 1994), 143.

50 John English, *The Decline of Politics* (Toronto: University of Toronto Press, 1977), 122.

51 On working-class gains in both purchasing power and leisure time, see Altman, "New Estimates of Hours of Work," 354. On per capita gains in consumption, see Monod, *Store Wars*, 110–11.

52 Fiamengo, *The Woman's Page*, 211, and Dianne M. Hallman, "Cultivating a Love of Canada through History: Agnes Maule Machar, 1837–1927," *Creating Historical Memory: English-Canadian Women and the Work of History*, ed. Beverly Boutilier and Alison Prentice (Vancouver: UBC Press, 1997), 25–26, 31.

53 The rise of the social gospel movement is associated with the shift towards a more secular world view; however, the timing and pace of change remains a subject of controversy. A useful overview is David B. Marshall, "Canadian Historians, Secularization and the Problem of the Nineteenth Century," *Canadian Catholic Historical Association, Historical Studies* 60 (1993–94): 57–81. Richard Allen recaps recent debates in Richard Allen, *The View from Murney Tower: Salem Bland, the Late Victorian Controversies, and the Search for a New Christianity* (Toronto: University of Toronto Press, 2008), xxix–xxiii. On the social gospel movement as a response to religious doubt and secular competition, see A.B. McKillop, *A Disciplined Intelligence* (Montreal and Kingston: McGill-Queen's University Press, 1979), 205–20; David B. Marshall, *Secularizing the Faith: Canadian Protestant Clergy and the Crisis of Belief, 1850–1940* (Toronto: University of Toronto Press, 1992), 25–48; Ramsay Cook, *The Regenerators: Social Criticism in Late Victorian English Canada* (Toronto: University of Toronto Press, 1985), 4, 26–40. Michael Gauvreau discerns less doubt and argues that the Canadian clergy greeted the challenges of modernity with confidence, seeing opportunity rather than crisis. Michael Gauvreau, *The Evangelical Century: College and Creed in English Canada from the Great Revival to the Great Depression* (Montreal and Kingston: McGill-Queen's University Press, 1991).

54 A.E. Smith, cited in Richard Allen, *The Social Passion: Religious and Social Reform in Canada, 1914–28* (Toronto: University of Toronto Press, 1971), 23.

55 *Grain Growers' Guide*, 30 June 1915, cited in Kenneth McNaught, *A Prophet in Politics: A Biography of J.S. Woodsworth* (Toronto: University of Toronto Press, 2001), 71.

56 Rev. Regina Mackinnon, "The Church and the New Patriotism," *Addresses Delivered at the Pre-Assembly Congress of the Presbyterian Church in Canada* (Toronto: Board of Foreign Missions, Presbyterian Church in Canada, 1913), 209.

57 Rev. A.G. Sinclair, "The Family at Home," *Addresses Delivered at the Pre-Assembly Congress*, 162–63.

58 Ibid., 168.

59 While they objected to economic exploitation and extremes of wealth and poverty, many progressive ministers were not opposed to industrialization per se. Rather, they made a distinction between the ability of the industrial system to produce abundance and its specific manifestation in a world subject to greed. Progressive ministers often described large-scale industry as a vehicle that could help to reconstitute society on a Christian basis. As Salem Bland, a radical minister frequently associated with socialism, explained, religious fellowship was "to be found in the process of industry and commerce." "God intends to use industrial life to bring His Kingdom on earth." Increased productivity and opportunities for increased consumption went hand in hand: the systematic organization of industry would equalize consumption. Salem Bland, *The New Christianity, or the Religion of the New Age* (Toronto: McClelland and Stewart, 1920), 8–9, 17, 88. People such as Bland viewed the techniques of industrial organization and the values of efficiency and orderly management as preparing the conditions for the Kingdom of God. See for other examples: *Social Service, Ottawa, 1914: Report of Addresses and Proceedings* (Toronto: Social Service Council of Canada, 1914), 42–45, and Allen, *The Social Passion*, 23–24.

60 Stewart Crysdale, *The Industrial Struggle and Protestant Ethics in Canada: A Survey of Changing Power Structures and Christian Social Ethics* (Toronto: Ryerson Press, 1961), 19–20.

61 Rev. Albert Carman, "The Gospel of Justice" (1891), cited in Marshall, *Secularizing the Faith*, 68, and Cook, *The Regenerators*, 134, 192.

62 Rev. C.W. Gordon, "The Canadian Situation," *Addresses Delivered at the Pre-Assembly Congress*, 92–3.

63 Rev. J.A. Macdonald, LLD, "The Relation of the Church to the Social and Industrial Situation," ibid., 218. See also Richard Allen, ed., *The Social Gospel in Canada: Papers of the Interdisciplinary Conference on the Social Gospel in Canada, March 21–24, 1973* (Ottawa: National Museums of Canada, 1975), 16–17; John Webster Grant, *The Church in the Canadian Era* (Burlington, ON: Welch Publishing, 1988), 112; Neil Semple, *The Lord's Dominion: The History of Canadian Methodism* (Montreal and Kingston: McGill-Queen's University Press, 1996), 340, 354.

64 On the Fred Victor Mission, see Semple, *The Lord's Dominion*, 298, and J.S. Woodsworth, *My Neighbour: A Study of City Conditions, a Plea for Social Service* (Toronto: Missionary Society of the Methodist Church, Young People's Forward Movement, 1911), 200–4. On All People's Church, see Woodsworth, *My Neighbour*, 208.

65 For a discussion of the standard of living as a tool of assimilation in American progressivism, see William R. Leach, *Land of Desire: Merchants, Power, and the Rise of a New American Culture* (New York: Pantheon Books, 1993), 242–43. The

identification of new material needs can also be understood as a response to concerns over social unrest rather than inequality. The social threat represented by poverty is not simply acts of violence, but the violation of community standards. Property serves to integrate the poor into the social order and, more importantly, into the defence of that order. Giovanna Procacci, "Social Economy and the Government of Poverty," in *The Foucault Effect: Studies in Governmentality*, ed. Graham Burchell, Colin Gordon, and Peter Miller (Chicago: University of Chicago Press, 1991), 151–68. On this theme, see also J.S. Woodworth, *Strangers within Our Gates: Or, Coming Canadians* (1909; repr., Toronto: University of Toronto Press, 1972).

66 Marshall, *Secularizing the Faith*, 23, 264.

67 Ibid., 127–28, 139–41; Kevin Kee, *Revivalists: Marketing the Gospel in English Canada, 1884–1957* (Montreal and Kingston: McGill-Queen's University Press, 2006), 7–9, 13–17, 40–52; Karr, *Authors and Audiences*, 35–36, 47; Nancy Christie and Michael Gauvreau, *A Full-Orbed Christianity: The Protestant Churches and Social Welfare in Canada, 1900–1940* (Montreal and Kingston: McGill-Queen's University Press, 1996), 37–39.

68 After more than a decade of debate, the 1910 General Conference of the Methodist Church dropped restrictions listing drinking, card-playing, dancing, and theatre attendance as forbidden activities. There was a new emphasis on "educated Christian conscience," rather than specific rules as the guide to morality. Phyllis D. Airhart, *Serving the Present Age: Revivalism, Progressivism and the Methodist Tradition in Canada* (Montreal and Kingston: McGill-Queen's University Press, 1992), 103.

69 Allen, *Social Gospel in Canada*, 33; Brian Clarke, "English Speaking Canada from 1854," in *A Concise History of Christianity in Canada*, ed. Terrence Murphy, Roberto Perin, and Gilles Chausse (Toronto: Oxford University Press, 1996), 333–34. For American parallels, see Ben Primer, *Protestants and American Business Methods* (Ann Arbor, MI: UMI Research Press, 1979). Religious periodicals opened their pages to consumer advertisements; however, on lingering tensions between the ethical emphasis of religious periodicals and consumer imperatives, see Johnston, *Selling Themselves*, 254–57.

70 Christie and Gauvreau, *A Full-Orbed Christianity*, 44–45, 47–48. Christie and Gauvreau argue that the concerns Marshall identifies occurred later; they point to the continuing strength of the church, particularly in rural Canada, before the Second World War.

71 On this theme, see Joan Shelley Rubin, "Salvation as Self-Realization," *Reviews in American History* 20, 4 (1992): 505–11.

72 Cited in George Emery, *The Methodist Church on the Prairies, 1896–1914* (Montreal and Kingston: McGill-Queen's University Press, 2001), 41.

73 Donohue, *Freedom from Want*, 113.

74 Generally, the more conservative regarded the salvation of the individual as the key to the salvation of society and called for legislation to force compliance; the more radical emphasized the need for social change as the basis for moral reform;

and the progressive sought a middle road, with a broad program of ameliorative social reform. Allen, *The Social Passion,* 17.

75 Alfred Marshall, *Principles of Economics,* Vol. 3, 3rd ed. (London: Macmillan, 1895), 212.

76 See discussions in Douglas J. Goodman and Mirelle Cohen, *Consumer Culture: A Reference Handbook* (Santa Barbara, CA: ABC-CLIO, 2004), 28–29, and David A. Reisman, *Alfred Marshall: Progress and Politics* (London: Routledge, 2011), 42–46.

77 James Livingston, *Pragmatism, Feminism, and Democracy: Rethinking the Politics of American History* (London: Routledge, 2001), 49–57; Charles F. McGovern, *Sold American: Consumption and Citizenship, 1890–1945* (Chapel Hill: University of North Carolina Press, 2006), 135–37.

78 Owram, *The Government Generation,* 13.

79 The first academic economists (William Ashley, John Davidson, and Albert Flux) arrived in Canada from Britain late in the nineteenth century. For the most part, they continued to work on the topics that had interested them before arriving in Canada and all left after several years. Although Canada's domestic economy was not the focus of attention, they did some work in the field, laying the groundwork for their successors. The slow development of economics as an academic discipline in Canada stood in marked contrast to the high degree of professionalization already achieved in the United States and Great Britain. Craufurd D.W. Goodwin, *Canadian Economic Thought: The Political Economy of a Developing Nation, 1814–1914* (Durham, NC: Duke University Press, 1961), 158, 172–75, 195–96; Robin Neill, *A History of Canadian Economic Thought* (London: Routledge, 1991), 120–21; Owram, *The Government Generation,* 10–13.

80 Goodwin, *Canadian Economic Thought,* 158–61, 186–93, 195–96. Shortt had intended to become a minister and studied philosophy at Queen's, Edinburgh, and Glasgow Universities before returning to take up the teaching of political economy at Queen's University. Mavor came to political economy from a background in the applied sciences. Although friends with a number of the leading economists in Britain and Europe, he had no formal training in economics. Leacock was educated in literature and the classics and had taught these subjects for eight years at Upper Canada College before going to the University of Chicago to do graduate work in economics. Skelton, who took over from Shortt at Queen's, had studied Latin and Greek and begun his doctoral work in classics. After three years working in Philadelphia as the assistant editor of *Booklovers Magazine,* he turned to the study of economics at the University of Chicago. On Shortt, see Shortt, *The Search for an Ideal,* 95–116; Barry Ferguson, *Remaking Liberalism: The Intellectual Legacy of Adam Shortt, O.D. Skelton, W.C. Clark, and W.A. Mackintosh, 1890–1925* (Montreal and Kingston: McGill-Queen's University Press, 1993); W.A. Mackintosh, "Adam Shortt, 1859–1931," *Canadian Journal of Economics and Political Science* 4, 2 (1938): 164–76. On Mavor, see Alan Bowker, "Truly Useful Men: Maurice Hutton, George Wrong, James Mavor and the University of Toronto, 1888–1927" (PhD thesis, York

University, 1975), 111–51; Shortt, *The Search for an Ideal*, 119–35; Paul Craven, *"An Impartial Umpire": Industrial Relations and the Canadian State, 1900–1901* (Toronto: University of Toronto Press, 1980), 44–51. On Skelton, who took over from Shortt at Queen's, see Ferguson, *Remaking Liberalism;* J.L. Granatstein, *The Ottawa Men: The Civil Service Mandarins, 1935–1957* (Toronto: University of Toronto Press, 1998), 28–34; and Terry Crowley, *Marriage of Minds: Isabel and Oscar Skelton Reinventing Canada* (Toronto: University of Toronto Press, 2003). On Leacock, with an emphasis on his work as an economist, see the introduction in Alan Bowker, ed., *The Social Criticism of Stephen Leacock: The Unsolved Riddle of Social Justice and Other Essays* (Toronto: University of Toronto Press, 1973), and Carl Berger, "The Other Mr. Leacock," *Canadian Literature* 55 (Winter 1973): 25–26, 32.

81 Adam Shortt, "The Evolution of the Relation between Capital and Labor," *Andover Review* 11, 62 (1889): 153; Adam Shortt, "The Nature and Sphere of Political Economy," *Queen's Quarterly* 1 (1893): 95–96; Ferguson, *Remaking Liberalism,* 47–49.

82 Adam Shortt, "The Influence of Daily Occupations on the Social Life of the People," *Sunday Afternoon Addresses, Series Three* (Queen's University: Alma Mater Society, 1893), 60.

83 Ibid., 67. The suggestion that changes in consumption could provide access to a more spiritual life also appears in the works of John Ruskin (1819–1900), William Morris (1834–96), and J.A. Hobson (1858–1940). It remains to be determined whether parallels between Shortt's ideas and those of these British thinkers were the result of direct links or of similar responses to similar conditions. On Hobson, see Martin Daunton and Matthew Hilton, *The Politics of Consumption: Material Culture and Citizenship in Europe and America* (Oxford: Berg, 2001), 66–68; and Matthew Hilton, "The Legacy of Luxury: Moralities of Consumption since the 18th Century," *Journal of Consumer Culture* 4, 1 (2004): 112–14.

84 Adam Shortt, "Some Aspects of the Social Life of Canada," *Canadian Magazine* 11, 1 (1898): 6.

85 Ibid.

86 In England, beginning in the mid-1800s, William Stanley Jevons led the development of marginalist theory, proposing that the ultimate value of goods depended on their ability to satisfy the market better than their alternatives. Technological improvements, he observed, encouraged growing demand. Later in the century, fellow British economist Alfred Marshall reinforced this shift, developing what would become the standard graphs of supply and demand, demonstrating the relationship between quantity and price. The concept of diminishing returns and the possibility of consumer and producer surpluses (increasingly common with developments in industry) were now accounted for in economic theory. Canadian economists working at this time did not advance marginalist theory; however, they were familiar with it. See, for example, Mavor's review of Alfred Marshall's "Elements of Economics of Industry," *International Journal of Ethics* 3, 2 (1893): 266–67. On marginal utility, see T.W. Hutchison, *A Review of Economic Doctrines, 1870–1929* (Oxford: Clarendon Press, 1953), 252; James Livingston, *Pragmatism*

and the Political Economy of Cultural Revolution, 1850–1940 (Chapel Hill: University of North Carolina Press, 1994), 49–53; McGovern, *Sold American*, 135–37.

87 Adam Shortt, "The Basis of Economic Value," *Queen's Quarterly* 2 (July 1894): 72–73.

88 Bowker, "Truly Useful Men," 115–19; Craven, *"An Impartial Umpire,"* 44–45.

89 James Mavor, *On Wage Statistics and Wage Theories* (Edinburgh: W. Brown, 1888), 9. The introduction of statistics (the "amoral vehicle of indifferent facts") in the discussion of poverty had begun with the economist Thomas Malthus and remained controversial. See Mary Poovey, *A History of the Modern Fact: Problems of Knowledge in the Sciences of Wealth and Society* (Chicago: University of Chicago Press, 1998), 285–90, 295–96.

90 James Mavor, "The Relation of Economic Study to Public and Private Charity," *Annals of the American Academy of Political and Social Science* 4 (July 1893): 39–40.

91 On Mavor as an advocate of market-based solutions for philanthropic endeavours, see Thomas Adam, *Buying Respectability: Philanthropy and Urban Society in Transnational Perspective, 1840s to 1930s* (Bloomington: Indiana University Press, 2009), 24–26, 81–82.

92 James Mavor, "Industry and Finance," *University Magazine* 17 (October 1919): 346; S.E.D. Shortt, *Search for an Ideal*, 134.

93 Stephen Leacock, *Arcadian Adventures with the Idle Rich: A Critical Edition*, ed. D.M.R. Bentley (Ottawa: Tecumseh Press, 2002), 196.

94 Stephen Leacock, "Democracy and Social Progress," in *The New Era in Canada: Essays Dealing with the Upbuilding of the Canadian Commonwealth*, ed. J.O. Miller (London: Dent, 1917), 32.

95 Berger, *The Sense of Power*, 32, 33.

96 Stephen Leacock, "Practical Economics: The Theory of Wages," *Saturday Night*, 4 March 1911. Although many aspects of Leacock's critique echoed the ideas of American economist Thorstein Veblen, under whom he had studied at the University of Chicago, Leacock did not share Veblen's faith in the technocratic expert. On Veblen's relationship to emerging consumer awareness, see Donohue, *Freedom from Want*, 35–37, 40, 78–79, 156–59, and McGovern, *Sold American*, 138–49. On Leacock and Veblen, see Berger, "The Other Mr. Leacock," 25–26, 32. The influence of Veblen on Leacock, Skelton, and Harold Innis, and through them on Canadian economic thought more generally, has often been noted in passing but remains to be fully examined.

97 O.D. Skelton, *Socialism: A Critical Analysis* (Boston: Houghton Mifflin, 1911), 147–48. On Skelton's thesis, which offered an extensive analysis of Marx's *Capital*, see Ferguson, *Remaking Liberalism*, 103–4, and Joseph Levitt, "In Praise of Reform Capitalism: The Economic Ideas of O.D. Skelton," *Labour/Le Travailleur* 11 (Spring 1983): 143–54.

98 Skelton, *Socialism*, 59. Economic expansion was not, however, a smooth process. Conflict was essential to growth in ways that required mediating state action. Ferguson, *Remaking Liberalism*, 115.

99 Skelton, *Socialism*, 117–27, 130–36; Ferguson, *Remaking Liberalism*, 109.

100 Skelton, *Socialism,* 169–70.

101 Ibid., 210–15, 17–18.

102 O.D. Skelton, *General Economic History of the Dominion, 1867–1912* (Toronto: Publishers' Association of Canada, 1913), 271–73.

103 Adam Shortt, "War and Economics," *Addresses Delivered before the Canadian Club of Montreal,* Season 1914–1915, 26 April 1915, 313–16.

104 Stephen Leacock, "Our National Organization for the War," in Miller, *The New Era in Canada,* 411–13.

105 Ibid., 418.

106 Ferguson, *Remaking Liberalism,* 180.

107 O.D. Skelton, "Canadian Federal Finance – II," *Queen's Quarterly* 26 (October 1918): 204.

108 Ibid.

109 O.D. Skelton, "Canadian Federal Finance," *Queen's Quarterly* 23 (July 1915): 87.

110 Skelton, "Canadian Federal Finance – II," 228.

111 Joshua Yates and James Davison Hunter, eds., *Thrift and Thriving in America: Capitalism and Moral Order from the Puritans to the Present* (Oxford: Oxford University Press, 2011), 11, 93, 95–96.

112 See Horowitz, *The Morality of Spending,* 166–67.

113 It is not clear how much direct connection there was among the members of this small community of intellectuals. Skelton was a prominent member of the Presbyterian Board of Social Service. His analysis of socialism was recommended in church reading courses. Stephen Leacock and the Reverend Charles Gordon wrote best-selling novels and were popular speakers. Andrew Macphail had a large presence in conservative circles. Religious commitments varied, but most intellectuals at this time believed that the church had an essential role to play in urban reform. See Christie and Gauvreau, *A Full-Orbed Christianity,* 76, 92; Brian J. Fraser, *The Social Uplifters: Presbyterian Progressives and the Social Gospel in Canada, 1875–1915* (Waterloo, ON: Wilfrid Laurier University Press, 1988), 81.

114 Shortt, "Some Aspects of the Social Life of Canada," 6.

CHAPTER 2: THE PROMISE OF A MORE ABUNDANT LIFE

1 Reports on food riots in Europe in the *Globe* (Toronto), one of Canada's major daily papers, included "Bread Riots Break Out in Lisbon," 5 August 1911, 1; "The French Food Riots Break Out a Fresh," 14 September 1911, 1; "Fierce Food Rioting," 18 September 1911, 2; and "Berlin Dear Food Riots," 25 October 1912, 4. See also Patricia MacLachlan and Frank Trentmann, "Civilizing Markets: Traditions of Consumer Politics in Twentieth-Century Britain, Japan and the United States," in *Markets in Historical Contexts: Ideas and Politics in the Modern World,* ed. Mark Bevir and Frank Trentmann (Cambridge: Cambridge University Press, 2004), 170–81. On protests in the United States, see Meg Jacobs, *Pocketbook Politics: Economic Citizenship in Twentieth-Century America* (Princeton, NJ: Princeton University Press, 2007), 42–44.

2 This interpretation draws on the essays collected in *The Foucault Effect: Studies in Governmentality*, ed. Graham Burchell, Colin Gordon, and Peter Miller (Chicago: University of Chicago Press, 1991); the discussion of systematic sorting in Michel Foucault, *Discipline and Punish: The Birth of the Prison* (New York: Vintage Books, 1995), especially 198ff; and Mary Poovey, *A History of the Modern Fact: Problems of Knowledge in the Sciences of Wealth and Society* (Chicago: University of Chicago Press, 1998). Also see Alain Desrosières, "How to Make Things Which Hold Together: Social Science, Statistics and the State," in *Discourses on Society: The Shaping of the Social Science Disciplines*, ed. Peter Wagner, Björn Wittrock, and Richard P. Whitley (Dordrecht: Kluwer, 1991).

3 Consumption of non-essentials seems to have been possible for half of Ontario's wage-earning families: David Monod, *Store Wars: Shopkeepers and the Culture of Mass Marketing, 1890–1939* (Toronto: University of Toronto Press, 1996), 102–9, 384n6.

4 Thomas A. Stapleford, *The Cost of Living in America: A Political History of Economic Statistics, 1880–2000* (Cambridge: Cambridge University Press, 2009), 62.

5 *Report of the Board of Inquiry into the Cost of Living* (Ottawa: King's Printer, 1915), 2: 1016–17.

6 Richard Hofstadter, *The Age of Reform* (New York: Vintage Books, 1955), 172–73.

7 Ibid. Meg Jacobs asserts that "pocketbook politics" should be recognized as central to the history of the United States in the twentieth century: these themes were used by politicians to mobilize voters and played a key role in the expansion and retraction of the state. Controversies over consumer purchasing power provided a medium through which competing factions battled for support. Jacobs, *Pocketbook Politics*, 2–5. Horowitz proposes that rising prices intensified the struggle between, on the one hand, adherence to a moralist tradition and, on the other, a fuller acceptance of new comforts and patterns of consumption within the American middle class. His study of the moral debates engendered by rising costs provides an interesting comparison with the Canadian experience. Daniel Horowitz, *The Morality of Spending: Attitudes toward the Consumer Society in America, 1875–1940* (Baltimore: Johns Hopkins University Press, 1985), 67–73. In Britain, Matthew Hilton argues that a consumer consciousness emerged around the turn of the century, when people formulated a sense of what they earned in terms of what they could buy. The ability to purchase, rather than simply the wage, became the focus of labour negotiations. Matthew Hilton, *Consumerism in Twentieth-Century Britain: The Search for a Historical Movement* (Cambridge: Cambridge University Press, 2003), 1, 51–52. On consumption as a motivating force for American wage earners, see Lawrence Glickman, *A Living Wage: American Workers and the Making of Consumer Society* (Ithaca: Cornell University Press, 1997).

8 See John Castell Hopkins, "The Increased Cost of Living in Canada," *Canadian Annual Review of Public Affairs* (Toronto: Canadian Annual Review Publishing Company, 1910), 298–304. Independent inquiries were conducted by Canada's major daily papers, including the *Toronto News*, the *Toronto Daily Star*, the *Winnipeg Telegram*, the *Montreal Star*, the *Montreal Herald*, the *Ottawa Citizen*, and the *Saint John Standard*. Investigations were discussed or carried out by provincial

governments in Ontario and Manitoba and municipal authorities in Regina and Toronto. Stephen Leacock weighed the merits of different arguments in "The High Cost of Living," *Addresses Delivered before the Canadian Club, Season 1913–1914*, 3 November 1913. See also M.A. MacKenzie, "The High Cost of Living," *Canadian Magazine* 60, 4 (1913): 368–76.

9　Hopkins, "Increased Cost of Living in Canada," 299.

10　Andrew Macphail, "The Cost of Living," *University Magazine* 11, 4 (1912): 531, 526, 543.

11　See "Sparks from Labour's Anvil," *Toronto Daily Star*, 8 July 1912, 8, for a discussion of labour action by waiters, carpenters, and pressmen. Farm and labour leaders noted that both constituencies were affected by rising costs of living, and objected that mergers and trusts fixed prices to the disadvantage of producers and consumers. Even though they recognized common interests and a common enemy, farm and labour leaders were unwilling to relinquish their distinctive identities. See *Toronto Daily Star*, 25 January 1912, 24; "C.P.R. Operators Demand a Raise," *Toronto Daily Star*, 30 March 1910, 1.

12　"Employees of Railways Go into Sale of Provisions," *Toronto Daily Star*, 11 May 1912, 14. Street railway workers prepared detailed family budgets to successfully support demands for wage increases. *Toronto Daily Star*, 2 July 1912.

13　The Calgary league, the first of its kind in Canada, was initiated under the auspices of the local branch of the National Council of Women. The organization achieved almost immediate success in its campaign to reinvigorate a dilapidated public market for the sale of fresh produce. The objective was to eliminate the middleman by having market gardeners and farmers in the surrounding regions ship produce directly to the Calgary market, where consumers could have access to fresh produce at lower prices. The league was besieged by requests from across the country for advice, written materials, and speakers. New consumer leagues, inspired by the Calgary model, were formed in Brandon, Red Deer, Edmonton, and Saskatoon. Articles appeared in daily newspapers from Victoria to Toronto and Quebec City. Inquiries came from as far away as New York City. See Bettina Liverant, "Making a Market for Consumers: The Calgary Consumers' League and the High Cost of Living," in *Shopping for Change: Consumer Activism and the Possibilities of Purchasing Power*, ed. Louis Hyman and Joseph Tohill (Ithaca, NY and Toronto: ILR Press/ Cornell University Press and Between the Lines Press, 2017), 41–52.

14　See, for example, "The Consumer behind the Counter," *Grain Growers' Guide*, 26 July 1911, 7. However, the emphasis on price alone was insufficient to sustain the movement. Committed to quick returns in the form of low prices rather than the principles of cooperation, most failed within a few short years. See Brett Fairbairn, *Building a Dream: The Co-operative Retailing System in Western Canada, 1928–1988* (Saskatoon: Western Producer Prairie Books, 1989), 15–19.

15　Alan Hunt, "Measuring Morals: The Beginnings of the Social Survey Movement in Canada, 1913–1917," *Histoire sociale/Social History* 35, 69 (2002): 171–94; Mariana Valverde, *The Age of Light, Soap and Water: Moral Reform in English Canada, 1885–1925* (Toronto: McClelland and Stewart, 1991), 20, 44, 46. Eric Rauchway, "The

High Cost of Living in the Progressives' Economy," *Journal of American History* 88, 3 (2001): 899–900, 923.

16 Academics provided theoretical supports for activist government, calling for the regulation of capitalism's excess and the mediation of relations between capital and labour to quell social unrest. The expert adviser replaced the generalist of sound character as the ideal public servant. As Adam Shortt explained, this was "an age of experts" and expertise was the key to efficiency. Both expertise and efficiency were business values, and the prominence of these terms in the discussion of civil service reform gives an indication of the penetration of business values into all areas of public life during this period. Doug Owram, *The Government Generation: Canadian Intellectuals and the State, 1900–1945* (Toronto: University of Toronto Press, 1986), 41–45, 73, 84–86. On parallels between the expansion of government in the American Progressive era and in early twentieth-century Canada, see V. Seymour Wilson, "The Influence of Organizational Theory in Canadian Public Administration," in *Canadian Public Administration: Discipline and Profession*, ed. Kenneth Kernaghan (Toronto: Butterworths, 1983), 106–8.

17 Robert Craig Brown and Ramsay Cook, *Canada: A Nation Transformed, 1896–1921* (Toronto: McClelland and Stewart, 1974), 193–94.

18 The scientific management and the classification movements in other nations were decisive influences on the development of government administration in Canada. The British tradition of administrative generalists was replaced by a hierarchical structure, with an emphasis on technical specialization and an ideology of business efficiency. Tasks of government were examined as mechanistic processes, civil service positions were classified by function, and examinations were devised to determine which candidates were best qualified to fill specific positions. Work was separated from worker. See J.E. Hodgetts, William McCloskey, Reginald Whitaker, and V. Seymour Wilson, *The Biography of an Institution: The Civil Service Commission of Canada, 1908–1967* (Montreal and Kingston: McGill-Queen's University Press, 1972), 65–66, 71; J.E. Hodgetts, "Implicit Values in the Administration of Public Affairs," in *Canadian Public Administration: Discipline and Profession*, ed. Kenneth Kernaghan (Toronto: Butterworths, 1983), 30; and "A Farwell Contribution from Griffenhage and Associates Limited," in *The Civilian: Canadian Civil Service Staff Publication* (February 1921), 69, cited by Wilson, "Influence of Organizational Theory," 106–7.

19 The values of the bureaucracy, it should be noted, were different than the political values of representation, responsibility, and responsiveness. These terms had been prominent in the eighteenth-century fight for responsible government and were associated with the building up of the nation during a period that also saw the build-up of private enterprise. The authority of management, however, was not rooted in politics, property, or labour, but in more diffuse forms of power exercised without ownership. On the rise of the professional managerial class, see Warren I. Susman, *Culture as History: The Transformation of American Society in the Twentieth Century* (New York: Pantheon Books, 1984), xxi–xxii.

20 James Livingston discusses the corporate form as the enabling condition of consumer society. Dispersing power broadened the terrain of political struggle, opening a middle ground that would become the terrain of cultural politics: Livingston, *Pragmatism, Feminism, and Democracy: Rethinking the Politics of American History* (London: Routledge, 2001), 54–55. Matthew Hilton argues that the politics of consumption has persistently offered itself as a middle way or "third" solution in the struggle between capital and labour. Hilton, *Consumerism in Twentieth-Century Britain*, 1, 12–14, 296–97.

21 R.H. Coats, *A National System of Statistics for Canada* (Ottawa: Census and Statistics Office, 1916), 7.

22 Ibid., 4–7. See also N. Keyfitz and H.F. Greenway, "Robert Coats and the Organization of Statistics," *Canadian Journal of Economics and Political Science* 27 (August 1961): 313–22.

23 On civil service reform as a tactic of bureaucratic expansion, see Ken Rasmussen, "Administrative Reform and the Quest for Bureaucratic Autonomy, 1867–1919," *Journal of Canadian Studies* 29, 3 (1994): 45–62. In its "managerial mode," the state requires statistical data, both as an indicator of performance and as a tool of administration. Stapleford, *The Cost of Living in America*, 60.

24 Stapleford, *The Cost of Living in America*, 57–58.

25 Rauchway, "The High Cost of Living," 899.

26 David A. Worton, *The Dominion Bureau of Statistics: A History of Canada's Central Statistics Office and Its Antecedents, 1841–1972* (Montreal and Kingston: McGill-Queen's University Press, 1998), 47.

27 Ibid., 48.

28 Both King and Coats were innovators in their respective fields. Coats would soon make himself Canada's foremost expert in the coordination of financial and economic data, as head of the Dominion Bureau of Statistics, a department he organized and subsequently led for forty years. He turned down offers from industry as well as an opportunity to become the chief statistician of the League of Nations, although he later became a statistical adviser to the United Nations. International honours included a term as president of the American Statistical Association.

King began this period in the civil service, before wining election to Parliament in 1908 and becoming Canada's first minister of labour. Upon losing his seat in 1911, he was invited to head the Rockefeller Foundation's new Department of Industrial Research. He was elected to Parliament again in 1919 and became prime minister in 1921. He held that office off and on for twenty-one years, making him the longest-serving prime minister in the British Empire. American historian James Livingston describes King as the man who "invented the 'human relations' brand of industrial psychology." Livingston regards this tactic of separating private property and labour from the management of the industrial process as a key step in the managerial revolution that accompanied the emergence of both large-scale industry and consumer culture. James Livingston, *Pragmatism and the Political Economy of Cultural Revolution, 1850–1940* (Chapel Hill: University of North Carolina Press, 1994), 94, 100, 328n18. See Irving Bernstein, *The Lean Years: A History of the American*

Worker, 1920–1933 (Cambridge: Riverside Press, 1960), 159–69 for a useful discussion of King as a professional intellectual.

29 On statistics and governmentality see Bruce Curtis, "Surveying the Social: Techniques, Practices, Power," *Histoire sociale/Social History* 35, 69 (2002): especially 90–91.

30 See Worton, *The Dominion Bureau of Statistics,* 49–50, for a detailed account of Coats' persistence and King's lack of response.

31 Ibid., 49.

32 Paul Craven, *"An Impartial Umpire": Industrial Relations and the Canadian State, 1900–1901* (Toronto: University of Toronto Press, 1980), 220; Worton, *The Dominion Bureau of Statistics,* 51.

33 Robert Hamilton Coats and the Canadian Department of Labour, *Wholesale Prices in Canada, 1890–1909, Special Report* (Ottawa: Government Print Bureau, 1910), 8.

34 *Labour Gazette,* February 1910, 894.

35 Coats, *Wholesale Prices in Canada,* 2.

36 Ibid., 3.

37 "Experimenting with Weighted Averages," in ibid., 12–15, and Appendix I, ibid., 433–89. Stephen Leacock, "The Movement of Prices and the Rise in the Cost of Living: Practical Political Economy VII," *Saturday Night,* 24 December 1910, 21–22.

38 Discussing the same developments in America, Thomas A. Stapleford observes that, prior to this period of public unrest, the government had no compelling reason to collect information on prices and wages, as retail prices had no role in the dominant concept of political economy. It was popular pressure and concerns about labour unrest that led to the cost of living index. Stapleford, *The Cost of Living in America,* 60.

39 Coats, *Wholesale Prices in Canada,* 489.

40 Mary Poovey describes organizing and interpreting data as a process of "making sense" that makes certain aspects of the world available for discussion. Poovey, *A History of the Modern Fact,* xi–xv, 1–5. Alain Desrosières similarly proposes that "the social category that is being described and measured is also being constructed and made visible." Desrosières, "How to Make Things Which Hold Together," 203.

41 Government effort on behalf of the Canadian consumer was not new but had generally been limited to the regulation of individual products and linked to the protection of public health and the control of fraud. With the move away from direct face-to-face transactions and the introduction of packaged and manufactured goods in which the nature and quality of products could potentially be disguised, it was regarded as necessary to devise substitutes for the informal controls of the neighbourhood market. Government controls provided a sort of "guarantee" that would improve trade by reassuring Canadians that it was fundamentally safe to participate in extended commercial networks. Investigation into the cost of living signalled an expansion of the state's interest in the private purchasing decisions of its citizens and a new understanding of the relationship between private consumption and the larger economy. See James Alexander Corry, *The Growth of Government Activities*

since Confederation (Ottawa: Royal Commission on Dominion-Provincial Relations, 1939), 20–28, 40, for a summary of early federal consumer legislation.

42 The *Toronto Daily Star,* for example, ran a series entitled "Why Is Toronto Housekeeping So Dear?" from 20 April 20 to 12 May 1911, culminating in an appeal to readers for practical suggestions to reduce the cost of living.

43 John Castell Hopkins, "The Increased Cost of Living and Its Causes," *Canadian Annual Review of Public Affairs* (Toronto: Annual Review Publishing Company, 1913), 313–21.

44 *Report of the Board of Inquiry into the Cost of Living* (Ottawa: King's Printer, 1915), 2: 1068.

45 Ibid., 1: 5.

46 See Worton, *The Dominion Bureau of Statistics,* 54–56, for a discussion of the negotiations involved in the production of the final report.

47 Horowitz's analysis of studies of working-class budgets conducted by the American Bureau of Labor in the late nineteenth century provides a useful model, highlighting differences in moral values and expectations between traditional and emerging patterns of consumption. Horowitz, *The Morality of the Spending,* 13–29.

48 *The Canadian Who's Who* (London: The Times, 1910), 155.

49 Worton, *The Dominion Bureau of Statistics,* 54.

50 *Report of the Board of Inquiry into the Cost of Living,* 1: 79.

51 Ibid., 16, 15–17, 12.

52 Ibid., 13–14.

53 Ibid., 15.

54 Ibid. See Horowitz, *The Morality of Spending,* 73–74, for a similar discussion of American attitudes, albeit forty years earlier, suggesting both the persistence of moral frameworks and a lag in development between Canada and the United States.

55 Coats' work in preparing the report received favourable attention in the community of professional economists, including praise from British economist Alfred Marshall and American economist Wesley Clair Mitchell, who described the investigation as "a real contribution to economic science" and "precisely the kind of work which is most needed for bettering our understanding of current economic developments, and for guiding our economic policy wisely." Worton, *Dominion Bureau of Statistics,* 57.

56 "Consumption and the Standard of Living," *Report of the Board of Inquiry into the Cost of Living,* 1: 46ff.

57 Ibid., 2: 1017.

58 Ibid., 2: 1068.

59 Coats was named the first dominion statistician in 1915. The Census and Statistics Office operated as a branch of the Department of Trade and Commerce until an act of Parliament formally established the Dominion Bureau of Statistics in 1918.

60 Livingston, *Pragmatism and the Political Economy of Cultural Revolution,* 20–1.

61 Poovey argues that the disinterested collection of data should be regarded as a fundamental marker of modernity. She proposes that the tension between first-hand

observation and systemic knowledge required a professional or disciplinary solution, with the result that knowledge production became the task of experts. Poovey, *A History of the Modern Fact,* xii–iv, 3. Alain Desrosières similarly notes, "In each case it is necessary to transcend the contingency of particular cases and circumstances and to make *things which hold together,* which display the qualities of generality and permanence ... The question is not: 'Are these objects *really* equivalent?' but: 'Who decided to treat them as equivalent and to what end?'" Desrosières, "How to Make Things Which Hold Together," 200–1 (emphasis in original).

62 William Lyon Mackenzie King, *Industry and Humanity: A Study in the Principles Underlying Industrial Reconstruction* (1918; repr., Toronto: University of Toronto Press, 1973), 32, 66, 78.

63 William Lyon Mackenzie King, "The Four Parties to Industry," *Address before the Empire Club of Canada, Toronto, 13 March 1919* (Toronto: Hunter Rose, 1919), 31–32.

64 F.A. McGregor, *The Fall and Rise of Mackenzie King, 1911–1929* (Toronto: Macmillan, 1962), 216–17.

65 In practice, the information available to the general public was often limited by arbitrators who used their personal skill to negotiate agreements that generally sought to balance labour's needs for a living wage with the prerogatives of property. In disputes arbitrated by Adam Shortt, for example, the goal was negotiated agreement rather than conciliation. Shortt, the most frequently appointed arbitrator on boards convened under the Industrial Disputes Investigation Act, rejected the utility of publicity, fearing that it would force disputants to become entrenched in their positions. His object was not to make a report that public opinion would compel the disputants to accept, but to achieve an agreement and then to report it. Craven, *"An Impartial Umpire,"* 296, 299–301; Robert C. Wallace, *Some Great Men of Queen's* (Toronto: Ryerson Press, 1941),124–25.

66 King, *Industry and Humanity,* 97.

67 Coal, King noted, not only was necessary in manufacturing and transportation, but was something that "as the recent experience has shown, much of happiness and life itself depends." W. L. Mackenzie King, "Settlement of Coal Miners Strike at Lethbridge, Alberta, Under the Conciliation Act," *Labour Gazette* 7, 6 (Ottawa: King's Printer, December 1906): 661–62.

68 King, *Industry and Humanity,* 28–29, 32.

69 Ibid.

70 Karl Mannheim, *Ideology and Utopia* (New York: Harcourt, 1985), 118–19.

71 Craven, *"An Impartial Umpire,"* 353.

CHAPTER 3: CULTURING CANADIAN PATRIOTISM

1 For three examples in different eras, see Paul Litt's discussion of the views held by the Royal Commission on National Development in the Arts, Letters and Sciences in the late 1940s and early 1950s in "The Massey Commission, Americanization, and Canadian Cultural Nationalism," *Queen's Quarterly* 98 (Summer 1991): 375–87;

John Herd Thompson and Allen Seager, "The Conundrum of Culture," in *Canada, 1922–1939: Decades of Discord* (Toronto: McClelland and Stewart, 1986), 159–92; and Jonathan Vance, *A History of Canadian Culture* (Toronto: Oxford University Press, 2009).

2 Arthur Lismer, cited in Angela Nairne Grigor, *Arthur Lismer, Visionary Art Educator* (Montreal and Kingston: McGill-Queen's University Press, 2002), 54.

3 Andreas Huyssen, *After the Great Divide: Modernism, Mass Culture, Postmodernism* (Bloomington: Indiana University Press, 1986), vii–x, 3–15. See also Pierre Bourdieu, *The Rules of Art: Genesis and Structure of the Literary Field* (Stanford: Stanford University Press, 1996), especially Chapter 3, "The Market for Symbolic Goods," 141–73.

4 Palmer describes the advance of mass culture in the interwar period as "the first act that gives sense of what was to come." Cultural historian Michael Kammen uses the term "proto-mass culture," arguing that mass culture requires not simply a mass of consumers, but also mass media, mass leisure, and mass accessiblity. Bryan D. Palmer, *Working Class Experience: Rethinking the History of Canadian Labour, 1800–1991* (Toronto: McClelland and Stewart, 1983), 230–35. Michael Kammen, *American Culture, American Tastes: Social Change and the 20th Century* (New York: Knopf, 1999), 17.

5 On the irregular advance of mass consumption, see Palmer, *Working Class Experience*, 231–32, and Veronica Strong-Boag, *The New Day Recalled: Lives of Girls and Women in English Canada, 1919–1939* (Toronto: Copp Clark Pitman, 1988), 113–14.

6 Mary Vipond, *The Mass Media in Canada* (Toronto: Lorimer, 2011), 30–47; Thompson and Seager, *Canada, 1922–1939*, 175–92.

7 Maria Tippett, *Making Culture: English-Canadian Institutions and the Arts before the Massey Commission* (Toronto: University of Toronto Press, 1990), 4, 28, 186.

8 Bourdieu, *The Rules of Art*, 161–65.

9 Joan Shelley Rubin, *The Making of Middlebrow Culture* (Chapel Hill: University of North Carolina Press, 1992), 18–19.

10 This analysis draws heavily on Bourdieu, but uses his concepts quite differently. See Bourdieu, *The Rules of Art*, 141–73; Kammen, *American Culture*, 36.

11 The term "cultural entrepreneur" is used by Ian McKay, *The Quest of the Folk: Antimodernism and Cultural Selection in Twentieth-Century Nova Scotia* (Montreal and Kingston: McGill-Queen's University Press, 1994), 57, 60, and Kammen, *American Culture*, 36.

12 Herbert J. Gans, *Popular Culture and High Culture: An Analysis and Evaluation of Taste*, rev. ed. (New York: Basic Books, 2008), 4.

13 Without the time or training needed for the consumption of high culture, members of the professional-managerial class strategically purchase high cultural signifiers to secure higher social status. John Guillory, "The Ordeal of Middlebrow Culture," *Transition* 67 (1995): 86–87. The term "professional-managerial class" is useful, but it has been criticized as a muddled concept, more accurate as a description of higher occupational status rather than as a coherent class. The term comes from

Barbara Ehrenreich and John Ehrenreich, "The Professional-Managerial Class," in *Between Labor and Capital*, ed. Pat Walker (Montreal: Black Rose Books, 1979), 19. See also James F. English, "Cultural Capital and the Revolutions of Literary Modernity, from Bourdieu to Casanova," in *A Handbook of Modernism Studies*, ed. Jean-Michel Rabate (Somerset, UK: John Wiley, 2013), 367–71.

14 On the persistent gendering as feminine that which is devalued, see Huyssen, *After the Great Divide*, 53.

15 For a discussion on differences between "popular" and "mass" culture, see Kammen, *American Culture*, 49.

16 Mary Vipond, "The Nationalist Network: English Canada's Intellectuals and Artists in the 1920s," *Canadian Review of Studies in Nationalism* 5 (Spring 1980): 32–52.

17 "Salutation," *Dalhousie Review* 1, 1 (1921): 3; Very Reverend Llwyd, "Good Books the Bulwark of Democracy," *Canadian Bookman* 1, 1 (1919): 8.

18 American cultural authorities had struggled with the same developments in the mid- and late nineteenth century; see Rubin, *The Making of Middlebrow Culture*, 18–19.

19 Candida Rifkind, "Labours of Modernity: The Literary Left in English Canada, 1929–1939" (PhD thesis, York University, 2003), 10.

20 Jennifer Scanlon, *Inarticulate Longings: The Ladies' Home Journal, Gender, and the Promises of Consumer Culture* (New York: Routledge, 1995), 12–13.

21 Cynthia Wright, "Feminine Trifles of Vast Importance: Writing Gender into the History of Consumption," in *Gender Conflicts: New Essays in Women's History*, ed. Franca Iacovetta and Mariana Valverde (Toronto: University of Toronto Press, 1992), 245.

22 "Salutation," *Dalhousie Review* 1, 1 (1921): 3. "Notes and Comments," *Canadian Historical Review* 1, 1 (1920): 1; "Editorial," *Canadian Forum* 1, 1 (1920): 3; B.K. Sandwell, "Bookishness in Canada," *Canadian Bookman* 1, 1 (1919): 11. This interpretation builds on Michael Warner, "Publics and Counterpublics," *Public Culture* 14, 1 (2002): 55–63.

23 B.K. Sandwell, "Free Trade in Debasing Literature," *Canadian Bookman* 1, 2 (1919): 9. For additional uses of the term "narcotic," see "The New Era," *Canadian Bookman* 1, 1 (1919): 3; Barker Fairley, "Artists and Authors," *Canadian Forum* 2, 15 (1921): 460, 462; and Marcus Adeney, "The Community Spirit," *Canadian Forum* 8, 85 (1927): 427.

24 Sandwell, "Bookishness in Canada," 11.

25 T. McGarry, "Cheap Magazines, Crime and Insanity," *Canadian Bookman* 1, 1 (1919): 11.

26 By the end of the decade, the *Dalhousie Review* had 500 subscribers, the *Canadian Bookman* had 1,800, and the *Canadian Forum* 2,500. At the end of 1925, the circulation numbers of the leading Canadian general interest magazines were: 82,013 for *Maclean's*, 68,054 for the *Canadian Home Journal*, 30,858 for *Saturday Night*, and 12,604 for *Canadian Magazine*. As of 30 June 1926, the circulation numbers for American bestsellers in Canada were 152,011 for the *Ladies' Home Journal*, 128,574 for the *Saturday Evening Post*, 128,320 for the *Pictorial Review*, and 103,209 for

McCall's Magazine. Mary Vipond, "Canadian Nationalism and the Plight of Canadian Magazines in the 1920s," *Canadian Historical Review* 58, 1 (1977): 43–44.

27 The first list of American "best-sellers" appeared in 1895. Clarence Karr, *Authors and Audiences: Popular Canadian Fiction in the Early Twentieth Century* (Montreal and Kingston: McGill-Queen's University Press, 2000), 26.

28 On the competing claims of popularity and literary prestige in the careers and lives of Pauline Johnson, Stephen Leacock, Lucy Maud Montgomery, and the Reverend Charles Gordon (writing as Ralph Connor), see Lorraine York, *Literary Celebrity in Canada* (Toronto: University of Toronto Press, 2007), chap. 2.

29 The literacy rates were measured by the ability to read and write in either English or French, and thus did not include immigrants who could read and write only in their mother tongues. Michel Verrette, "Measuring Literacy," in *History of the Book in Canada*, Volume 3, *1918–1980*, ed. Carole Gerson and Jacques Michon (Toronto: University of Toronto Press, 2007), 453. Vipond, "Canadian Nationalism and the Plight of Canadian Magazines," 43–44; Vipond, *The Mass Media in Canada*, 30–35.

30 Mary Hammond, *Reading, Publishing and the Formation of Literary Taste in England, 1880–1914* (Aldershot, UK: Ashgate, 2006), 136.

31 B.K. Sandwell, "The New Era," *Canadian Bookman* 1, 1 (1919): 3.

32 Sandwell, "Bookishness in Canada," 11–12.

33 On the efforts of the *Canadian Bookman* and the Canadian Authors' Association to build a middle ground between the "narcotic" of the mass periodical and academia, see Kathryn Chittick, "Making Literature Hum: Canadian Literary Journalism in the Twenties," *Studies in Canadian Literature* 6, 2 (1981), https://journals.lib.unb.ca/index.php/SCL/article/view/7968/9025.

34 George L. Parker, "Authors and Publishers on the Offensive: The Canadian Copyright Act of 1921 and the Publishing Industry 1920–1930," *Papers of the Bibliographical Society of Canada* 50, 2 (2012): 131–85.

35 Barker Fairley, "Editorial," *Canadian Forum* 1, 8 (1921): 230.

36 Barker Fairley, "Editorial," *Canadian Forum* 2, 14 (1921): 422.

37 B.K. Sandwell, "Correspondence: Canadian Authors Association," *Canadian Forum* 2, 15 (1921): 459.

38 B.K. Sandwell, "Editorial: Canadian Authors Week," *Canadian Bookman* 4, 1 (December 1921): 5–6.

39 Barker Fairley, "Artists and Authors," *Canadian Forum* 2, 15 (1921): 460–63.

40 Basil King, "To the Editor," *Canadian Forum* 2, 16 (1922): 491.

41 A.J.M. Smith, "Wanted – Canadian Criticism," *Canadian Forum* 8, 91 (1928): 600–1.

42 F.R. Scott, "To the Editor," *Canadian Forum* 8, 93 (1928): 697–98.

43 Douglas Bush, "Making Literature Hum," *Canadian Forum* 8 (December 1926): 72–73.

44 On the tension between commercial and artistic commitments, see James Mulvihill, "The 'Canadian Bookman' and Literary Nationalism," *Canadian Literature* 107

(Winter 1985): 48–59. Colin Hill argues that the valuable role the *Bookman* played in the development of Canadian literary modernism has been buried by those who associate it with commerce and popular reading and claim the heroic role of building national literature for themselves. Colin Hill, "*Canadian Bookman* and the Origins of Modern Realism in English-Canadian Fiction," *Canadian Literature* 195 (Winter 2007): 85–103.

45 Bourdieu, *Rules of Art*, 160, 224–25.

46 Carole Gerson, "The Canon between the Wars: Field-Notes of a Feminist Literary Archaeologist," in *Canadian Canons: Essays in Literary Value*, ed. Robert Lecker (Toronto: University of Toronto Press, 1991), 46–56; Peggy Kelly, "Anthologies and the Canonization Process: A Case Study of the English Canadian Literary Field, 1920–1950," *Studies in Canadian Literature* 25, 1 (2000): 73–94; Rubin, *The Making of Middlebrow Culture*, 18–19.

47 Gerson, "The Canon between the Wars," 54; Di Brandt, "A New Geneology of Canadian Literary Modernism," in *Wider Boundaries of Daring*, ed. Di Brandt and Barbara Godard (Waterloo, ON: Wilfrid Laurier University Press, 2009), 3; Peggy Kelly, "Politics, Gender, and *New Provinces:* Dorothy Livesay and F.R. Scott," *Canadian Poetry: Studies, Documents, Reviews* 53 (Fall/Winter 2003): 54–70, http://canadianpoetry.org/volumes/vol53/kelly.html.

48 Gerson, "The Canon between the Wars," 47.

49 Ruth B. Phillips and Christopher B. Steiner, eds., *Unpacking Culture: Art and Commodity in Colonial and Postcolonial Worlds* (Berkeley: University of California Press, 1999), 19, and Lynda Jessup, ed., *Antimodernism and Artistic Experience: Policing the Boundaries of Modernity* (Toronto: University of Toronto Press, 2001), 3–4.

50 "The dialectic of the lowest has the same value as the dialectic of the highest ... Both bear the stigmata of capitalism, both contain elements of change." Theodor Adorno to Walter Benjamin, March 1936, cited and discussed in John Hutnyk, "Culture," *Theory, Culture and Society* 23, 2–3 (2009): 353–55.

51 McKay, *Quest of the Folk*, 29. Ruth B. Phillips, "The Collecting and Display of Souvenir Arts: Authenticity and the 'Strictly Commercial,'" in *The Anthropology of Art: A Reader*, ed. Howard Morphy and Morgan Perkins (Oxford: Blackwell, 2006), 447. Lynda Jessup, "Bushwhackers in the Gallery: Antimodernism and the Group of Seven," in Jessup, *Antimodernism and Artistic Experience*, 131; Lynda Jessup, "The Group of Seven and the Tourist Landscape in Western Canada, or the More Things Change ...," *Journal of Canadian Studies* 37, 1 (2002): 156, 162–63; Vipond, "The Nationalist Network," 32–52.

52 Sharon Wall, "Totem Poles, Teepees, and Token Traditions: 'Playing Indian' at Ontario Summer Camps, 1920–1955," *Canadian Historical Review* 86, 3 (2005): 537.

53 On anti-modernism, see T. Jackson Lears, *No Place of Grace: Antimodernism and the Transformation of American Culture, 1880–1920* (New York: Pantheon, 1981), xi–xii, 6–7, 57–58; McKay, *The Quest of the Folk*, xv, 33, 37; Ross D. Cameron, "Tom Thomson, Antimodernism, and the Ideal of Manhood," *Journal of the Can-*

adian Historical Association 10, 1 (1999): 185–208; Lynda Jessup, "Antimodernism and Artistic Experience: An Introduction," in Jessup, *Antimodernism and Artistic Experience,* 3–12; Lynda Jessup, "Prospectors, Bushwhackers, Painters: Antimodernism and the Group of Seven," *International Journal of Canadian Studies* 17 (Spring 1998): 193–214.

54 In Britain, the perception of anarchy associated with modern commercial society was heightened by way of contrast with a romanticized vision of pre-mechanized England, where craftsmen took pride in their work and pleasure in their surroundings and possessed a "dignified notion" of their place in the community. German intellectuals similarly despaired with respect to the superficiality of mass culture. While some turned to Marx, others, including the philosopher Martin Heidegger, were convinced that renewal could be achieved by reviving organic ties with the land, language, and *volk.* For an interesting and relevant discussion of interwar British anti-modernism and a return to the land, see Frank Trentmann, "Civilisation and Its Discontents: English Neo-Romanticism and the Transformation of Anti-Modernism in Twentieth Century Western Culture," *Journal of Contemporary History* 29, 4 (1994): 583–625.

55 Benedict Anderson, "Staging Antimodernism in the Age of High Capitalist Nationalism," in Jessup, *Antimodernism and Artistic Experience,* 98–99. Expressing nationalism involves establishing both the difference from other nations, usually from specific nations such as the motherland or a neighbouring country, and the underlying unity of disparate groups within the nation-state.

56 On Canadian anti-modernism as inversion and reversal, see McKay, *The Quest of the Folk,* xv, 9, 29; Ian McKay, "Among the Fisherfolk: J.F.B. Livesay and the Invention of Peggy's Cove," in *Interpreting Canada's Past,* Volume 2, *After Confederation,* ed. J.M. Bumsted, 2nd ed. (Toronto: Oxford University Press, 1993), 496–99.

57 Rev. R.P. Bowles, "Culturing Canadian Patriotism," address to the Empire Club of Canada, 3 April 1924, http://speeches.empireclub.org/62650/data?n=8.

58 On these themes, see Anne Whitelaw, "'Whiffs of Balsam, Pine, and Spruce': Art Museums and the Production of a Canadian Aesthetic," in *Capital Culture: A Reader on Modernist Legacies, State Institutions,* ed. Jody Berland and Shelley Hornstein (Montreal and Kingston: McGill-Queen's University Press, 2000), 122–37; Cameron, "Tom Thomson, Antimodernism, and the Ideal of Manhood," 185–208; Ryan Edwardson, "A Canadian Modernism: The Pre–Group of Seven 'Algonquin School,' 1912–17," *British Journal of Canadian Studies* 17, 1 (2004): 81–86; Anderson, "Staging Antimodernism," 97–103; Ross King, *Defiant Spirits: The Modernist Revolution of the Group of Seven* (Vancouver: Douglas and McIntyre, 2010), 133; Paul Hjartarson, "'Virgin Land,' the Settler-invader Subject, and Cultural Nationalism: Gendered Landscape in the Cultural Construction of Canadian National Identity," in *Gender and Landscape: Renegotiating the Moral Landscape,* ed. Josephine Carubia, Lorraine Dowler, and Bonj Szczygiel (London and New York: Routledge, 2005), 203–20.

59 Whitelaw, "'Whiffs of Balsam, Pine, and Spruce,'" 123.
60 Anne Whitelaw, "Theorizing in the Bush: Camping Pedagogy, Tom Thomson, and Cultural Studies," *Review of Education, Pedagogy, and Cultural Studies* 29, 2–3 (2007): 194.
61 Barker Fairly, "Editorial," *Canadian Forum* 1, 1 (1921): 230.
62 Lawren Harris, "Winning a Canadian Background," *Canadian Bookman* 5, 2 (1923): 37.
63 Arthur Lismer, cited by F.B. Housser, "Ideas of a Painter," *Canadian Bookman* 7, 4 (1925): 70.
64 This paragraph draws from Cameron, "Tom Thomson, Antimodernism, and the Ideal of Manhood," 185–208, and Whitelaw, "Theorizing in the Bush," 187–209.
65 Frederick B. Housser, *A Canadian Art Movement: The Story of the Group of Seven* (Toronto: Macmillan, 1926), 28.
66 Ibid, 28, 40, 158, 166. On this theme, see Ross D. Cameron, "Tom Thomson, Antimodernism, and the Ideal of Manhood," *Journal of the Canadian Historical Association* 10, 1 (1999): 185–208; Lynda Jessup, "Prospectors, Bushwhackers, Painters: Antimodernism and the Group of Seven," *International Journal of Canadian Studies* 17 (Spring 1998): 193–214.
67 Lawren Harris, "Artist and Audience," *Canadian Bookman* 7, 12 (1925): 197.
68 Housser, *A Canadian Art Movement*, 15, and see similar examples on 17, 25, 28, 30, 31, 33, 42.
69 Frederick B. Housser, "Ideas of a Painter," *Canadian Bookman* 7, 4 (1925): 70; Grigor, *Arthur Lismer*, 56.
70 Arthur Lismer, "Canadian Art," *Proceedings of the Canadian Club* (Toronto, 1926–27), 170, 172, 176.
71 Harris, "Artist and Audience," 197.
72 On the appeal of the Group of Seven, see Tippett, *Making Culture*, 84; Whitelaw, "Theorizing in the Bush," 193–94; Douglas Cole, "Artists, Patrons and Public: An Enquiry into the Success of the Group of Seven," *Journal of Canadian Studies* 13, 2 (1978): 69–78. On the use of art produced by members of the Group of Seven for tourism and promotion, see Jessup, "The Group of Seven and the Tourist Landscape." On the success of the Group of Seven as producers of middle-brow art, see Thompson and Seager, *Decades of Discord*, 162–63.
73 Harris and Jackson, cited in Edwardson, "A Canadian Modernism," 87.
74 Tippett, *Making Culture*, 84–85.
75 Vipond, "The Nationalist Network," 32–52; Tippett, *Making Culture*, 83–85.
76 Tippet, *Making Culture*, 83–85; Jessup, "The Group of Seven and the Tourist Landscape," 144–78.
77 Phillips and Steiner, *Unpacking Culture*, 19; Christopher B. Steiner, "Authenticity, Repetition, and the Aesthetics of Servility," in Phillips and Steiner, *Unpacking Culture*, 88; Phillips, "The Collecting and Display of Souvenir Arts," 411–13.
78 Canada came late to the Museum Age, which art historian Ruth Phillips identifies as mid-nineteenth to early twentieth century. Rarity and age determined the value

of goods; however, by the early twentieth century, there were a number of challenges in building ethnographic collections for national museums. The professionalization of collecting programs and development of academic anthropology had created a taxonomy of pre-contact culture with slots waiting to be filled. By the time Canadian museums began to build their collections, there were not enough goods available to fill all of the slots. There was a good supply of souvenir goods and tourist art, but there were no slots for these goods. Phillips, "The Collecting and Display of Souvenir Arts, " 432, 437–38, 446.

79   Ibid., 437, 439, 444.

80   McKay, *The Quest of the Folk,* 38, 105, 108–9. Examining the work and life of folklorist and folk-song collector Helen Creighton, McKay identifies a self-serving contradiction between her efforts to commercialize the material she collected and her relationships with her informants in the field. Creighton, as presented by McKay, is snobbish, paternalistic, and often insensitive, expressing concern that better living conditions would "rob" her sources "of all their charm." Thinking of her contacts as living in a pre-capitalist state, McKay asserts, freed Creighton from the obligation to pay them. Other critics have been kinder, noting that Creighton's position as a cultural authority was hard won in the field and her circumstances always modest. McKay's point is that cultural blindness offers economic benefits and that the effects of cultivating the image of one group as the primitive counterpart of modernity linger.

81   Arthur Lismer, "Art a Common Necessity," *Canadian Bookman* 7, 10 (1925): 159–60. See also Lily Barry, "Soul of Canada," *Canadian Bookman* 7, 1 (1925): 1, 4–5. On Arthur Lower, see W.H. Heick, "The Character and Spirit of an Age: A Study of the Thought of Arthur R.M. Lower," in *His Own Man: Essays in Honour of Arthur Reginald Marsden Lower,* ed. W.H. Heick and Roger Graham (Montreal and Kingston: McGill-Queen's University Press, 1974), 22–24, 34–35. Writings by Gibbon include the four-volume *French Canadian Folk Songs* (1928) and *Canadian Mosaic* (1938). On Gibbon, see Leighann C. Neilson, "John Murray Gibbon (1875–1952): The Branding of a Northern Nation," *Conference on Historical Analysis and Research in Marketing, 2011 Proceedings* (New York: CHARM Association, 2011), 128–44; Antonia Smith, "'Cement for the Canadian Mosaic': Performing Canadian Citizenship in the Work of John Murray Gibbon," *Race/Ethnicity: Multidisciplinary Global Contexts* 1, 1 (2007): 37–60; Stuart Henderson, "'While There Is Still Time ...': J. Murray Gibbon and the Spectacle of Difference in Three CPR Folk Festivals, 1928–1931," *Journal of Canadian Studies* 39, 1 (2005): 139–74; and McKay, *The Quest of the Folk,* 57–58.

82   In this context, it is useful to remember Terry Eagleton's observation that the idea of culture is "symptomatic" of the division it offers to overcome. See Terry Eagleton, *The Idea of Culture* (Oxford: Blackwell, 2000), 31.

83   Anthropology, sociology, and geography can be characterized as institutionally based systems of knowledge. Each constitutes an independently organized "teaching factory," with researchers and research projects, teaching programs and degree

structures, publishing houses, theoretical schools, methods, debates, tenure processes, career tracks, course guides, reading lists, and so on. As a privileged system, anthropology reaches well beyond any specifically local instance of the cultural. Hutnyk, "Culture," 351–75.

84 A.J.M. Smith, "Wanted: Canadian Criticism," *Canadian Forum* 8, 91 (1928): 600. For a discussion of Sapir's "experiments in aesthetics," see Regna Darnell, *Edward Sapir: Linguist, Anthropologist, Humanist* (Berkeley: University of California Press, 1990), 151–69. See also Richard Handler, "Sapir's Poetic Experience," *American Anthropologist* 86, 2 (1984): 416–17.

85 On the importance of Sapir's theoretical work while in Canada, see Stephen O. Murray, "The Canadian Winter of Edward Sapir," *Historiographia Linguistica* 8, 1 (1991): 63–68.

86 Edward Sapir, "Culture, Genuine and Spurious," *Dalhousie Review* 2, 2 (1922): 175. Sapir's theorizing was consistent with his practical work for the National Museum of Canada. Championing the primitive as the locus of values lost in the course of Western industrialization places the carriers of this culture outside the larger economy. Phillips, "The Collecting and Display of Souvenir Arts," 437–39, 443.

87 Sapir, "Culture, Genuine and Spurious," 172, 173.

88 Robert. M. MacIver, *Community, A Sociological Study* (London: Macmillan, 1917).

89 Robert M. MacIver, *The Modern State* (New York: Oxford University Press, 1926), 325.

90 Robert M. MacIver, "Civilization versus Culture," *University of Toronto Quarterly* 1, 3 (1932): 316–32.

91 Sapir, "Culture, Genuine and Spurious," 176.

92 Edward Sapir, "Culture in New Countries," *Dalhousie Review* 2, 3 (1922): 361.

93 Cited in Doug Owram, *The Government Generation: Canadian Intellectuals and the State, 1900–1945* (Toronto: University of Toronto Press, 1986), 118–19.

94 Marcus Adeney, "The Community Spirit," *Canadian Forum* 8, 85 (1927): 427; Marcus Adeney, "The Amateur Spirit," *Canadian Forum* 8, 95 (1928): 756. For a very different view of Paris, Ontario, as a community developed around the presence of industry, see Joy Parr, *The Gender of Breadwinners: Women, Men, and Change in Two Industrial Towns, 1880–1950* (Toronto: University of Toronto Press, 1990).

95 Tippett, *Making Culture*, 4, 28.

96 On this theme in American culture, see Lears, *No Place of Grace*, 54–57, 306–7.

97 Suzanne Morton, *Ideal Surroundings: Domestic Life in a Working-Class Suburb in the 1920s* (Toronto: University of Toronto Press, 1995), 34–35, 127–28.

98 The phrase comes from Bourdieu, *Rules of Art*, 148.

99 C.R. Fay, "Capitalism and Counterpoise," *Dalhousie Review* 6, 1 (1926): 65; C.R. Fay, "Machinery and the Values of Life," *Dalhousie Review* 10, 1 (1930): 72–73.

100 The phrase comes from Bourdieu, *The Rules of Art*, 148.

101 Mary Vipond, "National Consciousness in English-Speaking Canada in the 1920s: Seven Studies" (PhD thesis, University of Toronto, 1974), 538–41; Vipond, "The Nationalist Network," 32–52; Bourdieu, *Rules of Art*, 162.

CHAPTER 4: MORALIZING THE ECONOMY

1 "Evils of Big Interests Challenged by Stevens," *Toronto Daily Star*, 16 January 1934, 1; "Big Stores Answer Stevens," *Globe*, 16 January 1934, 1; Larry A. Glassford, *Reaction and Reform: The Politics of the Conservative Party under R.B. Bennett, 1927–1935* (Toronto: University of Toronto Press, 1992), 139. It was no accident that Stevens' address received publicity. See David Monod, *Store Wars: Shopkeepers and the Culture of Mass Marketing, 1890–1939* (Toronto: University of Toronto Press, 1996), 304–6, for insight into Stevens' motives, a history of personal rivalry between Stevens and Prime Minister Bennett, and efforts taken to build a mass movement around Stevens' attack on big business.

2 "Quantity Buying Beneficial Not Unmoral, Eaton Replies," *Toronto Daily Star*, 18 January 1934, 1, 2.

3 Because it began as an inquiry before becoming a Royal Commission, the investigation was variously referred to by contemporaries as the Price Spreads Inquiry, the Royal Commission on Price Spreads and Mass Buying, the Stevens' Inquiry, and the Stevens' Commission.

4 Lara Campbell, *Respectable Citizens: Gender, Family, and Unemployment in Ontario's Great Depression* (Toronto: University of Toronto Press, 2009), 57–58.

5 Adam Ashforth, "Reckoning Schemes of Legitimation: On Commissions of Inquiry as Power/Knowledge Forms," *Journal of Historical Sociology* 3, 1 (1990): 1–22.

6 On the theory of moral economy, see E.P. Thompson, "The Moral Economy of the English Crowd in the Eighteenth Century," *Past and Present* 50 (February 1971): 76–136; Mark Granovetter, "Economic Action and Social Structures: The Problem of Embeddedness," *American Journal of Sociology* 91, 3 (1985): 481–510; John Lie, "Embedding Polanyi's Market Society," *Sociological Perspectives* 34, 2 (1991): 219–35; Karl Polanyi, *The Great Transformation: The Political and Economic Origins of Our Times* (New York: Farrar and Rinehart, 1944); Vivian A. Rotman Zelizer, *Morals and Markets: The Development of Life Insurance in the United States* (New Brunswick, NJ: Transaction Books, 1979).

7 Previous appeals had been made to Stevens. Monod, *Store Wars*, 303–4.

8 William Marchington, "Letters Pour in Telling Stevens about Complaints: Flood of Grievances Received by Trade and Commerce Minister," *Globe*, 3 February 1934, 1.

9 *Report of the Royal Commission on Price Spreads and Mass Buying* (Ottawa: King's Printer, 1937), xxvi.

10 Monod details the sequence of testimony in the early weeks of the inquiry. The hearings began with an investigation of sweatshops in the garment and footwear industries, revealing shockingly foul conditions and violations of minimum wage laws that academic experts and government officials implied were, in the main, the direct result of the pricing policies of mass manufacturers. This was followed by testimony from a succession of seemingly impartial expert business witnesses (many of whom were closely associated with the National Fair Trade Council of retail merchants); accountants detailing the profits made by the big stores while

manufacturers and small retailers suffered; former employees revealing the ways chains cheated the public and exploited workers; and finally managers and owners, who were asked to explain themselves. Monod, *Store Wars*, 306–8.

11 Glassford, *Reaction and Reform*, 149.

12 See the *Winnipeg Free Press*, 7 August 1934, for a transcript.

13 "Federal Administration and Politics," *Canadian Annual Review of Public Affairs* (Toronto: Annual Review Publishing, 1934), 40; "Capitalism under Fire," *Round Table: The Commonwealth Journal of International Affairs* 25, 98 (1935): 391.

14 The inquiry was reported on twenty-three of twenty-four publishing days in May 1934 on the front page of the *Toronto Daily Star*.

15 *Toronto Daily Star*, 5 May 1934, 1; *Globe*, 6 November 1934, 1.

16 "Photographers Code Aims at Price Cuts," *Toronto Daily Star*, 7 May 1934, 1; "Minimum Fee Scale Sought of Stevens," *Globe*, 12 March 1934, 5; "Probe Considered by United Church," *Montreal Gazette*, 4 June 1934, 3.

17 Wilfred Eggleston, "Mr. Stevens and Our Economic Ills," *Queen's Quarterly* 41 (1934): 532.

18 See, for example, "Economic Experiment in Canada," *Round Table: The Commonwealth Journal of International Affairs* 24, 95 (1934): 630; Vincent Bladen, *Bladen on Bladen: Memoirs of a Political Economist* (Toronto: Scarborough College, 1978), 60.

19 Duncan McArthur, "Public Affairs," *Queen's Quarterly* 41 (1934): 256.

20 "Bread Sales Methods Boost Cost 3 Cents," *Toronto Daily Star*, 1 May 1934, 1, 2; "Admits Combine Sets Bread Prices Here," *Toronto Daily Star*, 2 May 1934, 1, 4; "Bakers Attack Chain Stores," *Montreal Gazette*, 3 May 1934, 1; "Baking Industry Facing Problems," *Globe*, 2 May 1934, 3; "Special Board Control of Bakers Urged to Regulate Industry," *Globe*, 3 May 1934, 3; *Report of the Royal Commission*, 92–102. For an interesting discussion of responses to similar trends in Europe, see Victoria de Grazia, "Changing Consumption Regimes in Europe, 1930–1970: Comparative Perspectives on the Distribution Problem," in *Getting and Spending: European and American Consumer Societies in the Twentieth Century*, ed. Susan Strasser, Charles McGovern, and Matthias Judt (Cambridge: Cambridge University Press, 1998), 61–78.

21 Monod, *Store Wars*, 307–8.

22 *Report of the Royal Commission*, 92–93.

23 The *Montreal Gazette*, for example, covered the release of the report on the front page, and all of pages 10, 11, 12, and 13 of the 13 April 1935 edition; *Saturday Night* ran stories beginning on the front page with additional reportage on 13, 15, 16, 33, and 40 of the 20 April 1935 issue.

24 Credit for imposing a coherent structure on the extensive testimony and for producing largely unanimous recommendations in spite of party differences was widely given to future prime minster Lester B. Pearson, the commission's secretary, and to his staff of experts, including Queen's University economists Vincent Bladen and C.A. Curtis. Pearson was awarded an Order of the British Empire (OBE) for his work.

25 *Report of the Royal Commission*, 6.

26 Ibid., 106.

27 Ibid., 234.

28 King had placed some pressure on the Liberal members to support the findings, so that the party would not be seen as obstructing reform. H. Blair Neatby, *William Lyon Mackenzie King, 1932–1939: The Prism of Unity* (Toronto: University of Toronto Press, 1976), 102–3.

29 *Report of the Royal Commission,* 277–78.

30 Ibid., 293. Discussing his experiences as a member of the Price Spreads Inquiry, Young later explained that "witness after witness, not from any one class of society, but from every class," came before the commission asking for their competitors to be restrained in order that they be able to continue in their old occupations in their own way. E.J. Young, "A Western Farmer Looks at Business," *Addresses of the Canadian Club of Toronto, 1935–1936* (Toronto: Warwick Bros and Rutter, 1936).

31 *Report of the Royal Commission,* 293, 307. Young is paraphrasing the French economist Frederic Bastiat, known for popularizing free-market economics.

32 On this theme, see H.A. Innis, "For the People," *University of Toronto Quarterly* 5, 2 (1936): 279.

33 R.B. Bennett, *The Premier Speaks to the People: The Prime Minister's January Radio Broadcasts Issued in Book Form, The First Address* (Ottawa: Dominion Conservative Headquarters, 1935), 16.

34 Bennett, *The Premier Speaks to the People.*

35 V.W. Bladen, *An Introduction to Political Economy* (Toronto: University of Toronto Press, 1941), 213–15.

36 "Bennett Defends Gov't Record at Big Rally in City," *Calgary Herald,* 20 September 1935, 1, 12–13.

37 "Federal Administration and Politics," *Canadian Annual Review of Public Affairs 1935 and 1936* (Toronto: Annual Review Publishing, 1937), 60–62.

38 R.B. Bennett, "The Issues as I See Them," *Maclean's Magazine,* 15 September 1935, 10. On a similar theme in American political discourse, see Kathleen G. Donohue, *Freedom from Want: American Liberalism and the Idea of the Consumer* (Baltimore: Johns Hopkins University Press, 2003), 67.

39 See, for example, W.L. Mackenzie King, "The Issues as I See Them," *Maclean's Magazine,* 15 September 1935, 31, and W.L. Mackenzie King, "The Liberal Party's Position," National Liberal Federation of Canada, Ottawa, cited in D. Owen Carrigan, *Canadian Party Platforms, 1867–1968* (Toronto: Copp Clark, 1968), 130.

40 In addition to party literature, billboards, and radio broadcasts, this publicity included a series of articles (later collected and reprinted in pamphlet form) reexamining King's *Industry and Humanity* and drawing favourable comparisons with Franklin Roosevelt's National Recovery Administration; a new abridged version of *Industry and Humanity*; and a campaign biography of King prepared by Norman Rogers. See Reginald Whitaker, *The Government Party: Organizing and Financing the Liberal Party of Canada, 1930–58* (Toronto: University of Toronto Press, 1977), 81–83; and Neatby, *William Lyon Mackenzie King,* 97–98.

41 Norman Rogers, *Mackenzie King* (Toronto: T. Nelson and Sons, 1935), 190–93, 201.

42 Cited in the campaign version prepared by Bernard Rose: *Industry and Humanity: An Outstanding Contribution to the Understanding of Industrial Relations and the Need for Economic Justice, Analysis and Re-Valuation* (Montreal: Labour World, 1934), 18.

43 Neatby, *William Lyon Mackenzie King*, 102–3; D.F. Forster, "The Politics of Combines Policy: Liberals and the Stevens Commission," *Canadian Journal of Economics and Political Science* 28, 4 (1962): 515, 519.

44 Franklin D. Roosevelt, "Radio Address from Albany, New York: The 'Forgotten Man' Speech," 7 April 1932, http://www.presidency.ucsb.edu/ws/?pid=88408.

45 *Toronto Daily Star*, 20 September 1935.

46 "50 Household Articles Higher Here Than in U.S. Mrs. Thorburn Reveals," ibid., 20 September 1935, 1; "Mrs. Thorburn Talks," *Barrie Examiner*, 10 October 1935, 1.

47 The term "citizen-consumer" was first used by Lizabeth Cohen, *A Consumers' Republic: The Politics of Mass Consumption in Postwar America* (New York: Knopf, 2003). For a recent discussion, see Frank Trentmann, "Citizenship and Consumption," *Journal of Consumer Culture* 7, 2 (2007): 147–58.

48 H.H. Stevens, "The Issues as I See Them," *Maclean's Magazine*, 15 September 1935, 11.

49 "Text of Stevens Manifesto," *Globe*, 13 July 1935, 3.

50 The CCF's associated think tank, the League for Social Reconstruction, frequently cited evidence of price spreads to highlight the exploitation of ordinary Canadians by large businesses. Multiple references to the price spreads inquiry appear on 59 of 524 pages of the League for Social Reconstruction, Research Committee, *Social Planning for Canada* (Toronto: T. Nelson, 1935).

51 *The Social Credit Manual*, excerpted in William Aberhart and David Elliott, *Aberhart: Outpourings and Replies* (Calgary: Alberta Records Publication Board, Historical Society of Alberta, 1991), 29, 129; William Aberhart, "An Exposition of Social Credit," *Edmonton Journal*, 27 December 1934, cited in *William Aberhart and Social Credit in Alberta*, ed. L.H. Thomas (Toronto: Copp Clark, 1977), 68–69.

52 As commentators noted then and since, the magnitude of the Liberal victory and the Conservative loss was exaggerated by the structure of Canada's electoral system. Although the Liberals won control of the House, the difference between the two parties in the popular vote was less decisive. Over half of the voters preferred other parties. One in five Canadians voted for parties that had not existed at the time of the last election in 1930. The election results were as follows: Liberals (173 seats, 44.8 percent of the popular vote); Conservatives (40 seats, 29.6 percent of the popular vote); Social Credit (17 seats, 4.1 percent of the popular vote); CCF (7 seats, 8.8 percent of the popular vote); Reconstruction Party (1 seat, 8.7 percent of the popular vote); other (7 seats, 3.9 percent of the popular vote). In at least forty-five constituencies, the combined Conservative and Reconstruction vote would have won the seat. Thirty-six of these constituencies had been Conservative in the last Parliament. J.L. Granatstein, *The Politics of Survival: The Conservative Party*

of Canada, 1939–1945 (Toronto: University of Toronto Press, 1967), 8. Election analyses are available in J. Murray Beck, *Pendulum of Power: Canada's Federal Elections* (Scarborough: Prentice-Hall, 1968), 206–22; Escott Reid, "The Canadian Election of 1935 – and After," *American Political Science Review* 30, 1 (1936): 111–21; and John Herd Thompson and Allen Seager, *Canada, 1922–1939: Decades of Discord* (Toronto: McClelland Stewart, 1986), 274–76.

53 For example, see H.A. Innis and A.F.W. Plumptre, eds., *The Canadian Economy and Its Problems* (Toronto: Canadian Institute of International Affairs, 1934); and *Canadian Problems as Seen by Twenty Outstanding Men of Canada* (Toronto: Oxford University Press, 1933). For an overview of responses to the Depression by Canada's professional economists, see Bettina Liverant, "Buying Happiness: English Canadian Intellectuals and the Development of Canadian Consumer Culture" (PhD thesis, University of Alberta, 2008), 206–10, 214–21.

CHAPTER 5: CHARTING THE CONTOURS OF MODERN SOCIETY

1 Warren Susman notes that, beginning in the 1920s, one "of the more striking observed results of the structural changes in the social order was that a larger proportion of it was increasingly engaged in professional seeking to understand it, with a special calling to 'know' the world as writers, artists, intellectuals, journalists, scientists, social scientists, philosophers, teachers." Warren I. Susman, *Culture as History: The Transformation of American Society in the Twentieth Century* (New York: Pantheon Books, 1984), 107.

2 Many historians have found Warren Susman's focus on the cultural tensions that accompany social transformation useful. Specifically, Susman proposed that "a culture is defined by its tensions ... Cultures can actually be arguments or debates themselves." Ibid., xx, 288.

3 Leonard Marsh, *Canadians In and Out of Work* (Toronto: Canadian Scholars Press, 1940), 260; see also 391, 395, 457. R.H. Coats, "Statistics Comes of Age," *Canadian Journal of Economics and Political Science* 2, 3 (1936): 280.

4 In 1931, farmers and farm workers still made up 35 percent of the male working population in Canada, but only 22 percent in the United States and 6.4 percent in England and Wales. Marsh, *Canadians In and Out of Work*, 198–99.

5 Industrial Relations Section, School of Commerce and Administration, Queen's University, *The Economic Welfare of Canadian Employees: A Study of Occupations, Earnings, Hours and Other Working Conditions, 1913–1937* (Kingston: Queen's University, 1940), 54–55. The authors explained that simply measuring higher wages was simplistic because it failed to convey the impact of declines in hours of work per week, of periods of unemployment, or of the welfare of groups that contained both employed and unemployed members (24).

6 *Economic Welfare of Canadians*, 21, 24, 39. Gains in wage rates occurred primarily before 1923–24, during a period of increased industrial activity; paradoxically, increases in real earnings were achieved during periods of declining prices. This meant that the purchasing power of wage-earning families tended to decline during

the boom and increase during the Depression. Although the real value of hourly rates was 35 to 45 percent higher in 1938 than in 1921, annual real earnings per employed worker in Canada had risen by a more modest 5 percent when changes in the cost of living were taken into account.

7 Ibid., iii.

8 Dominion Bureau of Statistics, *Consumption of Luxuries in Canada, 1931 and 1932* (Ottawa: Dominion Bureau of Statistics, 1934), 1. The total value of the production of goods deemed as luxury (which the bureau rather unhelpfully described as "all those above the line of necessities") had risen from 12.7 to 13.3 percent of the total value of production of all Canadian manufactured goods, even though the overall dollar value of these goods had declined from just over $343 million in 1931 to just over $282 million in 1932.

9 Marsh, *Canadians In and Out of Work*, 4–27, 426.

10 Ibid., 164–65.

11 Ibid., 377. By way of comparison, Canadian labour historian Bryan Palmer argues that the development of mass consumer culture was an effective brake on the class struggle, undermining the cultural bonds that had united labour and redirecting attention from the workplace to the home. Marsh's analysis suggests that the effect was even more corrosive, remaking the socially significant markers of class difference. Bryan D. Palmer, *Working Class Experience: Rethinking the History of Canadian Labour, 1800–1991* (Toronto: McClelland and Stewart, 1983), 190. It should be noted that Palmer's assertion softened somewhat in the second edition (1992), 229, 232.

12 Ibid., 382.

13 Ibid., 377, 382, 383.

14 Coats noted that race and gender affected the likelihood of unemployment less than skill and occupation. In fact, because women often worked in sectors of the economy (such as personal services) that were less affected by downturns, they tended to fare better during hard times. R.H. Coats, "Science and Society," *Canadian Journal of Economics and Political Science* 5, 2 (1939): 164.

15 Coats, "Science and Society," 163, 165; see also Marsh, *Canadians In and Out of Work*, 301–2, 378–79.

16 Marsh, *Canadians In and Out of Work*, 339.

17 Ibid., 380.

18 T.H. Marshall, "The Recent History of Professionalism in Relation to Social Structure and Social Policy," *Canadian Journal of Economics and Political Science* 5, 3 (1939): 326.

19 Marsh, *Canadians In and Out of Work*, 389, 391.

20 Ibid., 400–1.

21 Marsh, *Canadians In and Out of Work*, 198–99. According to Marsh's calculations, the wages needed to allow for what he described as a small margin of comfort would be at least $1500 in the larger cities; this was the average earned by skilled tradesmen and white-collar workers. Potentially another 10 to 15 percent of working families could reach this level with contributions from wage-earning sons, daughters, or wives. However, Marsh suggested that, in reality, contributions by sons and

daughters tended to be small and short-lived insofar as they generally reached the age of marriage before they attained their maximum earnings. Since a larger number of wage earners also meant a larger number of consumers, the additional income did not tend to increase a family's overall standard of living. Moreover, the income brought into households by wage-earning women and children had the potential to add tensions to the negotiation of earnings and spending. Marsh, *Canadians In and Out of Work*, 170–73.

22 Ibid., 198–99.
23 Ibid., 199.
24 Dominion Bureau of Statistics, *Family Income and Expenditure in Canada, 1937– 1938: A Study of Urban Wage-earner Families, Including Data on Physical Attributes* (Ottawa: King's Printer, 1941).
25 The limitations with respect to lodgers and domestics did not apply to households in Quebec City and Montreal.
26 The study set entry to the middle class as requiring an annual wage of $2,500, the same number used by Marsh.
27 A larger proportion of these detailed records came from the middle-earnings range, reflecting "a more favorable reception to field workers than among families at higher earnings levels." At the low-earnings level, the authors had to discard records because of incomplete information. The results were analysed by income bracket, but the sample size available for each bracket was inconsistent. Dominion Bureau of Statistics, *Family Income and Expenditure in Canada*, 17.
28 Ibid., 28.
29 In the survey, debits were considered as the year-over-year increase carried forward and did not include debts incurred and paid off during the year.
30 Ibid., 34.
31 Ibid., 41.
32 Ibid., 31, 41. Other findings were less striking but were interesting in that detailed data on household expenditures had not previously been available in statistical form. For example, analysis showed that the proportion of total expenditure spent on basic living requirements (food, shelter, fuel, light) declined as family income mounted. Some costs, like furniture, moved upwards with income; others, like clothing, remained the same as a proportion of the total. The proportion of income spent on food did not decline as income rose, as families bought more varied and better quality food.
33 D.C. MacGregor, "Studies of the Cost of Living in Canada," *Canadian Journal of Economics and Political Science* 7, 4 (1941): 557–58.
34 J.A. Corry, *The Growth of Government Activities since Confederation: A Study Prepared for the Royal Commission on Dominion-Provincial Relations* (Ottawa: King's Printer, 1939), 78.
35 Corry obviously regarded increases in spending as money not saved; however, historian Martha Onley argues that working-class and middle-class North Americans perceived the purchase of some goods, particularly durable goods, as an

alternative form of investment and savings. See Martha Onley, *Buy Now, Pay Later: Advertising, Credit and Consumer Durables in the 1920s* (Chapel Hill: University of North Carolina Press, 1991).

36 Corry, *The Growth of Government Activities,* 78–79.

37 Rita Barnard, *The Great Depression and the Culture of Abundance: Kenneth Fearing, Nathanael West, and Mass Culture in the 1930s* (New York: Cambridge University Press, 1995), 16, 23.

38 Veronica Strong-Boag, *The New Day Recalled: Lives of Girls and Women in English Canada, 1919–1939* (Toronto: Copp Clark Pitman, 1988), 113–38; Candida Rifkind, "Labours of Modernity: The Literary Left in English Canada, 1929–1939" (PhD thesis, York University, 2003), 9–10.

39 Barnard, *The Great Depression and the Culture of Abundance,* 21; Rita Barnard, "Modern American Fiction," in *The Cambridge Companion to American Modernism,* ed. Walter Kalaidjian (Cambridge: Cambridge University Press, 2005), 61.

40 Barnard, *The Great Depression and the Culture of Abundance,* 24.

41 Susman, *Culture as History,* 106–7, 159–60; William Stott, *Documentary Expression in America in the Thirties* (Chicago: University of Chicago Press, 1973); Morris Dickstein, *Dancing in the Dark: A Cultural History of the Great Depression* (New York: W.W. Norton, 2009), 271–74.

42 Candida Rifkind, "Labours of Modernity," 153–54.

43 J. Grierson, "The Documentary Producer," *Cinema Quarterly* 2, 1 (1933): 7–9, discussed in Susan Kerrigan and Phillip McIntyre, "The 'Creative Treatment of Actuality': Rationalizing and Reconceptualizing the Notion of Creativity for Documentary Practice," *Journal of Media Practice* 11, 2 (2010): 111–30. Grierson became the first commissioner of the National Film Commission, subsequently renamed the National Film Board, in 1939.

44 Evelyn MacLure, "The Short Story in Canada: Development from 1935 to 1955" (MA thesis, University of British Columbia, 1969), 3.

45 Ibid., 10.

46 Alistair MacLeod, introduction to Morley Callaghan, *The Complete Short Stories,* volume 1 (Toronto: Exile Editions, 2003), xiv.

47 See for example, the following stories by Morley Callaghan: "The Blue Kimono," *Harper's Bazaar,* May 1935; "The Red Hat," *New Yorker,* 31 October 1931; "Very Special Shoes" and "A Cap for Steve" in *Now That April's Here and Other Stories* (Toronto: Macmillan, 1936); see also Sinclair Ross, "Circus in Town," *Queen's Quarterly* 43 (Winter 1936): 368–72.

48 Rifkind, "Labours of Modernity," 411.

49 James Livingston, "Modern Subjectivity and Consumer Culture," in *Getting and Spending: European and American Consumer Societies in the Twentieth Century,* ed. Susan Strasser, Charles McGovern, and Matthias Judt (Cambridge: Cambridge University Press, 1998), 413–29. See also McGovern's comments on Livingston in the same volume: Charles McGovern, "Consumption and Citizenship in the United States, 1900–1940," 57.

50 Mary Quayle Innis, "Holiday," *Canadian Forum* 12, 136 (1932): 140–42; Mary Quayle Innis, *Stand on a Rainbow* (Toronto: Collins, 1943), 162–63. For a full analysis of themes of consumption in the work of Innis, see Donica Belisle, "Guilty Pleasures: Consumer Culture in the Fiction of Mary Quayle Innis," in *Consuming Modernity: Changing Gendered Behaviours and Consumerism, 1919–1945,* ed. Cheryl Warsh and Dan Malleck (Vancouver: UBC Press, 2013), 258–73.

51 Colin Campbell, *The Romantic Ethic and the Spirit of Modern Consumerism* (Oxford: Basil Blackwell, 1987), 1–2, 185.

52 Innis, "Holiday." This short story is usefully read in conjunction with Cynthia Wright, "Feminine Trifles of Vast Importance: Writing Gender into the History of Consumption," in *Gender Conflicts: New Essays in Women's History,* ed. Franca Iacovetta and Mariana Valverde (Toronto: University of Toronto Press, 1992), which explores gender and class issues in the spatial organization of Eaton's College Street store in Toronto during the same period; see especially 244–50.

53 Catharine Robinson, "Some Effects of Social Change on the English Canadian Novel and Periodical Fiction, 1920–1955" (MA thesis, University of Western Ontario, 1960), 71. On the other hand, socialist writers tended to gender the class struggle, with images of a virile masculine proletariat and parasitic feminine bourgeoisie, often denoted by her upscale clothing and obliviousness to poverty. This pattern, however, was not common in stories that explicitly focused on consumption experiences. Candida Rifkind, "Modernism's Red Stage," in *The Canadian Modernists Meet,* ed. Dean Irvine (Ottawa: University of Ottawa Press, 2005), 194–95.

54 Stephen Leacock, "What Is Left of Adam Smith?" *Canadian Journal of Economics and Political Science* 1, 1 (1935): 49.

55 Ken Hughes argues that Canadian writers "knew" that the working class was neither large enough nor sufficiently united to win any revolutionary confrontations. He points instead to the presence of a radical tradition that explicitly promoted working-class consciousness, particularly through dramatizations of the dehumanization of mechanized production that forced workers to accept passive roles if they wanted to receive the income needed to feed their families. Kenneth J. Hughes, "Introduction," *Voices of Discord: Canadian Short Stories from the 1930s,* ed. Donna Phillips (Toronto: New Hogtown Press, 1979), 13, 67–71; Gary Cross, *An All-Consuming Century: Why Commercialism Won in Modern America* (New York: Columbia University Press, 2000), 74.

56 Frederick Philip Grove, *The Master of the Mill* (1944; repr., Toronto: McClelland and Stewart, 1961), 316. Depression-era joblessness was highest in sectors of the economy most associated with male employment and, in many ways, with manliness, including construction, small-business ownership, skilled labour, and work in the primary resource sector. Wage-earning opportunities tilted towards women, with growth in clerical work and in the sales and service sectors. High levels of male unemployment could increase a family's dependency on the wages earned by women and children, with the potential to add tensions to the negotiation of earnings and spending. However, this dynamic was not central in fictional accounts,

which generally hewed to conventional separate spheres plots, with beleaguered male breadwinners and challenged women consumers. Marsh, *Canadians In and Out of Work*, 170–73; Katrina Srigley, "'In Case You Hadn't Noticed!': Race, Ethnicity, and Women's Wage-Earning in a Depression-Era City," *Labour/Le Travail* 55 (Spring 2005): 69–105; Veronica Strong-Boag, "The Girl of the New Day: Canadian Working Women in the 1920s," *Labour/Le Travail* 4 (1979): 131–64.

57 Morley Callaghan, *They Shall Inherit the Earth* (1935; repr.,Toronto: McClelland and Stewart, 1962), 17.

58 Ibid., 149.

59 Irene Baird, *Waste Heritage* (Toronto: Macmillan, 1939).

60 On this theme, see James Livingston, *Pragmatism and the Political Economy of Cultural Revolution, 1850–1940* (Chapel Hill: University of North Carolina Press, 1994), 128, and Harold Innis, "The Passing of Political Economy," *Commerce Journal*, March 1938, 5.

61 Morley Callaghan, "The Plight of Canadian Fiction," *University of Toronto Quarterly* 7, 2 (1938): 152–61. See also Frederick Philip Grove, "The Plight of Canadian Fiction? A Reply," *University of Toronto Quarterly* 7, 4 (1938): 451–67.

62 Barry Ferguson and Doug Owram, "Social Scientists and Public Policy from the 1920s through World War II," *Journal of Canadian Studies* 15, 4 (1980–81): 6–7; Philip Massolin, *Canadian Intellectuals, the Tory Tradition, and the Challenge of Modernity* (Toronto: University of Toronto Press, 2001), 17–18.

63 While at the University of Toronto, Jackson consulted for the Bank of Nova Scotia, the Canada Cement Company, and Eaton's. Later in the 1930s, after leaving the university, he consulted with Canadian Pacific Railway, Canada Packers, Canadian Industries Ltd., and others. Jackson also used his connections in the business community to secure job placements for University of Toronto graduates. Don Nerbas, "Managing Democracy, Defending Capitalism: Gilbert E. Jackson, the Canadians Committee on Industrial Reconstruction, and the Changing Form of Elite Politics in Canada," *Histoire sociale/Social History* 46, 91 (2013): 180, 182.

64 On the federal level alone, the larger commissions included: the Royal Commission on Banking and Currency (1933); the Royal Commission on Price Spreads and Mass Buying (1934–35); the Royal Commission to Investigate the Penal System (1938); the Royal Commission on Dominion-Provincial Relations (1937–40); and the Royal Commission on the Textile Industry (1938).

65 Innis, "The Passing of Political Economy," 5. As the newly appointed head of the Department of Political Economy, Innis was asked to prepare an article for the university's *Commerce Journal* on a topic that would be of interest to businessmen as readers or as advertisers. Innis viewed this request as evidence of the passing of political economy.

66 Frank H. Knight, "Social Science and the Political Trend," *University of Toronto Quarterly* 3 (1934), in Frank H. Knight, *Freedom and Reform: Essays in Economics and Social Philosophy* (Indianapolis: Liberty Press, 1982), 43.

67 Ibid., 41.

68 Ibid., 40.

69 E.J. Urwick, "Wither Are We Drifting?" *Canadian Forum* 15 (July 1935): 306.

70 Leacock, "What Is Left of Adam Smith?" *Canadian Journal of Economics and Political Science* 1, 1 (1935): 42.

71 Ibid., 50.

72 Judith Stamps, *Unthinking Modernity: Innis, McLuhan, and the Frankfurt School* (Montreal and Kingston: McGill-Queen's University Press, 1995), 46–47.

73 H.A. Innis, "The Role of Intelligence: Some Further Notes," *Canadian Journal of Economics and Political Science* 1, 2 (1935): 280–87.

74 H.A. Innis, "Discussion in the Social Sciences," *Dalhousie Review* 15, 1 (1936): 401–13. Innis noted that this article was intended to compliment his earlier comments in the *Canadian Journal of Economics and Political Science*.

75 Ibid., 404. Innis believed that the mass-circulation commercial press deliberately used sensationalism and triviality, commoditizing news in order to reach readers with ever-lower levels of literacy in a spiraling effort to appeal to advertisers. Sustained thought on difficult problems was made impossible by the short attention spans cultivated by the desire for quick returns. Thus, the problems of marketing had "far reaching ramifications in a democracy." H.A. Innis, "Introduction," in *Marketing Organization and Technique,* ed. Jane McKee (Toronto: University of Toronto Press, 1940), xvii. In addition, he believed that journalism had moved from "a profession to a branch of commerce." Innis, cited in James P. Winter and Irving Goldman, "Comparing the Early and Late McLuhan to Innis's Political Discourse," *Canadian Journal of Communication* 14, 4 (1989): 93.

76 Innis, "The Role of Intelligence," 283; Stamps, *Unthinking Modernity*, 48–49.

77 Frank H. Underhill, "The Conception of a National Interest," *Canadian Journal of Economics and Political Science* 1, 3 (1935): 407.

78 Ibid., 405.

79 Other articles making explicit reference to this discussion include C.B. Macpherson, "Pareto's 'General Sociology': The Problem of Method in the Social Sciences," *Canadian Journal of Economics and Political Science* 3, 3 (1937), esp. 470–71, and E.K. Brown, "On Academic Freedom," *Dalhousie Review* 16, 2 (1936–37), esp. 222–23, 226–27.

80 MacGibbon studied at the University of Chicago and was the first professor of political economy at the University of Alberta, chair of Alberta's Royal Commission on Banking and Credit, and a long-serving member of the Board of Grain Commissioners for Canada.

81 D.A. MacGibbon, "Economics and the Social Order," *Canadian Journal of Economics and Political Science* 2, 1 (1936): 69, 73, 71, 72.

82 Mackintosh was a graduate of Queen's and Harvard and a professor of economics at Queen's. During this period, he also served as an adviser to government in many capacities, including acting as a member of the National Employment Commission in the 1930s. He would become one of Canada's most important civil servants during the war and reconstruction era.

83 W.A. Mackintosh, "An Economist Looks at Economics," *Canadian Journal of Economics and Political Science* 3, 3 (1937): 321, 314–15.
84 MacGibbon, "Economics and the Social Order," 71. See also Mackintosh, "An Economist Looks at Economics," 321.
85 British historian Matthew Hilton notes that Keynesian theory (which was rapidly gaining acceptance in the mid- to late 1930s) made consumption central to economic growth but abstracted it to such a degree that discussion of consumption at the micro level was unnecessary. The degree of abstraction, in other words, enabled advocates to avoid consideration of the political and ethical aspects of demand, even while in pursuit of its management at the macro level. As Keynes had written, "virtue and vice play no part." Matthew Hilton, "The Legacy of Luxury: Moralities of Consumption since the 18th Century," *Journal of Consumer Culture* 4, 1 (2004): 113–15.

CHAPTER 6: REGULATING THE CONSUMER

1 K.W. Taylor, "Canadian War-Time Price Controls, 1941–46," *Canadian Journal of Economics and Political Science* 13, 1 (1947): 81; A.F.W. Plumptre, *Mobilizing Canada's Resources for War* (Toronto: Macmillan, 1941), 20; F.H. Leacy, *Historical Statistics of Canada* (Ottawa: Statistics Canada, 1983), Series F56–75.
2 Plumptre, *Mobilizing Canada's Resources for War*, 2–3.
3 The statement from the finance minister dates from November 1940 and is cited in A.F.W. Plumptre, "An Approach to War Finance," *Canadian Journal of Economics and Political Science* 7, 1 (1941): 3; Plumptre, *Mobilizing Canada's Resources for War*, xviii; R.B. Bryce, "Financing the War," in *War and Reconstruction – Some Canadian Issues: Addresses Given at the Canadian Institute on Public Affairs, August 1942*, ed. Arthur R.M. Lower and Joseph Frederick Parkinson (Toronto: Ryerson Press, 1942), 13; Plumptre, *Mobilizing Canada's Resources for War*, 147–48.
4 W.L. Mackenzie King, *Controlling the Cost of Living: The Stabilization of Prices and Wages, October 18, 1941* (Ottawa: King's Printer, 1941), 5.
5 The most spectacular staged event was undoubtedly "If Day." Vividly described by historian Jody Perrun, "If Day" featured a simulated invasion of Winnipeg. The day began with the sounding of air raid sirens as RCAF aircraft representing German dive-bombers flew over Manitoba's major cities. Local reserves supported by defence troops stationed in the region staged an attack and then acted as occupation forces, raising swastika flags, patrolling the streets, arresting public figures, closing churches, surrounding and sandbagging department stores, taking over a local school, commandeering automobiles, and burning books outside the public library. The day concluded with a parade urging residents to buy bonds. The events, organized by the Public Relations Committee of the Manitoba Division of the National War Finance Committee to persuade ordinary wage earners of the need to buy bonds, received wide coverage in the media throughout Canada and the United States. Jody Perrun, *The Patriotic Consensus: Unity, Morale, and the Second World War in Winnipeg* (Winnipeg: University of Manitoba Press, 2014), 108–13.

On the campaigns to sell war savings bonds and certificates, see Jeffrey A. Keshen, *Saints, Sinners, and Soldiers: Canada's Second World War* (Vancouver: UBC Press, 2004), 31–35; Wendy Cuthbertson, "Pocketbooks and Patriotism: The 'Financial Miracle' of Canada's World War II Victory Bond Program," in *Canadian Military History since the 17th Century*, ed. Yves Tremblay (Ottawa: Directorate of History and Heritage, 2000), 179–80; Sheldon Garon, *Beyond Our Means: Why America Spends While the World Saves* (Princeton, NJ: Princeton University Press, 2011), 199; "1944: Shirley Temple Rings in Canada's Victory Loan," CBC Radio News Archives, Special Broadcast, 21 October1944, http://www.cbc.ca/archives/entry/1944-shirley-temple-rings-in-canadas-victory-loan.

6 Cuthbertson, "Pocketbooks and Patriotism," 181, 183; Vladimir Miller, "Canadian War Time Fiscal Policies" (BA thesis, McMaster University, 1945), 31.

7 Cuthbertson, "Pocketbooks and Patriotism," 178.

8 Keshen describes workplace sales tactics as "intense." Volunteers came to companies to deliver speeches prepared by the NWFC or the Wartime Information Board, after which sign-up papers were distributed among employees. Many work sites posted lists of those who had purchased bonds or participated in payroll deduction schemes. One woman, earning only $55.60 monthly as a Grade 1 clerk for the federal government recalled, "When a ... drive was on, we were given to understand that we were to buy and if we did not ... we were brought into the chief's office [who] mentioned love of country, duty ... and ... the error of trying to hold out." Keshen, *Saints, Sinners, and Soldiers*, 32; Perrun, *The Patriotic Consensus*, 87–89.

9 Mary Jane Lennon, *On the Homefront: A Scrapbook of Canadian World War II Memorabilia* (Erin, ON: Boston Mills Press, 1981), 60. Bonds generally paid 3 percent interest at a time when savings accounts paid 2 percent. In addition to bonds, every Canadian could also hold a maximum of $600 in war certificates, which, after seven years, would pay investors back five dollars for every four dollars spent.

10 Graham Broad, *A Small Price to Pay: Consumer Culture on the Canadian Home Front, 1939–1945* (Vancouver: UBC Press, 2013), 202.

11 "How Are Canadians Using Their War Earnings?" *Saturday Night*, 26 June 1943, 38–39.

12 Cuthbertson, "Pocketbooks and Patriotism," 178. This rate is consistent with savings rates in America (25%) and the United Kingdom (26%), although notably less than those in Japan (40%). Garon, *Beyond Our Means*, 221.

13 *Maclean's Magazine*, 1 July 1942, 28.

14 Lennon, *On the Homefront*, 60.

15 Ibid.

16 Perrun, *The Patriotic Consensus*, 95–96.

17 *Globe and Mail*, 4 November 1944, 8.

18 Ibid., 14 October 1944.

19 "Salesmen's Replies Regarding Public Attitude to the Eighth Victory Loan Campaign, August 1945," cited in Perrun, *The Patriotic Consensus*, 96, 250n47.

20 Plumptre, *Mobilizing Canada's Resources for War*, 147–48. Many Canadians began paying personal income taxes for the first time during the war. Beginning in June

1940, the National Defence Tax was the first tax to be deducted directly from pay-cheques, starting at an annual income of $660 for a single person and $1,200 for married taxpayers. Taxes continued rising. By the 1942 tax year, combined federal and provincial taxes and compulsory savings could exceed $5,000 on a $10,000 in-come. At one point, assuming no deductions, a taxpayer with a declared annual income of $500,000 would have paid $433,682 in taxes; however, investment in certain kinds of savings, including Victory Bonds, life insurance premiums, home mortgage, and pension payments, provided useful tax shelters.

The 1942 budget – which fully implemented the "pay-as-you-earn" system of at-source deductions – also contained assurances that increases in normal taxation would not reduce annual incomes below $800 for a single worker or $1,200 for mar-ried workers (with additional tax credits provided for a married spouse and depend-ent children). For these lower-income taxpayers, the refundable, compulsory savings portion was generally at least equal to the amount by which the budget had increased their tax liability. In effect, the tax system began to sanction the idea of a minimum income threshold. Keshen, *Saints, Sinners, and Soldiers*, 54; C. Campbell, "J.L. Ilsley and the Transformation of the Canadian Tax System, 1939–1943," *Canadian Tax Journal* 61, 3 (2013): 633–70; Joseph Tohill, "A Consumers' War: Price Control and Political Consumerism in the United States and Canada during World War II" (PhD thesis, York University, 2012), 51n11.

21 Livio Di Matteo, "Major Changes to the Federal Personal Income Tax, 1917–2017," in *The History and Development of Canada's Personal Income Tax: Zero to 50 in 100 Years*, ed. William Watson and Jason Clemens (n.p.: Fraser Institute, 2017), 12, http://www.fraserinstitute.org; David Perry, "Fiscal Figures: The Evolution of Tax Collection over the Past Half Century," *Canadian Tax Journal* 43, 5 (1995): 1094.

22 It is interesting to note that compulsory savings were recommended in the United Kingdom by Keynes but rejected by the government. Garon, *Beyond Our Means*, 197. In Canada, deductions from the minimum saving requirement were permitted for some types of personal savings, such as life insurance premiums and pension fund payments. The refundable portion of the tax was larger in the lower income brackets, thus serving the principle of equality of sacrifice. Tax rates were reduced and the refundable feature of the income tax was ended in the 1944 budget. Campbell, "J.L. Ilsley," 660–62; Miller, "Canadian War Time Fiscal Policies," 118.

23 J.F. Parkinson, ed., *Canadian War Economics* (Toronto: University of Toronto Press, 1941), 6; Keshen, *Saints, Sinners, and Soldiers*, 72.

24 Taylor, "Canadian War-Time Price Controls," 68. R.B. Bryce, at the time the assistant deputy minister of finance, similarly described the program as "the most daring and successful economic decision of the war." R.B. Bryce, "Prices, Wages and the Ceiling," in *War, Finance and Reconstruction: The Role of Canada's Depart-ment of Finance, 1939–1946*, ed. David W. Slater (Ottawa: D.W. Slater, 1995), 127. Plumptre suggested that Canada's efforts to control monetary policy were based on economic understandings that had "seldom if ever been set down in black and white." Plumptre, "An Approach to War Finance," 1. In his address to the nation, Prime Minister King described the program as an "experiment hitherto untried on

this continent and perhaps having regard to its breadth and variety, hitherto untried by the will and consent of any free people anywhere." King, *Controlling the Cost of Living,* 3.

25 Taylor, "Canadian War-Time Price Controls," 68.

26 The government stepped in on occasion to negotiate a rollback of the freeze within industry groups, offering direct subsidies to prevent increases that would trigger cost-of-living bonuses. Taylor outlined some of the prioritization and production directives, raw material allocation mechanisms, distribution controls, and selective service regulations in ibid., 87–94. Sheila I. Stewart, "Statutes, Orders, and Official Statements Relating to Canadian War-Time Economic Controls," *Canadian Journal of Economics and Political Science* 13, 1 (1947): 99–114, provides an extensive list of the principal federal statutes and regulations that emerged under the emergency needs of the wartime economy. Christopher Waddell offers a comprehensive examination of the activities of the WPTB. Christopher Robb Waddell, "The Wartime Prices and Trade Board: Price Control in Canada in World War II" (PhD thesis, York University, 1981).

27 Taylor, "Canadian War-Time Price Controls," 87. WPTB chair Donald Gordon was similarly convinced that, if Canadians believed that price control and rationing worked, much of the board's enforcement effort would become unnecessary. See Waddell, "The Wartime Prices and Trade Board," 548, 611, and Daniel J. Robinson, *The Measure of Democracy: Polling, Market Research, and Public Life, 1930–1945* (Toronto: University of Toronto Press, 1999), 113.

28 "Here Is One Big War Job Which You Alone Can Do," *Toronto Daily Star,* 18 December 1941, 33.

29 Tohill, "A Consumers' War," 233, 250. Tohill's insightful comparative history of consumer activism in wartime Canada and the United States situates national experiences in their respective institutional and political frameworks, enriching our understanding of the successes and failures of different paths.

30 Consumers associations had been part of both radical and mainstream women's movements for decades, particularly with respect to single issues. See, for example, Toronto housewives organizing around the politics of affordable milk, as discussed in Julie Guard, "A Mighty Power against the Cost of Living: Canadian Housewives Organize in the 1930s," *International Labor and Working-Class History* 77, 1 (2010): 27–47; and Ruth A. Frager, *Sweatshop Strife: Class, Ethnicity, and Gender in the Jewish Labour Movement of Toronto, 1900–1939* (Toronto: University of Toronto Press, 1992), 36–37. For an example of more sustained protest, see Joan Sangster, "Consuming Issues: Women on the Left, Political Protest, and the Organization of Homemakers, 1920–1960," in *Framing Our Past: Canadian Women's History in the Twentieth Century,* ed. Sharon Anne Cook, Lorna R. McLean, and Kate O'Rourke (Montreal and Toronto: McGill-Queen's University Press, 2001), 240–47.

31 On Byrne Hope Sanders, see Tohill, "A Consumers' War," 225–26.

32 On more than one occasion, the Consumer Branch successfully challenged restrictions it considered ill advised. For example, the WPTB had planned to shift sugar rationing from the honour system to coupon rationing on 1 July 1942. When the

Consumer Branch argued that introducing sugar rationing in the middle of jam-making season was unwise, sugar rationing was postponed, making tea and coffee the first commodities to be rationed by coupon in Canada. Stacey Jo-Anne Barker, "Feeding the Hungry Allies: Canadian Food and Agriculture during the Second World War" (PhD thesis, University of Ottawa, 2008), 197.

33 Ian Mosby, *Food Will Win the War: The Politics, Culture, and Science of Food on Canada's Home Front* (Vancouver: UBC Press, 2014); Broad, *A Small Price to Pay*, 32–47; 70–74; Tohill, "A Consumers' War," 250, 267–68, 284; Magda Fahrni, *Household Politics: Montreal Families and Postwar Reconstruction* (Toronto: University of Toronto Press, 2005), 111–14; and Ruth Roach Pierson, *"They're Still Women After All": The Second World War and Canadian Womanhood* (Toronto: McClelland and Stewart, 1986), 37–38, 43–44.

34 This gendering was apparent in the government's larger announcements, and was accepted as common sense in countless small ways. For example, in reporting changes to sugar rationing, the Canadian Press used the term "Mrs. Consumer" throughout, beginning with the first line in the story: "Mrs. Canadian Consumer is going to have to learn a few new tricks." "Rules Inflexible in Sugar Rations: All to Share Equally under Compulsory Plan," *Globe and Mail*, 2 July 1942, 9.

35 Pierson, *"They're Still Women After All,"* 41; *Toronto Daily Star*, 17 March 1942.

36 Lizabeth Cohen, *A Consumer's Republic: The Politics of Mass Consumption in Postwar America* (New York: Alfred A. Knopf, 2003), 75, 83; Meg Jacobs, "How About Some Meat? The Office of Price Administration, Consumption Politics, and State Building from the Bottom Up, 1941–46," *Journal of American History* 84, 3 (1997): 920–25; Pierson, *"They're Still Women After All,"* 33, 41; Tohill, "A Consumers' War," 227–31, 262–63, 284.

37 Lennon, *On the Homefront*, 38; Pierson, *"They're Still Women After All,"* 41–44; Brennan McConnell, "A Course for Victory: Gender, Class and Nation Depicted through Food in *Chatelaine* Magazine" (MA thesis, Carleton University, 2014); Mosby, *Food Will Win the War. The Miracle of Making Old Things New: A Remake Review* (Ottawa: Wartime Prices and Trade Board, 1943), a forty-eight-page booklet prepared with contributions from pattern companies, reveals the degree to which business and government shared an interest in cultivating appropriate consumer behaviours during the war. See also Lillian Millar, "Price Control Depends Largely on Women," *Saturday Night*, 10 October 1942, 20. As the introduction noted, "This article is designed to inform the women of Canada – on whose loyal support its success very largely depends – on the whys and wherefores of price control." In a flourish of militaristic rhetoric, Millar announced, "You women are a much more important factor than you realize in Canada's fight to control inflation. You belong to a vast army three million strong – homemakers and business women – and to you the government entrusted the task of seeing that price control works. The future security of your family depends upon how you carry out this duty."

38 Questions were asked to gauge support for economic controls, but also to determine sugar usage, driving patterns, the number of dresses and suits people had and the minimum they required per year, what an average Canadian family ate in the

course of a day, how many Canadians were planning gardens, and what major purchases Canadians were planning for after the war. Analysis of the responses also became increasingly sophisticated, with results broken down by gender and region.

39 Canadian communications historian Daniel Robinson observes that the consumer surveys conducted by the WPTB and those developed by business to market goods utilized the same techniques to different ends: the information gathered by the WPTB was used to constrain and channel rather than increase consumption. Robinson, *The Measure of Democracy*, 120–25; Robinson, "Polling Consumers and Citizens: Opinion Sample Surveys and the Rise of the Canadian Marketing Polity, 1928–1945" (PhD thesis, York University, 1996), 246–50.

40 Keshen, *Saints, Sinners, and Soldiers*, 73. In December 1941, 75 percent of Canadians endorsed the price freeze. Although public approval declined as the war continued, even after the war ended in 1945 polls revealed support for the retention of price controls for a period to prevent inflation and allow the diversion of supplies to Europe.

41 Broad, *A Small Price to Pay*, 35–42. For a complete study of the management of Canada's food supply during the war, see Barker, "Feeding the Hungry Allies," which discusses the evolution of rationing policies on 14, 134–35, 145–200.

42 Jeff Keshen, "One for All or All for One: Government Controls, Black Marketing and the Limits of Patriotism, 1939–1947," *Journal of Canadian Studies* 29, 4 (1994): 111–43.

43 "Corsets, Girdles on Banned List," *Toronto Daily Star*, 16 January 1942, 23.

44 Wartime Price and Trade Board, "Loyal Citizens Do Not Hoard!" *Fraser Valley Record*, 9 April 1942, 2, Mission Community Archives, http://app.ufv.ca/fvhistory/studentsites/wwII/wareffortconservation/Consumerexperiences.html.

45 Keshen, *Saints, Sinners, and Soldiers*, 106.

46 Tohill, "A Consumers' War," 243–44, 246, 250.

47 On resistance to aggressive bond sales tactics, see Cuthbertson, "Pocketbooks and Patriotism," 181, and Perrun, *The Patriotic Consensus*, 89.

48 Shirley Tillotson, "Warfare State, Welfare State, and the Selling of the Personal Income Tax, 1942–1945," *Canadian Tax Journal* 63, 1 (2015): 53–90; Shirley Tillotson, "The Family as Tax Dodge: Partnership, Individuality, and Gender in the Personal Income Tax Act, 1942 to 1970," *Canadian Historical Review* 90, 3 (2009): 400–4.

49 Tohill suggests that the focus on securing standards of living diverted labour protest away from wages and working conditions. Joseph Tohill, "'No Meat, No Work': Labour's Response to Consumer Rationing in Canada and the United States during the Second World War" (paper presented at the Canadian Historical Association annual meeting, Halifax, 2003).

50 Keshen, "One for All"; Broad, *A Small Price to Pay*, 33–34. Robert Morrison claims that a disproportionate number of violations came from western Canada, where civilians asserted that shortages had been artificially created by WPTB administrators favouring central Canada, and where there were greater opportunities to obtain

rationed goods from Americans who were stationed in Edmonton to work on the Alaska Highway. Robert Morrison, "Be Patient, Some Goods Are Scarce: Edmonton's Wartime Black Markets, 1939–1945," Edmonton City as Museum Project, http://citymuseumedmonton.ca/2015/12/01/edmontons-wartime-black -markets/.

51 Keshen, "One for All," 111.

52 "Who Said You Can't Buy Happiness?" advertisement, *Ottawa Citizen*, 15 May 1942, 21; *Globe and Mail*, 12 May 1942, 7.

53 *Maclean's Magazine*, 1 April 1943; Lennon, *On the Homefront*, 47.

54 "Don't Delay ... Do You Realize It Is Your Patriotic Duty to Safeguard Your Furs ... to Make Them Last for the Duration!" advertisement, *Globe and Mail*, 30 April 1943, 12.

55 *Maclean's Magazine*, 1 November 1942, 6, and 15 May 1945, inside front cover; Dominion Oilcloth and Linoleum advertisement, *Maclean's Magazine*, 15 April 1943, inside front cover. On the evolution of wartime advertising, see Broad, *A Small Price to Pay*, 71–124.

56 F.H. Leacy, ed., *Historical Statistics of Canada* (Ottawa: Statistics Canada, 1983), F76–90. The effect of the war on civilian incomes varied considerably. Employment opportunities, whether in industry or the armed forces, dramatically improved the lives of those who had been unable to find work during the Depression. Hourly wage rates were frozen in 1941 but extended hours of work in wartime industries often meant more take-home pay. On the other hand, the enlistment of the principal breadwinner, especially if that person was a skilled worker with dependants, could have the effect of reducing the family's living standards. Changing attitudes to consumer spending were apparent in unexpected locations. Historian Nancy Christie argues that the administration of discretionary grants to dependants of enlisted soldiers often treated overspending and the desire to save for postwar expenditures with some sympathy. Nancy Christie, *Engendering the State: Family, Work, and Welfare in Canada* (Toronto: University of Toronto Press, 2000), 261–62.

57 By comparison, the value of consumer purchases in Britain fell 22 percent between 1938 and 1944. Tohill, "A Consumers' War," 36. Parr argues that "there was no wartime spending splurge," pointing out that spending on consumer durables, as a proportion of disposable income, declined by two-thirds. There is evidence to support both interpretations: while durable goods were unavailable, non-durable consumer goods were, and, as incomes rose, Canadians spent. Joy Parr, *Domestic Goods: The Material, the Moral, and the Economic in the Postwar Years* (Toronto: University of Toronto Press, 1999), 25. Interestingly, it was at this time that the University of Toronto added marketing to its curriculum, publishing a series of studies on retail merchandising, installment selling, market research, and the importance of goodwill, which made virtually no reference to the war. Harold Innis, by then the head of the Department of Political Economy at the university, introduced one such study, discussing the far-reaching ramifications of marketing, which affected not only the advertising policies of large organizations but also control of the media, political practice, and, ultimately, the possibility of democracy. H.R.

Kemp, ed., *Canadian Marketing Problems: Ten Essays* (Toronto: University of Toronto Press, 1939) and Jane McKee, ed., *Marketing Organization and Technique* (Toronto: University of Toronto Press, 1940). See also Harold Innis, "The Changing Structure of the Canadian Market," in McKee, ibid., xvii-xiii.

58 Magda Fahrni, *Household Politics: Montreal Families and Postwar Reconstruction* (Toronto: University of Toronto Press, 2005), 487.

59 Hon. Ian Mackenzie, 30 April 1942, cited in Robert A. Young, "Reigning in James: The Limits of the Task Force," *Canadian Public Administration* 24, 4 (1981): 598. A. Brady, "Reconstruction in Canada: A Note on Policies and Plans," *Canadian Journal of Economics and Political Science* 8, 3 (August 1942): 460–68.

60 Leonard Kuffert, *A Great Duty: Responses to Modern Life and Mass Culture in Canada, 1939–1967* (Montreal and Kingston: McGill-Queen's University Press, 2003), 78–79 and 267n56.

61 In October 1943, a national public opinion poll was conducted that was notable for its emphasis on postwar concerns, with eight of seventeen topics focused on postwar matters. Concerns about what would happen in Canada after the war ranked higher than concerns about price controls. Robinson, *The Measure of Democracy*, 115–19; Robinson, "Polling Consumers and Citizens," 238–39.

62 Robert Bothwell and William Kilbourn, *C.D. Howe: A Biography* (Toronto: McClelland and Stewart, 1979), 181. Robert Bothwell, Ian Drummond, and John English, *Canada since 1945*, rev. ed. (Toronto: University of Toronto Press, 1981), 46. In the spring of 1943, reporter Bruce Hutchinson noted that the "newest and the most fundamental fact in our current Canadian politics ... is this: The politicians of all sorts have promised us permanent prosperity." Bruce Hutchinson, "Pie in the Sky," *Maclean's Magazine*, 1 April 1943. Leonard Marsh similarly observed that commitments were being made "on a scale never seen before" and "entirely new as far as the major political parties are concerned." Leonard Marsh, *Report on Social Security for Canada* (Toronto: University of Toronto Press, 1975), xiii. For a good overview of the range of reconstruction discussion, in which "it seemed as if everyone had a postwar program, scheme, or counterproposal to add to the mix," see Peter McInnis, "Planning Prosperity: Canadians Debate Postwar Reconstruction," in *Uncertain Horizons: Canadians and Their World in 1945*, ed. Greg Donaghy (Ottawa: Canadian Committee for the History of the Second World War, 1997), 231–59. McInnis suggests that much of the debate revolved around the degree of state involvement in the postwar economy. For a discussion of reconstruction debates within the civil service, see Doug Owram, *The Government Generation: Canadian Intellectuals and the State, 1900–1945* (Toronto: University of Toronto Press, 1986), 292–306. Also of interest is Gail Cuthbert Brandt, "'Pigeon-Holed and Forgotten': The Work of the Subcommittee on the Post-War Problems of Women, 1943," *Histoire sociale/Social History* 15, 29 (1982): 239–59.

63 Quote from John Deutsch, then a young economist with the Bank of Canada, in *Canadian Economic Policy since the War: A Series of Six Public Lectures in Commemoration of the Twentieth Anniversary of the 'White Paper' on Employment and Income of 1945, Delivered at Carleton University, Ottawa, September–November 1965,*

ed. S.F. Kaliski (Montreal: Canadian Trade Committee, 1966), 128. W.A. Mackintosh offered similar recollections, ibid., 13. See also Robert M. Campbell, *Grand Illusions: The Politics of the Keynesian Experience in Canada, 1945–1975* (Peterborough, ON: Broadview Press, 1987), 19; Parr, *Domestic Goods*, 31.

64 D.C. MacGregor, "The Project of Full Employment and Its Implications," in *Canada after the War: Studies in Political, Social and Economic Policies for Postwar Canada*, ed. Alexander Brady and F.R. Scott (Toronto: Macmillan, 1944), 191, 193.

65 The reporter was Grant Dexter of the *Winnipeg Free Press*, cited in Owram, *The Government Generation*, 301.

66 Deutsch, in Kaliski, *Canadian Economic Policy since the War*, 123–24, 128. W.A. Mackintosh offered similar recollections, ibid., 13. See also David Slater, "Behaving as Canadians: British Columbians, 1945–1947," in *Uncertain Horizons: Canadians and Their World in 1945*, ed. Greg Donaghy (Ottawa: Canadian Committee for the History of the Second World War, 1997), 193–94; Bryce, "Prices, Wages and the Ceiling," 93–210; and Parr, *Domestic Goods*, 10, 31–36.

67 Slater, *War, Finance and Reconstruction*, 274–76; Albert Rose, "Postwar Consumption Program," *Canadian Forum* 24 (November 1944): 177.

68 Advisory Committee on Reconstruction, *Report, September 24, 1943* (Ottawa: King's Printer, 1944), 13.

69 Historian Nancy Christie places the Marsh report at the centre of postwar conservative reaction to the social security state. The secularization of social welfare and focus on economic rather than spiritual security provoked a backlash that united university educators, church leaders, and conservative opinion-makers. Nancy Christie, "The Search for a Conservative Modernist Consensus," in *Cultures of Canadian Citizenship in Post-war Canada, 1940–1955*, ed. Nancy Christie and Michael Gauvreau (Montreal and Kingston: McGill-Queen's University Press, 2004), 65. On progressive responses see "Planning Post-War Canada," a regular monthly section in *Canadian Forum* in April, May, June, July, and August 1943. For examples of the conservative intellectual response, see S.D. Clark, "England's Road to Social Security: From the Statute of Laborers in 1349 to the Beveridge Report of 1942 by Karl de Schweinitz, and: Report on Social Security for Canada, Prepared by Dr. L.C. Marsh, for the Advisory Committee on Reconstruction, and: The Dawn of Ampler Life: Some Aids to Social Security by Charlotte Whitton (review)," *Canadian Historical Review* 25, 1 (1944): 63–66; and J.A. Corry, "Recent Books on Reconstruction," *Canadian Historical Review* 24, 4 (1943): 410–13. For examples of progressive responses, see "Planning Post-War Canada," *Canadian Forum*, May, June, July, and August 1943. Also, P.T. Rooke and R.L. Schnell, *No Bleeding Heart: Charlotte Whitton, A Feminist on the Right* (Vancouver: UBC Press, 1987), 111–14, for a discussion of the philosophical and religious roots of Whitton's response.

70 Leonard Marsh, *Report on Social Security for Canada* (Ottawa: King's Printer, 1943), 12, 18, 28.

71 Charlotte Whitton, *The Dawn of an Ampler Life* (Toronto: Macmillan, 1943), 23, 15–16, 83.

72 Christie, "The Search for a Conservative Modernist Consensus," 6–8, 17; Kuffert, *A Great Duty,* 53–55, 58, 63.

73 Owram, *The Government Generation,* 296–97, and Parr, *Domestic Goods,* 65, 73.

74 Some historians argue that the practical impact of this competition for authority may have been overstated, as there was considerable continuity in key personnel. W.A. Mackintosh, for example, was an ex-officio member of the James Committee and the head of the Economic Advisory Committee's subcommittee on reconstruction before assuming the role of director general of economic research in the Department of Reconstruction and Supply, where he became the principal author of the White Paper. On the rivalry that developed between the Advisory Committee on Reconstruction and the civil service, see J.L. Granatstein, *The Ottawa Men: The Civil Service Mandarins, 1935–1957* (Toronto: University of Toronto Press, 1998), 161–63; and Owram, *The Government Generation,* 283–86.

75 On the "floor and ceiling" approach to consumer spending, see Owram, *The Government Generation,* 306–7, and Granatstein, *The Ottawa Men,* 165.

76 Owram, *The Government Generation,* 298, 300, 310–15, locates the origins of postwar family allowance legislation in the Department of Finance rather than the social reform movement. See also Christie, *Engendering the State,* 294–95. On universality and the elimination of stigma, see James Struthers, "Family Allowances, Old Age Security, and the Construction of Entitlement in the Canadian Welfare State," in *The Veterans Charter and Post–World War II Canada,* ed. Peter Neary and J.L. Granatstein (Montreal and Kingston: McGill-Queen's University Press, 1997), 183–84.

77 Christie, *Engendering the State,* 280, 297.

78 Jill Wade, "Wartime Housing Limited, 1941–1947: Canadian Housing Policy at the Crossroads," *Urban History Review* 15, 1 (1986): 41–49, 51–53, 55–56.

79 Leonard Kuffert, "'Stabbing Our Spirits Broad Awake': Reconstructing Canadian Culture, 1940–1948," in *Cultures of Citizenship in Postwar Canada, 1940–1955,* ed. Nancy Christie and Michael Gauvreau (Montreal and Kingston: McGill-Queen's University Press, 2004), 27–62.

80 Peter Neary, "Canadian Universities and Canadian Veterans of World War II," in Neary and Granatstein, *The Veterans Charter,* 142; Thomas Lemieux and David Card, "Education, Earnings, and the 'Canadian GI Bill,'" *Canadian Journal of Economics* 34, 2 (2001); 313–44; Peter S. McInnis, *Harnessing Labour Confrontation: Shaping the Postwar Settlement in Canada, 1943–1950* (Toronto: University of Toronto Press, 2002), 97, 122; Christie, *Engendering the State,* 256.

81 Jeff Keshen, "Revisiting Canada's Civilian Women during World War II," *Histoire sociale/Social History* 30, 60 (1997): 257–58.

82 The incentives devised to stimulate the various components of aggregate demand were supposedly determined by economic merit. Parr convincingly argues that these decisions embodied gender discrimination and moral judgments that privileged the largest producers and neglected the interests of Canadian consumers. Parr, *Domestic Goods,* 65, 73.

83 W.A. Mackintosh, "The White Paper on Employment and Income in Its 1945 Setting," in Kaliski, *Canadian Economic Policy since the War,* 14–15; Campbell, *Grand Illusions,* and Robert M. Campbell, *The Full Employment Objective in Canada, 1945–85: Historical, Conceptual and Comparative Perspectives* (Ottawa: Economic Council of Canada, 1991), 1–5.

CHAPTER 7: BUYING HAPPINESS

1 Magda Fahrni, "Under Reconstruction: The Family and the Public in Postwar Montreal, 1944–1949" (PhD thesis, York University, 2011), 254. See also the educational pamphlet, J.F. Parkinson, *Price Controls for Victory* 9, 1 (Ottawa: Canadian Affairs, 1944).
2 *Canada Year Book,* 1962, 708–9.
3 Joseph Tohill, "A Consumers' War: Price Control and Political Consumerism in the United States and Canada during World War II" (PhD thesis, York University, 2012), 401–7.
4 K.W. Taylor, "Canadian War-Time Price Controls, 1941–46," *Canadian Journal of Economics and Political Science* 13, 1 (1947): 98.
5 Magda Fahrni, "Counting the Costs of Living: Gender, Citizenship, and a Politics of Prices in 1940s Montreal," *Canadian Historical Review* 83, 4 (2002): 491.
6 Some members of the federal government believed that rising prices would help limit domestic consumption, freeing resources to create an exportable surplus that would enable Canada to fulfil commitments to supply humanitarian relief in Europe. "Ottawa Glad Food Prices Drain Cash," *Globe and Mail,* 10 January 1948, 15.
7 Fahrni proposes that a sense of "economic citizenship" had been cultivated during the war, leading many to assert their right to a reasonable standard of living and a reasonable cost of living in the immediate postwar period. Lack of money to meet basic household needs was regarded as data to support political action rather than a source of private shame. Magda Fahrni, *Household Politics: Montreal Families and Postwar Reconstruction* (Toronto: University of Toronto Press, 2005), 51, 55–56, 62, 108–10, 279.
8 This account draws on Tohill, "A Consumers' War," 410–21, and Joy Parr, *Domestic Goods: The Material, the Moral, and the Economic in the Postwar Years* (Toronto: University of Toronto Press, 1999), 84–100. The Consumers' Association of Canada was known as the Canadian Association of Consumers until 1962. On the early history of the organization, see Helen Jones Dawson, "The Consumers' Association of Canada," *Canadian Public Administration* 6, 1 (1963): 92–118. On other consumer organizations active in the immediate postwar period, see also Fahrni, "Counting the Costs of Living," 492–94, 501–3.
9 Thelma Craig, "New Association of Consumers to Be Voice of United Women," *Saturday Night,* 1 November 1947, 31.
10 Tohill, "A Consumers' War," 420–24.

11	"Week to See Testing Consumer Resistance to Soaring Food Prices," *Globe and Mail,* 12 January 1948, 3. Protest was particular vehement around the topic of rising milk and butter prices. W.H. Heick, *A Propensity to Protect: Butter, Margarine and the Rise of Urban Culture in Canada* (Waterloo, ON: Wilfrid Laurier University Press, 1991), 69–71. Tohill, "A Consumers' War," 421–22.

12	Tohill, "A Consumers' War," 365, 424–35.

13	"Report of the Royal Commission on Prices," *Labour Gazette* 49, Part 1 (January–June 1949): 700–2.

14	Federal rent controls, necessitated by severe shortages in housing, were removed only when the federal government handed responsibility over to the provinces on 31 March 1951. The Supreme Court had previously upheld the federal government's power to regulate rents in peacetime on the grounds of "peace, order and good government"; however, rent control was increasingly unpopular with tenants as well as landlords, motivating Ottawa to relinquish its authority to the provinces. John C. Bacher, *Keeping to the Marketplace: The Evolution of Canadian Housing Policy* (Montreal and Kingston: McGill-Queen's University Press, 1993), 197–98. "Decontrol Is Ottawa's Job," *Globe and Mail,* 2 March 1950, 6.

15	Parr, *Domestic Goods,* 85–86. On the CAC, see also Thelma Craig, "New Association of Consumers to Be Voice," and "The Voice of the Consumer to Be Heard via Women's Organization," *Saturday Night,* 3 May 1947, 22–23. As Parr notes, the orientation of the Housewives' Consumers Association was announced in its name.

16	Jeff Keshen, "Revisiting Canada's Civilian Women during World War II," *Histoire sociale/Social History* 30, 60 (1997): 244; Tohill, "A Consumers' War," 445, 450; Parr, *Domestic Goods,* 99–100.

17	Tohill, "A Consumers' War," 424–34.

18	Parr, *Domestic Goods,* 97.

19	Per capita food consumption declined after 1945, and it was not until the late 1950s that Canadians' average food consumption levels would again reach their wartime highs. See http://wartimecanada.ca/essay/eating/food-home-front-during -second-world-war. On the federal government policies that created prolonged shortages of durable goods, see Parr, *Domestic Goods,* 66–77.

20	Craig, "The Voice of the Consumer to Be Heard," 23.

21	Peter McInnis, "Planning Prosperity: Canadians Debate Postwar Reconstruction," in *Uncertain Horizons: Canadians and Their World in 1945,* ed. Greg Donaghy (Ottawa: Canadian Committee for the History of the Second World War, 1997), 129–38; Parr, *Domestic Goods,* 73, 77–78.

22	Lillian D. Millar, "More 'Know-How' for Housewife Might Balance Shrinking Dollar," *Saturday Night,* 5 October 1946, 34.

23	See ibid. and the following articles by Lillian D. Millar: "Good Buymanship Can Add Thirty Per Cent to Your Dollar's Worth," *Saturday Night,* 26 October 1946; "Even the House Cat Is a Factor in the Budget for Recreation," *Saturday Night,* 29 March 1947; "Wisdom of the Housewifely Arts vs. the Shrinking Food Dollar," *Saturday Night,* 14 June 1947, 46; "Why Budgets Don't Work," *Saturday Night,* 9 October 1948; "Master Your Finances," *Chatelaine,* March 1947, 88.

24 Millar, "Good Buymanship."

25 Millar, "Master Your Finances," 88.

26 Millar, "More 'Know-How,'" 34.

27 Robert Bothwell, Ian Drummond, and John English, *Canada since 1945*, rev. ed. (Toronto: University of Toronto Press, 1981), 68–69.

28 John Porter, *Canadian Social Structure: A Statistical Profile* (Toronto: McClelland and Stewart, 1967), 91. GNP in constant dollars almost quadrupled from 1945 to 1960. Job prospects and wages grew faster than the population, and the official unemployment rate from 1945 to 1956 averaged 2.5 percent. Inflation was low and real wage rates for unionized workers rose. At the same time, prosperity was not well distributed. Twenty-seven percent of Canada's non-farm families spent 60 percent or more of their income on basic food, clothing, and shelter. Alvin Finkel, *Our Lives: Canada after 1945*, 2nd ed. (Toronto: James Lorimer, 1997), 6–10.

29 "Sees No Reason for Canada to Distrust Future," *Ottawa Journal*, 7 May 1949, 9. Also cited in Kenneth Wilson, "Sister If You've Never Kept a Budget ... You'd Better Start Now," *Chatelaine*, January 1951, 56.

30 Doug Owram discusses the centrality of a romanticized, idealized view of home in the immediate postwar period. Doug Owram, "Canadian Domesticity in the Postwar Era," in *The Veterans Charter and Post–World War II Canada*, ed. Peter Neary and J.L. Granatstein (Montreal and Kingston: McGill-Queen's University Press, 1997), 207–13; Mona Gleason, "Psychology and the Construction of the 'Normal' Family in Postwar Canada, 1945–60," *Canadian Historical Review* 78, 3 (1997): 449–51. On this theme, see also Derek Schilling, "Everyday Life and the Challenge to History in Post War France: Braudel, Lefebvre, Certeau," *Diacritics* 33, 1 (2003): 23–40.

31 On attention to the suburban "phenomenon" in the popular media, see Doug Owram, *Born at the Right Time: A History of the Baby Boom Generation* (Toronto: University of Toronto Press, 1996), 55.

32 On the representativeness of *Chatelaine* readers as a segment of the Canadian population, see Valerie Korinek, "'Mrs. Chatelaine' vs. 'Mrs. Slob': Contestants, Correspondents and the *Chatelaine* Community in Action, 1961–1969," *Journal of the Canadian Historical Association* 7, 1 (1996): 257–61.

33 The magazine's business department gave feminist-oriented editors and writers considerable leeway to challenge and even critique aspects of women's role in Canadian society, as long as magazine sales remained strong. Ibid., 253–54.

34 However, Valerie Korinek suggests that a "tradition of anti-consumerism" lingered at *Chatelaine*, possibly the legacy of the magazine's commitments to helping women through the Depression and its role as "a right-hand helper" in the rationing and conservation campaigns of the Second World War. Ibid., 295.

35 Owram, *Born at the Right Time*, 22.

36 On this theme in the United States, see Lendol Calder, *Financing the American Dream: A Cultural History of Consumer Credit* (Princeton, NJ: Princeton University Press, 1999), 349.

37 Charlene Champness, "Rich on $40 a Week," *Chatelaine*, February 1949, 14–16, 26–27.

38 Ibid., 14.

39 Ibid., 27, 16.

40 On the role of fathers in upgrading and building homes in an era that celebrated home-centred living, see Robert Rutherdale, "New 'Faces' for Fathers: Memory, Life-Writing, and Fathers as Providers in the Post Consumer Era," in *Creating Postwar Canada: Community, Diversity, and Dissent, 1945–75*, ed. Magda Fahrni and Robert Rutherdale (Vancouver: UBC Press, 2008), 248–50.

41 Ibid., 27, 14.

42 American historian Warren Susman discussed the shift from a culture of character (associated with producer society) to a culture of personality that emphasized external appearance and likeability (associated with consumer society) in *Culture as History: The Transformation of American Society in the Twentieth Century* (New York: Pantheon Books, 1984).

43 The author noted that Marie had encouraged Bill to take a job with Bell Telephone because it was a company of "standing" that offered opportunities for advancement and retirement benefits.

44 Champness, "Rich on $40 a Week," 15.

45 Martha Bennett King, "More Money Isn't the Answer," *Chatelaine*, March 1951, 24.

46 Wilson, "Sister If You've Never Kept a Budget," 15, 56; King, "More Money Isn't the Answer," 50.

47 Sidney Margolius, "We Sent an Expert to Help This Family Make Both Ends Meet," *Chatelaine*, January 1954, 14–15, 49–51; "Remember the Woods Family," *Chatelaine*, September 1954, 23–24; "A Year Ago the Woodses Went on a Budget – Look at Them Now," *Chatelaine*, December 1954, 24, 42, 44, 46–47; "More Advice for the Woods Family," *Chatelaine*, March 1954, 3; "Woods Family Remembered," *Chatelaine*, June 1954, 3. By this time, all postwar restrictions, including those limiting consumer credit, had ended.

48 Champness, "Rich on $40 a Week," 14; Margolius, "We Sent an Expert," 14, 15.

49 Professional counselling by self-help experts was characteristic of the North American way of life at least since the interwar period. In the postwar period, new experts stepped forward to teach Canadians how to be more effective consumers. High rates of literacy and access to the radio and, later, to television, helped experts disseminate advice aimed at solving a wide range of social problems associated with rapid change and increasing affluence. While it is difficult to know if the recommendations of experts were followed, labelling some behaviours as positive and others as negative served to transmit social conventions, helping to generate "spontaneous" consent for desirable ideals. On the role of postwar psychologists, see Mona Gleason, *Normalizing the Ideal: Psychology, Schooling, and the Family in Postwar Canada* (Toronto: University of Toronto Press, 1999), 6–9. On the emergence of marriage experts in the 1950s, see Owram, *Born at the Right Time*, 21–22, 33–34. On the popularity of childrearing experts, see ibid., 33, 38–37.

50 Margolius, "We Sent an Expert", 49. On the trope of the hapless father in postwar Canadian society, see Chris Dummitt, "Finding a Place for Father: Selling the Barbecue in Postwar Canada," *Journal of the Canadian Historical Association* 9 (1998): 218–19. Dummitt further suggests that mocking the domestic skills of Dad served to confirm that his true position lay outside the home.

51 On Margolius in the United States, see Gary Cross, *An All-Consuming Century: Why Commercialism Won in Modern America* (New York: Columbia University Press, 2000), 147–48. In postwar Canada, Chatelaine was not the only source of information available to Canadian consumers. By 1957, some 17,000 Canadians subscribed to the American publication *Consumer Reports,* and another 20,000–25,000 copies were sold on Canadian newsstands each month. In 1962, the CAC added product testing to its mandate and began to publish results in its *Bulletin* and in periodic Program Kits focusing on purchases of special interest to consumers (for example, "Gifts for the Bride"). For the most part, these efforts to align good consumer practices with the purchase of goods associated upward mobility with the progressive accumulation of more things, rather than with, for example, non-material forms of acquisition. Valerie Korinek, *Roughing It in the Suburbs: Reading Chatelaine Magazine in the Fifties and Sixties* (Toronto: University of Toronto Press, 2000), 274; Jean L. Whitehill, "We Help a Nation Buy," *Food for Thought* 18, 3 (1957): 120–21, 148–49.

52 Margolius, "We Sent an Expert," 51.

53 Ibid.

54 Russ' efforts to earn more in order to spend more were far from unique. Canadian economist David Slater noted at that time that new research suggested that household incomes were increasingly a function of consumption: it was the desire for goods and the conviction that they could be had that drove Canadians to work longer and harder. David W. Slater, *Consumption Expenditures in Canada* (Ottawa: Royal Commission on Canada's Economic Prospects, 1957), 49–50.

55 Margolius, "A Year Ago the Woodses Went on a Budget," 24. Consumers such as Joie could be assured they were making the right decision by reading the publications of not-for-profit consumer testing associations, such as the American-based Consumers Union, and those provided by commercially driven organizations such as *Chatelaine* and *Good Housekeeping,* to confirm that the family's income was being deployed on goods that offered the best value. By the late fifties, features explaining "how to budget" were being replaced by those explaining how to spend. "Should a dryer be your next appliance?" asked *Chatelaine* in April 1959. Expert advice was one of *Chatelaine*'s selling points. The magazine's "Seal of Approval" was featured prominently, both within its pages and on product packaging in the late 1950s, certifying that certain goods had been tested by the *Chatelaine* Institute and found worthy. The prototype was the American magazine *Good Housekeeping,* which began in 1924 to test household products and issue a "Seal of Guarantee" to those items that met minimum standards. Insofar as consumers were seen to need guidance rather than protection, the Seal of Guarantee would safeguard shoppers from

exploitation by unscrupulous manufacturers while continuing to promote a free market ethic. Seals of approval offered by private associations were singled out in the 1960s by consumer advocates for their links with advertisers and manufacturing associations. Matthew Hilton, *Consumerism in Twentieth-Century Britain: The Search for a Historical Movement* (Cambridge: Cambridge University Press, 2003), 172–73; Franca Iacovetta and Valerie J. Korinek, "Jell-O Salads, One-Stop Shopping, and Maria the Homemaker: The Gender Politics of Food," in *Sisters or Strangers? Immigrant, Ethnic, and Racialized Women in Canadian History,* ed. Marlene Epp and Franca Iacovetta (Toronto: University of Toronto Press, 2004), 199–200.

56 Margolius, "A Year Ago the Woodses Went on a Budget," 44.

57 Richard L. Edsall, "This Changing Canada," *Canadian Business* 27, 10 (1954): 72–74. Median incomes rose with the age of the family head, peaking when the heads were in their forties, and dropping sharply after age sixty-five; Richard L. Edsall, "Soaring Family Incomes Add New Dimension to Buying Power," *Canadian Business* 29, 11 (1956): 78, 80, 81–82.

58 Sidney Margolius, "How Much Money Should Your Family Owe?" *Chatelaine,* January 1956, 22.

59 Steuart Hendersen Britt, *The Spenders: Where and Why Your Money Goes* (New York: McGraw-Hill, 1960), 102–3; "The Consumer Comes Through," *Canadian Business Magazine,* October 1954, 18; Barry E.C. Boothman, "Mammoth Market: the Transformation of Food Retailing in Canada, 1946–1965," *Journal of Historical Research in Marketing* 3, 3 (2011): 294; Rom J. Markin, *The Supermarket: An Analysis of Growth, Development, and Change* (Pullman: Washington State University Press, 1968), 67–68; *Report of the Royal Commission on Price Spreads on Food Products,* 2 (Ottawa: Queen's Printer, 1959), 38–66.

60 See, for example, James Lorimer, *The Developers* (Toronto: James Lorimer, 1978), 186, 188.

61 Mary Jukes, "How to Borrow Wisely," *Chatelaine,* February 1951, 53–54, 64; Sidney Margolius, "How Much Money Should Your Family Owe?" *Chatelaine,* January 1956, 22, 27–30.

62 Elizabeth Loosley, "Opinion," *Food for Thought* 18, 3 (1957): 107, 109.

63 Attitudes to the use of credit were complex. Buying goods on instalment freed income to be spent in other ways. *Canadian Business* magazine suggested that, in the early 1950s, the average family was earning more, spending more, taking on more debt, and also building up their savings. Rising incomes and high rates of employment, decreases in the prices of basic necessities, and the use of instalment debt allowed Canadians to save more at the same time that they were spending more; indeed, total personal savings were growing even faster than total spending on consumer goods and services. Parr proposes that rising criticism of consumer credit in the late 1950s and through the 1960s was linked to criticism of commodity culture, which was intensifying as manufacturers responded to saturated markets by emphasizing style and engineering obsolesce. On the other hand, she notes that working-class families often regarded the ability to take on and repay debt not as moral weakness, but as evidence of trustworthiness and good character. The

repayment of debt required a steady income and self-discipline. On attitudes to the expansion of consumer credit during this period, see Edsall, "Soaring Family Incomes," 78, 80, 81–82; Dominion Bureau of Statistics, *National Accounts Income and Expenditure, 1926–1956* (Ottawa: Queen's Printer, 1958), 34–35; Parr, *Domestic Goods,* 101–18; Kathleen Rex, "Consumer Education on the Air," *Food for Thought* 18, 3 (1957): 118–19. Also valuable is David Steigerwald, "Did the Protestant Ethic Disappear? The Virtue of Thrift on the Cusp of Postwar Affluence," *Enterprise and Society* 9, 4 (2008): 788–815. On the myth of lost economic virtue and the tendency to see "credit revolutions" rather than evolving practices, see Calder, *Financing the American Dream,* 23–26.

64 "101 Ways to Save Money – and Look Better, Dress Better, Eat Better, and Live Better," *Chatelaine,* January 1962. Subsections of the feature include Jessie London, "Every Family Needs a Budget to Save"; Vivian Wilcox (Chatelaine fashion editor), "How to Perform a Miracle with a Makeover – and Save"; Eveleen Dollery (Chatelaine beauty editor), "You Can Be Your Own Best Hairdresser and Save $26"; Chatelaine Institute, "How to Eat Better and Save $200"; Alan Campaigne (Chatelaine home planning editor), "Have the Furniture You Really Want in 5 Years and Save."

65 On the "absent presence" of breadwinner fathers, see Cynthia Comacchio, "Bringing Up Father: Shaping a Modern Canadian Fatherhood," in *Family Matters: Papers in Post-Confederation Canadian Family History,* ed. Edgar-André Montigny and Lori Chambers (Toronto: Canadian Scholars Press, 1998), 289–308; and Veronica Strong-Boag, "Home Dreams: Women and the Suburban Experiment in Canada, 1945–60," *Canadian Historical Review* 72, 4 (1991): 471–504.

66 From 1945 to 1962, real average hourly and weekly wages rose substantially for a number of reasons, including low inflation through the 1950s, cost-of-living increases for unionized workers, technological changes that favoured skilled over unskilled workers, and increases in seniority among the generation taking up jobs after the war.

67 Wilcox, "How to Perform a Miracle," 38–39.

68 French cultural theorist Jean Baudrillard has observed that "few objects today are offered *alone,* without a context of objects to speak for them. And the relation of the consumer to the object has consequently changed: the object is no longer referred to in relation to a specific utility, but as a collection of objects in their total meaning ... The arrangement directs the purchasing impulse towards *networks* of objects in order to seduce it and elicit ... a maximal investment, reaching the limits of economic potential. Clothing, appliance, and toiletries thus constitute object *paths,* which establish inertial constraints on the consumer who will proceed *logically* from one object to the next. The consumer will be caught up in a *calculus* of objects, which is quite different from the frenzy of purchasing and possession which arises from the simple profusion of commodities." Jean Baudrillard, "Consumer Society," in *Consumer Society in American History: A Reader,* ed. Lawrence B. Glickman (Ithaca, NY: Cornell University Press, 1990), 35.

69 Only the Woods family mentioned one of the most significant phenomena of the era: television. Although television came relatively late to Canada, it spread rapidly.

The first Canadian television stations arrived only in 1952; by 1960, there were fifty-nine stations capable of reaching 90 percent of the population. In 1952, the average set cost over $400, or almost 20 percent of an average annual income. By 1956, the cost of a basic set had fallen to under $170. By the end of the decade, more Canadians owned televisions than telephones. The impact was especially powerful for children, who watched more or less the same shows and were encouraged to buy – or ask their parents to buy – the same products. Television, writes Canadian historian Doug Owram, helped to give a generation a common perspective on the world and their place in it. Owram, *Born at the Right Time*, 87–96.

70 London, "Every Family Needs a Budget," 48.

71 Sidney Margolius, "Who Should Handle the Family's Money," *Maclean's Magazine*, 1 October 1950, 12–13, 52.

72 Sidney Katz, "Why Husbands and Wives Fight over Money," *Maclean's Magazine*, 8 October 1960, 24–25, 53–55.

73 Both parenting and financial authorities believed that providing children with a regular allowance was vital to the development of future money-management skills and family happiness. An allowance, it was often explained, was neither a wage earned for chores around the home nor a bribe for good behaviour, but the child's rightful share of the family earnings. The opportunity to practise spending was regarded as critical to the formation of good spending habits because the ability to use money wisely was "not something you're born with, but something you learn." The *Canadian Banker* agreed, noting, "the main thing is to see that the allowance is prompt and regular and to leave the spending of it to the child." See Dorothy Sangster, "Finance in the Nursery," *Maclean's Magazine*, 15 December 1948, 14–15, 24, 26–27; N.B. Mallovy, "Teach Your Child the Value of Money," *Canadian Banker, Journal of the Canadian Banker's Association* 66, 1 (1959); Dr. Blatz, "Training Your Child," *Chatelaine*, June 1947.

74 Loosley, "Opinion," 107–8.

75 "Business and Government Listen to This Consumer's Voice," *Canadian Business*, February 1956, 72–78.

76 On masculine relationships to consumer spending, see Robert Rutherdale, "Fatherhood and Masculine Domesticity during the Baby Boom: Consumption and Leisure in Advertising and Life Stories," in *Family Matters: Papers in Post-Confederation Canadian Family History*, ed. Lori Chambers and Edger Andre Montignay (Toronto: Canadian Scholars Press, 1998), 309–33; and in Dummitt, "Finding a Place for Father," 209–23.

77 Baudrillard, "Consumer Society," 50.

78 A "concern with thriftiness permeated most of the food articles" in *Chatelaine* throughout the 1950s and 1960s. Korinek, *Roughing It in the Suburbs*, 192–93. Similarly, some homemakers resisted the lure of technological innovations they regarded as unsuited to Canadian conditions. Preferring simpler, more durable, wringer washers to mass-produced automatic washers, they continued to trade off personal labour for appliances that consumed less fuel and water and produced less waste. Parr, *Domestic Goods*, 240–42. Whether these examples of resistance were the result

of economic necessity, a cautious attitude to new technologies, or moral commitments remains an open question.

79 Household Finance, *Your Shopping Dollar* (Toronto and Chicago: Household Finance Corporation, 1962).

80 Korinek, *Roughing It in the Suburbs*, 290–91, 358, 421n18.

81 While the *Chatelaine* families were urban and entering the middle class, *Chatelaine* readers tended to be more rural and slightly less well off than the national average. Korinek, "'Mrs. Chatelaine' vs. 'Mrs. Slob,'" 261.

82 "Woods Family Remembered," *Chatelaine*, June 1954, 3.

83 "More Advice for the Woods Family," *Chatelaine*, March 1954, 3.

84 Ibid.

85 Cross, *An All-Consuming Century*, 98, 103, 109.

CHAPTER 8: ACADEMIC ENCOUNTERS

1 See, for example, Philip Massolin, *Canadian Intellectuals, the Tory Tradition, and the Challenge of Modernity* (Toronto: University of Toronto Press, 2001).

2 Daniel Horowitz has written a trilogy of carefully researched and thoughtful studies documenting the evolution of intellectual responses to consumer society, primarily in the United States, as they pass from condemnation to "reluctant fascination" to the pleasures of consumption. The studies provide a guide to similar trends in Canada. Works relevant to this chapter are Daniel Horowitz, *The Anxieties of Affluence: Critiques of American Consumer Culture, 1939–1979* (Amherst: University of Massachusetts Press, 2004) and *Consuming Pleasures: Intellectuals and Popular Culture in the Postwar World* (Philadelphia: University of Pennsylvania Press, 2012). On the decline of moral critique and the rising appreciation of consumption, see especially *Consuming Pleasures*, 7–8. See also Angus Burgin, "Review – *Consuming Pleasures: Intellectuals and Popular Culture in the Postwar World* by Daniel Horowitz," *Journal of Interdisciplinary History* 44, 2 (2013): 250–52.

3 The most influential of these studies were W.W. Rostow, *The Stages of Economic Growth: A Non-Communist Manifesto* (Cambridge: Cambridge University Press, 1960), and Seymour Martin Lipset, *Political Man: The Social Bases of Politics* (London: Doubleday, 1963). On the powerful influence of modernization theory on postwar historiography, see John Brewer, "Microhistory and the Histories of Everyday Life," *Cultural and Social History* 7, 1 (2010): 93–95, and Frank Trentmann, "Consumer Society: RIP – A Comment," *Contemporary European History* 20, 1 (2001): 27–31.

4 For an overview of capitalism's most influential American critics in the decades immediately following the war, see Horowitz, *The Anxieties of Affluence*. The list of influential critiques of modern American society should include, in addition to works by Galbraith, Packard, Riesman, and Whyte, those by Rachel Carson, *Silent Spring* (Boston: Houghton Mifflin, 1962) and Betty Friedan, *The Feminine Mystique* (New York: W.W. Norton, 1963).

5 John Seeley, R. Alexander Sim, and Elizabeth Loosley, *Crestwood Heights: A Study of the Culture of Suburban Life* (Toronto: University of Toronto Press, 1956), 355.

6 Horowitz, *Consuming Pleasures*, 127. On the "axes" of sociological accounts of consumption, see Silvia Rief, "Outlines of a Critical Sociology of Consumption: Beyond Moralism and Celebration," *Sociology Compass* 2, 2 (2008): 562–65.

7 The volume was issued in the United States as John Seeley, *Crestwood Heights: A North American Suburb* (New York: Basic Books, 1956). On the complex and competitive relationship between the co-authors, see Paul R. Bentley, "Martyr for Mental Health: John R. Seeley and the Forest Hill Village Project, 1948–1956" (PhD thesis, University of Toronto, 2013), 321–43.

8 Seeley et al., *Crestwood Heights*, 3–7, 20.

9 It is interesting that American, but not Canadian, reviewers commented on the high degree of role differentiation between Crestwood Heights spouses, in which the woman developed her expertise in the realm of consumer culture while the male focused almost exclusively on work. See, for example, David Riesman, "Introduction," in Seeley et al., *Crestwood Heights*, xii; Donald L. Foley, "Crestwood Heights: A Study of the Culture of Suburban Life," *Public Opinion Quarterly* 21, 1 (1957): 219; and Robert Rappaport, "Crestwood Heights: A Study of the Culture of Suburban Life," *American Anthropologist* 60, 1 (1958): 170.

10 Seeley et al., *Crestwood Heights*, 43, 46, 47, 49, 51, 189–90.

11 Ibid., 6, 42.

12 Ibid., 135.

13 Michael Rossman, "The Fool of Sociology: A Professional Biography of John R. Seeley," http://www.mrossman.org/uncollectedessays/seeley1.html.

14 Seeley et al., *Crestwood Heights*, 61, 343–44.

15 Ibid., 371–73, 416–21. When the study was completed, most of the senior personnel experienced sharp breaks in their careers. Two of the senior authors ceased to be practising social scientists. Elizabeth Loosley became involved in Canadian Association for Adult Education and for a time was the editor of *Food for Thought*, including the issue cited in the previous chapter. Alexander Sim became the chief liaison officer for Canada's Department of Citizenship and Immigration. Witnessing the convergence of consumer values and the discipline of sociology, Seeley came to doubt that the social sciences could offer neutral, constructive knowledge in a consumer society. He did not leave academia but became a prominent critic of psychological and sociological research, particularly when it involved children. On the impact of rapid change and the problem of self-consciousness among researchers working in suburban communities, see John R. Seeley, "Social Values, the Mental Health Movement, and Mental Health," *Annals of the American Academy of Political and Social Science* 286 (March 1953): 22–23, and John R. Seeley, "Social Science in Social Action," *Canadian Journal of Economics and Political Science* 17, 1 (1951): 89.

16 The release of the book in both Canada and the United States was delayed by several weeks after it was selected by the Basic Book Club. "The Fly Leaf," *Globe and Mail*, 12 May 1956, 31.

17 See the following items in the *Globe and Mail*: "Why Do People Want to Move to Crestwood Heights? Why Do They Work So Hard to Stay There?," 2 June 1956,

8; "Does Any Family Feel at Home in Crestwood Heights?," 19 May 1956, 18; "Is There Such a Thing as the 'Family' in Crestwood Heights?," 12 May 1956, 31; "The School or the Family: Which Counts More in Crestwood Heights?," 5 May 1956, 35; "Why Is the Child the Focus of Life in Crestwood Heights?," 21 April 1956, 12; "What Counts in Crestwood Heights? What You Are or What You Have?," 14 April 1956, 10.

18 On the reception of the book, also see Bentley, "Martyr for Mental Health," 344–49.

19 David Riesman and Howard Roseborough, "Careers and Consumer Behavior," in *Consumer Behavior II,* ed. Lincoln Clark (New York: New York University Press, 1955), 1–18. Roseborough's dissertation on the sociology of consumer spending and this essay, written in collaboration with David Riesman, received considerable attention. See Francis X. Sutton and Gregory P. Stone, "Comments on 'Careers and Consumer Behavior" in *Consumer Behavior II,* ed. Lincoln Clark (New York: New York University Press, 1955), 19–27; also, Talcott Parsons and Neil Smelser, *Economy and Society: A Study in the Integration of Economic and Social Theory* (London: Routledge and Kegan Paul, 1956), 222nn2–3. Riesman was a prolific networker. His insightful introduction to *Crestwood Heights* helped draw attention to that study. For Riesman's thinking on consumer society, see Horowitz, *Consuming Pleasures,* 122–36. Horowitz finds common ground between the work of Riesman and McLuhan, noting that both were "trying to figure out how to think about commercial culture," fascinated by, but also ambivalent towards, what they observed (122, 162).

20 Riesman and Roseborough, "Careers and Consumer Behavior," 15, 14.

21 Howard Roseborough, "Some Sociological Dimensions of Consumer Spending," *Canadian Journal of Economics and Political Science* 26, 3 (1960): 461.

22 Ibid., 463–64.

23 Ibid., 453.

24 Dominik Schrage, "The Domestication of Luxury in Social Theory," *Social Change Review* 10, 2 (2012): 177–93.

25 S.D. Clark, "The Suburban Community," in *Urbanism and the Changing Canadian Society,* ed. S.D. Clark (Toronto: University of Toronto Press, 1961), 28.

26 S.D. Clark, *The Suburban Society* (Toronto: University of Toronto Press, 1966), 120. Clark, long interested in the social consequences of economic change, began to study the suburbs in the 1950s. *The Suburban Society* was the culmination of work begun in a 1960 study commissioned by the Canada Mortgage and Housing Corporation, a new federal agency with a mandate to support housing through design and planning policy as well as through financial assistance.

27 Clark, "The Suburban Community," 1–2, 20–21, 34–38; Clark, *The Suburban Society,* 100–13.

28 *The Vertical Mosaic* was the culmination of eleven years of research and writing. Substantial portions had appeared as articles in the *Canadian Journal of Economics and Political Science* (1955, 1956, 1957, and 1958) and in *Social Purpose for Canada* (1961). Rick Helmes-Hayes and James Curtis, eds., *The Vertical Mosaic Revisited* (Toronto: University of Toronto Press, 1998), 6, 32.

29 John Porter, *The Vertical Mosaic: An Analysis of Social Class and Power in Canada* (Toronto: University of Toronto Press, 1965). The book was a much-discussed Canadian best-seller, for a while more popular among the patrons of the Toronto Public Library than Truman Capote's *In Cold Blood*. "The Vertical Mosaic: A Surprise $15 Bestseller," *Toronto Daily Star*, 18 June 1966, 25. On the impact of the book on Canadian sociology, see Helmes-Hayes and Curtis, *The Vertical Mosaic Revisited*, 7–8.

30 Porter, *The Vertical Mosaic*, 4, 125.

31 Ibid., 4, 11–12, 125. Porter specifically references *Crestwood Heights* in this regard. On Porter's use of "class," see Helmes-Hayes and Curtis, *The Vertical Mosaic Revisited*, 20–21, 43, 120.

32 John Porter, "Freedom and Power," in *Social Purpose for Canada*, ed. Michael Oliver (Toronto: University of Toronto Press, 1961), reprinted in John Porter, *The Measure of Canadian Society: Education, Equality, and Opportunity* (Toronto: Gage, 1979), 214–15, 219.

33 Porter, *The Vertical Mosaic*, 35.

34 Ibid., 126.

35 Ibid.

36 Porter, and before him Leonard Marsh, asserted that Canada's middle-class consumption ideal was based largely on American standards; however, neither made clear whether these standards were real even for Americans or were entirely the product of Hollywood and the advertising media.

37 Porter, *The Vertical Mosaic*, 9–12.

38 Ibid., 6.

39 Ibid., 129–31, 6, 457–59; John Porter, "Elite Groups: A Scheme for the Study of Power in Canada," *Canadian Journal of Economics and Political Science* 21, 4 (1955): 499, 511.

40 Leonard Kuffert, "'Stabbing Our Spirits Broad Awake': Reconstructing Canadian Culture, 1940–1948," in *Cultures of Citizenship in Postwar Canada, 1940–1955*, ed. Nancy Christie and Michael Gauvreau (Montreal and Kingston: McGill-Queen's University Press, 2004), 16, 19, 24, 27–28.

41 Leonard Kuffert, *A Great Duty: Responses to Modern Life and Mass Culture in Canada, 1939–1967* (Montreal and Kingston: McGill-Queen's University Press, 2003), 103, 173.

42 Hilda Neatby, *A Temperate Dispute* (Toronto: Clarke Irwin, 1954), cited in Philip Massolin, *Canadian Intellectuals*, 183.

43 The Royal Commission for the National Development in the Arts, Letters and Sciences has been the focus of a number of excellent studies, which portray it as both a key event in the development of Canadian national culture and a watershed moment in the conservative defence of the values and traditions of high culture. See Paul Litt, *The Muses, the Masses and the Massey Commission* (Toronto: University of Toronto Press, 1992); Massolin, *Canadian Intellectuals*, 155–95; Kuffert, *A Great Duty*, 146–53; Karen Finlay, *The Force of Culture, Vincent Massey and Canadian Sovereignty* (Toronto: University of Toronto Press, 2004), 210–38; and

Zoe Druick, "Remedy and Remediation: The Cultural Theory of the Massey Commission," *Review of Education, Pedagogy, and Cultural Studies* 29 (2007), http://dx.doi.org/10.1080/10714410701196468.

44 Royal Commission on National Development in the Arts, Letters and Sciences, *Report* (Ottawa: King's Printer, 1951), 271, 5.

45 On McLuhan's life, thoughts, and his significance as a scholar of consumer culture, see Horowitz, *Consuming Pleasures*, 136–62.

46 Most notably advocated by F.R. Leavis in *Mass Civilization and Minority Culture* (Cambridge: Minority Press, 1930). Blaming machine technology, Leavis argued that modern "man" had "lost all powers of discrimination." Only the literary elite could preserve the most essential creative achievements of Western civilization and prevent further descent into the abyss of modernity that was progressively destroying individual intelligence, choice, will, and critical judgment. Matthew Hilton, "The Legacy of Luxury: Moralities of Consumption since the 18th Century," *Journal of Consumer Culture* 4, 1 (2004): 110–11; Ross Alloway, "Selling the Great Tradition," *Book History* 6 (2003): 227–50.

47 Marshall McLuhan, *The Mechanical Bride: Folklore of Industrial Man* (New York: Vanguard Press, 1951), 43, v.

48 Ibid. Gordon notes that Poe's parable was a "perennial favorite" in McLuhan's teaching and writing. W. Terrence Gordon, *McLuhan: A Guide for the Perplexed* (New York: Continuum, 2010), 2.

49 For example, McLuhan noted at the outset of *The Mechanical Bride* "the advantage I have enjoyed in reading unpublished work of Professor David Riesman on the consumer mentality" (vi).

50 This paragraph draws on Philip Marchand, *Marshall McLuhan: The Medium and the Messenger* (Toronto: Random House, 1989), 73–75; Janine Marchessault, "Mechanical Brides and Mama's Boys: Gender and Technology in Early McLuhan," in *Marshall McLuhan: Theoretical Elaborations*, Volume 2, ed. Gary Genosko (London: Routledge, 2005), 161–63, 169, 175–78; and Arthur Asa Berger, *Television as an Instrument of Terror* (New Brunswick, NJ: Transaction Publishers, 2007), 75–76.

51 McLuhan, *The Mechanical Bride*, 93.

52 Ibid., 40, 21.

53 Ibid., 21, 58, 117–18. The title, McLuhan explained, referenced the Hollywood glamour girl, alluding to both technology and the distortion of culture by the economics of mass production and mass consumption.

54 Gordon, *McLuhan*, 77.

55 *The Mechanical Bride* also had very practical outcomes for McLuhan's career, helping to win him a grant from the Ford Foundation that funded a series of seminars in communication and culture at the University of Toronto, which were critical in shifting his focus to non-literary forms of communication.

56 On the rise and fall of McLuhan as a public intellectual, see James C. Morrison, "Marshall McLuhan: No Prophet without Honor," *AmeriQuests* 3, 2 (2006), http://www.mit.edu/~saleem/ivory/ch2.htm; Glen Willmott, *McLuhan, or Modernism in Reverse* (Toronto: University of Toronto Press, 1996), 144–45.

57 For an analysis of the complicated rivalry of McLuhan and Frye and the intellectual context of their work, see B.W. Powe, *Marshall McLuhan and Northrop Frye: Apocalypse and Alchemy* (Toronto: University of Toronto Press, 2014).

58 The book began to take form as a series of lectures presented at Princeton University in 1954. Parts had been previously published as essays, some as much as a decade earlier. The "Polemical Introduction" was a revised version of "The Function of Criticism at the Present Time," *University of Toronto Quarterly* 19, 1 (1949): 1–16.

59 Northrop Frye, *Anatomy of Criticism* (Princeton, NJ: Princeton University Press, 1957), 3, 4.

60 Ibid., 344.

61 Diane Dubois, *Northrop Frye in Context* (Newcastle, UK: Cambridge Scholars, 2013), 26–29; Northrop Frye, *The Critical Path: An Essay on the Social Context of Literary Criticism* (Bloomington: Indiana University Press, 1971), 170.

62 Jonathan Hart, *Northrop Frye: The Theoretical Imagination* (London: Routledge, 1994), 181.

63 Frye, *Anatomy of Criticism*, 348.

64 Ibid., 345–46, 115, 348.

65 Northrop Frye, *The Educated Imagination* (1963; repr., Toronto: House of Anansi Press, 1993), 56.

66 Ibid., 59–66.

67 Dubois, *Northrop Frye in Context*, 29.

68 Jonathan Hart, *Textual Imitation: Making and Seeing in Literature* (New York: Palgrave, 2013), 81–82.

69 B.S. Kierstead, "Economic Man in Relation to His Natural Environment," *Canadian Journal of Economics and Political Science* 15, 2 (1949): 232–35; C. Reinold Noyes, "What Kind of Psychology Does Economics Need?" *Canadian Journal of Economics and Political Science* 16, 2 (1950): 210–15; B.S. Kierstead, "The Nature of Economic Man: A Rejoinder," *Canadian Journal of Economics and Political Science* 17, 2 (1951): 221–24; C. Reinold Noyes, "The Nature of Economic Man: A Reply," *Canadian Journal of Economics and Political Science* 17, 2 (1951): 225–28; Clarence L. Barber, "The Concept of Disposable Income," *Canadian Journal of Economics and Political Science* 15, 2 (1949): 227–29; Simon A. Goldberg, "The Concept of Disposable Income: A Reply," *Canadian Journal of Economics and Political Science* 15, 4 (1949): 539–42.

70 Dominion Bureau of Statistics, *The Consumer Price Index, January 1949–August 1952 (Including an Explanatory Statement)* (Ottawa: Queen's Printer, 1952), 10–12, 31.

71 David W. Slater, *Consumption Expenditures in Canada* (Ottawa: Royal Commission on Canada's Economic Prospects, 1957), 1.

72 Ibid., 49–50.

73 Ibid., 4.

74 Ibid., 49, 173.

75 John K. Galbraith, *The Affluent Society* (New York: Mentor Books, 1958). On Galbraith as a critic of consumer society, see Horowitz, *The Anxieties of Affluence,* 14–15, 102–8.

76 D.E. Moggridge, *Harry Johnson: A Life in Economics* (Cambridge: Cambridge University Press, 2008), 234, 239. On Johnson's writings on consumer society, see W. Paul Strassman, "Optimum Consumption Patterns in High-Income Nations," *Canadian Journal of Economics and Political Science* 28, 3 (1962): 364–72, and Richard E. Caves, "Harry Johnson as a Social Scientist," *Journal of Political Economy* 92, 4 (August 1984): 642–58.

77 Harry G. Johnson, *The Canadian Quandary: Economic Problems and Policies* (Montreal and Kingston: McGill-Queen's University Press, 2005), 232. The book comprises previously published essays, the most relevant of which appeared earlier as "The Political Economy of Opulence," *Canadian Journal of Economics and Political Science* 26, 4 (1960); "The Social Policy of an Opulent Society" (paper presented at the 41st Annual Meeting and Conference of the Canadian Welfare Council, Ottawa, 29 May 1961); "Advertising in Today's Economy," *Queen's Quarterly* 19, 4 (1963); and "Apologia for Ad Men" (address to the Toronto chapter of the American Marketing Association, 26 February 1963).

78 Johnson, *The Canadian Quandary,* 232.

79 Ibid., 236, 238, 274.

80 Ibid., 237.

81 Ibid., 264.

82 Ibid., 249, 256–61.

CONCLUSION

1 Joseph Tohill, "A Consumers' War: Price Control and Political Consumerism in the United States and Canada during World War II" (PhD thesis, York University, 2012), 208, 212; Joy Parr, *Domestic Goods: The Material, the Moral, and the Economic in the Postwar Years* (Toronto: University of Toronto Press, 1999), 232–36.

2 Elizabeth Loosley, "Opinion," *Food for Thought* 18, 3 (1957): 109.

3 Warren I. Susman, *Culture as History: The Transformation of American Society in the Twentieth Century* (New York: Pantheon Books, 1984), xx, 288; Richard Wilk, "Consuming Morality," *Journal of Consumer Culture* 1, 2 (2001): 254; Angus Burgin, "Review: Consuming Pleasures: Intellectuals and Popular Culture in the Postwar World by Daniel Horowitz," *Journal of Interdisciplinary History* 44, 2 (2013): 252.

4 On this theme see David Scott, "The Temporality of Generations: Dialogue, Tradition, Criticism," *New Literary History* 45, 2 (2014): 157–81.

5 Clifford Geertz, *The Interpretation of Cultures* (New York: Basic Books, 1973), 5.

INDEX